"John Owen is one of the church's greatest minds. His theology is exegetically robust, expansive in scope, and penetratingly insightful. Barrett and Haykin ably guide readers through Owen's work and mine many brilliant gems. I highly recommend this book for anyone weary of banal and Christless spirituality."

J. V. Fesko, Academic Dean and Professor of Systematic and
Historical Theology, Westminster Seminary California

"The writings of John Owen constitute an entire country of biblical, exegetical, doctrinal, spiritual, casuistical, practical, ecclesiastical, controversial, and political theology. Massive in size, Oweniana cannot be visited on a day trip. Indeed a lifetime hardly suffices for all there is to explore. But hire as your tour guides Matthew Barrett and Michael Haykin, and the daunting journey seems possible after all. With these seasoned scholars and enthusiasts as companions, visiting the varied counties, the significant towns, and the great cities of Oweniana is as enjoyable as it is instructive. *Owen on the Christian Life* simply excels as an outstanding contribution to an already first-class series."

Sinclair B. Ferguson, Professor of Systematic Theology,
Redeemer Seminary, Dallas, Texas

"Theologically rich, carefully researched, and historically grounded, this book leads us into the wisdom of one of the greatest theologians of all time. Barrett and Haykin's study of John Owen expands our view of the Christian life to embrace the knowledge of God's glory in Jesus Christ. As our Lord reminded us, that is life indeed (John 17:3). Once you finish this book, you will definitely want to read Owen himself!"

Joel R. Beeke, President, Puritan Reformed Theological Seminary

"John Owen's work is well worth knowing, especially since he was one of the giants who understood that all good theology is inevitably pastoral. Matthew Barrett and Michael A. G. Haykin strongly believe this as well; therefore, they prove able guides committed to introducing key theological emphases that not only inform Owen's own conception of the Christian life but should guide ours as well."

Kelly M. Kapic, Professor of Theological Studies, Covenant College

"All that Owen wrote sought to promote contemplation of God and pursuit of godliness. This clear and loving account of his theology provides a sure guide to the spiritual riches of a magnificent Christian thinker."

John Webster, Professor of Systematic Theology, University of Aberdeen

"I am delighted to be able to commend this guide to the Christian life drawn so deftly from the writings of John Owen by Drs. Barrett and Haykin. The authors are familiar with the Owen corpus and have drawn widely from the available materials. The result is a delightfully lucid work. When one first comes to Owen's writings, the sheer bulk may be daunting. Owen was a pastor, and this guidebook is a delight to read and study. Anyone who ventures into these pages will find the result richly rewarding and hopefully will turn to the sources. As I read this book, repeatedly I thought of what a blessing this would have been to me in the late 1950s when I acquired unexpectedly an almost complete set of Owen's *Works*."

Robert W. Oliver, Retired Pastor and Seminary Lecturer; writer on English Nonconformist and Baptist History

"*Owen on the Christian Life* is one of the most valuable accounts yet published of the practical theology of the most eminent English Puritan. Owen's theology has become known for its difficulty and polemic, and yet, as Barrett and Haykin demonstrate, it was driven by and was intended to develop a life of discipline and devotion. This book will be one of the best studies of Owen's thinking to be published in anticipation of his anniversary year."

Crawford Gribben, Professor of Early Modern British History, Queen's University

"John Owen was arguably the most important Puritan; his mind, the most penetrating; and his understanding of the Bible and theology, preeminent. As a pastor, he had a deep concern for the spiritual well-being of his hearers and readers. It is gratifying that this excellent discussion of Owen's consideration of the Christian life brings his work to a wider readership."

Robert Letham, Director of Research and Senior Lecturer in Systematic and Historical Theology, Wales Evangelical School of Theology

"As Barrett and Haykin make clear, John Owen always wrote for life: truth is not just to be believed but also to be experienced. Their book explores many of the great truths of the Christian faith in the hands of this great thinker. They translate the wisdom of his age for the benefit of ours, all in a way that helps us faithfully to live in the reality of God's holiness, love, and grace."

Tim Cooper, Associate Professor of Church History, University of Otago, New Zealand

OWEN

on the Christian Life

THEOLOGIANS ON THE CHRISTIAN LIFE

EDITED BY STEPHEN J. NICHOLS AND JUSTIN TAYLOR

Augustine on the Christian Life:
Transformed by the Power of God,
Gerald Bray

Bavinck on the Christian Life:
Following Jesus in Faithful Service,
John Bolt

Bonhoeffer on the Christian Life:
From the Cross, for the World,
Stephen J. Nichols

Calvin on the Christian Life:
Glorifying and Enjoying God Forever,
Michael Horton

Edwards on the Christian Life:
Alive to the Beauty of God,
Dane C. Ortlund

Luther on the Christian Life:
Cross and Freedom,
Carl R. Trueman

Newton on the Christian Life:
To Live Is Christ,
Tony Reinke

Owen on the Christian Life:
Living for the Glory of God in Christ,
Matthew Barrett and Michael A. G. Haykin

Packer on the Christian Life:
Knowing God in Christ, Walking by the Spirit,
Sam Storms

Schaeffer on the Christian Life:
Countercultural Spirituality,
William Edgar

Warfield on the Christian Life:
Living in Light of the Gospel,
Fred G. Zaspel

Wesley on the Christian Life:
The Heart Renewed in Love,
Fred Sanders

OWEN
on the Christian Life

LIVING FOR THE GLORY
OF GOD IN CHRIST

MATTHEW BARRETT AND
MICHAEL A. G. HAYKIN

FOREWORD BY CARL R. TRUEMAN

CROSSWAY

WHEATON, ILLINOIS

Owen on the Christian Life: Living for the Glory of God in Christ

Copyright © 2015 by Matthew Barrett and Michael A. G. Haykin

Published by Crossway
        1300 Crescent Street
        Wheaton, Illinois 60187

Cover design: Josh Dennis
Cover image: Richard Solomon Artists, Mark Summers

First printing 2015

Printed in the United States of America

All Scripture quotations are from the King James Version or John Owen's translation.

Trade paperback ISBN: 978-1-4335-3728-8
ePub ISBN: 978-1-4335-3731-8
PDF ISBN: 978-1-4335-3729-5
Mobipocket ISBN: 978-1-4335-3730-1

Library of Congress Cataloging-in-Publication Data

Barrett, Matthew, 1982–
   Owen on the Christian life: living for the glory of God in Christ / Matthew Barrett and Michael A. G. Haykin; foreword by Carl R. Trueman.
      pages   cm.— (Theologians on the Christian life)
      Includes bibliographical references and index.
      ISBN 978-1-4335-3728-8 (tp)
      1. Owen, John, 1616–1683. 2. Christian life. 3. Theologians—England—Biography. 4. Dissenters, Religious—England—Biography. I. Haykin, Michael A. G. II. Title.
BX5207.O88B37   2015
285'.9092—dc23   2014037746

Crossway is a publishing ministry of Good News Publishers.

VP	25	24	23	22	21	20	19	18	17	16	15
15	14	13	12	11	10	9	8	7	6	5	4	3	2	1

To my son, Charles—
may you find a friend in John Owen
and together meditate on the glory of God in Christ.

—Matthew Barrett

———

To Trinity Baptist Church,
Burlington, Ontario—
where I learned much about John Owen
and his vision of the Christian life.

—Michael A. G. Haykin

All solid, learned, sober endeavours for the vindication of the absolute-ness, freedom, independency, and pre-eminence of that grace in Jesus Christ, whereby we are saved, will doubtless find acceptance with the children of Gospel-wisdom and all that love the glory of him that bought us.

JOHN OWEN, LETTER TO READER, NOVEMBER 7, 1653,
IN W. EYRE, *VINDICIAE JUSTIFICATIONIS
GRATUITAE* (1654)

CONTENTS

SERIES PREFACE

Some might call us spoiled. We live in an era of significant and substantial resources for Christians on living the Christian life. We have ready access to books, DVD series, online material, seminars—all in the interest of encouraging us in our daily walk with Christ. The laity, the people in the pew, have access to more information than scholars dreamed of having in previous centuries.

Yet for all our abundance of resources, we also lack something. We tend to lack the perspectives from the past, perspectives from a different time and place than our own. To put the matter differently, we have so many riches in our current horizon that we tend not to look to the horizons of the past.

That is unfortunate, especially when it comes to learning about and practicing discipleship. It's like owning a mansion and choosing to live in only one room. This series invites you to explore the other rooms.

As we go exploring, we will visit places and times different from our own. We will see different models, approaches, and emphases. This series does not intend for these models to be copied uncritically, and it certainly does not intend to put these figures from the past high upon a pedestal like some race of super-Christians. This series intends, however, to help us in the present listen to the past. We believe there is wisdom in the past twenty centuries of the church, wisdom for living the Christian life.

Stephen J. Nichols and Justin Taylor

FOREWORD

We live in an age when the challenges to Christianity, theological and practical (if one can separate such), are pressing in from all sides. Perhaps the most obvious challenge is the issue of homosexuality. Given the high pastoral stakes in this matter, it is important that we make the right decisions.

What has this to do with the thought of a man who died nearly 350 years ago? Simply this: in our era much practical thinking is driven by emotions. Emotions are enemies of fine distinctions. And yet the ethical and practical issues facing the church today demand precisely such fine distinctions if we are to do our task as pastors and church members: comfort the brokenhearted and rebuke those at ease in their sin. And John Owen was of an era when fine distinctions were part of the very fabric of practical theology.

Like one of his great theological heroes, Augustine, Owen was an acute psychologist of the Christian life. Further, as part of the great post-Reformation elaboration and codification of Reformed orthodoxy, he was adept at careful distinctions and precise argument. Finally, as a pastor and preacher, he constantly brought these two things together in practical ways in his congregation. We might add that the pastoral problems in the seventeenth century—greed, sex, anxiety, marital strife, petty personal vendettas—have a remarkably familiar and contemporary feel.

Owen thus wrestled with what he as pastor and his congregants could expect from the Christian life. Is such a life to be marked merely by an increasing appreciation for justification in Christ? Or is it also to involve the steady slaying of sin within our bodily members? Certainly it is hard to read the New Testament and see Paul's imperatives as simply pointing to legal impossibilities in order to drive us to despair. If they were simply that, why does he typically place them at the end of his letters, after talking about the work that is done in Christ?

Further, Owen wrestled with the nature of sin and temptation. Is it sinful to be tempted? Well, that cannot be true in the simplest and most straightforward way because the New Testament teaches that Christ was sinless while tempted in every way as we are. This is where fine distinctions become helpful. Owen distinguishes between external temptations and internal. Thus one might pass a suggestive poster outside a shop that tempts one to have a lustful thought and yet resist that temptation and not sin. Or one may be sitting at home daydreaming and start to have inappropriate thoughts about a neighbor's wife. The one represents an external temptation; the other, internal.

That difference is crucial and surely plays into current discussions of same-sex attraction. Some say that the tendency itself is not wrong because temptation itself is not wrong. Owen would reply that it depends on how one is using the term *temptation*. Thus, Owen has much to say to perhaps the most pressing pastoral issue of our day.

Yet our culture is against Owen. That is not so much a theological statement as a comment on our intellectual life. Owen is hard to read. He wrote in long sentences and sometimes arcane and technical vocabulary. I suspect his theology is not so much rejected by the church today as simply not read. The effort is too great, whatever the actual reward might be.

For this reason, it is a pleasure to write the foreword to this book. Here the neophyte will find Owen's understanding of the Christian life explained in concise and clear prose. And for committed Owen aficionados, the authors provide a helpful overview. Hopefully, it will be the gateway for many who have never read Owen themselves to now be encouraged to do so. Given the times in which we live, when the most important questions both without and within the church relate to practical, pastoral ministry, a sound understanding of the Christian life is of paramount importance. There is no better place to start than Owen, and this is a fine introduction to the great man on precisely that topic.

Carl R. Trueman
Paul Woolley Professor of Church History
Westminster Theological Seminary

PREFACE

A book on John Owen on the Christian life is especially difficult to write for the simple reason that no one book can do justice to the rich depth of Owen's writings and theology. To begin with, the sheer *volume* of works Owen wrote in his lifetime is truly remarkable. He stands alongside Augustine, Luther, and Calvin when one considers the large corpus of his writings, including not only theological treatises but also his commentary on Hebrews, as well as his sermons before Parliament and the local church. But even more impressive is the *quality* of those works. In other words, Owen's greatness owes not merely to his having written so many large theological tomes—many theologians have done that—but rather the rich content contained in those doctrinal works. Each of his works is like a deep well. One lets down his bucket to draw up water, and it returns full every time.

Therefore, this book is an exercise in the impossible. To write on such a herculean theologian like John Owen is a daunting task to say the least. How can we do justice to a man who wrote so many books on almost every theological topic, preached a multitude of sermons on a cornucopia of biblical texts, and contributed in significant ways to the development of seventeenth-century Puritanism in an evolving European context? Therefore, a few words are in order about how we wrote this book and how you might approach reading it.

The Task at Hand

Owen on the Christian Life is not meant to be exhaustive. It would be a tremendous and enormous project for an author (or, more likely, a group of authors) to tackle a comprehensive study of Owen's theology. But that was not our assignment in this book. Instead, we have chosen a select number of doctrines and topics that we believe were central to Owen's thought. In doing so, this book aims to introduce the reader to the fundamentals of Owen's theology with special attention to its application to the Christian life.

Moreover, *Owen on the Christian Life* is not a typical historical-theological study. It is a part of Crossway's Theologians on the Christian Life series. So while we focus on Owen's theology, we do so with the intention all along of applying his thought to the Christian life. As authors, we need not stretch Owen's theological works to somehow apply them to the Christian life. Owen was a theologian who always had this purpose in mind when he sat down to write. Whether it was the Trinity, the person of Christ, or the doctrines of predestination, regeneration, or justification, Owen continually sought to show how these glorious truths shape how we live for the glory of God in the face of Christ. For Owen, theology and doxology go hand and hand, like a married couple, impossible to divorce from one another.

How Is This Book Different?

Additionally, we are not the first, nor will we be the last, to write on John Owen. Nor do we wish to be so. It must be acknowledged that a number of outstanding scholars have written books on Owen before us. Perhaps the book closest to our own is that of Sinclair Ferguson, *John Owen on the Christian Life*. Ferguson's book is excellent in many ways, and we would encourage every reader to sink his or her teeth deep into it. Our book is not meant to replace Ferguson's outstanding volume, nor is it designed to improve upon it. Rather, ours is meant to complement the work of Ferguson (and many other worthy scholars). Likewise, our hope is that our book will add to the ongoing study of Owen, encouraging others to probe areas where we do not tread.

However, our book does differ from Ferguson's in notable ways. For example, Ferguson's volume does not devote significant attention to divine providence, predestination, justification, the person of Christ, or the nature of the atonement. Therefore, among many other topics, we have also spent considerable space treating these doctrines not only because they were of great importance to Owen, but also to avoid overlapping territory with Ferguson too much. On the other hand, while Ferguson gives lengthy attention to topics like covenant theology, law and gospel, assurance, apostasy, the sacraments, and prayer, our utilization of these themes in Owen is intentionally minimal. Nonetheless, the keen eye will notice many of these themes sprinkled throughout the book and even assumed in various ways. So while we do attend to many of those areas Ferguson has touched on, our book seeks to look at Owen from another angle, addressing several doctrines that Owen wrote on extensively and that need to be unearthed. Our hope is that this book will add to the ongoing study of Owen, encouraging others to probe areas where we do not tread.

Who Should Read *Owen on the Christian Life*?

For whom did we write this book? There are several excellent books on Owen that are meant for an academic audience, and we have provided a Select Bibliography at the end of this volume for that purpose. However, this book, and the entire series, is not written for the academic elite. It is written for any and every Christian interested in what this Puritan giant had to say about the Christian life. Therefore, while we do not pass over or ignore the weightiness of Owen's theology, nevertheless, the book is written with a very practical and pastoral focus in mind. So if you want to be introduced to Owen, his theology, and how he applied that theology to Christian living, then you have picked up the right book. Our hope is that, with Owen's help, you will walk away with a deep sense of some of the most important truths of the Christian faith, and that you will see just how important theology is for living the Christian life. If you do, then not only have we succeeded, but we have also represented Owen well, since his aim, as both a theologian and a pastor, was to demonstrate that what we think about God should transform everything about us. Again, theology and doxology go together, and the latter flows naturally from the former.

One other word is in order. For the average layperson, the Puritans are not easy to read, especially John Owen. Puritan thought is embedded in what to many is increasingly archaic English. Sadly, many have picked up a book by Owen and minutes later set it down indefinitely because of the difficulty of comprehending him. We are not ignorant of the fact that for many, reading Owen is a fearful task. What we have tried to do in this book, therefore, is translate Owen for those who are not familiar with the Puritans and their style of writing. Where Owen is famously (or for others, infamously) long-winded, exploring one digression after another, we have done our best to summarize his main points, and to footnote those places we did not cover but welcome every reader to explore.

At the same time, we have also tried to avoid "dumbing-down" Owen. One of Owen's strengths is his ability to leave no stone unturned. Owen has the extraordinary skill of describing a theological truth in such depth that he brings to the surface aspects of that truth you had never thought of or imagined could exist. Therefore, though we have tried to make Owen digestible for the novice, nevertheless, there are many times when you just need to hear Owen for yourself, unchecked, unbridled, unabridged, and unedited. In that light, we have, as much as possible, quoted him so that you can hear this great Puritan thinker unfiltered.

Why We Need to Read and Learn from John Owen

Why should we read, get to know, and learn from a Puritan like John Owen? As J. I. Packer has argued, we need to read the Puritans, and John Owen especially, because we are spiritual dwarfs by comparison.[1] Far too often in the recent past the focus of Christians has shifted away from the glory of God and the gospel of Jesus Christ and has instead made Christianity man-centered and success-oriented. Consequently, Christian spirituality has become sentimental and self-indulgent. In short, we lack spiritual maturity.

In contrast, John Owen was a spiritual giant. Many reasons could be listed as to why, but we will focus on just three. First and foremost, Owen had a big view of God and a passion to see this great God lifted up in worship. The glory of God in Christ was at the very core of Owen's thought, suffusing his writing and preaching at every turn. Owen was radically God-centered. But for Owen, and for the Puritans altogether, intellectual knowledge was not enough. Rather, one must *know* God experientially, or, as Owen would put it, experimentally. In other words, it was not enough for God to be studied; God had to be served, adored, and worshiped. Truly understanding who God is and what he has done in redemptive history is meant to arouse our affections for God. Head knowledge always has to be accompanied by heartfelt experience, which leads us to our next point.

Second, we can learn much from the quality of Owen's spirituality. In knowing God, Owen knew humanity.[2] While human beings have been

---

[1] J. I. Packer, *A Quest for Godliness: The Puritan Vision of the Christian Life* (Wheaton, IL: Crossway, 1990), 22.

[2] Owen sounds much like Calvin before him. See John Calvin, *Institutes of the Christian Religion*, ed. John T. McNeil, trans. Ford Lewis Battles (Philadelphia: Westminster John Knox, 1960), 1.1.1.

made in God's image, sin has radically distorted them in every way. Every person stands guilty before a holy God and every person is corrupt, unwilling and unable to turn to Christ. For Owen, it is only through the effectual and gracious work of the Spirit that sinners are converted to Christ and thereafter grow in holiness and likeness to Christ. It is no wonder that Owen's assistant, David Clarkson, wrote of him, "It was his great Design to promote Holiness in the Life and Exercise of it among you."[3] And for Owen, this communion with the triune God was at the very center of the Christian's sanctification and growth in holiness.

Third, Owen sought reformation, not only in the individual believer but also in the corporate church. Owen was serious about both the Christian life and the church's godliness, which in his mind was to occur through the preaching and teaching of God's Word, the administration of the sacraments, and the practice of church discipline. In this sense Owen was in line with the best of the sixteenth-century Reformers. If there was any man who sought to initiate and cultivate genuine reformation in England, it was John Owen. If we desire to see spiritual renewal in our own day, we will do well to pay heed to the lessons we can glean from the life and writings of Owen.

It is sad that many Christians today have never heard of John Owen, let alone read this colossal Puritan. Owen simply is not read and celebrated to the extent of others such as Martin Luther, John Calvin, and Jonathan Edwards. Nevertheless, he should be. Owen's writings are a gold mine just waiting to be dug up and discovered anew. Therefore, it is our aim both to introduce you to Owen's understanding of the Christian life, and to instill within each reader a thirst to imbibe Owen, drinking deeply from this Puritan well. In so doing, our ultimate goal is not to create merely a renewed interest in Owen, as important as that is. Rather, our aspiration is to allow Owen to speak for himself, giving us a glimpse into the majesty, glory, and supremacy of our great God, as well as a renewed passion to see the gospel of Jesus Christ take root both in the church and in the life of the believer.

Living for the Glory of God in Christ

Last, a word is needed about the subtitle of this book, *Living for the Glory of God in Christ*. Clarkson said in his sermon at the funeral of John Owen:

---

[3] Quoted in Sinclair B. Ferguson, *John Owen on the Christian Life* (Edinburgh: Banner of Truth, 1987), xiii.

I need not tell you of this who knew him, that it was his great Design to promote Holiness in the Life and Exercise of it among you: But it was his great Complaint, that its Power declined among Professors. It was his Care and Endeavor to prevent or cure spiritual Decays in his own Flock: He was a burning and a shining Light, and you for a while rejoiced in his Light. Alas! It was but for a while; and we may Rejoyce in it still.[4]

Clarkson has well captured the *raison d'etre* of the life of Owen. Owen's books and sermons drip with this ever-flowing, ever-radiant emphasis on Christian holiness. At the core of this emphasis was his desire to live a life of purity and godliness, one that magnified, glorified, and pleased God and his Savior Christ Jesus. Like Owen, we also lament that few today understand and experience what it is like to live in this way. But also like Owen, we aim in this book to help prevent and cure spiritual decay in the church. So if you are lacking in your zeal for Christ and are weary in your struggle against sin and your pursuit of godliness, then you have come to the right place. Drink deeply.

Soli Deo gloria

---

[4] Quoted in ibid., xiii.

CHRONOLOGY

1616   John Owen is born to Rev. Henry Owen and his wife, Hester.

1625   James I is succeeded by Charles I.

1626   Owen begins grammar school.

1628   Owen enters Oxford University.

1629   Charles I dissolves Parliament.

1630   William Laud becomes chancellor of Oxford.
        Puritans leave for New England and are led by John Winthrop.

1632   Owen graduates with a BA.

1633   Laud is appointed archbishop of Canterbury.

1635   Owen is awarded an MA; begins a seven-year BD program.

1637   Owen leaves Oxford University.

1640   The Long Parliament (1640–1653) convenes.

1642   The English Civil War begins; Owen moves to London and gains assurance of salvation.

1643   Owen takes up a pastorate in Fordham, Essex; Owen marries Mary Rooke (c. 1618–1676).
        The Westminster Assembly convenes.
        The Solemn League and Covenant is signed.

1644   Parliamentarians gain an important victory at the Battle of Marston Moor.

1645   Laud is executed; the decisive Battle of Naseby is fought.

1646   Owen preaches before Parliament (April 29).
        He is inducted as vicar of Coggeshall, Essex.
        Owen becomes a Congregationalist.

1647   The Westminster Confession of Faith is completed.

1648   The First Civil War comes to an end.

1649   Charles I is executed; England is declared a commonwealth.
        As Oliver Cromwell's chaplain, Owen travels to Ireland.

1650   Owen is appointed preacher to the Council of State and a chaplain to
        Cromwell with the expedition to Scotland.

1651   Owen is appointed dean of Christ Church, Oxford University.

1652   Owen is appointed vice-chancellor of Oxford.

1653   Cromwell dissolves Parliament and is appointed Lord Protector.
        Owen is awarded an honorary DD from Oxford.

1657   Owen opposes the offer of the crown to Cromwell.
        Owen is no longer vice-chancellor.

1658   Owen takes a leading role at the Savoy Assembly.
        Cromwell dies (September 3).

1660   The monarchy is restored under Charles II.
        Owen leaves Christ Church and Oxford (March); he lives at Stadhampton.

1662   The Act of Uniformity seeks to impose Anglican uniformity; two thou-
        sand Puritan ministers are ejected on St. Bartholomew's Day (August 24);
        Owen moves to Stoke Newington.

1664   The Conventicle Act prohibits Nonconformist pastors from preaching.

1665   The Great Plague kills many in London; the Five Mile Act prohibits Non-
        conformist ministers from returning to parishes.

1666   The Great Fire in London destroys much of the city.

1669–1670   Owen discusses Nonconformist unity with Richard Baxter.

1672   Limited religious freedom is granted by the Declaration of Indulgence.

1673   Owen's church unites with that of Joseph Caryl; the congregation now
        meets in Leadenhall Street, London.

1675   Owen's first wife, Mary, dies.

1676   Owen marries Dorothy D'Oyley.

1683   Owen dies (August 24); he is buried in Bunhill Fields (September 4).

1689   The Toleration Act receives royal assent.

CHAPTER I

BEING JOHN OWEN

The Puritan John Owen . . . was one of the greatest of English theologians. In an age of giants, he overtopped them all. C. H. Spurgeon called him the prince of divines. He is hardly known today, and we are the poorer for our ignorance. [1]

"I Would Gladly Relinquish All My Learning"

Charles II (r. 1660–1685) once asked one of the most learned scholars that he knew why any intelligent person should waste time listening to the sermons of an uneducated tinker and Baptist preacher by the name of John Bunyan (1628–1688).[2] "Could I possess the tinker's abilities for preaching, please your majesty," replied the scholar, "I would gladly relinquish all my learning." The name of the scholar was John Owen (1616–1683), and this small story—apparently true and not apocryphal—says a good deal about the man and his Christian character. His love of and concern for the preaching of the Word reveals a man who was Puritan to the core. And the fragrant humility of his reply to the king was a virtue that permeated all of his writings, in which he sought to glorify the triune God and help God's people find the maturity that was theirs in Christ.[3]

---

[1] J. I. Packer, *A Quest for Godliness: The Puritan Vision of the Christian Life* (Wheaton, IL: Crossway, 1990), 191.

[2] Parts of this chapter are taken from Michael A. G. Haykin, *The Reformers and Puritans as Spiritual Mentors* (Ontario: Joshua, 2012), chap. 9. For permission to use this material here, the authors are indebted to Joshua Press.

[3] For the story, see Andrew Thomson, *Life of Dr Owen*, in *The Works of John Owen* (1850; repr., London: Banner of Truth, 1965), 1:xcii; Allen C. Guelzo, "John Owen, Puritan Pacesetter," *Christianity Today* 20 (May 21, 1976): 14; Peter Toon, *God's Statesman: The Life and Work of John Owen: Pastor, Educator, Theologian*

In his own day some of Owen's fellow Puritans called him the "Calvin of England."[4] More recently, Roger Nicole has described Owen as "the greatest divine who ever wrote in English," and J. I. Packer says of him that during his career as a Christian theologian, he was "England's foremost bastion and champion of Reformed evangelical orthodoxy."[5] Despite his theological brilliance, it needs noting that Owen's chief interest was not in producing theological treatises for their own sake, but in advancing the personal holiness of God's people.[6]

"Bred Up from My Infancy": Owen's Early Years

John Owen was born in 1616, the same year that William Shakespeare died. Owen grew up in a Christian home in a small village now known as Stadhampton, then called Stadham, about five miles southeast of Oxford.[7] His father, Henry Owen, was a Puritan and the minister of the parish church there. The names of three of his brothers have also come down to us: his older brother, William, who became the Puritan minister at Remenham, just north of Henley-on-Thames; and his two younger brothers: Henry, who fought as a major in the New Model Army of Oliver Cromwell (1599–1658), and Philemon, who was killed fighting under Cromwell in Ireland in 1649.[8]

Of Owen's childhood years only one reference has been recorded. "I was bred up from my infancy," he remarked in 1657, "under the care of my father, who was a nonconformist all his days, and a painful labourer [that is, diligent worker] in the vineyard of the Lord."[9] If we take as our cue the way that other Puritans raised their children, we can presume that as a small boy Owen, along with his siblings, would have been taught to pray, to read the Bible, and to obey its commandments. At least once a day there

---

(Exeter: Paternoster, 1971), 162. Subsequent references to the works of Owen throughout this book are cited according to the title of the work, as well as the volume and page numbers in *The Works of John Owen*, ed. William H. Goold, 23 vols. (1850–1855; repr., London: Banner of Truth, 1965–1968). References to Owen's commentary on Hebrews are cited in the same fashion, the Hebrews volumes being vols. 17–23 of the *Works*. Where pertinent, the biblical text being commented upon will also be referenced.

[4] Guelzo, "John Owen, Puritan Pacesetter," 14; Richard L. Greaves, "Owen, John (1616–1683)," *Oxford Dictionary of National Biography* (Oxford: Oxford University Press, 2004); online ed., May 2009, http://www.oxforddnb.com.libaccess.lib.mcmaster.ca/view/article/21016, accessed June 16, 2013.

[5] Guelzo, "John Owen, Puritan Pacesetter," 14; Packer, *Quest for Godliness*, 81.

[6] Guelzo, "John Owen, Puritan Pacesetter," 15–16.

[7] For a good account of Owen's life, see Toon, *God's Statesman*. For Owen's theology, the best studies are undoubtedly Carl R. Trueman, *The Claims of Truth: John Owen's Trinitarian Theology* (Carlisle: Paternoster, 1998), and now Kelly M. Kapic and Mark Jones, eds., *The Ashgate Research Companion to John Owen's Theology* (Burlington, VT: Ashgate, 2012). See also Sinclair B. Ferguson, *John Owen on the Christian Life* (Edinburgh: Banner of Truth, 1987); and Robert W. Oliver, ed., *John Owen: The Man and His Theology* (Phillipsburg, NJ: P&R, 2002).

[8] Toon, *God's Statesman*, 2.

[9] Owen, *A Review of the True Nature of Schism*, in *Works*, 13:224.

would have been time set aside for family worship when he would have listened to his father explain a portion of God's Word and pray for their nation, his parishioners, and each of his children.[10] It needs noting that this is the only personal remark about his family that Owen makes in any of his published works. There was clearly a reticence on his part to open up his life to his readers. As James Moffatt remarked at the turn of the twentieth century: "Owen never trusts himself to his readers. . . . Hence his private life and feelings remain for the most part a mystery."[11]

At twelve years of age, Owen was sent by his father to Queen's College, the University of Oxford. Here he obtained his BA on June 11, 1632, when he was sixteen. He went on to study for the MA, which he was awarded on April 27, 1635. Everything seemed to be set for Owen to pursue an academic career. It was not, however, a good time to launch out into world of academe. The archbishop of Canterbury, William Laud (1573–1645), had set out to suppress the Puritan movement, which was seen as radical, even revolutionary, by the leadership of the state church. Laud thus began a purge of the churches and universities. By 1637 Owen had no alternative but to leave Oxford and to become, along with many other Puritans who refused to conform to the established church, a private chaplain. He eventually found employment in the house of Lord Lovelace, a nobleman sympathetic to the Puritan cause. Laud's policies, supported by the monarch Charles I (r. 1625–1649), alienated the Puritan cause and pushed the Puritans to the point where many of them believed they had no choice but to engage in a civil war against their sovereign. In the early stages of the English Civil War, which broke out in 1642, Lord Lovelace decided to support the king, and Owen, whose sympathies were with Parliament, left his chaplaincy and moved to London.

A "Clear Shining from God"

The move to London was providential in a couple of ways. First of all, it brought him into contact with the some of the leading defenders of the parliamentary cause, Puritan preachers who viewed the struggle between the king and Parliament in terms of the struggle between Christ and anti-Christian forces. Moreover, it was during these initial days in London that he had an experience he would never forget. By 1642 Owen was convinced

---

[10] Toon, *God's Statesman*, 2.
[11] James Moffatt, *The Golden Book of John Owen* (London: Hodder & Stoughton, 1904), 19–20.

that the final source of authority in religion was the Holy Scriptures and, moreover, that the doctrines of orthodox Calvinism were biblical Christianity. But he had yet to experience personally the Holy Spirit bearing witness to his spirit and giving him the assurance that he was a child of God.[12]

Owen found this assurance one Sunday when he decided to go with a cousin to hear Edmund Calamy the Elder (1600–1666), a famous Presbyterian preacher, at St. Mary's Church, Aldermanbury. On arriving at this church, they were informed that Calamy was not going to preach that morning. Instead a country preacher (whose name Owen never did discover) was going to fill in for the Presbyterian divine. Owen's cousin urged him to go with him to hear Arthur Jackson (c. 1593–1666), another notable Puritan preacher, at nearby St. Michael's. But Owen decided to remain at St. Mary's. The preacher took as his text Matthew 8:26: "Why are ye fearful, O ye of little faith?" It proved to be a message that Owen needed to hear and embrace. Through the words of a preacher whose identity is unknown, God spoke to Owen and removed once and for all his doubts and fears as to whether he was truly regenerate. He now knew himself to be born of the Spirit.[13]

The impact of this spiritual experience cannot be overestimated. It gave Owen the deep, inner conviction that he was indeed a child of God and chosen in Christ before the foundation of the world, that God loved him and had a loving purpose for his life, and that this God was the true and living God. In practical terms, it meant a lifelong interest in the work of God the Holy Spirit that would issue thirty years later in his monumental study of the Holy Spirit, *Pneumatologia; or, A Discourse concerning the Holy Spirit*.[14] As he later wrote, "Clear shining from God must be at the bottom of deep labouring with God."[15]

Pastoral Ministry and Preaching before Parliament

In 1643 Owen was offered the pastorate in the village of Fordham, six miles or so northwest of Colchester in Essex. Owen was here till 1646, when he became the minister of the church at the market town of Coggeshall, some five miles to the south. Here, as many as two thousand people would fill

---

[12] Toon, *God's Statesman*, 12.
[13] Ibid., 12–13.
[14] Ibid., 13. It also meant Owen would write on the doctrine of assurance. See Owen, *A Practical Exposition upon Psalm 130*, in *Works*, 6:324–648.
[15] Quoted in Peter Barraclough, *John Owen (1616–1683)* (London: Independent Press, 1961), 6.

the church each Lord's Day to hear Owen preach.[16] Thus, although Owen would later speak slightingly of his preaching to King Charles II—as seen in the anecdote with which this chapter began—it is evident that he was no mean preacher.

It is also noteworthy that this change in pastorates began an ecclesiological shift to Congregationalism. Up until this point Owen had been decidedly Presbyterian in his understanding of church government. However, Owen began to change his mind after reading *The Keyes of the Kingdom of Heaven* by John Cotton (1584–1652), which had been published in 1644, and by 1648 he was a confirmed Congregationalist. It was also at Coggeshall that he wrote the classic work on particular redemption *The Death of Death in the Death of Christ* (1647).[17] The backdrop for these early years of Owen's pastoral ministry was the English Civil War, when England knew the horrors of bloody fields of battle, and father was ranged against son and neighbor against neighbor on the battlefield. Well has this period been described as "the world turned upside down." It needs to be noted, though, that little of the early fighting actually took place in Essex or remotely near Coggeshall; hence at this time, Owen saw little of the bloody horrors of civil war.[18]

During these tumultuous days Owen clearly identified himself with the parliamentary cause. Like others who ardently supported Parliament in their struggle against the king, Owen would look back on some of the decisive parliamentary victories in the 1640s as a clear vindication of their cause by God.[19] He also developed a friendship with the rising military figure Oliver Cromwell and was frequently invited to preach before Parliament. By late 1648 some of the parliamentary army officers had begun to urge that Charles I be brought to trial on charges of treason since he had fought against his own people and Parliament. Charles was accordingly put on trial in January 1649, and by the end of that month a small group of powerful Puritan leaders had found him guilty and sentenced their king to death. On January 31, the day following the public execution of the king, Owen was asked to preach before Parliament.

Owen used the occasion to urge upon the members of Parliament that

---

[16] Robert W. Oliver, "John Owen (1616–1683)—His Life and Times," in Oliver, *John Owen*, 16.

[17] For a study of this work, see Jack N. Macleod, "John Owen and the Death of Death," in *Out of Bondage* (London: The Westminster Conference, 1983), 70–87.

[18] Tim Cooper, "Why Did Richard Baxter and John Owen Diverge? The Impact of the First Civil War," *Journal of Ecclesiastical History* 61 (2010): 507–11.

[19] As he once stated, "Where is the God of Marston Moor, and the God of Naseby? is an acceptable expostulation in a gloomy day." Quoted in Moffatt, *Golden Book of John Owen*, 112.

for them, now the rulers of England, in order to obtain God's favor in the future they must remove from the nation all traces of false worship and superstition and wholeheartedly establish a religion based on Scripture alone. Owen based his sermon on Jeremiah 15. He made no direct reference to the events of the previous day, nor did he mention, at least in the version of his sermon that has come down to us, the name of the king. Nevertheless, his hearers and later readers would easily have been able to deduce from his use of the Old Testament how he viewed the religious policy and end of Charles. From the story of the wicked king Manasseh that is recorded in 2 Kings 21 and with cross-references to Jeremiah 15, he argued that the leading cause for God's judgments upon the Jewish people had been such abominations as idolatry and superstition, tyranny and cruelty. He then pointed to various similarities between the conditions of ancient Judah and the England of his day. At the heart of the sermon was a call to Parliament to establish a Reformed style of worship, to disseminate biblical Christianity, to uphold national righteousness, and to avoid oppression. He assured the Puritan leaders who heard him that day that God's promise of protection to Jeremiah was also applicable to all who in every age stood firmly for justice and mercy.[20]

Ireland and Oxford

Later that same year, Owen accompanied Cromwell on his campaign in Ireland, where he stayed from August 1649 to February 1650. Though ill much of this time, he preached frequently to "a numerous multitude of as thirsting a people after the gospel as ever yet I conversed withal."[21] When he returned to England the following year, he confessed, "The tears and cries of the inhabitants of Dublin after the manifestations of Christ are ever in my view." Accordingly, he sought to convince Parliament of the spiritual need of this land and asked:

> How is it that Jesus Christ is in Ireland only as a lion staining all his garments with the blood of his enemies; and none to hold him out as a lamb sprinkled with his own blood to his friends? Is it the sovereignty and interest of England that is alone to be there transacted? For my part, I see no farther into the mystery of these things but that I could heartily rejoice,

---

[20] Owen, "Righteous Zeal Encouraged by Divine Protection," in *Works*, 8:133–62; Toon, *God's Statesman*, 33–34.
[21] Owen, *Of the Death of Christ*, in *Works*, 10:479.

that, innocent blood being expiated, the Irish might enjoy Ireland so long as the moon endureth, so that Jesus Christ might possess the Irish. I would there were for the present one gospel preacher for every walled town in the English possession in Ireland. . . . If they were in the dark, and loved to have it so, it might something [to some extent] close a door upon the bowels of our compassion; but they cry out of their darkness, and are ready to follow every one whosoever, to have a candle. If their being gospelless move not our hearts, it is hoped their importunate cries will disquiet our rest, and wrest help as a beggar doth an alms.[22]

Although Owen's pleas were heeded and this period saw the establishment of a number of Puritan congregations—both Congregationalist and Baptist—in Ireland, Crawford Gribben has shown that the inability of the Puritans in Ireland to work together with like-minded brethren for the larger cause of the kingdom of Christ hindered their witness.[23]

By the early 1650s, Owen had become one of Cromwell's leading advisors, especially in national affairs having to do with the church. There is little doubt that Owen was a firm supporter of Cromwell in this period. As Owen told him on one occasion in 1654, for example, "The series and chain of eminent providences whereby you have been carried on and protected in all the hazardous work of your generation, which your God hath called you unto, is evident to all."[24] Two years later, though, when Cromwell was urged to become the monarch of England, Owen was among those who opposed this move. As it turned out, Cromwell did not accept the crown. But Owen's friendship with Cromwell had been damaged, and the two men were nowhere near as close as they had been.[25] This would have distressed Owen since he had viewed Cromwell with enormous admiration. This rupture in his friendship with Cromwell may well have reinforced a tendency in Owen's character to be self-reliant.[26]

Cromwell had appointed Owen to the oversight of Oxford University in 1652 as its vice-chancellor. From this position Owen helped to reassemble the faculty, who had been dispersed by the war, and to put the university back on its feet. He also had numerous opportunities to preach

---

[22] Owen, "The Steadfastness of the Promises, and the Sinfulness of Staggering," in *Works*, 8:235–36.

[23] Crawford Gribben, *The Irish Puritans: James Ussher and the Reformation of the Church* (Darlington: Evangelical Press, 2003), 91–115.

[24] Owen, *The Doctrine of the Saints' Perseverance Explained and Confirmed*, in *Works*, 11:5.

[25] Oliver, "John Owen (1616–1683)," 26; Toon, *God's Statesman*, 97–101.

[26] See the remarks on Owen's friendships by Moffatt, *Golden Book of John Owen*, 19–20, and Tim Cooper, "Owen's Personality: The Man behind the Theology," in Kapic and Jones, *Ashgate Research Companion to John Owen's Theology*, 215–26.

to the students at Oxford. Two important works on holiness came out of his preaching during this period. *Of Temptation*, first published in 1658, is essentially an exposition of Matthew 26:4. It analyzes the way in which believers fall into sin. A second work, *Of the Mortification of Sin in Believers* (1656), is in some ways the richest of all of Owen's treatises on this subject. It is based on Romans 8:13 and lays out a strategy for fighting indwelling sin and warding off temptation. Owen emphasizes that in the fight against sin the Holy Spirit employs all our human powers. In sanctifying us, Owen insists, the Spirit works

> in us and upon us, as we are fit to be wrought in and upon; that is, so as to preserve our own liberty and free obedience. He works upon our understandings, wills, consciences, and affections, agreeably to their own natures; he works in us and with us, not against us or without us; so that his assistance is an encouragement as to the facilitating of the work, and no occasion of neglect as to the work itself.[27]

Not without reason does Owen lovingly describe the Spirit in another place as "the great beautifier of souls."[28]

Oliver Cromwell died in September 1658, and the "rule of the saints," as some called it, began to fall apart. In the autumn of that year, Owen, now a key leader among the Congregationalists, played a vital role in drawing up what is known as the Savoy Declaration, which would give the Congregationalist churches fortitude for the difficult days ahead. Only a few days after Cromwell's death, Owen met with around two hundred other Congregationalist leaders, including men like Thomas Goodwin (1600–1680), Philip Nye (c. 1596–1672), and William Bridge (c. 1600–1671),[29] in the chapel of the old Savoy Palace in London. One of the outcomes of this synod was a recommendation to revise the Westminster Confession of Faith for the Congregationalist churches. Traditionally Owen has been credited with writing the lengthy preface that came before the Savoy Declaration. In it he rightly argued, anticipating a key issue over the rest of his life:

---

[27] In *Works*, 6:20. See also the comments of J. I. Packer, "'Keswick' and the Reformed Doctrine of Sanctification," *Evangelical Quarterly* 27 (1955): 156.

[28] Owen, *The Nature, Power, Deceit, and Prevalency of the Remainders of Indwelling Sin in Believers*, in *Works*, 6:188. For further discussion of this area of Owen's teaching, see Michael A. G. Haykin, "The Great Beautifier of Souls," *Banner of Truth* 242 (1983): 18–22, and below in chap. 8.

[29] For biographical sketches of these three men, see William S. Barker, *Puritan Profiles: 54 Influential Puritans at the Time When the Westminster Confession of Faith Was Written* (Fearn, Ross-shire: Christian Focus, 1996), 69–94 passim.

The Spirit of Christ is in himself too *free*, great and generous a Spirit, to suffer himself to be used by any human arm, to whip men into belief; he drives not, but *gently leads into all truth*, and *persuades* men to *dwell in the tents* of *like precious faith*; which would lose of its preciousness and value, if that sparkle of freeness shone not in it.[30]

The following year Owen preached again before Parliament. But the times were changing, and this proved to be the last of such occasions.

"The Church in a Storm": Owen, a Leader in a Time of Persecution, 1660–1683

In 1660 a number of Cromwell's fellow Puritan leaders, fearful that Britain was slipping into full-fledged anarchy, asked Charles II, then living in exile on the Continent, to return to England as her monarch. Those who came to power with Charles were determined that the Puritans would never again hold the reins of political authority. During Charles's reign and that of his brother James II (r. 1685–1688), the Puritan cause was thus savagely persecuted. After the Act of Uniformity in 1662, which required all religious worship to be according to the letter of the Book of Common Prayer, and other legislation enacted during the 1660s, all other forms of worship were illegal.

A number of Owen's close friends, including John Bunyan, suffered fines and imprisonment for not heeding these laws. Although Owen was shielded from actual imprisonment by some powerful friends, such as Lord Philip Wharton (1613–1696), he led at best a precarious existence till his death. He was once nearly attacked by a mob, which surrounded his carriage.[31] Between 1663 and 1666 he was tempted to accept the offer of a safe haven in America when the Puritan leaders in Massachusetts offered him the presidency of Harvard.[32] Owen, though, recognized where he was needed most, and he wrote prodigiously in defense of Nonconformity. This polemical defense, though, took its toll. In 1672, he told the New England Puritan John Eliot (1604–1690), "There is scarce any one alive in the world that hath more reproaches cast upon him than I have," and as he was experiencing "a dry and barren spirit," he begged Eliot to pray for him that God

---

[30] Preface to the Savoy Declaration in *The Creeds of Christendom*, ed. Philip Schaff and rev. David S. Schaff, vol. 3 (1931; repr., Grand Rapids: Baker, 1983), 709; emphasis original. For a recent edition of this confession, see *The Savoy Declaration of Faith* (Millers Falls, MA: First Congregational Church, 1998).
[31] Barraclough, *John Owen*, 15.
[32] Greaves, "Owen, John."

would "water me from above."[33] Two years later, in a letter to Charles Fleetwood (c. 1618–1692), one of Cromwell's sons-in-law, he described himself as a "poor withering soul" and he expressed his fear that

> we shall die in the wilderness; yet ought we to labour and pray continually that the heavens would drop down from above, and the skies pour down righteousness—that the earth may open and bring forth salvation, and that righteousness may spring up together [see Ps. 85:10–11]. . . . I beseech you to contend yet more earnestly than ever I have done, with God, with my own heart, with the church, to labour after spiritual revivals.[34]

Owen's fears were not unfounded: he would die without seeing any turning of the tide for the Nonconformists, and the spiritual state of England would continue to decline until the revivals of the mid-1730s.

Owen's first wife, Mary, died in 1676. When he remarried the following year, his second wife, Dorothy D'Oyley, was the widow of a wealthy Oxfordshire landowner whom Owen would have known from his connections to his home village of Stadhampton.[35] Added to the toil and anxieties of these years were physical challenges, especially asthma and kidney stones. But these years were also ones of prodigious literary fruitfulness. His exhaustive commentary on Hebrews appeared between 1668 and 1684, which he regarded in many ways as his magnum opus.[36] A Discourse concerning the Holy Spirit came out in 1674, and an influential work on justification, The Doctrine of Justification by Faith, in 1677. Owen's Meditations and Discourses on the Glory of Christ, which Robert Oliver has rightly termed

---

[33] Letter to John Eliot (1672), in The Correspondence of John Owen, ed. Peter Toon (Cambridge: James Clarke, 1970), 154.

[34] Letter to Charles Fleetwood, July 8 (1674), in Toon, Correspondence of John Owen, 159. Owen was not the only Puritan leader urging prayer for revival in the 1670s. Four years after Owen wrote this letter, John Howe (1630–1705) preached a series of sermons based on Ezekiel 39:29 in which he dealt with the subject of the outpouring of the Holy Spirit. In one of these sermons he told his audience: "When the Spirit shall be poured forth plentifully I believe you will hear much other kind of sermons, or they will, who shall live to such a time, than you are wont to do now-a-days. . . . It is plain, too sadly plain, there is a great retraction of the Spirit of God even from us; we know not how to speak living sense [i.e., felt reality] unto souls, how to get within you; our words die in our mouths, or drop and die between you and us. We even faint, when we speak; long experienced unsuccessfulness makes us despond; we speak not as persons that hope to prevail. . . . When such an effusion of the Spirit shall be as is here signified . . . [ministers] shall know how to speak to better purpose, with more compassion and sense, with more seriousness, with more authority and allurement, than we now find we can." The Prosperous State of the Christian Interest before the End of Time, by a Plentiful Effusion of the Holy Spirit: Sermon IV, in The Works of the Rev. John Howe, M. A. (New York: John P. Haven, 1838), 1:575. For the explanation of "living sense" as "felt reality," see J. I. Packer, God In Our Midst: Seeking and Receiving Ongoing Revival (Ann Arbor, MI: Servant, 1987), 33.

[35] Oliver, "John Owen (1616–1683)," 35.

[36] See John W. Tweeddale, "John Owen's Commentary on Hebrews in Context," in Kapic and Jones, Ashgate Research Companion to John Owen's Theology, 52, 54–55.

"incomparable,"[37] was written under the shadow of death in 1683 and represents Owen's dying testimony to the unsurpassable value and joy of living a life for the glory of Christ.

He fell asleep in Christ on August 24, 1683. His final literary work is a letter to his friend Charles Fleetwood, written but two days before his death. "Dear Sir," he wrote:

> I am going to him whom my soul hath loved, or rather who hath loved me with an everlasting love; which is the whole ground of all my consolation. The passage is very irksome and wearysome through strong pains of various sorts which are all issued in an intermitting fever. All things were provided to carry me to London today attending to the advice of my physician, but we were all disappointed by my utter disability to undertake the journey. I am leaving the ship of the church in a storm, but whilst the great Pilot is in it the loss of a poore under-rower will be inconsiderable. Live and pray and hope and waite patiently and doe not despair; the promise stands invincible that he will never leave thee nor forsake thee.[38]

Owen was buried on September 4 in Bunhill Fields, where the bodies of so many of his fellow Puritans were laid to rest until that tremendous day when they—and all the faithful in Christ—shall be raised to glory.

---

[37] Oliver, "John Owen (1616–1683)," 35.
[38] Toon, *Correspondence of John Owen*, 174.

CHAPTER 2

LIVING BY THE SCRIPTURES

Many men have invented several ways to lessen the authority of the Scripture, and few are willing to acknowledge an immediate speaking of God unto them therein. Various pretences are used to subduct the consciences of men from a sense of his authority in it. But whatever authority, efficacy, or power the word of God was accompanied withal, whether to evidence itself so to be, or otherwise to affect the minds of men unto obedience, when it was first spoken by the Holy Ghost, the same it retains now it is recorded in scripture, seeing the same Holy Ghost yet continues to speak therein. [1]

One of the challenges that exercised Owen has been a perpetual issue for humanity: the issue of authority. Without any hint of embarrassment, Owen gave a ringing endorsement of divine authority throughout his written corpus: for the seventeenth-century Puritan, God's authority was seen as that which "motivates rather than manacles, and renews rather than restricts." [2] And for Owen God's authority was perfectly expressed in the Holy Scriptures, "whose authority and truth are the only unerring

---

[1] Owen, *Hebrews*, in *Works*, 20:21, comment on Heb. 3:7–11. This chapter is taken from Michael A. G. Haykin, "'The One and Only, Absolute and Perfect, Rule': John Owen and the Challenge of the Quakers," in *John Owen—The Man and His Theology*, ed. Robert W. Oliver (Darlington: Evangelical Press; Phillipsburg, NJ: P&R, 2002), 131–55. For permission to use this material here, we are indebted to Evangelical Press and P&R Publishing.
[2] John Wesley Campbell, "John Owen's Rule and Guide: A Study in the Relationship between the Word and the Spirit in the Thought of Dr John Owen" (ThM thesis, Regent College, 1991), 84.

rule and immoveable basis of divine faith, and its properest touch-stone."[3] *Infallible*—"incapable of erring"[4]—was the normal term that Owen used to describe the Scriptures' freedom from error.[5] This much is evident in his *Of the Divine Original of the Scripture* (1659) and *The Causes, Ways, and Means of Understanding the Mind of God* (1678).[6]

Owen developed this understanding of Scripture in response to a variety of challenges: from various groups who emphasized the primacy of reason, such as the Socinians, who denied the Trinity, and the Cambridge Platonists, who stressed the divinity of human reason; from Roman Catholic apologists, who stressed the authority of the church alongside Holy Scripture; and from the Quakers, who essentially exalted their experience of the Spirit's inner working over God's Word.[7] Owen's response to the last of this trio of challenges will provide an excellent vantage point to see his conception of the Scriptures' authority for the Christian life in action.

Meeting with Some Quakers

In June 1654, Elizabeth Fletcher (c. 1638–1658) and Elizabeth Leavens (d. 1665), two Quakers from Kendal, Westmoreland, visited Oxford. They were the first to bring the Quaker message to the university town.[8] They sought to warn the students there about the ungodly nature of academia and convince them that their real need was not intellectual illumination but the inner light given by the Holy Spirit. Their message, though, fell largely on deaf ears. Fletcher felt led by God to resort to a more dramatic testimony to arrest the students' attention. She stripped off her clothing and

---

[3] John Owen and Samuel Annesley, "To the Christian Reader," in Elisha Coles, *A Practical Discourse of God's Sovereignty*, 3rd ed. (London, 1678), 6.
[4] *The Oxford Universal Dictionary on Historical Principles*, ed. William Little, H. W. Fowler, J. Coulson and revised by C. T. Onions, 3rd ed. (Oxford: Clarendon, 1955), s.v.
[5] Stanley N. Gundry, "John Owen on Authority and Scripture," in *Inerrancy and the Church*, ed. John D. Hannah (Chicago: Moody Press, 1984), 203.
[6] Owen, *The Causes, Ways, and Means of Understanding the Mind of God*, in *Works*, 4:118–235; Owen, *Of the Divine Original of the Scriptures*, in *Works*, 16:296–344. Also see Owen, *Integrity and Purity of the Hebrew and Greek Text*, in *Works*, 16:345–423.
[7] For details on Owen's response to these various groups, see Campbell, "John Owen's Rule and Guide," 81–114.
[8] For brief biographical sketches of these two women, see R. L. Greaves, "Fletcher, Elizabeth," in *Biographical Dictionary of British Radicals in the Seventeenth Century*, ed. R. L. Greaves and Robert Zaller, 3 vols. (Brighton: Harvester, 1982–1984), 1:292; and D. P. Ludlow, "Leavens, Elizabeth," in *Biographical Dictionary of British Radicals in the Seventeenth Century*, 2:182. For the following account of their visit to Oxford, see William Sewel, *The History of the Rise, Increase and Progress of the Christian People Called Quakers*, vol. 1 (New York: Baker & Crane, 1844), 120–21; and Peter Toon, *God's Statesman: The Life and Work of John Owen: Pastor, Educator, Theologian* (Exeter: Paternoster, 1971), 76. For a similar account of the entrance of Quakerism into Cambridge University, see John Twigg, *The University of Cambridge and the English Revolution 1625–1688* (Cambridge: Cambridge University Press, 1990), 193–95.

walked semi-naked through the streets of Oxford as "a signe against the Hippocriticall profession they then made there, being then Presbetereans & Independants, which profession she told them the Lord would strip them of, so that their Nakedness should appear."[9] Fletcher's "going naked as a sign," a practice not uncommon among the early Quakers,[10] sparked a hostile reaction among the students. Some of the students seized her and her companion, dragged them through a miry ditch, and then half-drowned them under the water pump on the grounds of St John's College. At some point Fletcher was also either thrown over a gravestone or pushed into an open grave, sustaining injuries that plagued her for the rest of her short life.

It appears, though, that this ordeal did little to dampen the spirits of the two women. The following Sunday they visited an Oxford church where they interrupted the service in order to give a divine warning to the congregation. This time they were arrested and imprisoned in the Bocardo prison. The following day, John Owen, who, as university vice-chancellor was responsible for discipline within the university, accused the two Quakers of blaspheming the Holy Spirit and profaning the Scriptures. Convinced that if their behavior were left unpunished it would incite disorder in the university, he ordered the women to be whipped and expelled from the town.

Two years later Owen had another memorable encounter with the Quakers. This time it was a theological debate in Whitehall Palace with the man who would come to be viewed as the foremost figure in the seventeenth-century British Quaker community, George Fox (1624–1691).[11] Fox later recounted what transpired when he and another Quaker, Edward Pyott (d. 1670), visited Oliver Cromwell, who was then ruling England as Lord Protector.

> Edward Pyott and I went to Whitehall after a time and when we came before him [i.e., Cromwell] there was one Dr. John Owen, Vice-Chancellor of Oxford with him: so we was moved to speak to Oliver Cromwell concerning the sufferings of Friends and laid them before him and turned him to the light of Christ who had enlightened every man that cometh into the world: and he said it was a natural light and we showed him the contrary and how it was divine and spiritual from Christ the spiritual and

---

[9] Kenneth L. Carroll, "Early Quakers and 'Going Naked as a Sign,'" *Quaker History* 67, no. 2 (1978): 80.
[10] For two excellent studies of this phenomenon, see ibid., 69–87, and Richard Bauman, *Let Your Words Be Few: Symbolism of Speaking and Silence among Seventeenth-Century Quakers* (Cambridge: Cambridge University Press, 1983), 84–94.
[11] For a biography of Fox, see H. Larry Ingle, *First among Friends: George Fox and the Creation of Quakerism* (New York: Oxford University Press, 1994).

heavenly man, which was called the life in Christ, the Word and the light in us. And the power of the Lord God riz in me, and I was moved to bid him lay down his crown at the feet of Jesus. Several times I spoke to him to the same effect, and I was standing by the table; and he came and sat upon the table's side by me and said he would be as high as I was. And so he continued speaking against the light of Christ Jesus.[12]

These two incidents display some of the central features of early Quakerism: its emphasis on the divine light within every human being (a conviction drawn from John 1:9), its fiery proselytizing, its contempt of university learning, and its reliance on dramatic and socially disruptive gestures.

Quakerism during the Commonwealth

The Quaker movement was a product of the turmoil of the English Civil War, when familiar social, political, and religious boundaries were being swept away by the tide of conflict, and when tried-and-true religious practices and beliefs no longer seemed to carry any weight. Numerous individuals, many of them raised in a Puritan environment with its emphasis on radical depravity and the need for the sovereign converting work of the Spirit, had begun seeking a God who would bring peace to their souls in the midst of the massive upheaval of the times. Some of these so-called "Seekers" longed for a restoration of the charismatic vitality and simplicity they believed to be characteristic of the apostolic church. As J. F. McGregor points out, they regarded the sign of a true church of Christ to be "its possession of the grace given to the apostles and demonstrated through miracles." Since none of the Puritan congregations claimed to be in possession of such charismatic gifts, the Seekers felt that they had to withdraw from them and wait for what they hoped would be a new divine dispensation.[13] For many Seekers, that divine dispensation appeared with the advent of the Quakers and their message.

Although there were a number of key figures in Quakerism's early days, men such as Edward Burrough (1634–1662), William Dewsbury (1621–1688), and James Nayler (c. 1618–1660), it was George Fox who served as the principal catalyst to bring together many of these Seekers into "a loose kind of church fellowship with a coherent ideology."[14] By the late 1660s

---

[12] *The Journal of George Fox*, ed. John L. Nickalls (Philadelphia: Religious Society of Friends, 1985), 274–75.

[13] J. F. McGregor, "Seekers and Ranters," in *Radical Religion in the English Revolution*, ed. J. F. McGregor and B. Reay (Oxford: Oxford University Press, 1984), 122–23.

[14] Barry Reay, *The Quakers and the English Revolution* (New York: St. Martin's Press, 1985), 9.

most of these early Quaker leaders were dead, and Fox survived to become the nucleus around which the Quaker community eventually coalesced in the late seventeenth century. A one-time shepherd and shoemaker, "literate, but not learned,"[15] Fox left his native village of Drayton-in-the-Clay (now Fenny Drayton), Leicestershire, in 1643 and for lengthy periods of time over the next four years tramped through the Midlands and as far south as London. His goal during this period of physical wandering seems to have been the acquisition of spiritual wisdom. He spent a considerable amount of time with the General (i.e., Arminian) Baptists, whose influence on him may be seen in his later rejection of orthodox Puritan soteriology, in particular, the doctrine of predestination.[16]

Finally, in 1647 and 1648 Fox wrote that he found wisdom "without the help of any man, book or writing."[17] Through a series of what he called "openings," experiences of inner enlightenment, he became convinced, among other things, "that being bred at Oxford or Cambridge was not enough to fit and qualify men to be ministers of Christ,"[18] and that genuine Christianity was essentially a matter of inward spiritual experience. "The Lord God," Fox later recalled in his *Journal*,

> opened to me by his invisible power how that every man was enlightened by the divine light of Christ; and I saw it shine through all, and that they, that believed in it came out of condemnation and came to the light of life and became the children of it, but they that hated it, and did not believe in it, were condemned by it, though they made a profession of Christ. This I saw in the pure openings of the Light without the help of any man, neither did I then know, where to find it in the Scriptures; though afterwards, searching the Scriptures, I found it. For I saw in that Light and Spirit which was before Scripture was given forth, and which led the holy men of God to give them forth, that all must come to that Spirit, if they would know God, or Christ, or the Scriptures aright, which they that gave them forth were led and taught by.[19]

John 1:9 ("that was the true Light, which lighteth every man that cometh into the world"), to which Fox alludes in the earlier part of this passage, was at the core of Fox's distinctive message and that of his fellow

---

[15] Gordon Rupp, *Religion in England 1688–1791* (Oxford: Clarendon, 1986), 139.
[16] For this contact with Baptists, see Ingle, *First among Friends*, 35–38, 42.
[17] Nickalls, *Journal of George Fox*, 11.
[18] Ibid., 7.
[19] Ibid., 33.

Quakers. They understood this text to teach that every individual was born with the light of Christ, which, though darkened by sin, was never fully extinguished. For those who became convinced by the Quaker message, this light had succeeded in breaking through the barrier of sin to unite their souls with Christ.[20] This verse thus described what they knew "experimentally," to use Fox's own description of his spiritual illumination. Moreover, this light of Christ shone within their dark hearts, they believed, independently of the various means of grace normally stressed by the Puritans, such as the reading of the Scriptures.

This text from the Gospel of John also helped define the Quaker mission. After his conversion, for instance, Fox was conscious of being commanded "to turn people to that inward light, spirit and grace, by which all might know their salvation, and their way to God; even that divine spirit, which would lead them into all Truth, and which I infallibly knew would never deceive any."[21] "[We] call All men to look to the Light within their own consciences," another Quaker convert, Samuel Fisher (1605–1665), who had been a Baptist, declared as the goal of Quaker proselytizing. "By the leadings of that Light," he continued, "they may come to God, and work out their Salvation."[22]

In the first decade of the Quaker movement, this message enjoyed phenomenal success. Historians often regard 1652 as the start of Quakerism.[23] It was during the spring of that year that Fox took his message north to the Pennines and Westmoreland. On Whitsunday that year, Fox preached to a large gathering of a thousand Seekers not far from Kendal. "As soon as I heard him declare . . . that the Light of Christ in man was the way to Christ," recalled Francis Howgill (1618–1669), a local preacher and one-time Baptist, "I believed the eternal word of truth, and that of God in my conscience sealed to it." Not only was he convinced of the truth of Fox's message, but, he remembered, so were "many hundred more, who thirsted after the Lord."[24]

The Quaker message took deep root in northern England, in particular,

---

[20] Michael R. Watts, *The Dissenters*, vol. 1 (Oxford: Clarendon, 1978), 203; T. L. Underwood, *Primitivism, Radicalism, and the Lamb's War: The Baptist-Quaker Conflict in Seventeenth-Century England* (New York: Oxford University Press, 1997), 105–11.
[21] Nickalls, *Journal of George Fox*, 34–35. See the comments of Underwood on this passage: *Primitivism, Radicalism, and the Lamb's War*, 112.
[22] Quoted in Reay, *Quakers and the English Revolution*, 33.
[23] Hugh Barbour, *The Quakers in Puritan England* (New Haven, CT: Yale University Press, 1964), 45; Arthur O. Roberts, "George Fox and the Quakers," in *Great Leaders of the Christian Church*, ed. John D. Woodbridge (Chicago: Moody Press, 1988), 273.
[24] *The Inheritance of Jacob* (1656), in *Early Quaker Writings*, ed. Hugh Barbour and Arthur O. Roberts (Grand Rapids: Eerdmans, 1973), 173.

in the counties of Westmoreland, Lancashire, Yorkshire, and Cumberland. Over the next decade it spread south and had a profound impact on at least four other areas: Cheshire; London and those counties directly to the north and east of the capital (Hertfordshire, Buckinghamshire, Cambridgeshire, and Essex); the town of Bristol, along with Somerset and Wiltshire; and the Midlands counties of Warwickshire and Worcestershire.[25] Quaker missionary endeavors were not confined to the British Isles, however. By 1660 zealous Quaker evangelists had gone as far afield as Massachusetts, Germany, Rome, Malta, and Jerusalem.[26] As a result of these endeavors, it is estimated that there were at least thirty-five thousand to forty thousand Quakers in Britain alone by the early 1660s. According to Barry Reay, there may have been as many as sixty thousand.[27]

Exalting the Spirit at the Expense of the Word

Alongside the Quaker emphasis on the illumination that came from the light within, which the Quakers variously called the indwelling Christ or indwelling Spirit,[28] there was, as Richard Bauman has noted, the vigorous assertion that Quaker experience involved hearing a divine inner voice. The Quakers did not deny that God could and did speak to people mediately through the written text of Scripture, but they were convinced that they also knew and enjoyed the Spirit's immediate inspiration and guidance like the apostles and saints of the New Testament era.[29] In the words of the Quaker theologian William Penn (1644–1718), immediate experiences of the Spirit "once were the great Foundation of both their [i.e., New Testament believers'] Knowledge and Comfort, though now mockt at . . . with great Derision in a Quaker."[30] In Bauman's words, "Direct personal communion with God speaking within was the core religious experience of early Quakerism."[31]

Bauman's comment is well borne out by a letter that Isaac Penington the Younger (1616–1679) wrote to a fellow Quaker, Nathanael Stonar, in 1670. Penington, who is "a prime example of the intellectual sophistication" of a

---

[25] Reay, *Quakers and the English Revolution*, 27–29.
[26] Barbour, *Quakers in Puritan England*, 67–70.
[27] B. G. Reay, "Early Quaker Activity and Reactions to It, 1652–1664" (DPhil diss., University of Oxford, 1979), 218–20; Reay, *Quakers and the English Revolution*, 26–27; Underwood, *Primitivism, Radicalism, and the Lamb's War*, 10.
[28] Underwood, *Primitivism, Radicalism, and the Lamb's War*, 105–7.
[29] Ibid., 26–27, 32–33.
[30] Quoted in ibid., 26.
[31] Bauman, *Let Your Words Be Few*, 24–25.

number of early Quaker converts,[32] told his correspondent that one of the main differences between themselves and other "professors," by whom he meant Congregationalists and Baptists, was "concerning *the rule*." While the latter asserted that the Scriptures were the rule by which men and women ought to direct their lives and thinking, Penington was convinced that the indwelling Spirit of life is "nearer and more powerful, than the words, or outward relations concerning those things in the Scriptures." As Penington noted:

> The Lord, in the gospel state, hath promised to be present with his people; not as a wayfaring man, for a night, but to *dwell in them and walk in them*. Yea, if they be tempted and in danger of erring, they shall hear a voice behind them, saying, "This is the way, walk in it." Will they not grant this to be a rule, as well as the Scriptures? Nay, is not this a more full direction to the heart, in that state, than it can pick to itself out of the Scriptures? . . . the Spirit, which gave forth the words, is greater than the words; therefore we cannot but prize Him himself, and set Him higher in our heart and thoughts, than the words which testify of Him, though they also are very sweet and precious to our taste.[33]

Penington thus affirmed that the Quakers esteemed the Scriptures as "sweet and precious," but he was equally adamant that the indwelling Spirit was to be regarded as the supreme authority when it came to direction for Christian living and thinking.[34]

Similarly George Fox, listening to a sermon on 2 Peter 1:19 in which the preacher told the congregation "that the Scriptures were the touchstone and judge by which they were to try all doctrines, religions, and opinions," found himself unable to contain his disagreement. He cried out, "Oh no, it is not the Scriptures." He then proceeded to tell the presumably shocked audience that the touchstone and judge was "the Holy Spirit, by which the holy men of God gave forth the Scriptures, whereby opinions, religions, and judgements were to be tried; for it led into all Truth, and so gave the knowledge of the Truth."[35] And when some Baptists in Huntingdonshire and Cambridgeshire

---

[32] J. W. Frost, "Penington, Isaac (the Younger)," in *Biographical Dictionary of British Radicals in the Seventeenth Century*, 3:23.

[33] *Letters of Isaac Penington*, 2nd. ed. (repr., London: Holdsworth and Ball, 1829), 202–3. For access to this text we are indebted to Heinz G. Dschankilic of Cambridge, Ontario.

[34] See also the remarks by Richard Dale Land, "Doctrinal Controversies of English Particular Baptists (1644–1691) as Illustrated by the Career and Writings of Thomas Collier" (DPhil diss., Regent's Park College, Oxford University, 1979), 205–11.

[35] Nickalls, *Journal of George Fox*, 39–40.

became Quakers they were quick to assert that henceforth the "light in their consciences was the rule they desire to walk by," not the Scriptures.[36]

Quakerism thus tended to exalt the Spirit at the expense of the Word.[37] And on not a few occasions this led the early Quakers into quite bizarre patterns of behavior and speech. Elizabeth Fletcher's going half-naked for a sign is but one example. Others would include Margaret Fell (1614–1702), Fox's future wife, describing Fox as "the fountain of eternal life" to whom "all nations shall bow";[38] the acclamation made by Richard Sale (d. 1658) to Fox, "Praises, praises, eternal praises to thee forevermore, who was and is and is to come, who is god over all, blessed forever";[39] and James Nayler's shocking reenactment of Christ's ride into Jerusalem at Bristol in 1656.[40] It was this willingness on the part of the Quakers to appear to go "behind and beyond" the Scriptures that explains much of the "unmitigated abhorrence" for them found in Puritan writings of the time.[41]

John Owen was one of Puritanism's sharpest critics of the Quakers. Unlike some of his Puritan contemporaries, though, his critique is informed not primarily "by vituperation, but by close and careful argument."[42]

John Owen, Critic of the Quakers

Discarding the Means of Grace in Worship

Owen is quite prepared to admit that some "edification" can be found in the "silent [worship] meetings" of the Quakers.[43] On the whole, however, he sees this group as "poor deluded souls."[44] Their teaching about the inner light is an attack on the work and person of the Holy Spirit, a "pretended light," and possibly even "a dark product of Satan."[45] When they point to

---

[36] Quoted in Reay, *Quakers and the English Revolution*, 34.

[37] For a different perspective on this issue, see James L. Ash Jr., "'Oh No, It Is Not the Scriptures!' The Bible and the Spirit in George Fox," *Quaker History* 63, no. 2 (1974): 94–107.

[38] Watts, *Dissenters*, 209.

[39] Quoted in Richard G. Bailey, "The Making and Unmaking of a God: New Light on George Fox and Early Quakerism," in *New Light on George Fox (1624 to 1691)*, ed. Michael Mullett (York: William Sessions, Ebor, 1991), 114.

[40] For a succinct account of this event, see Watts, *Dissenters*, 209–11. See also Charles L. Cherry, "Enthusiasm and Madness: Anti-Quakerism in the Seventeenth Century," *Quaker History* 74, no. 2 (1984): 7–9.

[41] Geoffrey F. Nuttall, "The Quakers and the Puritans," in Nuttall, *The Puritan Spirit: Essays and Addresses* (London: Epworth, 1967), 170, 174–75.

[42] Maurice A. Creasey, "Early Quaker Christology with Special Reference to the Teaching and Significance of Isaac Penington 1616–1679" (PhD diss., University of Leeds, 1956), 158. Creasey's thesis has been extremely helpful in following Owen's overall critique of Quaker teaching. See 154–58.

[43] Owen, *A Discourse concerning the Holy Spirit*, in *Works*, 4:331.

[44] Ibid., 3:66.

[45] Ibid., 3:36–37. See also John Owen, *A Defense of Sacred Scripture against Modern Fanaticism*, trans. Stephen P. Westcott, in Owen, *Biblical Theology* (Pittsburgh: Soli Deo Gloria, 1994), 777, where he suggests that the Quakers, or as some called them, "quiverers," were moved "by the power of the evil spirit."

the trembling and quaking that sometimes grips men and women in their meetings as evidence of the Spirit's powerful presence, Owen sees only "a spirit of bondage" that throws them "into an un-son-like frame."[46] Their worship is further flawed by their discarding of the "sacraments, . . . baptism and the supper of the Lord, which are so great a part of the mystical worship of the church." Owen is not surprised, though. Both of these ordinances speak about the heart of the Christian faith, "the sanctifying and justifying blood of Christ." But the Quakers, Owen is convinced, have forsaken the gospel's emphasis on the objective, atoning work of Christ for a focus upon the "light within men," and these two ordinances cannot "contribute any thing to the furtherance, increase, or establishment, of that light."[47] At the heart of this erroneous focus of the Quakers, Owen sees a failure to grasp the Trinitarian nature of the work of redemption. "Convince any of them of the doctrine of the Trinity," he comments in 1674, "and all the rest of their imaginations vanish into smoke."[48]

Misunderstanding the Role of the Spirit

Owen argues that the Quaker lauding of the light within, which they often identify with the Spirit, seems to be a subtle exaltation of the Spirit by the Spirit. Jesus's statement in John 16:14 ("he [i.e., the Spirit] shall glorify me; for he shall receive of mine, and shall show it to you") is crucial to understanding the salvific work of the Trinity, and it reveals that the message of the Quakers is actually an inversion of "the order of the divine dispensations." The Holy Spirit has not come to glorify himself. According to Owen's reading of John 16:14, the Father sent the Spirit in love to make the Son "glorious, honourable, and of high esteem in the hearts of believers" and to shed "abroad the love of God in our hearts." The Spirit's mission in this regard runs parallel, as it were, to the Son's being sent by the Father "to suffer at Jerusalem . . . for us" and bring glory to the one who sent him.[49]

---

[46] Owen, *Of Communion with God the Father, Son, and Holy Ghost*, in *Works*, 2:258; hereafter *Of Communion with God*.

[47] Owen, *Nature and Causes of Apostasy from the Gospel*, in *Works*, 7:219–20.

[48] Owen, *A Discourse concerning the Holy Spirit*, in *Works*, 3:66.

[49] Owen, *Of Communion with God*, in *Works*, 2:257–58. On the crucial importance of the Trinity for Owen's theology, see Carl R. Trueman, *The Claims of Truth: John Owen's Trinitarian Theology* (Carlisle: Paternoster, 1998); Robert Letham, "John Owen's Doctrine of the Trinity in Its Catholic Context," in *The Ashgate Research Companion to John Owen's Theology*, ed. Kelly M. Kapic and Mark Jones (Burlington, VT: Ashgate, 2012), 185–97.

Defending the Sacred Scriptures

Owen's most concentrated attack on the Quakers is found in his *Pro Sacris Scripturis Exercitationes adversus Fanaticos*—literally, *A Defense of the Sacred Scriptures against the Fanatics*—which was published in 1659.[50] In Peter Toon's biography of the Congregationalist theologian, Toon suggests that the writing of the treatise in Latin is a deliberate affirmation of traditional learning in the face of the Quakers' denigration of university education.[51] Toon may well be right, for Owen devotes a substantial portion of the second chapter of this treatise to a defense of sound exegesis and exegetical techniques, many of which would be learned in the university environment of the theological college.[52]

Scripture Is the Word of God

The treatise is divided into four chapters. In the first, Owen refutes the claim of the Quakers that Scripture should not be termed "the Word of God" since, they argued, this title properly belongs to Christ alone.[53] Owen, of course, knows that there are biblical texts which do call Christ "the Word," passages such as John 1:1, John 1:14, and Revelation 19:13. Owen can thus agree with the Quakers: "Christ Himself is the Word of God, the essential Word."[54] Yet, this term is frequently used by the Bible as a self-description, as Owen easily shows. He cites Mark 7:13, for example, where Jesus accuses the Pharisees of preferring their traditions to the commands of the Old Testament and so "making the Word of God of no effect." The Scriptures are also to be considered a spoken declaration of the will and mind of God and, as such, his Word. Owen then points his readers to verses like Exodus 34:1 and Revelation 21:5, which refer to this inscripturation of God's speaking. He also notes a passage like Colossians 3:16, which mentions "the Word of Christ," which, he rightly states, cannot be Christ himself. "Scripture," he concludes, "is God's written Word, speaking of him to us."[55] Owen's quarrel with the Quakers over the use of this phrase "Word of God" is no mere issue of semantics. As he would later write in

---

[50] This is readily available in the English translation by Westcott, *A Defense of Sacred Scripture*, in Owen, *Biblical Theology*, 775–854. For the date of this treatise, see Donald K. McKim, "John Owen's Doctrine of Scripture in Historical Perspective," *Evangelical Quarterly* 45 (1973): 198 and note 16.

[51] Toon, *God's Statesman*, 76n4.

[52] Owen, *Defense of Sacred Scripture*, in *Biblical Theology*, 805–16.

[53] For this claim, see Underwood, *Primitivism, Radicalism, and the Lamb's War*, 28.

[54] Owen, *Defense of Sacred Scripture*, in *Biblical Theology*, 781–82, 791.

[55] Ibid., 790–91.

his 1678 treatise *The Causes, Ways, and Means of Understanding the Mind of God as Revealed in His Word*:

> Our belief of the Scriptures to be the word of God, or a divine revelation, and our understanding of the mind and will of God as revealed in them, are the *two springs* of all our interest in Christian religion. From them are all those streams of light and truth derived whereby our souls are watered, refreshed, and made fruitful unto God.[56]

The Sufficiency and Necessity of God's Word

The second chapter of *Pro Sacris Scripturis* opens with what initially appears to be an extraneous issue—a refutation of the claim of the Roman Catholic magisterium to be "the one, perfect, independent, visible judge and expositor" of Scripture.[57] The link between the Roman Catholic view of the Scriptures and that of the Quakers in Owen's mind seems to be that both groups effectively undermined the authority of God's Word.[58] Roman Catholics of that day rejected its sufficiency, while the Quakers denied its necessity. There is an area, though, where Owen is in agreement with seventeenth-century Roman Catholic thought: proper public interpreters of God's Word are necessary.

Among the English Puritans, however, the question of who could publicly expound the Word of God was hotly debated.[59] Those who were more conservative, like Richard Baxter (1615–1691), insisted that ordination was the regular pathway to preaching. Owen disagreed.

> A faithful man . . . being furnished with the knowledge of God and the requisite Spiritual gifts for the edification of others (graciously bestowed upon him by God), and also having the time and other things necessary for the right performance of this duty granted him by providence, then I certainly would allow him to interpret the Scriptures and to meet with others for their edification, even though he does not intend ever to holy orders—providing only that he makes no interruption of

---

[56] In *Works*, 4:121. For further discussion of other aspects of this first chapter of Owen's *Defense of Sacred Scripture*, see Trueman, *Claims of Truth*, 67–71.

[57] Owen, *Defense of Sacred Scripture*, in *Biblical Theology*, 793–98.

[58] Trueman, *Claims of Truth*, 65–66. The same linkage is made in Owen, *The Causes, Ways, and Means of Understanding the Mind of God as Revealed in His Word*, chaps. 1–3, in *Works*, 4:121–60.

[59] For the debate, see especially, Geoffrey F. Nuttall, *The Holy Spirit in Puritan Faith and Experience*, 2nd ed. (repr., Chicago: University of Chicago Press, 1992), 75–89; and Richard L. Greaves, "The Ordination Controversy and the Spirit of Reform in Puritan England," *Journal of Ecclesiastical History* 21 (1970): 225–41.

an established ministry. . . . Where Christ has provided the gifts there *must* be a vocation.[60]

Owen's insistence that lay preaching not be an "interruption of an established ministry" is an important point in this statement. It indicates his opposition to those radicals, like the Quakers, who wanted to go even further and secure the complete freedom of the pulpit for anyone who wished to express his opinions.[61]

Having demonstrated the necessity of fit expositors of God's Word, Owen can now tackle the Quaker dislike of exposition and expository techniques, as well as their rejection of the use of commentaries and other books to ascertain the meaning of the Scriptures. God's gift of human reason, which sets humanity apart from animals, and the necessity of Scripture knowledge so as to be instructed in the ways of God require these very things the Quakers despise.[62] "God, in his infinite wisdom, not only arranged the declaration of his will in the Scripture," Owen remarks, "but also arranged that declaration in such a manner as absolutely necessitates the duty of exposition as a function of the Church as long as the Scriptures shall last."[63]

The Perfection of God's Word

Chapter 3 of *Pro Sacris Scripturis* deals with the "perfection" of the Scriptures. From personal conversation with Quakers and perusal of some of their books,[64] Owen lists a number of major Quaker opinions with regard to the Scriptures that he wishes to refute. Two in particular receive detailed attention in Owen's rebuttal. He notes their denial that "the Scriptures are the settled, ordinary, perfect and unshakable rule for divine worship and human obedience." The Quakers also argued, he records, that the goal of the Scriptures is to bring men and women to heed the "inner light" within them, and once that has been achieved, the Bible's main purpose has been fulfilled.[65]

Owen's refutation of the first of these convictions begins by stressing

---

[60] Owen, *Defense of Sacred Scripture*, in *Biblical Theology*, 802–3.
[61] Greaves, "Ordination Controversy," 227. For further discussion of Owen's thought on the issue of the interpretation of Scripture, see Ferguson, *John Owen on the Christian Life* (Edinburgh: Banner of Truth, 1987), 196–99; J. I. Packer, "John Owen on Communication from God," in Packer, *A Quest for Godliness: The Puritan Vision of the Christian Life* (Wheaton, IL: Crossway, 1990), 93–95; Campbell, "John Owen's Rule and Guide," 153–207; Trueman, *Claims of Truth*, 84–90.
[62] Owen, *Defense of Sacred Scripture*, in *Biblical Theology*, 806–14.
[63] Ibid., 814.
[64] Ibid., 822.
[65] Ibid., 823–24. See also 833–35.

that the Scriptures were given to fulfill two broad purposes. In line with his Reformed heritage, Owen reasons that the ultimate purpose of Scripture is doxological, namely, the glory of God. "Since God does all that he does for his own sake and for his own glory, and as he has produced this surpassing achievement of the written Scripture, given by his absolute sovereign will, then he can have given it for no less supreme purpose." A secondary purpose of the Scriptures is soteriological. It has been given for the salvation of sinners, "the instructing of men in the knowledge and worship of God." Owen insists that these two purposes dovetail, for it is as men and women are brought by the instruction of Scripture to salvation that God's glory is secured. Since Scripture perfectly achieves that for which it has been given, it must be deemed "the one and only, absolute and perfect, rule for the whole of divine worship and obedience."[66] A series of Bible verses is given as support.

> [Scripture's] purpose . . . is to engender faith. "These things have been written, that ye might believe" (John 20:31); "Faith cometh by hearing, and hearing by the word of God' (Romans 10:17). It is "the certainty of those things" (Luke 1:4) which is able "to make thee wise unto salvation" (2 Timothy 3:15); "a sure word of prophecy" (2 Peter 1:19), through which we may be "thoroughly furnished unto all good works" (2 Timothy 3:17), and it is by it that we gain life eternal (John 5:39, 20:31). . . . "The law of the LORD is perfect, converting the soul" (Psalm 19:7), and so it is "a lamp unto my feet, and a light unto my path" (Psalm 119:105), it is "the power of God unto salvation" (Romans 1:16), that which is "able to make thee wise unto salvation" (2 Timothy 3:15) and "thoroughly furnished unto all good works" (verse 17). It is that which "is able to save your souls" (James 1:21). So Scripture accomplishes all things which are necessary for God's glory and man's salvation.[67]

Other arguments for Scripture's perfection are drawn from biblical texts that condemn adding to the Scriptures, and from the frequency of God's command in his Word that his people diligently heed the Scriptures. Owen also adduces the work of deception carried on by Satan, who has used the "mask of pretended revelations and interior inspiration" throughout

---

[66] Ibid., 824–25. Gundry ("John Owen on Authority and Scripture," 194) notes only the soteriological purpose of the Bible.

[67] Owen, *Defense of Sacred Scripture*, in *Biblical Theology*, 828–29. For a brief summary of Owen's conception of the purposes of Scripture, see Ferguson, *John Owen on the Christian Life*, 199–201.

history to ensnare human beings. In order to provide "a constant aid and guide" to embattled humanity, God thus caused his Word to be carefully inscripturated.[68]

Refutation of the other major Quaker argument, namely, the doctrine of the "inner light," is deemed so important to Owen that he devotes the fourth and final chapter of his work to this subject.

The Inner Light and John 1:9

Owen initially sets his reply to the Quaker doctrine of the inner light within the context of a discussion of two central aspects of the history of salvation. First, there is the fact of the fall, an event that extinguished the "inborn spiritual light" which Adam and Eve possessed in the paradisal state. There was, in Owen's words, an "actual inrush of spiritual shade" when they fell, and they, as did their progeny, henceforth lived and walked in darkness. This situation did not essentially change until the coming of Christ, though the darkness of humanity was alleviated to some degree by the light cast by the Old Testament prophets. It was the coming of Christ, the true light of the entire world, and the outpouring of his Spirit that brought sight to the spiritually blind and so transformed "his people from the domain of darkness into the glory of his most marvelous light."[69] Owen's point in reciting these facts is to stress that any remnant of Adamic light which remains in human nature has power enough only to reveal that all human beings are "by nature dead, blind, deaf, darkened of intellect, nay, are very blindness and darkness itself." Salvation therefore requires "the infusion of an outside and spiritual light to irradiate hearts and minds."[70]

Owen rightly understands the Quaker concept of the inner light to be an assertion that the fall was not as radical an event as Reformed theology maintains, and thus that the "inborn spiritual light" possessed prior to the fall can still give a saving knowledge of God.[71] Although Owen is prepared to admit that this light can attain to some valid knowledge about God,[72] he essentially rejects the Quaker position. As he stated a number of years later in his *Christologia; or, A Declaration of the Glorious Mystery of the Person of*

---

[68] Owen, *Defense of Sacred Scripture*, in *Biblical Theology*, 829–32 passim.

[69] Ibid., 841–43.

[70] Ibid., 846–47.

[71] For the Quaker notion of the "Spirit in every man," see Nuttall, *Holy Spirit*, 159–62.

[72] See Creasey, "Early Quaker Christology," 164–65, and the texts quoted there. Cf. Owen's remarks in *Defense of Sacred Scripture*, in *Biblical Theology*, 853: "There are remains, although feeble ones, of creation light surviving in all men, but I strongly refute the suggestion that these remnants may be in any degree saving."

Christ—God and Man (1679), when he had occasion to comment on the best of Greek philosophical thought:

> There was a notion, even among the philosophers, that the principal en-
> deavour of a wise man was to be like unto God. But in the improvement
> of it, the best of them fell into foolish and proud imaginations. Howbeit,
> the notion itself was the principal beam of our *primigenial light*, the last
> relic of our natural perfections. . . . But those persons who had nothing
> but the absolute essential properties of the divine nature to contemplate
> on in the light of reason, failed all of them, both in the notion itself of
> conformity unto God, and especially in the practical improvement of it.[73]

The Quaker notion of the inner light as a common possession of all men is also disproved by what Scripture tells us about the gift of the Spirit, which the Quakers often equated with the inner light. Owen notes that a passage like Jude 19 declares that "the Spirit of Christ is expressly *not* possessed by some." And referring to Romans 8:9 ("if any man have not the Spirit of Christ, he is none of his"), Owen deduces that "Christ does not bestow his Holy Spirit . . . on all and sundry."[74]

Not surprisingly Owen devotes some space to the exegesis of John 1:9 ("that was the true Light, which lighteth every man that cometh into the world"), the textual linchpin of the Quaker position.[75] The Quaker reading of this verse assumed that the participle "cometh" refers back to "every man." Owen's exposition of this text, on the other hand, is informed by his remarks earlier in the chapter about the history of salvation. Christ, the true light, by means of his incarnation gives light to sinners who are sitting "shrouded in deep shadow." Thus Owen states, "It is not said that Christ illuminates every man coming into the world, but rather that he, coming into the world, illuminates every man." In other words, Owen understands the referent of the participle "coming" to be the "true Light."

Owen's interpretation means that the illumination about which the Johannine text speaks is spiritual, not a natural one of which all human beings partake. In Owen's words, it is "a fruit of renewal by grace, rather than infusion by creation." As Owen further recognizes, his reading of the passage commits him to taking "every man" in a relative sense, as meaning

---

[73] Owen, *Christologia; or, A Declaration of the Glorious Mystery of the Person of Christ—God and Man*, in *Works*, 1:172–73.
[74] Owen, *Defense of Sacred Scripture*, in *Biblical Theology*, 848–49.
[75] Ibid., 850–54.

"all of God's people," and not in an absolute sense, as "all people without exception."[76] The means by which this saving enlightenment comes is "the Word and the Spirit."[77] As Owen argues in his later treatise *Christologia*, the Word is the objective light by which knowledge of Christ is conveyed to our minds. Without the Scriptures we can see nothing of Christ. The Spirit, on the other hand, is the light that illuminates the mind, by means of the Scriptures, to spiritually "behold and discern the glory of God in the face of Christ."[78] Quaker assertions of the inner light and their apparent devaluing of the Scriptures thus cut the nerve of true vital experience of the saving light of Christ. Nearly twenty years later, Owen would sum up the difference between those of his persuasion and the Quakers along these very lines:

> We persuade men to take the Scripture as the *only rule*, and the holy promised Spirit of God, sought by ardent prayers and supplications, in the use of all means appointed by Christ for that end, *for their guide*. They deal with men to turn into themselves, and to attend unto the light within them. Whilst we build on these most distant principles, the difference between us is irreconcilable, and will be eternal. . . . Until, therefore, they return unto "the law and testimony,"—without which, whatsoever is pretended, there is no *light* in any,—we have no more to do but, labouring to preserve the flock of Christ in the profession of the "faith once delivered unto the saints," to commit the difference between the *word and Spirit* on the one hand, and the *light within* on the other, unto the decision of Jesus Christ at the last day.[79]

Conclusion

Though we live in quite different times than Owen, his arguments for the supremacy of Scripture are as valid today as they were in his day when he responded to the Quakers. In our day, certain charismatic groups and preachers maintain a position similar to that of the Quakers: the Scriptures are indeed inspired by God, but the Spirit who indwells believers is still giving fresh words for the church today, some of which clearly undermine the teaching of the Scriptures. Owen's response to the Quakers is essentially

---

[76] Ibid., 852.
[77] Ibid.
[78] In *Works*, 1:74–75. On the Trinitarian foundation of Owen's thought here, see Trueman, *Claims of Truth*, 70–71.
[79] Owen, *The Causes, Ways, and Means of Understanding the Mind of God*, in *Works*, 4:159–60.

the response we must make: the one sure word we know to be from the Holy Spirit is the sixty-six books of the Bible. Since that is the case, all that claims to be from God the Holy Spirit today must be tested and validated by those books. The Spirit did not give his Word over the millennia and then preserve it for the church in what we call the Bible to have it trumped by later so-called prophetic words. And so, as Owen was a man of the Word, we too must be, lest we find ourselves out of step with the Spirit of God.

CHAPTER 3

COMMUNING WITH THE TRINITY

There was no more glorious mystery brought to light in and by Jesus Christ than that of the holy Trinity, or the subsistence of the three persons in the unity of the same divine nature. . . . And this revelation is made unto us, not that our minds might be possessed with the notions of it, but that we may know aright how to place our trust in him, how to obey him and live unto him, how to obtain and exercise communion with him, until we come to the enjoyment of him. [1]

If we, either intentionally or unintentionally, dispense with the doctrine of the Trinity, then we cannot, in any Christian sense, know God. Or as Owen says, "The doctrine of the Trinity is the foundation of all our Communion with God, and comfortable Dependence upon him." [2] Owen, in other words, draws a direct line from the Trinity to the Christian life, a line that cannot be broken. To know God, to have fellowship with him, to commune with him, is to converse with the three members of the Godhead in their proper order and role. Owen explains this communion in his classic *Of Communion with God the Father, Son, and Holy Ghost, Each Person Distinctly, in Love, Grace, and Consolation; or, The Saints' Fellowship with the Father, Son, and*

---

[1] Owen, *A Discourse concerning the Holy Spirit*, in *Works*, 3:158.
[2] Savoy Declaration 2.3.

Holy Spirit Unfolded (1657).[3] In this book, says Brian Kay, Owen "breaks new ground" not only by "emphasizing the Trinity as the foundational substructure upon which is constructed almost the entirety of Christian soteriology," but also "by showing how the Christian's devotional response to God takes on a distinctively trinitarian shape."[4]

Before we look at this work, it is crucial to remember that Owen's discussion about communion with the triune God took place in an increasingly volatile context with regard to the doctrine of the Trinity. While it would be wrong to think that anti-Trinitarian thought was as developed or as widespread as it would be in the 1690s, a dozen years or so after Owen's death, when a wave of anti-Trinitarianism swept through certain Anglican and Dissenting circles, nevertheless a critical rejection of this foundation of the Christian faith was beginning to make itself felt during Owen's lifetime. During the 1640s and 1650s, in particular, Socinianism or Unitarianism (represented by Paul Best and John Biddle) and Arianism (as found in the thinking of John Knowles) were being explicitly taught. To Owen, these Socinians and other anti-Trinitarians were on a par with Muslims and atheists.

Union and Communion

What marks Owen's treatment as unique, at least in part, is how he defines our communion in relation to each distinct person within the triune Godhead.[5] But at the outset, it is important to distinguish between union and communion. Kelly Kapic makes the astute observation that for Owen "union" refers to the sinner's union with Christ, whereby the sinner is totally passive and God works monergistically. "This union is a unilateral action by God, in which those who were dead are made alive, those who lived in darkness begin to see the light, and those who were enslaved to sin are set free to be loved and to love." Therefore, when "one speaks of 'union,' it

---

[3] For a detailed outline of the book, see John Owen, *Communion with the Triune God*, ed. Kelly M. Kapic and Justin Taylor (Wheaton, IL: Crossway, 2007), 51–83. Also note that Owen's book was criticized by William Sherlock, to whom Owen responded in *A Vindication of Some Passages in a Discourse concerning Communion with God*, in *Works*, 2:275–365. For the background to this debate, see Kapic, *Communion with God: The Divine and the Human in the Theology of John Owen* (Grand Rapids: Baker Academic, 2007), 151–57.
[4] Brian K. Kay, *Trinitarian Spirituality: John Owen and the Doctrine of God in Western Devotion* (Milton Keynes: Paternoster, 2007), 115–16.
[5] For example, in one of his many Trinitarian summaries, Owen writes: "There is no grace whereby our souls go forth unto God, no act of divine worship yielded unto him, no duty or obedience performed, but they are distinctly directed unto Father, Son, and Spirit. Now, by these and such like ways as these, do we hold communion with God; and therefore we have that communion distinctly, as hath been described." Owen, *Of Communion with God*, in *Works*, 2:15.

must be clear that the human person is merely receptive, being the object of God's gracious action."[6] On the other hand, "communion," the subject of this chapter, is something distinct, though not unrelated. While an individual is passive in union, he or she is called to action in communion. In fact, it is union with Christ that results in and brings about a person's communion with the triune God. Communion, therefore, occurs within the context of what we today call sanctification.[7] As Kapic explains, "Those who are united to Christ are called to respond to God's loving embrace. While union with Christ is something that does not ebb and flow, one's experience of communion with Christ can fluctuate." Kapic continues:

> This is an important theological and experiential distinction, for it protects the biblical truth that we are saved by radical and free divine grace. Furthermore, this distinction also protects the biblical truth that the children of God have a relationship with their Lord, and that there are things they can do that either help or hinder it. . . . Let there be no misunderstanding—for Owen, Christian obedience was of utmost importance, but it was always understood to flow out of this union and never seen as the ground for it.[8]

Kapic's point will become more evident as we continue, especially in our chapters on regeneration, justification, and the indwelling of the Holy Spirit. For now, suffice it to say that while we are *passive* in being united with Christ through the Spirit's work in effectually calling us to the Son, granting us new life in regeneration, once we have been made alive, we are now *active* as the Spirit's sanctifying grace conforms us more and more into the image of Christ and we pursue godliness. In sanctification, therefore, we have communion with God, whereby we either enjoy fellowship with each distinct person of the Trinity according to his proper role or, sadly, at times fall into sin and hinder the progress of our communion. Obedience, therefore, is crucial in our communion. While obedience in no way grounds or conditions our union, regeneration, or

---

[6] Kelly M. Kapic, "Worshiping the Triune God," in Kapic and Taylor, *Communion with the Triune God*, 21.
[7] "Sanctification" is used here in the contemporary sense, referring to the ongoing and progressive pursuit of holiness by the power of the Spirit. However, to complicate matters, at times Owen uses the word *sanctification* to refer to the Spirit's work in bringing about union with Christ and regeneration, which we experience as a "mere passive reception, as a vessel receives water." Owen, *Of Communion with God*, in *Works*, 2:231. He then uses the word *consolation* to refer to an aspect of what we today call sanctification. In consolation the Spirit comforts the believer and the believer in return actively seeks his comfort (ibid., 2:233).
[8] Kapic, "Worshiping the Triune God," 21–22.

justification (see chaps. 6 and 7), it does play a significant role in our sanctification, and the sweetness of our communion with God can be greatly affected by it.[9]

Communion with God Defined

Owen's entire book *Of Communion with God* is built upon the Trinitarian nature of our fellowship with God as seen in 1 John 1:3. There the apostle John is clear that the fellowship we have with God is a fellowship or communion both with God the Father and with God the Son, Jesus Christ. But for Owen the fundamental question is how such a communion is possible given the entrance of sin into the world. While God is holy, we are by nature children of wrath and therefore can never dwell in his presence. "He [God] is light, we darkness; and what communion hath light with darkness? He is life, we are dead,—he is love, and we are enmity; and what agreement can there be between us?"[10] As Ephesians 2:12 and 4:18 demonstrate, we are alienated from the life of God. What is needed, therefore, is for God to restore such a communion by manifesting his "grace and pardoning mercy, which is the only door of entrance into any such communion," a door opened only through the blood of Jesus Christ.[11]

Such a predicament can be seen in the Old Testament. As Owen explains, "This communion and fellowship with God is not in express terms mentioned in the Old Testament. The thing itself is found there; but the clear light of it, and the boldness of faith in it, is discovered in the gospel, and by the Spirit administered therein." Owen makes his case by arguing that though certain Old Testament saints had fellowship with God more directly (e.g., Abraham, David, Enoch), "the way into the holiest was not yet made manifest whilst the first tabernacle was standing." Yes, communion existed under the old covenant, but there was no "boldness and confidence in that communion."[12] Owen makes such a point obvious by drawing our attention to the role of the high priest. Israel's sin barred her from enter-

---

[9] All of this should be qualified, however, in that Owen does, at times, seem to use the word *communion* in a broad, as well as a narrow, sense. This is captured in how Ferguson summarizes Owen: "Both the union with Christ which gives the Christian his status before God, and the communion with God which is the fruit of that status, are thus subsumed under the notion of communion, and this is the sense in which Owen generally employs the expression." Sinclair B. Ferguson, *John Owen on the Christian Life* (Edinburgh: Banner of Truth, 1987), 75. Also see Joel R. Beeke and Mark Jones, *A Puritan Theology: Doctrine for Life* (Grand Rapids: Reformation Heritage, 2012), 105–6.

[10] Owen, *Of Communion with God*, in *Works*, 2:6.

[11] Ibid.

[12] Ibid.

ing the presence of a holy God. Therefore, the high priest had to intercede on behalf of Israel on the Day of Atonement, entering the Most Holy Place with the blood of the sacrifice. The high priest served as the mediator on behalf of God's people, Israel. "But now in Christ we have boldness and access with confidence to God" (2 Cor. 3:15–16; Eph. 3:12; Heb. 4:16; 10:19), something the "saints of old were not acquainted with."[13] Christ is both the Great High Priest and the sacrifice (see chap. 5). Through his own flesh Christ has made a new and living way that was previously shut up (Heb. 10:20). Through Christ the sinner now has access by one Spirit to the Father (Eph. 2:12–14, 18).

What is the consequence of this great salvation accomplished by the blood of Christ? For Owen, the answer is found in Ephesians 2: we now have been brought near. No longer are we alienated, but now we can draw near to God with full confidence and assurance. The dividing wall of hostility has been broken down and therefore we have peace with God through Christ. In Owen's own words, it is upon the foundation of the blood of Christ that we "are sinners admitted unto communion with God, and have fellowship with him." This is nothing short of amazing, as Owen says: "For sinners to have fellowship with God, the infinitely holy God, is an astonishing dispensation."[14]

Now that we know how our communion and fellowship with God is possible in the first place, what does this communion look like? The answer to this question occupies Owen for the remainder of his book. He first provides us with a definition: "Our communion, then, with God consisteth in his communication of himself unto us, with our returnal unto him of that which he requireth and accepteth, flowing from that union which in Jesus Christ we have with him."[15] For Owen, such a reciprocal communion works itself out in two ways. First, there is what he calls the "perfect and complete" communion, whereby "in the full fruit of his glory" and the "total giving up of ourselves to him" we rest in him as our utmost end. We will finally enjoy such a communion when we see him as he is. Second, there is the "initial and incomplete" communion. In contrast to the former, this latter communion is the "firstfruits and dawnings of that perfection which we have here in grace." It is this second type of communion

---

[13] Ibid., 2:7.
[14] Note how Owen defines communion: "To speak a little of it in general—Communion relates to things and persons. A joint participation in any thing whatever, good or evil, duty or enjoyment, nature or actions, gives this denomination to them so partaking of it" (ibid.).
[15] Ibid., 2:8.

that Owen will focus on, for it is a "mutual communication in giving and receiving, after a most holy and spiritual manner, which is between God and the saints while they walk together in a covenant of peace, ratified in the blood of Jesus."[16]

Before moving on, however, it must be stressed that Owen's aim in this study of communion with God is that God our Father—who has rescued us through the blood of his own Son and by the "riches of his own grace," recovering us "from a state of enmity into a condition of communion and fellowship with himself"—might give us a taste of "his sweetness and excellencies," stirring us up to have a greater longing "after the fullness of his salvation, and the eternal fruition of him in glory."[17]

The Works of the Trinity Undivided

The beauty of Owen's understanding of our fellowship with God is that it is Trinitarian through and through.[18] Owen takes us back to the Scriptures, where we see each person of the Trinity at work in bringing about our salvation, from beginning to end. Grace, says Owen, is communicated from "several persons of the Deity," and therefore believers must "have distinct communion with them." Such grace is communicated by the Father's "original authority," the Son's "purchased treasury," and the Spirit's "immediate efficacy."[19] There is no division within the Godhead in the work of redemption. Rather, the work of redemption is by nature Trinitarian. All three persons of the Trinity work together to accomplish salvation, and no one person works by himself, apart from the other two.

Such an emphasis by Owen is both inherently biblical and entirely Augustinian. Augustine asserted that since the three persons are inseparable in their divine unity and essence, so also their work is inseparable.[20] Therefore, our salvation has an intentional triadic pattern to it: from the Father, through the Son, by the Holy Spirit. Consequently, for both Augustine and Owen, every act of redemption involves not just one person but all three

---

[16] Ibid., 2:9.
[17] Ibid.
[18] We do not have space here to lay out Owen's biblical and theological defense of the Trinity, but see *A Brief Declaration and Vindication of the Doctrine of the Trinity as Also of the Person and Satisfaction of Christ*, in *Works*, 2:365–454. There Owen defines the Trinity as follows: "God is one;—that this one God is Father, Son, and Holy Ghost; that the Father is the Father of the Son; and the Son, the Son of the Father; and the Holy Ghost, the Spirit of the Father and the Son; and that, in respect of this their mutual relation, they are distinct from each other" (ibid., 2:377).
[19] Owen, *Of Communion with God*, in *Works*, 2:16–17.
[20] Augustine, *The Trinity* 1.2.8.

persons of the Trinity so that the external works of the Trinity are undivided (*opera ad extra trinitatis indivisa sunt*).[21]

It is through this Trinitarian lens that Owen views our communion and fellowship with God. He writes, "When I assign any thing as peculiar wherein we distinctly hold communion with any person, I do not exclude the other persons from communion with the soul in the very same thing." Therefore, "by what act soever we hold communion with any person, there is an *influence* from every person to the putting forth of that act."[22] Consider, for example, how we receive faith. It is "bestowed on us by the Father" (Matt. 11:25; Eph. 2:8), "purchased for us by the Son" (Luke 17:5; Eph. 1:3; Phil. 1:29), and "wrought in us by the Spirit" (Rom. 8:11; Eph. 1:19–20).[23] Yet, at the same time, one particular person in the Trinity may take on the focal role at a specific point in redemptive history. For example, says Owen, creation is appropriated to the Father, while redemption is to the Son.[24] Each person of the Trinity has a specific role to play in our redemption, and yet each leg of our redemption is the work of the entire Trinity, as no one person works apart from the others. Each of these divine persons, particularly each person's distinct role, deserves our attention, beginning with the Father, the "original authority."

Communing with the Father

The Love of the Father

What is it that defines our communion with the Father? The answer, for Owen, is love—"free, undeserved, and eternal love."[25] Owen sees the gospel itself wrapped in the love of the Father for his elect.

> This is the great discovery of the gospel: for whereas the Father, as the fountain of the Deity, is not known any other way but as full of wrath, anger, and indignation against sin, nor can the sons of men have any other thoughts of him (Rom. 1:18; Isa. 33:13, 14; Hab. 1:13; Ps. 5:4–6; Eph. 2:3),—here he is now revealed peculiarly as love, as full of it unto us; the manifestation whereof is the peculiar work of the gospel, Tit. 3:4.[26]

---

[21] Owen, *Of Communion with God*, in *Works*, 2:18, see especially note 1. Also see Owen, *A Discourse concerning the Holy Spirit*, in *Works*, 3:162, 198–200.
[22] Owen, *Of Communion with God*, in *Works*, 2:18.
[23] Ibid.
[24] Ibid.
[25] Ibid., 2:19.
[26] Ibid.

Owen points us to 1 John 4:8, where John teaches us that most basic and important truth: "God is love." Owen believes this passage has in mind God the Father in particular, since the text goes on to distinguish him from the Son, whom he sends into the world. But notice, the phrase the "Father is love" refers not only to his infinitely gracious, tender, compassionate, and loving nature (Ex. 34:7), but also to the way he "eminently and peculiarly dispenseth himself unto us in free love."[27] Such love is demonstrated in the Father's sending his Son into the world to be the propitiation for our sins (1 John 4:9–10).[28] Perhaps no verse better describes the love of the Father for sinners than John 3:16: "For God so loved the world, that he gave his only begotten Son, that whosoever believeth in him should not perish, but have everlasting life." Those who do believe in Christ will experience this unfathomable love of the Father firsthand, as Jesus promised in John 14:23.

However, Owen recognizes how difficult it can be for believers to accept and truly embrace this divine love from the Father. Often we allow an unbiblical picture of the Father's stance toward us to creep in. In a very pastoral tone, Owen writes with much concern, "Christians walk oftentimes with exceedingly troubled hearts, concerning the thoughts of the Father towards them. They are well persuaded of the Lord Christ and his goodwill; the difficulty lies in what is their acceptance with the Father,—what is his heart towards them?" (see John 14:8).[29] Yes, God is a God of wrath and judgment, but he is also filled with great love for us, for he has sent Christ to be our sin- and wrath-bearing substitute, and by the power of the Spirit we have now been united to Christ and, as a result, have communion with God as Father.[30] Peace has been made by the blood of the cross; we are no longer God's enemies but his children; he no longer is our condemning Judge, but our Father.

Therefore, we must rid our minds of the conception that when we sin and fail him, we must run away from him, as if we are no longer accept-

---

[27] Ibid.

[28] Owen appeals to a variety of other passages that support the love of the Father: John 14:23; 16:26–27; 16:16; Rom. 5:5; 2 Cor. 13:11, 14; Eph. 1:4–6.

[29] Owen, *Of Communion with God*, in *Works*, 2:21–22. Owen notes that we can be tempted to think wrongly of Christ as well: "I fear thou dost not love me, that thou hast forsaken me; because I know I deserve not to be beloved. These thoughts are hard as hell; they give no rest to the soul" (ibid., 2:128). Owen counsels us otherwise: "And let our souls be persuaded of his sincerity and willingness in giving himself, in all that he is, as mediator unto us, to be ours; and let our hearts give up themselves unto him. Let us tell him that we will be for him, and not for another: let him know it from us; he delights to hear it" (ibid., 2:59).

[30] Ferguson makes an important point: For Owen "the death of Christ did not purchase the Father's love, but is the way in which that love is communicated. The death of Christ is not the cause of the Father's love, but is its effect." Ferguson, *John Owen on the Christian Life*, 76–77. Also see Kay, *Trinitarian Spirituality*, 127ff.

able. To the contrary, because we are clothed in the righteousness of Christ, we must run to him! As Owen says, "Assure thyself, then, there is nothing more acceptable unto the Father, than for us to keep up our hearts unto him as the eternal fountain of all that rich grace which flows out to sinners in the blood of Jesus."[31] Owen once again reminds us of the Father's benevolence by turning our attention to what Scripture says. For example, Owen draws our attention to Titus 3:3–7, where Paul spells out our wickedness and then God's great mercy. It was while we were foolish, disobedient, led astray, slaves to various passions and pleasures, passing our days in malice and envy, hated by others and hating one another that God reached down and saved us at the cost of his own Son's blood! Therefore, Owen concludes, "There is love in the person of the Father peculiarly held out unto the saints, as wherein he will and doth hold communion with them."[32]

The Christian's Response to the Father's Love Is Love

So far we have described the central motif in the Father's communion with his people, namely, love, most explicitly demonstrated in the sending of his own Son to die for sinners. But Owen is not finished. In order for this communion between the Father and the redeemed sinner to be complete, there must be an appropriate and proper response from the believer. Owen observes that there are two requirements: (1) that believers receive the love of the Father; (2) that they make suitable returns unto the Father.

First, it is essential that the believer *receive the love of the Father*. "Communion consists in giving and receiving. Until the love of the Father be received, we have no communion with him therein."[33] But how exactly is one to receive the Father's love? Owen answers: by faith. Indeed, as 1 John 5:1 states, "Whosoever believeth that Jesus is the Christ is born of God: and every one that loveth him that begat loveth him also that is begotten of him." In other words, love for the Father is the natural response of one who believes in Jesus, and believing in Jesus is always the result of regeneration. Stated otherwise, God's supernatural work of regeneration brings about faith, and faith always results in a love for the Father.

Nonetheless, even here we witness the entire Trinity at work, for the believer's love for the Father is not an "immediate acting of faith upon the

---

[31] Owen, *Of Communion with God*, in *Works*, 2:35. On this point especially see Ferguson, *John Owen on the Christian Life*, 76–77; Kapic, "Worshiping the Triune God," 29–32.
[32] Owen, *Of Communion with God*, in *Works*, 2:22.
[33] Ibid.

Father, but by the Son."[34] Such a point is supported by 1 John 5:1. It is by believing in Christ that one then loves the Father. In other words, we come to the Father *through the Son*, for he is the "merciful high priest over the house of God, by whom we have access to the throne of grace" (see 1 Pet. 1:21).[35] Christ is the stream that leads us to the fountain. If the believer would recognize this, his or her spiritual walk with God would be greatly improved.

Undoubtedly having his parishioners in mind, Owen reflects upon the "dark and disturbing thoughts" that many have, resulting in such a handicap that they are unable to "carry up their hearts and minds to this height by faith, as to rest their souls in the love of the Father." Instead, says Owen, they live below it, "in the troublesome region of hopes and fears, storms and clouds."[36] In reply, Owen reminds such weary souls that only the love of the Father will deliver rest to their soul. This was Christ's very purpose, to reveal the Father (John 1:18), to manifest his name to those whom the Father gave to the Son out of the world (John 17:6), and to effectually lead sinners to the Father as he is the "only way of going to God as a Father" (John 14:5–6).[37]

Second, the believer must *love the Father in return*. "God loves, that he may be beloved."[38] As Owen says, "When the soul sees God, in his dispensation of love, to be love, to be infinitely lovely and loving, rests upon and delights in him as such,—then hath it communion with him in love."[39] Our salvation begins with God loving us (Eph. 1:4), but it ends with us loving God (Luke 10:27).

Because the Father first loved us, we in return love him. But in what ways are these two loves similar and different? They are similar in two ways. In the first place, they are each a love of rest, complacency (i.e., contentment), and delight. Appealing to Zephaniah 3:17, Owen says that God rejoices over those whom he loves with singing! He is a God whose heart is glad and has the greatest delight in his children. Therefore, he always has our good in mind and can even be said to be working all things for our good. And his children love their Father in return. They find their rest in him (Ps. 116:7), for he is their greatest desire and delight. As the psalmist

---

[34] Ibid.
[35] Ibid., 2:23.
[36] Ibid., 2:22.
[37] Owen makes the same point throughout his *Discourse concerning the Holy Spirit* as well.
[38] Owen, *Of Communion with God*, in *Works*, 2:24. Owen is careful to define love: "Generally, love is an affection of union and nearness, with complacency therein."
[39] Ibid.

sings, "Whom have I in heaven but thee? And there is none upon earth that I desire beside thee" (Ps. 73:25; cf. 63:3).[40]

These two loves are also similar in that each is rooted and grounded in Christ. "The Father," says Owen, "communicates no issue of his love unto us but through Christ; and we make no return of love unto him but through Christ."[41] Christ is the "treasury" where the Father places all the riches of his grace, which itself is taken from his "eternal love." And since Christ is our Great High Priest, it is into his hands that we place all of our "offerings" to our Father in return. Therefore, says Owen, Scripture always speaks of the Father loving the Son—not merely as his eternal Son (see Prov. 8:30, where he is said to be the delight of the Father's soul before the foundation of the world), but also as our Mediator. Christ, in other words, is the very means by which the Father conveys his love to us (Matt. 3:17; John 3:35; 5:20; 10:17; 15:9; 17:24). "And we are said through him [Christ] to believe in and to have access to God."[42] Owen believes there are many ways we see and experience the love of the Father toward us. For example, his love is manifested in divine election (see chap. 6). Before the foundation of the world he chose us and blessed us with all spiritual blessings in the heavenly places in Christ (Eph. 1:3–4). Additionally, the Father then displays his love by pouring out the Holy Spirit "richly upon us, through Jesus Christ our Saviour" (Titus 3:6).[43]

God's love and our love differ in significant ways as well. Owen lists three. First, the love of God is a love of bounty, but our love for him is a love of duty. Concerning the former, Owen explains that God's love is one that descends to us and does great things for us. Nowhere is this love more explicit than in God's sending his own Son to die for us, thereby blessing us with all spiritual blessings. Our love, however, is one of duty, like the love of a child. While God's love "descends upon us in bounty and fruitfulness; our love ascends unto him in duty and thankfulness."

---

[40] "Thus the soul gathers itself from all its wanderings, from all other beloveds, to rest in God alone,—to satiate and content itself in him; choosing the Father for his present and eternal rest" (ibid., 2:26).

[41] Ibid., 2:27.

[42] Ibid.

[43] Owen, however, qualifies this statement: "Though the love of the Father's purpose and good pleasure have its rise and foundation in his mere grace and will, yet the design of its accomplishment is only in Christ. All the fruits of it are first given to him; and it is in him only that they are dispensed to us. So that though the saints may, nay, do, see an infinite ocean of love unto them in the bosom of the Father, yet they are not to look for one drop from him but what comes through Christ. He is the only means of communication. Love in the Father is like *honey in the flower*;—it must be in the comb before it be for our use. Christ must extract and prepare this honey for us. He draws this water from the fountain through union and dispensation of fullness;—we by faith, from the wells of salvation that are in him" (ibid.).

To clarify, while God's love "adds to us," our love adds nothing to him.[44] Therefore, "though he requires our love, he is not benefited by it" (Job 22:2–3; 35:5–8; Rom. 11:35). Here Owen is simply applying the Reformed doctrine of divine aseity, the belief that God does not need us, either ontologically or relationally, but is eternal, self-existent, and self-sufficient (Acts 17:24–25). In other words, before the foundation of the world God was not lonely, but in the triune Godhead each person enjoyed perfect fellowship with the others (John 17:5). The same is true with our salvation. God was not obligated to save us, nor did he need to in order to fill a void within himself. Instead, out of pure mercy and grace, he chose to redeem us and enter into a covenant relationship with us, and in his doing so it is his love that benefits us, not vice versa. Therefore, when Owen applies divine aseity (God's independence from the world for his existence or happiness) to our relationship with God, it becomes clear that God's love is the root of our love for him.

It follows, second, that the Father's love for us is antecedent, but our love is consequent. First John 4:10 expresses this truth powerfully: "Herein is love, not that we loved God, but that he loved us [first]."[45] By nature we are children of wrath (Rom. 1:30) or, as Owen says, "haters of God." Therefore, any mutual love between God and the sinner must begin with God. As Paul explains in Romans 5:8, "God shows his love for us in that while we were still sinners, Christ died for us." Owen elaborates:

> Sin holds out all of unloveliness and undesirableness that can be in a crea-ture. The very mention of that removes all causes, all moving occasions of love whatever. Yet, as such, have we the commendation of the Father's love unto us, by a most signal testimony. Not only when we have done no good, but when we are in our blood, doth he love us;—not because we are better than others, but because himself is infinitely good. His kindness

---

[44] "Our goodness extends not unto him. Though our love be fixed on him immediately, yet no fruit of our love reacheth him immediately" (ibid., 2:28). Owen goes on to explain that we hold communion with God by our (1) rest, (2) delight, (3) reverence, and (4) obedience. "Hence God calls that love which is due to him as a father, 'honour'" (see Mal. 1:6) (ibid., 2:29).

[45] Later on Owen responds with force to the objection: "I cannot find my heart making returns of love unto God. Could I find my soul set upon him, I could then believe his soul delighted in me." Returning once again to 1 John 4:10–11, Owen responds, "This is the most *preposterous* course that possibly thy thoughts can pitch upon, a most ready way to rob God of his glory. 'Herein is love,' saith the Holy Ghost, 'not that we loved God, but that he loved us' first, 1 John 4:10, 11. Now, thou wouldst invert this order, and say, 'Herein is love, not that God loved me, but that I love him first.' This is to take the glory of God from him: that, whereas he loves us without a cause that is in ourselves, and we have all cause in the world to love him, thou wouldst have the contrary,—namely, that something should be in thee for which God should love thee, even thy love to him; and that thou shouldst love God, before thou knewest any thing lovely in him,—namely, whether he love thee or no. This is a course of flesh's finding out, that will never bring glory to God, nor peace to thy own soul" (ibid., 2:37).

appears when we are foolish and disobedient. Hence he is said to "love the world"; that is, those who have nothing but what is in and of the world, whose whole [portion] lies in evil.[46]

God's saving love is not conditioned on anything in us. On the contrary, his love comes to us by grace. It is an unconditional love, meaning that nothing in us moved him to love us. He did not love us because we were better than others—indeed, due to our sinfulness, there was nothing in us to love! The unconditionality of God's saving love is evident in that he placed his covenant love on us while we were in the grip of sin, bound and enslaved. In short, while the believer's relationship with God is one of mutual love, in the beginning it was not our love that moved God to love us, but rather his love that effectually moved us to love him.[47]

Third, the love of God is like himself—equal, constant, not capable of augmentation or diminution.[48] But our love is like ourselves—unequal, increasing, waning, growing, and declining. The Father's love is equal, meaning that those whom he loves "he loves unto the end, and he loves them always alike."[49] It is also constant, for God is not like man that he should repent. "On whom he fixes his love, it is immutable; it doth not grow to eternity, it is not diminished at any time. It is an eternal love, that had no beginning, that shall have no ending; that cannot be heightened by any act of ours, that cannot be lessened by any thing in us."[50] Such divine love from the Father, says Owen, should lead us into a sweet fellowship with him, to delight in him, and to "make our abode with him."[51]

Regretfully, many "saints have no greater burden in their lives, than that their hearts do not come clearly and fully up, constantly to delight

---

[46] Ibid., 2:29.

[47] Owen observes yet another difference, namely, that while there is nothing in us to move God to love us (after all, we are sinners deserving only condemnation), everything in God commends our love to him. "God must be revealed unto us as lovely and desirable, as a fit and suitable object unto the soul to set up its rest upon, before we can bear any love unto him. The saints (in this sense) do not love God for nothing, but for that excellency, loveliness, and desirableness that is in him." Owen appeals to Ps. 116:1 (ibid.).

[48] Owen also describes God's love as eternal, free, unchangeable, and distinguishing. See ibid., 2:33.

[49] Ibid., 2:30.

[50] Ibid. However, Owen does qualify such a point by explaining that when God's love is manifested in space and time, it may look different. Therefore, "in respect of its fruits," says Owen, "it may sometimes be greater, sometimes less; its communications are various" (ibid.). In responding to an objection, Owen goes on to ask whether God alters his love toward us. He answers, "Not the *purpose* of his will, but the *dispensations* of his grace. He *rebukes* them, he *chastens* them, he *hides* his face from them, he *smites* them, he *fills* them with a sense of [his] indignation; but woe, woe would it be to us, should he change in his love, or take away his kindness from us! Those very things which seem to be demonstrations of the change of his affections toward his, do as clearly proceed from love as those which seem to be the most genuine issue thereof" (ibid., 2:31).

[51] Ibid., 2:35.

and rejoice in God," walking closely with him. But why? Owen believes it is because they neglect to commune with the Father in love. For if we truly know the "eminency of the Father's love," then we "cannot choose but be overpowered, conquered, and endeared unto him."[52] So what then should we do to know this overpowering love of the Father? One must exercise his thoughts upon the "eternal, free, and fruitful love of the Father," so that one's heart will delight in him.

> I dare boldly say, believers will find it as thriving a course as ever they pitched on in their lives. Sit down a little at the fountain, and you will quickly have a farther discovery of the sweetness of the streams. You who have run from him, will not be able, after a while, to keep at a distance for a moment.[53]

Not only is communion with the Father irresistibly sweet, but he himself is our safe haven. Though we will undergo reproach from the world, nevertheless, we have in God a mighty fortress, a safe retreat. Using the illustration of a child, Owen explains, "When a child is abused abroad in the streets by strangers, he runs with speed to the bosom of his father; there he makes his complaint, and is comforted."[54] Likewise, the same is true with us and our heavenly Father. We are abused by the world, enduring persecution. So we run with "moanings" to our Father to be comforted (Isa. 66:13). He is compassionate, and if we go to him he will satisfy us, for his kindness is better than life itself. "There is in my Father's love every thing desirable: there is the sweetness of all mercies in the abstract itself, and that fully and durably."[55]

Communing with the Son

If communion with the Father is sweet, so also is communion with his Son. Scripture everywhere affirms that we, as believers, have fellowship with Jesus Christ, the Son of God (Prov. 9:1–5; Song 2:1–7; 1 Cor. 1:9; Rev. 3:20).[56] Owen, basing his thought on Song of Solomon 2:1–7,[57] uses four terms to describe our communion with Christ.

---

[52] Ibid., 2:36.
[53] Ibid.
[54] Ibid., 2:38.
[55] Ibid.
[56] For Owen, the entire book of the Song of Solomon "is taken up in the description of the communion that is between the Lord Christ and his saints" (ibid., 2:46).
[57] For many it may appear strange that Owen turns to the Song of Solomon to describe our communion with Christ. However, Owen views the Song of Solomon as a picture of the church's marriage to Christ.

Sweetness. Our communion with Christ is one characterized by grace, mercy, love, and kindness, all of which are revealed in the gospel, applied to us by the Holy Spirit.

Delight. Owen says:

> Upon discovery of the excellency and sweetness of Christ in the banqueting-house, the soul is instantly overpowered, and cries out to be made partaker of the fullness of it. She is "sick of love": not (as some suppose) fainting for want of a sense of love, under the apprehension of wrath; but made sick and faint, even overcome with the mighty actings of that divine affection, after she had once tasted of the sweetness of Christ in the banqueting-house. [58]

Owen goes on to explain that once we have a glimpse of the "King in his beauty," having tasted the fruit of righteousness, our soul "melteth in longing after him." Christ becomes our greatest desire and delight in life.

Safety. Verse 4 says, "He brought me to the banqueting house, and his banner over me was love." What is the purpose of this banner? "The banner is an emblem of safety and protection,—a sign of the presence of an host." For example, when you are in an army, you encamp under its banner in security. Also, the banner is a "token of success and victory" (see Ps. 20:5). What then is the banner that Christ has over us? Love. And as his bride we shall have all the protection his love can give us. We are safeguarded from hell, death, and our enemies. "Whatever presses on them [his people], it must pass through the banner of the love of the Lord Jesus. They have, then, great spiritual safety; which is another ornament or excellency of their communion with him." [59]

Support and consolation. As verse 6 states, "His left hand is under my head, and his right hand doth embrace me." "Christ here," says Owen, "hath the posture of a most tender friend towards any one in sickness and sadness. The soul faints with love,—spiritual longings after the enjoyment of his presence; and Christ comes in with his embraces. He nourisheth and cherisheth his church" (Isa. 63:9; Eph. 5:29). [60]

Owen explains his own hermeneutic when he writes: "This sense of the love of Christ, and the effect of it in communion with him, by prayer and praises, is divinely set forth in the Book of Canticles. The church therein is represented as the spouse of Christ; and, as a faithful spouse, she is always either solicitous about his love, or rejoicing in it." Owen, *Christologia; or, A Declaration of the Glorious Mystery of the Person of Christ—God and Man*, in *Works*, 1:116. Also see Owen, *Of Communion with God*, in *Works*, 2:46.

[58] Owen, *Of Communion with God*, in *Works*, 2:44.

[59] Ibid., 2:45.

[60] Ibid.

But Owen presses deeper, seeking to understand the very basis for our fellowship with Christ. Owen believes that basis is to be found in divine grace itself. Such grace has been manifested by God in sending Christ into the world to dwell among us. Christ himself is full of grace and truth (John 1:14, 17), and from him we have received grace (Zech. 4:7; John 1:16; 2 Cor. 13:14; 2 Thess. 3:17–18). That is, "we have communion with him in grace; we receive from him all manner of grace whatever; and therein have we fellowship with him."[61] Owen categorizes grace in three ways: (1) grace of personal presence and comeliness, which he believes is the subject of half of the Song of Solomon (see also Ps. 45:2); (2) grace of free favor and acceptance, which is the very grace that saves us, that is, the "free favour and gracious acceptation of God in Christ" (Gen. 39:21; 41:37; 1 Sam. 2:26; 2 Kings 25:27; Acts 7:10; James 4:6); and (3) the fruits of the Spirit, which play the role of "sanctifying and renewing our natures, enabling unto good, and preventing from evil" (see 2 Cor. 8:6–7; Col. 3:16; Heb. 12:28). The first of these three Owen calls "personal grace," to which we will devote the majority of our time in this chapter. The latter two Owen calls "purchased grace" because Christ purchased them for us. Accordingly, we have communion with him in his sufferings and in the power of his resurrection (Phil. 3:10).[62] In other words, purchased grace has to do with Christ's active and passive obedience, his intercession, and the justification of the believer.[63]

What is especially notable is not only how Owen exalts Christ as our Savior, but also how he instructs the believer to relate to Christ as Savior. Christ, says Owen, is fit to save by virtue of the union of his two natures (one human, one divine) in his one person (Isa. 9:6; John 1:14; Rom. 1:3; 9:5). And because he is fit to save, he is able to satisfy all the desires of our soul. Owen writes:

> He hath a fitness to save, having pity and ability, tenderness and power, to carry on that work to the uttermost; and a fullness to save, of redemption and sanctification, of righteousness and the Spirit; and a suitableness to the wants of all our souls: whereby he becomes exceedingly desirable, yea, altogether lovely; as afterward will appear in particular.

---

[61] Ibid., 2:47.
[62] Ibid., 2:48.
[63] Owen also divides "purchased grace" into three further categories: (1) grace of acceptance with God, (2) grace of sanctification, and (3) grace of privilege (i.e., adoption). Since chaps. 5 and 7 address these, we will limit ourselves to "personal grace." For a treatment of each, see Kay, *Trinitarian Spirituality*, 147–60; Kapic, *Communion with God*, 186–92.

And as to this, in the first place, the saints have distinct fellowship with the Lord Christ.[64]

Yet Owen does not leave the reader here. Rather, he takes us one step further, asking us where Christ sits in our hearts. Does Christ have "his due place in your hearts"? Is he "your all," and "does he dwell in your thoughts?" Do "you know him in his excellency and desirableness"? Do you "account all things 'loss and dung' for his exceeding excellency"? Or do you "prefer almost anything in the world before it"?[65] For Owen, Christ is worthy of our all. He alone is the greatest of treasures; he alone is more desirable than anything this world has to offer. He alone deserves first place in our hearts.[66]

Therefore, our communion with Christ is one in which we cherish Christ above all things. Owen explains how this looks in the life of a believer:

> Let us receive him in all his excellencies, as he bestows himself upon us;—be frequent in thoughts of faith, comparing him with other beloveds, sin, world, legal righteousness; and preferring him before them, counting them all loss and dung in comparison to him. And let our souls be persuaded of his sincerity and willingness in giving himself, in all that he is, as mediator unto us, to be ours; and let our hearts give up themselves unto him. Let us tell him that we will be for him, and not for another: let him know it from us; he delights to hear it, yea, he says, "Sweet is our voice, and our countenance is comely";—and we shall not fail in the issue of sweet refreshment with him.[67]

The fellowship between Christ and the believer is so intimate that Owen, following Scripture (Eph. 5:22–33), appeals to the metaphor of marriage itself. "Christ makes himself over to the soul, to be his, as to all the love, care, and tenderness of a husband; and the soul gives up itself wholly unto the Lord Christ, to be his, as to all loving, tender obedience."[68] According to Owen, the love between Christ and his bride is mutual, though it begins with Christ. Christ bestows his love on us, a love that is characterized by the tenderness of a husband, and in return the soul gives itself up entirely to Christ. Owen elaborates:

---

[64] Owen, *Of Communion with God*, in *Works*, 2:50.
[65] Ibid., 2:53–54.
[66] For Owen's warning to those who reject Christ, ibid., 2:53.
[67] Ibid., 2:59.
[68] Ibid., 2:56.

Christ gives himself to the soul, with all his excellencies, righteousness, preciousness, graces, and eminencies, to be its Saviour, head, and husband, for ever to dwell with it in this holy relation. He looks upon the souls of his saints, likes them well, counts them fair and beautiful, because he hath made them so.

In response, says Owen, Christ's saints find it to be their "free, willing consent to receive, embrace, and submit unto the Lord Jesus, as their husband, Lord, and Saviour,—to abide with him, subject their souls unto him, and to be ruled by him for ever."[69]

When the believer has a taste of this communion with his Savior, sin is bitter on the tongue. Furthermore, says Owen, the believer is on guard against sin, lest it should interrupt and disrupt this sweet communion he enjoys so much with his Savior. Owen writes:

When once the soul of a believer hath obtained sweet and real communion with Christ, it looks about him, watcheth all temptations, all ways whereby sin might approach, to disturb him in his enjoyment of his dear Lord and Saviour, his rest and desire. How doth it charge itself not to omit any thing, nor to do any thing that may interrupt the communion obtained![70]

Owen goes on to explain that no temptation, no proposal or allurement can compare to the delight one has in Christ. The believer who has Christ in his arms is like the man who discovers "great spoils" or the "pearl of price." He is like the man Jesus speaks of, who finds treasure buried in a field and then, in his joy, sells everything he owns in order to purchase the field (Matt. 13:44).

For Owen, Christ does not merely delight in his saints, however; he values them as well, something that is obvious from his incarnation and suffering for sinners in their stead (2 Cor. 8:9; Phil. 2:6–7; Heb. 2:14–16).[71] Such servanthood, such sacrifice, only serves to demonstrate how great the Savior's love for us truly is. For our sake Christ became obedient even to the point of death on a cross. As he says in John 17:19, "For their sakes I sanctify myself, that they also might be sanctified through the truth." Owen elaborates:

---

[69] Ibid., 2:56, 58. Owen spends considerable space elaborating on how this communion is enjoyed, even giving practical examples. See ibid., 2:117–32.
[70] Ibid., 2:126.
[71] Ibid., 2:118–35.

And if we might stay to consider a little what was in this death that he underwent for them, we should perceive what a price indeed he put upon them. The curse of the law was in it [Gal. 3:13], the wrath *of God* was in it [2 Cor. 5:21], the loss of God's presence was in it [Ps. 22:1]. It was a fearful cup that he tasted of, and drank of, that they might never taste of it [Matt. 26:39].

In other words, the cross—where Christ bore the penalty, the punishment of our sin, satisfying the wrath of God that we deserve—displays and exhibits the love of Christ for sinners. Certainly there is no greater love. As we read in John 15:13, "Greater love hath no man than this, that a man lay down his life for his friends." Owen remarks:

> It is impossible there should be any greater demonstration or evidence of love than this. What can any one do more? . . . Such a death, in such a manner, with such attendancies of wrath and curse,—a death accompanied with the worst that God had ever threatened to sinners,—argues as high a valuation of us as the heart of Christ himself was capable of.[72]

Yet, not only is the love of Christ manifested in his death, but so too is the love of the Father. As we discover in Romans 5:8, "God commendeth his love toward us, in that, while we were yet sinners, Christ died for us."[73] God could have judged us, and he would have been just to do so. Instead, he loved us, something we did not deserve as sinners.

Owen, as usual, does not miss a chance to apply such a rich doctrine to the Christian personally and individually. Because Christ loved us so much even to die for us, we are, in the eyes of our Savior, precious and valuable. Because he suffered for us, interceding on our behalf, and thereby delivering us from condemnation, we are considered the "apple of his eye, his jewel, his diadem, his crown."[74] All the world is nothing to Christ in comparison to his bride, whom he purchased with his own blood. "They are his garden; the rest of the world, a wilderness" (see Song 4:12). They are his inheritance, but everyone else—those who have no regard for Christ—are his enemies (Isa. 43:3–4).

Why does the Lord deal this way with his people in contrast to everyone else? Owen answers, it is "because he loves her."[75] He loves her, will move na-

---

[72] Ibid., 2:135.
[73] Ibid.
[74] Ibid., 2:136.
[75] Ibid.

tions to benefit her (Amos 9:9), and even appoints angels to minister to her (Heb. 1:14). The implication for even the weakest believer is astounding. "In a word, there is not the meanest, the weakest, the poorest believer on the earth, but Christ prizeth him more than all the world besides. Were our hearts filled much with thoughts hereof, it would tend much to our consolation."[76]

Not only does Christ value believers, but believers, in response, value Christ. They say of him in their hearts continually, following the example of David, "Whom have I in heaven but thee? and there is none upon earth that I desire beside thee" (Ps. 73:25). Owen gives three ways believers desire Christ above all else.

In the first place, they value him above all other things and persons. "Christ and a dungeon, Christ and a cross, is infinitely sweeter than a crown, a scepter without him, to their souls."[77] This much was true of Moses, for example, who esteemed the reproach of Christ greater riches than the treasures all of Egypt had to offer (Heb. 11:26).[78] Hence, Christ himself tells his listeners that if they love anything, even their own mother or father, more than Christ, then they are not worthy of him (Luke 14:26). Therefore, says Owen, a "despising of all things for Christ is the very first lesson of the gospel. 'Give away all, take up the cross and follow me,' was the way whereby he tried his disciples of old; and if there be not the same mind and heart in us, we are none of his."[79]

Believers also value him above their lives. The apostle Paul is a prime example. Consider his words in Acts 20:24, "My life is not dear, that I may perfect my course with joy, and the ministry I have received of the Lord Jesus." Owen enlists not only Paul as an example, but Ignatius as well. When Ignatius was martyred he said, "Let what will come upon me, only so I may obtain Jesus Christ." Therefore, believers of old rejoiced when they were counted worthy of suffering and dishonor for the name of Christ (Acts 5:41; Hebrews 11): "The lives they have to live, the death they have to die, is little, is light, upon the thoughts of him who is the stay of their lives and the end of their death. Were it not for the refreshment which daily they receive by thoughts of him, they could not live,—their lives would be a burden to them."[80]

---

[76] Ibid.
[77] Ibid., 2:137.
[78] "The reproach of Christ is the worst consequent that the wickedness of the world or the malice of Satan can bring upon the followers of him" (ibid.).
[79] Ibid.
[80] Ibid.

Finally, they value Christ above all spiritual excellencies and all other righteousness whatever. Owen finds support in Philippians 3:7–8, where Paul looks back at all his works as a "Hebrew of Hebrews," and he considers them all loss and dung.[81] So is it the same for every believer whose soul cries out, "In the Lord Jesus only is my righteousness and glory."[82] Only then does Christ appear all-satisfying. Owen concludes, "The glory of his Deity, the excellency of his person, his all-conquering desirableness, ineffable love, wonderful undertaking, unspeakable condescensions. Effectual mediation, complete righteousness, lie in their eyes, ravish their hearts, fill their affections, and possess their souls."[83]

It is crucial to understand that Owen recognizes the enormous challenges one faces in knowing Christ. On one occasion toward the close of his ministry, in a conversation that Owen had with Richard Davis (1658–1714), who later had a powerful ministry,[84] Owen reflected on times in his life when he felt little toward Christ, struggling to know Christ as he knew he ought. In a rare moment of transparency, Owen confessed a lack of "experimental acquaintance" with "God through Christ" at one point early in his life. In his own words:

> I myself preached Christ some years, when I had but very little, if any, experimental acquaintance with access to God through Christ; until the Lord was pleased to visit me with sore affliction, whereby I was brought to the mouth of the grave, and under which my soul was oppressed with horror and darkness; but God graciously relieved my spirit by a powerful application of Psalm 130:4, "But there is forgiveness with thee, that thou mayest be feared"; from whence I received special instruction, peace, and comfort, in drawing near to God through the Mediator.[85]

As we will see next, it was the Holy Spirit who comforted Owen. But notice, Owen says that during this time of "horror and darkness," he was able to draw near to God through Christ, his Mediator.

In *Of Communion with God*, Owen has much more to say about Christ, particularly in regard to Christ's acting as our substitute.[86] We shall re-

---

[81] For Owen's understanding of "works" after the believer's conversion, see ibid., 2:147.
[82] Ibid., 2:138.
[83] Ibid., 2:139.
[84] On Davis, see Peter Beale, "Richard Davis of Rothwell and Evangelistic Passion," in *The Power of God in the Life of Man* (London: Westminster Conference, 2005), 85–105.
[85] Quoted in W. H. Goold, "Prefatory Note" to *A Practical Exposition upon Psalm 130*, in *Works*, 6:324.
[86] Also note how Owen connects communion with the Son to our adoption as sons. With the Son, and because of what he has done, we have "fellowship in *name*; we are (as he is) sons of God"; "fellowship in

visit this topic in chapter 5, seeking to understand what it means for Christ to act vicariously, both in his life and in his death, and what the implications are for the Christian life. Now, however, we must move on to the communion we have with the Holy Spirit, the third person of the Trinity.

Communing with the Holy Spirit

In order to understand how the believer has fellowship with the third person of the Trinity, the Holy Spirit, we must begin by comprehending the Spirit's mission. Owen helps us grasp the mission of the Spirit by turning our attention to John 16. There Christ informs his disciples that he is about to depart. As the disciples will later realize, Christ is preparing them for not only his death and resurrection, but also his ascension, where he will ascend to the right hand of the Father and no longer be physically present with his followers. Understandably, the disciples are troubled and sorrowful. But Christ has good news for them: he will send them the Comforter, previously referred to as the Spirit of truth (John 15:26), who will reveal all truth to the sons of men.

Christ is clear that unless he goes away, the Comforter will not come. But if he goes, he will send him (John 16:7; cf. 14:16; 15:26). What is so remarkable, however, is that Jesus says not merely that he is sending the Spirit from the Father, but also that the presence of the Spirit is far better. "This is the sum," Owen states; "the presence of the Holy Ghost with believers as a comforter, sent by Christ for those ends and purposes for which he is promised, is better and more profitable for believers than any corporeal presence of Christ can be, now he hath fulfilled the one sacrifice for sin which he was to offer."[87] Certainly this must come as a shock to Christ's disciples. How could the Spirit, who is invisible to them, be far better than Christ who is with them physically? In order to understand the answer to such a perplexing question, we must first know who the Holy Spirit is and what his role involves.

---

title and right; we are heirs, co-heirs with Christ"; "fellowship in *likeness* and conformity; we are predestinated to be like the firstborn of the family"; "fellowship in *honour*; he is not ashamed to call us brethren"; "fellowship in *sufferings*; he learned obedience by what he suffered, and every son is to be scourged that is received"; "fellowship in his *kingdom*; we shall reign with him." Owen, *Of Communion with God*, in *Works*, 2:222. One other area of communion with the Son is the Lord's Supper. As Owen explains, "There is, in the ordinance of the Lord's supper, an especial and peculiar communion with Christ, in his body and blood, to be obtained." Owen, *Sacramental Discourses*, in *Works*, 9:523. Also see Beeke and Jones, *A Puritan Theology*, 111.

[87] Owen, *Of Communion with God*, in *Works*, 2:226.

First, the Holy Spirit is the Spirit of sanctification to God's elect, "to convert them and make them believers."[88] When we first receive the Spirit, it is "a mere passive reception, as a vessel receives water." He comes upon us like the wind "on Ezekiel's dead bones, and makes them live; he comes into dead hearts, and quickens them, by an act of his almighty power."[89] As a consequence of the quickening work of the Spirit, the Spirit is then received by faith. As Galatians 3:2 makes plain, the Spirit was received not by works of the law, but by "hearing of faith." In other words, "the preaching of the gospel, begetting faith in them, enabled them to receive the Spirit." Therefore, says Owen, "believing is put as the qualification of all our receiving the Holy Ghost" (John 7:39). Owen is referring not to what we call regeneration (the new birth), but rather to conversion (faith and repentance), whereby the sinner, who has been made alive, now believes and receives the indwelling Spirit by faith. As Owen explains, "It is believers that thus receive the Spirit; and they receive him by faith." "It is faith alone that makes profit of the benefit of the promises" (see Gal. 3:14; Eph. 1:13; Heb. 4:2).[90]

Second, he is the Spirit of consolation to believers. He is the one who gives them the "privileges of the death and purchase of Christ."[91] Elsewhere Owen explains that the Spirit of consolation indwells us for he is the Spirit of sanctification. He indwells us as in a temple, which he makes holy (Rom. 8:11; 1 Cor. 6:19). As our Comforter, he abides in us always, just as Christ promised (John 14:16). But now Owen runs into a significant problem. If the Spirit of sanctification dwells in us always, it is therefore impossible "that we should lose utterly our holiness." However, if it is the case that the Comforter abides in us forever, how can it be that "we may yet utterly lose our comfort"?[92]

Owen answers, "The Comforter may always abide with us, though not always comfort us." In other words, "in truth, as to the essence of holiness, he cannot dwell in us but withal he must make us holy; for the temple of God is holy;—but as to his comforting, his actings therein are all of his sovereign will; so that he may abide and yet not actually comfort us." The Spirit as a sanctifier comes "with power to conquer an unbelieving heart." However, the Spirit as a Comforter "comes with sweetness, to be received in a believing heart." In this subsequent role, the Spirit speaks to us, but at times we do not believe it is his voice. He "tenders the things of consolation, and we

---

[88] Ibid.
[89] Ibid., 2:231.
[90] Ibid.
[91] Ibid., 2:226.
[92] Ibid., 2:232.

receive them not." We are like David, who refused to be comforted. That said, Owen concludes that the Spirit will never "absolutely and universally leave a believing soul without consolation." The believer "may be darkened, clouded, refuse comfort,—actually find none, feel none; but radically he hath a foundation of consolation, which in due time will be drawn forth."[93]

The Procession of the Spirit

How exactly the Spirit is sent into this world is Owen's first concern, since it has major implications for what it means for the Spirit to sanctify and console the believer. According to Owen, the Spirit's coming can be referred to as the "procession" of the Spirit. John 15:26 teaches that the Spirit "proceedeth from the Father," who is the "fountain of this dispensation." The Spirit's procession is twofold: he proceeds in respect to his substance and personality, and he proceeds in respect to his work of grace. Concerning the former, the Spirit's procession is eternal. This, says Owen, is certainly one of the great mysteries, which requires the "bare acquiescence of faith" in what God has revealed.[94] Regarding the latter, Owen describes the Spirit's procession as a work of grace in that he comes to the world to testify about Christ, "which cannot be assigned to him in respect of his eternal procession, but of his actual dispensation; as it is said of Christ, 'He came forth from God.'"[95] There is an order to our communion, argues Owen, that follows the ordering of the Trinity itself: Father, Son, and Holy Spirit. We have "communion with the Father in love, the Son in grace, and the Holy Ghost in consolation."[96] It is the Spirit in particular who blesses us with all the privileges of salvation in time and space.

The Giving, Sending, and Pouring Out of the Spirit

The Spirit's salvific blessings can be seen in how he works in the souls of believers. The Spirit is given to believers freely, with authority, and is said

---

[93] Therefore, says Owen, "when God promises that he will heal sinners, and restore comfort to them, as Isa. 57:18, it is not that they were without any, but that they had not so much as they needed, that that promise is made" (ibid., 2:233).

[94] Ibid., 2:227.

[95] Owen goes on, "And this relation *ad extra* (as they call it) of the Spirit unto the Father and the Son, in respect of operation, proves his relation *ad intra*, in respect of personal procession; whereof I spake before" (ibid.). Furthermore, lest one think that the Spirit's eternal procession means he is inferior in deity, Owen is quick to explain that it does not. "Frequent mention is made (as we shall see afterward) of his being sent, his being given, and poured out; [but] that it might not be thus apprehended, either that this Spirit were altogether an *inferior, created* spirit, a mere servant, as some have blasphemed, nor yet merely and principally, as to his personality, the virtue of God, as some have fancied, he hath ἰδιώματα ὑποστατικά, personal properties, applied to him in this work, arguing his personality and liberty" (ibid.).

[96] Ibid., 2:228.

to be poured out. First, he is given freely, meaning that he is given as a gift to be received. And that which is a gift, says Owen, is free. "The Spirit of grace is given of grace: and not only the Spirit of sanctification, or the Spirit to sanctify and convert us, is a gift of free grace, but in the sense whereof we speak, in respect of consolation, he is of gift also; he is promised to be given unto believers."[97] Therefore, Owen argues, in texts like Galatians 3:2 the Spirit is said to be received not by the law, but by the gospel. He is received "of mere grace, and not of our own procuring." All his works, in other words, are to be called "free donations."[98]

Second, the Spirit not only comes freely but also comes with authority. He is said to be sent, according to John 14:26, 15:26, and 16:7. Again, the order of the Trinity's work of redemption follows the ordering of their persons.

> This mission of the Holy Ghost by the Father and the Son, as it answers the order of the persons' subsistence in the blessed Trinity, and his procession from them both, so the order voluntarily engaged in by them for the accomplishment, as was said, of the work of our salvation. There is in it, in a most special manner, the condescension of the Holy Ghost, in his love to us, to the authoritative delegation of Father and Son in this business; which argues not a disparity, dissimilitude, or inequality of essence, but of office, in this work.[99]

In other words, there is an ordering, a taxis, when it comes to the Trinity, but not in regard to essence (since all three persons of the Trinity are equally and fully divine), but rather in respect to their functioning roles. Concerning the Spirit, he is our Advocate and Comforter, sent authoritatively by the Father and the Son. And yet, though he submits to the Father and the Son in being sent, he is equal in deity. As Owen explains, "This subjection (if I may so call it), or inequality in respect of office, doth no ways prejudice the equality of nature which he hath with Father and Son; no more than the mission of the Son by the Father doth his."[100]

Lest one think this is a matter of little significance, Owen discerns how a "right apprehension of many mysteries in the gospel," as well as

---

[97] Owen appeals to Neh. 9:20; John 14:16; 7:39; 20:22; Acts 2:38; 5:32; 8:15; 10:47; 15:8; 19:2; Rom. 5:5; 1 Cor. 2:12; 6:19; 12:7; 1 Thess. 4:8; 1 John 4:13 (ibid.).
[98] Ibid.
[99] Ibid., 2:229.
[100] Ibid.

"the ordering of our hearts in communion with him," depends upon this authoritative mission of the Spirit.[101] Take, for example, the unpardonable sin against the Holy Spirit (Matt. 12:31). Why is such a sin so rebellious, so unforgivable? Owen answers:

> Because he [the Spirit] comes not, he acts not, in his own name only, though in his own also, but in the name and authority of the Father and Son, from and by whom he is sent; and therefore, to sin against him is to sin against all the authority of God, all the love of the Trinity, and the utmost condescension of each person to the work of our salvation.[102]

Or consider a second example: prayer. We are instructed to pray to the Father and the Son to give us the Spirit (Luke 11:13). It is true that the Holy Spirit, since he is God, is "no less to be invocated, prayed to, and called on, than the Father and the Son." But how do we, in particular, ask the Father for the Spirit, praying that the Spirit would come and visit us and abide with us? Again, Owen answers:

> In our prayers that are directed to himself, we consider him as essentially God over all, blessed for evermore; we pray for him from the Father and Son, as under this mission and delegation from them. And, indeed, God having most plentifully revealed himself in the order of this dispensation to us, we are (as Christians generally do) in our communion to abound in answerable addresses; that is, not only to the person of the Holy Ghost himself, but properly to the Father and the Son for him, which refers to this dispensation.[103]

Likewise, grieving the Holy Spirit (Eph. 4:30) also proves the point at hand. It is such a crime to grieve the Spirit "because he comes to us in the name, with the love, and upon the condescension, of the whole blessed Trinity."[104] It is the Spirit who is sent to believers from the Father and the Son, "commissioned with their love and grace, to communicate them to their souls."[105]

Third, the Spirit is said to be poured out upon us (Titus 3:6). He is shed on us abundantly. Such a truth was axiomatic in the Old Testament (see

---

[101] Ibid.
[102] Ibid.
[103] Ibid., 2:230.
[104] Ibid.
[105] Ibid.

Isa. 32:13–15; 44:1–4; Zech. 12:10), which, for Owen, reveals to us that the Father is pleased to pour the Spirit out upon us for our salvation.

In summary, Owen believes that these three expressions—giving, sending, and pouring out the Spirit—give us the "great properties of the covenant of grace."[106]

The Spirit as the Pledge of God's Love

Building on Jesus's promise in John 14:26 that the Spirit would teach his disciples all things and assist them in remembering what he had taught them, Owen draws out the implications for the Christian life. First, the Spirit works *powerfully*. He comforts us with the words and promises of Christ, which "break in through all opposition into the saddest and darkest condition imaginable."[107] In doing so, the Spirit can make men sing in the darkest of dungeons, rejoice in the midst of flames, and glory in tribulation. Whether we are thrown into prisons, are tormented by temptation, or have to walk through life's greatest distresses, the Spirit will move our hearts to rejoice because of Christ. The Spirit, says Owen, "works effectually," bringing to our remembrance the promises of Christ in order to console us. Neither "Satan nor man, sin nor world, nor death, shall interrupt our comfort."[108] Owen elaborates:

> Sometimes the heavens are black over them, and the earth trembles under them; public, personal calamities and distresses appear so full of horror and darkness, that they are ready to faint with the apprehensions of them;—hence is their great relief, and the retrievement of their spirits; their consolation or trouble depends not on any outward condition or inward frame of their own hearts, but on the powerful and effectual workings of the Holy Ghost, which by faith they give themselves up unto.[109]

Notice, the believer's comfort and consolation in the midst of life's worst trials lies not in himself or in some external condition. Rather, the believer's security rests in the Spirit, whose work in us and for us cannot fail.

Therefore, the Spirit's work of consolation is absolutely necessary. When a sense of sin fills our hearts with "troubles and disquietness," it

---

[106] On the covenant of grace, see ibid., 2:230–31. Also see Ferguson, *John Owen on the Christian Life*, 24–25.
[107] Owen, *Of Communion with God*, in *Works*, 2:238.
[108] Ibid.
[109] Ibid. Also see ibid., 2:241, where Owen picks up the imagery of a courtroom to further his point.

is the Spirit who gives us peace in Christ.[110] Owen lists the consequences, should we not receive the consolations of the Spirit:

> Without them, we shall either despise afflictions or faint under them, and God be neglected as to his intendments in them.
>
> Without them, sin will either harden us to a contempt of it, or cast us down to a neglect of the remedies graciously provided against it.
>
> Without them, duties will either puff us up with pride, or leave us without that sweetness which is in new obedience.
>
> Without them, prosperity will make us carnal, sensual, and to take up our contentment in these things, and utterly weaken us for the trials of adversity.
>
> Without them, the comforts of our relations will separate us from God, and the loss of them make our hearts as Nabal's.
>
> Without them, the calamity of the church will overwhelm us, and the prosperity of the church will not concern us.
>
> Without them, we shall have wisdom for no work, peace in no condition, strength for no duty, success in no trial, joy in no state,—no comfort in life, no light in death.[111]

Owen pities those who do not have the consolations of the Spirit. They have to face the giants that oppose them in their own strength! And even if they should conquer these giants, they are still left with nothing but the "misery of their trials!"[112]

Second, the Spirit works *voluntarily*. The Spirit is sovereign, distributing to everyone as he will. At one point, the Spirit may choose to work in us in such a way that we are full of joy and consolation even in the midst of great distress. Every "promise brings sweetness when his [the believer's] pressures are great and heavy." At another point, however, even in the smallest of trials, the believer may seek comfort and search the promises of God, only to find that they are far away.[113] God works differently with different people. To "some each promise is full of life and comfort; others taste little all their days;—all upon the same account."[114] It all depends upon the sovereign will of the Spirit. We are to simply wait upon him, for him to accomplish his good pleasure.

---

[110] Ibid., 2:261.
[111] Ibid.
[112] Ibid.
[113] Ibid., 2:238.
[114] Ibid.

Third, the Spirit works *freely*. The Spirit often provides us with comfort unexpectedly, "when the heart hath all the reasons in the world to look for distress and sorrow."[115] This is good news for the "backsliding soul." Just when he feels as though he is "utterly cast off," the Spirit surprisingly shows up to restore his soul. How the Spirit restores the downtrodden soul is especially important. The Spirit turns our eyes to the promises of Jesus, for he is where the life and soul of all our comforts "lie treasured up."[116] These promises of Christ "break upon the soul with a conquering, endearing life and vigour" as our faith considers the promises and then waits upon the Spirit. "No sooner doth the soul begin to feel the life of a promise warming his heart, relieving, cherishing, supporting, delivering from fear, entanglements, or troubles, but it may, it ought, to know that the Holy Ghost is there; which will add to his joy, and lead him into fellowship with him."[117]

However, Owen does not limit himself to John 14:26, but also utilizes John 16:14 to describe the Spirit's role in the Christian life. There Jesus promises that the Spirit, the Comforter, shall glorify him, for "he shall receive of mine, and shall show it unto you." The work of the Spirit, says Owen, is to glorify Christ. In fact, Owen observes that this qualification is exactly how we, as Christians, are able to identify a false spirit. If a spirit does not glorify Christ, then it is not from Christ. In contrast to all false spirits, the Holy Spirit not only reveals Christ to us for our benefit, but actually applies all that Christ has purchased to us as recipients. Or as Owen puts the matter:

> He reveals to the souls of sinners the good things of the covenant of grace, which the Father hath provided, and the Son purchased. He shows to us mercy, grace, forgiveness, righteousness, acceptation with God; letteth us know that these are the things of Christ, which he hath procured for us; shows them to us for our comfort and establishment.[118]

It is for our good that the Spirit effectually applies the saving benefits of Christ's redeeming work to us. While the Father set his electing love on us in eternity past, the Son purchased us on the cross, and the Spirit then applies this redeeming and saving grace to us in space and time. Stated otherwise, mercy, grace, forgiveness, righteousness, and acceptance with God

---

[115] Ibid.
[116] Ibid., 2:239.
[117] Ibid.
[118] Ibid., 2:239–40.

are all "things of the Father, prepared from eternity in his love and good-will; as purchased for them by Christ, and laid up in store in the covenant of grace for their use." Christ then is "magnified and glorified" in the hearts of the elect, so that they "know what a Saviour and Redeemer he is." How does this occur but by the Spirit? "A soul," writes Owen, "doth never glorify or honour Christ upon a discovery or sense of the eternal redemption he hath purchased for him, but it is in him a peculiar effect of the Holy Ghost as our comforter."[119] Hence, Paul can write to the Corinthians, "No man can say that Jesus is the Lord, but by the Holy Ghost" (1 Cor. 12:3).

Additionally, Owen appeals to Romans 5:5 where we learn that the Spirit "sheds the love of God abroad in our hearts." Notice, says Owen, the text does not say "our love to God" but the "love of God to us."[120] The love Paul has in mind is a good love, a love where God intends to do us good. How does the Spirit shed this divine love into our hearts? The "Comforter gives a sweet and plentiful evidence and persuasion of the love of God to us, such as the soul is taken, delighted, satiated withal. This is his work, and he doth it effectually."[121] What a merciful love this is!

> To give a poor sinful soul a comfortable persuasion, affecting it through-out, in all its faculties and affections, that God in Jesus Christ loves him, delights in him, is well pleased with him, hath thoughts of tenderness and kindness towards him; to give, I say, a soul an overflowing sense hereof, is an inexpressible mercy.[122]

The Spirit of Adoption

Not only does the Spirit shed the love of God into our hearts, but as Owen also enlists Romans 8:16 to demonstrate, the Spirit is the *Spirit of adoption*. "The Spirit itself beareth witness with our spirit, that we are the children of God." By nature we are children of Satan, cursed, and under the wrath of God. But by the Spirit "we are put into another capacity, and are *adopted to be the children of God*, inasmuch as by receiving the Spirit of our Father we become the children of our Father."[123]

Owen uses the analogy of a lawcourt to make his point. In a judicial

---

[119] Ibid., 2:240.
[120] Ibid.
[121] Ibid.
[122] Ibid. On the Spirit's work of assurance of salvation and in helping the believer to pray, which Owen also treats in *Of Communion with God*, see chap. 8.
[123] Owen, *Of Communion with God*, in *Works*, 2:241. Owen also speaks of our adoption in relation to communion with the Son. See ibid., 2:173, 207.

proceeding one sits before the judge and his adversaries accuse him. Suddenly "a person of known and approved integrity comes into the court, and gives testimony fully and directly on the behalf of the claimer; which stops the mouths of all his adversaries, and fills the man that pleaded with joy and satisfaction."[124] Similarly, the Spirit intercedes on our behalf before the throne of God. We are brought before the law of God, and there our plea is that we are a child of God, that we belong to God's family on the basis of what Christ has done for us. Satan, however, opposes us, brings sin and the law against us, exposing our flaws. "In the midst of the plea and contest the Comforter comes, and, by a word of promise or otherwise, overpowers the heart with a comfortable persuasion (and bears down all objections) that his plea is good, and that he is a child of God."[125] Therefore, when we plead our right and title, it is the Spirit who comes in and "bears witness on our side," and at the same time enables us to "put forth acts of filial obedience, kind and child-like," whereby we cry out, "Abba, Father" (Gal. 4:6). Returning to the categories already discussed, Owen reminds us that the Spirit does all of this "effectually, voluntarily, and freely."[126] The Spirit is like Christ, who, with one word, stills the raging sea and wind (Luke 8:24–27). Likewise, the Spirit, with one word, "stills the tumults and storms that are raised in the soul, giving it an immediate calm and security."[127]

Sealed by the Spirit

Owen also turns to Ephesians 1:13 to show not only that the Spirit is the Trinitarian agent of our adoption, but also that this same Spirit seals us. "We are sealed by the Holy Spirit of promise." Or as Paul says in Ephesians 4:30, "Grieve not the Holy Spirit of God, whereby ye are sealed unto the day of redemption." Owen admits that he is not "very clear in the certain peculiar intendment of this metaphor." Nonetheless, he does not pretend to be ignorant of any meaning. It is clear that to seal a thing is to "stamp the character of the seal on it." "In this sense, the effectual communication

---

[124] Ibid., 2:241.
[125] Ibid. Owen elaborates, however, on how this process may not be easy. "Hence sometimes the dispute hangs long,—the cause is pleading many years. The law seems sometimes to prevail, sin and Satan to rejoice; and the poor soul is filled with dread about its inheritance. Perhaps its own witness, from its faith, sanctification, former experience, keeps up the plea with some life and comfort; but the work is not done, the conquest is not fully obtained, until the Spirit, who worketh freely and effectually, when and how he will, comes in with his testimony also; clothing his power with a word of promise, he makes all parties concerned to attend unto him, and puts an end to the controversy" (ibid., 2:241–42).
[126] Ibid., 2:241.
[127] Ibid., 2:242.

of the image of God unto us should be our sealing. The Spirit in believers, really communicating the image of God, in righteousness and true holiness, unto the soul, sealeth us."[128] Owen goes on to observe that having this "stamp" of the Spirit is evidence that we are accepted with God.

But what is the purpose and end of this sealing? Owen lists two interpretations: there is a sense in which the word *seal* conveys a confirming or ratifying, but there is also a sense in which the word means "appropriate, distinguish, and keep safe."[129] Concerning the latter, we are "marked with God's mark" (Ezek. 9:4) to be heirs of the "purchased inheritance, and to be preserved to the day of redemption."[130] If this is what Scripture means by sealing, writes Owen, then sealing "denotes not an act of sense in the heart, but of security to the person." And this is a Trinitarian work to be sure. "The Father gives the elect into the hands of Christ to be redeemed; having redeemed them, in due time they are called by the Spirit, and marked for God, and so give up themselves to the hands of the Father."[131] But, asks Owen, which one of these meanings is chiefly intended: to confirm and ratify or to appropriate, distinguish, and keep safe? For Owen, it is the first, though not to the exclusion of the second. "We are sealed to the day of redemption, when, from the stamp, image, and character of the Spirit upon our souls, we have a fresh sense of the love of God given to us, with a comfortable persuasion of our acceptation with him."[132]

Furthermore, the Spirit who seals us is also the "earnest" or guarantee of our inheritance (2 Cor. 1:22; 5:5; Eph. 1:13–14; cf. Gal. 4:6).[133] What does this mean exactly? An "earnest" is "part of the price of any thing, or part of any grant, given beforehand to assure the person to whom it is given that at the appointed season he shall receive the whole that is promised him."[134] Therefore, in regard to spiritual matters, the Spirit is this earnest. "God gives us the promise of eternal life. To confirm this to us, he giveth us his

---

[128] Ibid.

[129] For Owen's nuances on each of these, see ibid., 2:242–43.

[130] Ibid., 2:243.

[131] Ibid. Also see 2:262–63.

[132] "Thus, then, the Holy Ghost communicates unto us his own likeness; which is also the image of the Father and the Son. 'We are changed into this image by the Lord the Spirit,' 2 Cor. 3:18; and herein he brings us into fellowship with himself. Our likeness to him gives us boldness with him. His work we look for, his fruits we pray for; and when any effect of grace, any discovery of the image of Christ implanted in us, gives us a persuasion of our being separated and set apart for God, we have a communion with him therein" (ibid., 2:243). Of course, Owen addresses this issue in his book *Perseverance of the Saints*, which we will look at in chap. 6.

[133] Owen notes, however, that in 2 Cor. 1:22 and 5:5 we are said to have the guarantee or earnest of the Spirit, while in Eph. 1:13–14 the Spirit himself is said to be our earnest or guarantee.

[134] Owen, *Of Communion with God*, in *Works*, 2:244.

Spirit; which is, as the first part of the promise, to secure us of the whole. Hence he is said to be the earnest of the inheritance that is promised and purchased."[135] How the Spirit acts in this role is twofold.

First, the Spirit is an earnest or guarantee *on the part of God* "in that God gives him as a *choice part* of the inheritance itself. . . . The full inheritance promised, is the fullness of the Spirit in the enjoyment of God." The full inheritance promised is received when the Spirit perfectly takes away all sin and sorrow, and we are one day able "to enjoy the glory of God in his presence."[136] Not only has God granted us numerous securities—"his word, promises, covenant, oath, the revelation and discovery of his faithfulness and immutability in them all"—but also he is pleased to graciously give us one who will be with us (Isa. 59:21), namely, the Spirit himself, so that we may "have all the security we are capable of." Owen asks rhetorically, "What can more be done? He hath given us of the Holy Spirit;—in him the first-fruits of glory, the utmost pledge of his love, the earnest of all."[137]

Second, the Spirit is an earnest *on the part of believers* because he gives them an acquaintance with the love of God (Rom. 8:17; Gal. 4:6; 1 John 3:24) and their inheritance (1 Cor. 2:9–10). Owen applies this truth to the Christian life and explains why it must lead us to great joy and satisfaction:

> So much as we have of the Spirit, so much we have of heaven in perfect enjoyment, and so much evidence of its future fullness. Under this apprehension of him in the dispensation of grace do believers receive him and rejoice in him. Every gracious, self-evidencing act of his in their hearts they rejoice in, as a drop from heaven, and long for the ocean of it. Not to drive every effect of grace to this issue, is to neglect the work of the Holy Ghost in us and towards us.[138]

Owen concludes that the Spirit not only seals the believer and is the believer's guarantee, but also *anoints believers* (2 Cor. 1:21; 1 John 2:20, 27) and is our means of supplication (i.e., the Spirit of supplication; cf. Zech. 12:10; Rom. 8:26–27). Additionally, we are right to say that the Spirit convicts and illuminates, sanctifies, and brings about our consolation. Regarding "consolation," the Spirit makes "sweet, useful, and joyful to the soul,

---

[135] Ibid., 2:244. And again: "So is he [the Spirit] in all respects completely an earnest,—given of God, received by us, as the beginning of our inheritance, and the assurance of it. So much as we have of the Spirit, so much we have of heaven" (ibid., 2:246).

[136] Ibid., 2:245.

[137] Ibid.

[138] Ibid., 2:246.

the discoveries that are made of the mind and will of God in the light of the Spirit of sanctification."[139] How tragic it is, Owen grieves, that so many have so little "taste and sweetness and relish in their souls of those truths which yet they savingly know and believe." However, when the Spirit anoints us, "how sweet is every thing we know of God!"[140] The Spirit teaches us the "love of God in Christ" and, as David says, puts gladness into our hearts (Ps. 4:6–7). Owen articulates well the effect that the Spirit has in the believer's sanctification:

> We have this, then, by the Spirit:—he teacheth us of the love of God in Christ; he makes every gospel truth as wine well refined to our souls, and the good things of it to be a feast of fat things;—gives us joy and gladness of heart with all that we know of God; which is the great preservative of the soul to keep it close to truth. The apostle speaks of our teaching by this unction, as the means whereby we are preserved from seduction. Indeed, to know any truth in the power, sweetness, joy, and gladness of it, is that great security of the soul's constancy in the preservation and retaining of it. They will readily change truth for error, who find no more sweetness in the one than in the other.[141]

According to Owen, such a great truth concerning the Spirit brings us back to the gospel itself and reminds us that it is because of the Spirit that we see the gospel as glorious. "When we find any of the good truths of the gospel come home to our souls with life, vigour, and power, giving us gladness of heart, transforming us into the image and likeness of it,—the Holy Ghost is then at his work, is pouring out of his oil."[142]

Finally, we cannot forget the Spirit's power of supplication, as promised in Zechariah 12:10 and declared in Romans 8:26–27 and Galatians 4:6. We are told to "pray in the Holy Ghost." Prayer therefore is a spiritual duty that God requires of us, "wrought in us by the Spirit of sanctification, which helps us to perform all our duties, by exalting all the faculties of the soul for the spiritual discharge of their respective offices in them," and also a means of retaining communion with God, "whereby we sweetly ease our hearts in the bosom of the Father, and receive in refreshing tastes of his love." Owen concludes, "The soul is never more raised with the love of God

---

[139] Ibid., 2:248.
[140] Ibid.
[141] Ibid.
[142] Ibid.

than when by the Spirit taken into intimate communion with him in the discharge of this duty; and therein it belongs to this Spirit of consolation, to the Spirit promised as a comforter."[143]

In sum, the Spirit is the Trinitarian agent who brings us to the Father through the Son:

> All the consolations of the Holy Ghost consist in his acquainting us with, and communicating unto us, the love of the Father and the grace of the Son; nor is there any thing in the one or the other but he makes it a matter of consolation to us: so that, indeed, we have our communion with the Father in his love, and the Son in his grace, by the operation of the Holy Ghost.[144]

In other words, the Spirit is always working so as to draw the believer into deeper fellowship with the Father in his love and through the Son by his grace.

Conclusion

In his exposition on Psalm 130, Owen says that "the nature of all gospel truths" is that they are "experienced by a believing soul." And what gospel truth is "so high, glorious, and mysterious as the doctrine of the ever-blessed Trinity"? The Trinity, therefore, is a doctrine that is to be not only believed but also experienced by the believer. In other words, to know God is to have fellowship with each person in the Godhead. In this fellowship, one comes to understand the Trinity in a way that is far greater than someone who merely understands the Trinity in his mind, without it penetrating into the depths of his soul.[145]

Today, however, evangelicalism struggles with the opposite temptation. We desire to experience God but have no intention to know him as he has made himself known. In other words, we have the tendency to bypass

---

[143] Ibid., 2:249. Far more can be said about communion with the Spirit. See, for example, ibid., 2:249–74. Owen summarizes: "And this is the next thing to be considered in our communion with the Holy Ghost,—namely, what are the peculiar effects which he worketh in us, and towards us, being so bestowed on us as was declared, and working in the way and manner insisted on. Now, these are,—his bringing the promises of Christ to remembrance, glorifying him in our hearts, shedding abroad the love of God in us, witnessing with us as to our spiritual estate and condition, sealing us to the day of redemption (being the earnest of our inheritance), anointing us with privileges as to their consolation, confirming our adoption, and being present with us in our supplications. Here is the wisdom of faith,—to find out and meet with the Comforter in all these things; not to lose their sweetness, by lying in the dark [as] to their author, nor coming short of the returns which are required of us" (ibid., 2:249).

[144] Ibid., 2:262.

[145] Owen, *A Practical Exposition upon Psalm 130*, in *Works*, 6:459.

knowing God so that we can go directly to experiencing God. Owen, looking to Scripture itself, counters such contemporary spirituality. We cannot fully experience God unless we have a proper knowledge of who he is and what he has done. Therefore, both extremes must be avoided. We should not be deceived into thinking God is content with our having a mere cognitive knowledge of him. No, that knowledge must move from our head to our heart, impacting our affections for God and one another. Likewise, zeal without knowledge will not do either, lest we run the risk of basking ourselves in an experience not rooted in truth. Our heartfelt affections must be grounded in right doctrine as we worship God for who he truly is rather than create a deity after our own imagination.

CHAPTER 4

BEHOLDING THE GLORY OF CHRIST

I have had more advantage by private thoughts of Christ, than by any thing in this world; and I think, when a soul hath satisfying and exalting thoughts of Christ himself, his person, and his glory, it is the way whereby Christ dwells in such a soul. If I have observed any thing by experience, it is this, a man may take the measure of his growth, and decay in grace, according to his thoughts and meditations upon the person of Christ, and the glory of Christ's kingdom, and of his love. A heart that is inclined to converse with Christ, as he is represented in the gospel, is a thriving heart; and if estranged from it, and backward to it, it is under deadness and decays. [1]

It would be difficult to overemphasize the importance of the person of Christ in John Owen's theology. Owen's understanding of Christ penetrates his theology as a whole, giving each of his writings a Christ-centered, gospel-saturated flavor. But what is often forgotten is that many of his works on the person of Christ are intended to be applied to the Christian life. For Owen, this is the purpose of christology. Not only is Christ to be studied, but our study of Christ should lead us to worship him and consequently live out our lives for his glory.

The christological focus of Owen is apparent from the very start of his

---

[1] Owen, "The Excellency of Christ," in *Works*, 9:475.

ministry.[2] In the year 1643, at the young age of twenty-seven, Owen began his first pastorate in Fordham, Essex. Immediately, he recognized that his people were "grossly ignorant" of the person of Christ and the gospel.[3] To help them he began to write two catechisms, published in 1645: *Two Short Catechisms, wherein the Principles of the Doctrine of Christ Are Unfolded and Explained. Proper for All Persons to Learn Before They Be Admitted to the Sacrament of the Lord's Supper and Composed for the Use of All Congregations in General.* In these two catechisms, the first a Lesser Catechism for children (see chap. 11) and the second a Greater Catechism for adults, Owen's chief focus is on the person and work of Christ.[4]

Owen's later writings would center on christology as well. While his 1679 book *Christologia; or, A Declaration of the Glorious Mystery of the Person of Christ—God and Man* (hereafter, *The Person of Christ*), defends Chalcedonian christology (i.e., an orthodox understanding of the person of Christ defended by the church at the council of Chalcedon in AD 451), the book is especially noteworthy for showing how this doctrine shapes Christian living.[5] The same can be said of Owen's book *Meditations and Discourses on the Glory of Christ, in His Person, Office, and Grace: with the Differences between Faith and Sight; Applied unto the Use of Them That Believe* (published posthumously in 1684 [part 1] and 1689 [part 2]),[6] as well as his sermon series "The Excellency of Christ."[7] Of course, in other places Owen gives serious attention to defending the orthodox view of the person of Christ as well, especially against the Socinians of his day who attacked it. This much is apparent in his weighty polemic of 1655, *Vindiciae Evangelicae; The Mystery of the Gospel Vindicated and Socinianism Examined*, in which Owen takes on John Biddle's *Twofold Catechism* (1654), his version of *The Racovian Catechism* (1605).[8]

---

[2] For a recent study of this theme, see Suzanne McDonald, "Beholding the Glory of God in the Face of Jesus Christ: John Owen and the 'Reforming' of the Beatific Vision," in *The Ashgate Research Companion to John Owen's Theology*, ed. Kelly M. Kapic and Mark Jones (Burlington, VT: Ashgate, 2012), 141–58.

[3] Owen, *The Lesser Catechism*, in *Works*, 1:465.

[4] For more historical background, see Sinclair Ferguson, "John Owen and the Doctrine of the Person of Christ," in *John Owen: The Man and His Theology*, ed. Robert W. Oliver (Darlington: Evangelical Press, 2002), 69–100.

[5] For this treatise, see *Works*, 1:1–415.

[6] In *Works*, 1:273–415; hereafter *Meditations and Discourses on the Glory of Christ*. Also see *Meditations and Discourses on the Glory of Christ, Applied unto Unconverted Sinners and Saints under Spiritual Decays*, in *Works*, 1:417–61.

[7] In *Works*, 9:462–89.

[8] John Owen, *Vindiciae Evangelicae; The Mystery of the Gospel Vindicated and Socinianism Examined*, in *Works*, 12:1–617; hereafter *The Mystery of the Gospel*. For the seventeenth-century background to christological heresies, see Richard Daniels, *The Christology of John Owen* (Grand Rapids: Reformation Heritage, 2004), 22–75. Carl Trueman describes Biddle's view: "The basic idea underlying Biddle's thinking at this point is that Christ is not essentially God, but earns his position as Son of God through his work." And

The Importance of Christology for the Christian Life

What stands out in Owen's many works is not only his meticulous defense of orthodox christology, but how Owen believed the person of Christ makes all the difference in how we live as Christians. Therefore, while we will briefly look at Owen's rigorous defense of orthodox christology in this chapter, we especially want to devote our attention to how Owen applies his christology to the life of the believer. Such an emphasis is consistent with Owen himself. As Ferguson explains, while Owen believed attention to in-depth theological argument to be of utmost importance, nevertheless, the person of Christ is not "for Owen a subject for technical analysis, but a person, coming to us 'clothed with his gospel' as Calvin put it." We read the Scriptures so that in understanding who Christ is we might be brought to our knees in worship of him.[9]

Right at the start of *The Person of Christ*, in his preface, Owen tells us how christology relates to Christian living. For the sinner who has believed in Christ for his salvation, Christ is precious. "In, from, and by him, is all their spiritual and eternal life, light, power, growth, consolation, and joy here; with everlasting salvation hereafter."[10] Through Christ, and him alone, the sinner receives deliverance from "wo[e]ful apostasy from God." Christ keeps him safe from that which is "evil, noxious, and destructive." Christ brings the believer into the "nearest cognation, alliance, and friendship with God, the firmest union unto him, and the most holy communion with him, that our finite natures are capable of, and so conducted unto the eternal enjoyment of him."[11] The "principal design" of our entire life is to acquaint ourselves with Christ and to trust in him, casting on him the greatest concerns of our soul. Our chief purpose is to "endeavour after conformity to him, in all those characters of divine goodness and holiness which are represented unto them in him." In this, says Owen, is the "soul, life, power, beauty, and efficacy of the Christian religion." Though one may play the part of a Christian by all outward appearances, if one does not truly know, cherish, and treasure Christ, all external formalities are useless. Or

---

concerning the Racovian Catechism, Trueman notes: "While allowing that Christ can be called divine, the *Catechism* insists that the word must in this context be reconstrued in such a way that it does not imply any kind of equality or identity with the Father." Trueman, *The Claims of Truth: John Owen's Trinitarian Theology* (Carlisle: Paternoster, 1998), 152, 153. See also Trueman, *Claims of Truth*, 153–64, for the Socinian argument and Owen's response to it.

[9] Ferguson, "John Owen and the Doctrine of the Person of Christ," 72.

[10] Owen, *The Person of Christ*, in *Works*, 1:3.

[11] Ibid.

as Owen says, they are but a "lifeless carcass."[12] Knowing and having Christ are of supreme importance (Phil. 3:8–12). Such a perspective, such a heart-felt desire, is "predominant and efficacious in them unto whom Christ is precious."

> So it is the highest duty of them unto whom he is precious, whose principal design is to be found built on him as the sure foundation, as to hold the truth concerning him, (his person, spirit, grace, office, and authority,) and to abound in all duties of faith, love, trust, honour, and delight in him—so also to declare his excellency, to plead the cause of his glory, to vindicate his honour, and to witness him the only rest and reward of the souls of men, as they are called and have opportunity.[13]

The Person of Christ

Before we can further understand how christology impacts the Christian life, however, we should first take a moment to review the basics of the hypostatic union, allowing Owen to be our guide.

Christ Is Fully God, Possessing a Divine Nature

Owen lived in a day when the deity of Christ, as well as the atoning work he accomplished on the cross (see the next chapter), was questioned and rejected by the Socinians. For Owen, there could be no greater offense to the glory of Christ than what the Socinians taught. Their doctrine is the very antithesis of evangelical truth. "The holy Trinity they blaspheme—the incarnation of the Son of God they scorn—the work of his mediation in his oblation and intercession, with the satisfaction and merit of his obedience and suffering, they reject."[14] If ever there was a valid slippery-slope argument to be made, Owen believes it is with Socinianism. Not only do the Trinity, the deity of Christ, and the satisfaction of Christ come under attack, but so do the divine attributes (e.g., immutability, immensity, prescience), human depravity (Socinianism finding an ally in Pelagianism!), the Spirit's sovereign and supernatural work of regeneration, and much more. The Socinians do violence to all of Christianity, argues Owen, and the person of Christ is one of the first doctrines they have corrupted by their disbelief. Tragically, all of Christianity unravels with Socinianism.

---

[12] Ibid., 1:4.
[13] Ibid., 1:5.
[14] Ibid., 1:83.

Dissolve the knot, centre, and harmony in the most beautiful composition or structure—and every part will contribute as much unto the deformity and ruin of the whole, as it did before unto its beauty and consistency. So is it with every doctrine—so is it with the whole system of evangelical truth. Take the person of Christ out of them, dissolve their harmony in relation thereunto—whereby we no longer hold the Head in the faith and profession of them—and the minds of men cannot deliver them from an irreconcilable difference among themselves.[15]

The Socinians have abandoned and lost the very center of Christianity: the person and work of Jesus Christ. The consequences for justification, sanctification, the salvation of the church, and the Christian life could not be overstated. All of these are but "esteemed fables" if "what we believe concerning the person of Christ" is not true.

Owen considered his debates with the Socinians to be of first importance in the defense of the gospel. Hence the name of his massive polemic against Socinianism: *Vindiciae Evangelicae; The Mystery of the Gospel Vindicated and Socinianism Examined.*[16] The gospel itself is at stake in the person and work of Christ. However, our goal here is not to replay that awesome treatise point by point. Rather, our first objective is to see that Owen defends Christ as the eternal Son, the second person of the Trinity, and as one who is fully divine, equal in deity to the Father, sharing that one, divine essence or nature.

To begin with, Owen is very aware of the christological heresies—or, as he calls them, "pernicious errors"—that have colored church history. The Ebionites in the second century, for example, while affirming the virgin birth, nevertheless denied the deity of Christ and instead believed him to be a "mere man, and no more." Others, such as the Docetists, also in the second century, went in the other direction, denying the full humanity of Christ. They "denied him to have any real human nature, but [alleged him] to have been a phantasm, an appearance, a dispensation, a mere cloud acted by divine power."[17]

With the advent of the third and fourth centuries, the Arians became

---

[15] Ibid., 1:84.

[16] Owen, *The Mystery of the Gospel*, in *Works*, 12:1–617.

[17] Others said he "was made of heavenly flesh, brought from above, and which is some also affirmed, was a parcel of the divine nature. Some affirmed that his body was not animated, as ours are, by a rational soul, but was immediately acted by the power of the Divine Being, which was unto it in the room of a living soul; some, that his body was of an ethereal nature, and was at length turned into the sun; with many such diabolical delusions." Owen, *The Person of Christ*, in *Works*, 1:39–40.

a serious threat to biblical Christianity as they entered into conflict with Athanasius, the Cappadocian fathers, and the Council of Nicaea. The Arians, writes Owen, "in words acknowledge his divine person; but added, as a limitation of that acknowledgment, that the divine nature which he had was originally created of God, and produced out of nothing." Owen calls this a double blasphemy because they denied that Jesus is "the true God" and simultaneously made a "god of a mere creature."[18] So Christ, said the Arians, was created, and had a beginning, and for this reason is not equal in deity to the Father.

The fifth-century errors of Nestorianism presented their own challenge as well. They granted that Christ possessed a divine nature and a human nature, but denied the "personal union between these two natures."

> God did, as they imagined, eminently and powerfully manifest himself in the man Christ Jesus—had him in an especial regard and love, and did act in him more than in any other. But that the Son of God assumed our nature into personal subsistence with himself—whereby whole Christ was one person, and all his mediatory acts were the acts of that one person, of him who was both God and man—this they would not acknowledge.[19]

If they were right, Owen argues, then all that Christ accomplished for us would be "only as a man—which would have been altogether insufficient for the salvation of the church, nor had God redeemed it with his own blood."[20]

Many more christological heresies could be mentioned (Eutychianism, Apollinarianism, etc.), but the point is that "the principal opposition of the gates of hell unto the church lay always unto the building of it, by faith, on the person of Christ."[21] In other words, Satan knows very well that if he is to lead people into hell, the person of Christ is always the key doctrine to distort and pervert, because it is at the very center of the gospel, the very blood of Christianity itself. The Socinians, in Owen's day, make this point all too obvious.

In contrast to these christological heresies, and especially Socinian-

---

[18] Ibid.
[19] Ibid., 1:40.
[20] Ibid. Owen believes this heresy has been reincarnated in his own day.
[21] Ibid., 1:41. For a helpful overview of these heresies, as well as the church fathers and councils that responded to them, see Stephen J. Nichols, *For Us and for Our Salvation: The Doctrine of Christ in the Early Church* (Wheaton, IL: Crossway, 2007).

ism, Owen stands with the great fathers and councils of the early church (e.g., Nicaea, Chalcedon) in affirming the full deity, as well as the full humanity, of Christ. The Son, the second person of the Trinity, had no beginning. He was not created by the Father, coming into existence at a certain point in time. To the contrary, as the second person of the Trinity he is eternal, with no beginning or end. Moreover, he shares the one divine essence or nature, which means that he is fully God, equal to the Father (and the Spirit) in deity. Nothing changes, either, when he becomes incarnate, taking on a human nature. He remains fully God, not abandoning his divine nature or turning off his divine nature as if it were inactive during his incarnate state. As we will see, he is one person with two natures, a divine nature and a human nature. Therefore, as the God-man he is fully capable and absolutely qualified to act as our Mediator. Or to be more precise, only if he is fully God and fully man can he act as our Mediator, our Savior, in his life, death, and resurrection.

Owen believes that Scripture everywhere attests to the full deity of Christ.[22] While we will not explore Owen's meticulous and extensive defense from Scripture on this matter, we can summarize Owen's conclusions. First, the New Testament authors appeal to a multitude of Old Testament texts that speak of God and apply these to Jesus Christ (e.g., Heb. 1:10 and Ps. 102:25–27). Second, the works Jesus performs are works exclusively attributed to God (e.g., John 1:3 and creation). Third, the attributes Jesus possesses are exclusively attributed to God (e.g., John 5:23). And fourth, the titles given to Christ are titles exclusively belonging to God.[23] Besides these points, one must also acknowledge that only one who is fully divine can save sinners. As Ferguson says, "Here is his [Owen's] Calvin-like consciousness that deity and genuine soteriology belong together in an indivisible way; loosen our grip on one and we inevitably lose our grasp on the other."[24] To conclude, Owen's expansive biblical examination demonstrates that Christ is indeed fully God, the second person of the Trinity.

[22] Space does not permit a survey of Owen's biblical presentation of the deity of Christ, but see *The Mystery of the Gospel*, in *Works*, 12:1–617; Owen, *A Brief Declaration and Vindication of the Doctrine of the Trinity as Also of the Person and Satisfaction of Christ*, in *Works*, 2:365–454. In the latter he appeals to Isa. 7:14; 9:6; Matt. 1:20–23; John 1:14; 3:13, 31; 6:62; 16:28; Acts 20:28; Rom. 1:3–4; Gal. 4:4; Phil. 2:5–7; 1 Tim. 3:16; Heb. 2:14; 1 John 3:16.

[23] See Ferguson, "John Owen and the Doctrine of the Person of Christ," 80. Owen will appeal to other points as well, including the eternal generation of the Son by the Father, based on John 5:19–23, a doctrine Owen believes demonstrates that the Son is God. For other proofs, see Carl R. Trueman, *John Owen: Reformed Catholic, Renaissance Man* (Hampshire: Ashgate, 2007), 50ff.

[24] Ferguson, "John Owen and the Doctrine of the Person of Christ," 80.

Christ Is Fully Man, Possessing a Human Nature

Our human nature, says Owen, was assumed "into hypostatic union with the Son of God," and this meant a "constitution of one and the same individual person in two natures so infinitely distinct as those of God and man." No doubt there is much mystery here in how the "Eternal was made in time, the Infinite became finite, the Immortal mortal, yet continuing eternal, infinite, immortal."[25] The eternal Son, the second person of the Trinity, became incarnate, adding to himself a human nature, but not giving up his divine nature in the process.[26] As Scripture tells us, he did so in the most humble of circumstances, being born as a babe of a virgin in a manger. Yet, though he took the form of a servant (Phil. 2:6–7), he was the Son of God. As Paul says, the Son of God "was manifest in the flesh" (1 Tim. 3:16). Or as John explains, "The Word was made flesh, and dwelt among us" (John 1:14).

But who is this "Word"? asks Owen. "That which was in the beginning, which was with God, which was God, by whom all things were made, and without whom was not any thing made that was made; who was light and life."[27] Owen carefully explains that the Word was made flesh "not by any change of his own nature or essence, not by a transubstantiation of the divine nature into the human, not by ceasing to be what he was, but by becoming what he was not, in taking our nature to his own, to be his own, whereby he dwelt among us."[28] In other words, the Son did not become incarnate by subtraction—as if becoming human meant he must give up his divine nature—but rather by addition, namely, adding to himself a human nature, uniting the human nature with the divine nature in his one person, though not blurring the distinction between the two natures.

Furthermore, lest anyone doubt Christ's humanity, Owen observes that he was human in every sense of the word, taking on the "lowest state and condition of human nature."[29] As we will see in the next chapter, he took on human flesh in order to mediate on behalf of God's people, atone for their sin, and accomplish salvation on their behalf.[30] And, given God's decree to

---

[25] Owen, *The Person of Christ*, in *Works*, 1:46.

[26] Trueman clarifies that for Owen and Chalcedonian orthodoxy, "it was not a human person who was assumed in the Incarnation, but a human nature which received its personhood in union with the divine." See Trueman, *John Owen*, 50–53. And again, "Before the Logos assumed the human nature, that human nature had no personal subsistence of itself." Trueman, *Claims of Truth*, 155.

[27] Owen, *The Person of Christ*, in *Works*, 1:46.

[28] Ibid.

[29] Ibid., 1:47. Elsewhere Owen makes a point to add that Christ, in taking on a human nature, was without sin (cf. ibid., 1:215).

[30] "It is by the exercise and discharge of the office of Christ—as the king, priest, and prophet of the church—that we are redeemed, sanctified, and saved. Thereby doth he immediately communicate all

redeem elect sinners, it was necessary for the Son to become incarnate, for apart from doing so, he could not fulfill his salvific role as prophet, priest, and king. Owen explains:

> For in his divine nature, singly considered, he had no such relation unto them for whom he was to discharge his offices, as was necessary to communicate the benefit of them, nor could he discharge their principal duties. God could not die, nor rise again, nor be exalted to be a prince and a saviour, in his divine nature. Nor was there that especial alliance between it and ours, as should give us an especial interest in what was done thereby.[31]

In affirming the full humanity of Christ, Owen is careful not to confuse the divine nature with the human nature. He does not hesitate, for example, to say that in regard to his human nature, Christ is a "creature, finite and limited." Owen does not ascribe "the infusion of omniscience, of infinite understanding, wisdom, and knowledge, into the human nature of Christ."[32] Nevertheless, the human nature was filled with "light and wisdom to the utmost capacity of a creature."[33] Yet this was not because it was changed into a divine nature, but rather because of the "communication of the Spirit unto it without measure."[34]

To recap, Owen provides us with a point-by-point summary. Here is what the condescension of the Son in the incarnation does *not* mean:

1. "This condescension of the Son of God did not consist in a laying aside, or parting with, or separation from, the divine nature, so as that he should cease to be God by being man."
2. "Much less did this condescension consist in the conversion of the divine nature into the human" (i.e., Arianism).
3. "There was not in this condescension the least change or alteration in the divine nature" (i.e., Eutychianism).
4. This condescension did not mean that Jesus's divine nature and divine glory were explicit at all times. "The apostle tells us that he 'humbled

---

Gospel benefits unto us—give us an access unto God here by grace, and in glory hereafter; for he saves us, as he is the mediator between God and man" (ibid., 1:85).
[31] Ibid., 1:86.
[32] "Hence some things, as he was a man, he knew not, (Mark 13:32,) but as they were given him by revelation, Rev. 1:1" (ibid., 1:93).
[33] Ibid., 1:225.
[34] Ibid., 1:93. Also note what others have called Owen's "Spirit-Christology." See Alan Spence, *Incarnation and Inspiration: John Owen and the Coherence of Christology* (London: T&T Clark, 2007), 39–46, 61; Oliver D. Crisp, *Revisioning Christology: Theology in the Reformed Tradition* (Burlington, VT: Ashgate, 2011), 91–90; Daniels, *Christology of John Owen*, 269–73.

himself, and made himself of no reputation,' (Phil. 2:7, 8). He veiled the glory of his divine nature in ours, and what he did therein, so as that there was no outward appearance or manifestation of it." Yet, as point 1 says, he did not give up his divine nature, but remained fully God, as Jesus himself reveals in John 8:58–59 and 10:33.

5. "This condescension of Christ was not by a phantasm or an appearance only" (i.e., Docetism).[35]

On the other hand, the incarnation does mean the following:

1. The "eternal person of the Son of God, or the divine nature in the person of the Son, did, by an ineffable act of his divine power and love, assume our nature into an individual subsistence in or with himself; that is, to be his own, even as the divine nature is his."

2. "By reason of this assumption of our nature, with his doing and suffering therein, whereby he was found in fashion as a man, the glory of his divine person was veiled, and he made himself of no reputation."

3. "In the assumption of our nature to be his own, he did not change it into a thing divine and spiritual; but preserved it entire in all its essential properties and actings."[36]

These summary points lead us to the natural question, What does it mean for Christ to be one person but with two natures? Here we come to the very center of the hypostatic union.

Christ Is One Person with Two Natures

Simply put, although there are two natures—one divine, the other human—the two are not to be confused or mixed, nor divided or separated; there is but one person. Therefore, there is a union between the divine nature and the human nature in the one person of Christ. As Owen says, "The divine nature may be said to be united unto the human, as well as the human unto the divine."[37] The two natures subsist in the one person of Christ.

Isaiah 9:6 bears witness to this union: "Unto us a child is born, unto us a son is given; and his name shall be called . . . The mighty God." Notice, Owen observes, how the "child and the mighty God are the same person."[38]

---

[35] These points can be found in Owen, *The Person of Christ*, in *Works*, 1:327–29.
[36] Ibid., 1:329–30.
[37] Ibid., 1:226.
[38] Ibid., 1:233.

In the former we see the humanity of Christ, and in the latter his divinity. Yet, this is one and the same person being referenced. As many other biblical texts attest,

> the Son of God took on him "the seed of Abraham," was "made of a woman," did "partake of flesh and blood," was "manifest in the flesh,"—whereby God "purchased the church with his own blood,"—are all spoken of one and the same person, and are not true but on the account of the union of the two natures therein.[39]

How these two natures function—and especially how they relate to one another—in the one person of Christ is a complex matter. Owen makes three observations.[40]

First, "each nature doth preserve its own natural, essential properties, entirely unto and in itself; without mixture, without composition or confusion, without such a real communication of the one unto the other, as that the one should become the subject of the properties of the other." Here Owen echoes the Council of Nicaea (AD 325) and especially the Council of Chalcedon (AD 451) before him. The divine nature, he says, is not "made temporary, finite, limited, subject to passion or alteration by this union." In other words, the union of the two natures does not compromise Christ's possession of those divine attributes that characterize his divine nature, nor does it deactivate his use of them during his earthly ministry.[41] Likewise, the human nature is not rendered "immense, infinite, omnipotent." Miss this crucial point, Owen warns, and we will not preserve the distinction between the two natures of Christ.[42]

Second, "each nature operates in him according unto its essential

---

[39] Ibid.

[40] Owen prefaces these three observations by commenting on the "communication of properties" (*communicatio idiomatum*) and shows himself to adhere to a Reformed, rather than Lutheran, christology (see ibid.). Also see Owen, *Of Communion with God*, in *Works*, 2:51. As Crisp says, "Here, in keeping with the Reformed tradition Owen defends the view that the communication of idioms or attributes from the human to the divine, or the divine to the human natures of Christ is routed through his person. . . . It is not the case that the attributes of one nature are assimilated to that of the other nature in Christ, as the Lutherans believed." See Crisp, *Revisioning Christology*, 96. Also see Spence, *Incarnation and Inspiration*, 39–41, 63; Trueman, *Claims of Truth*, 166, 175–79.

[41] Ferguson helpfully explains, "The divine nature knows all things, upholds all things, rules all things, acts by its presence everywhere. The human nature was born, yielded obedience, died and rose again. But it is the same person, the same Christ who does all these things, the one nature being no less active than the other." Ferguson, "John Owen and the Doctrine of the Person of Christ," 90. Owen, therefore, was a believer in the *extra-calvinisticum*: "While Christ lay in the manger he continued as the Son of God to uphold the universe by his divine power. So there is great condescension, but that does not imply abnegation of his personal being. Nor was the divine nature exchanged for the human, changed into the human, or mixed with the human" (ibid., 92).

[42] Owen, *The Person of Christ*, in *Works*, 1:234.

properties." Owen, sounding like Calvin before him, explains what this looks like: "The divine nature knows all things, upholds all things, rules all things, acts by its presence everywhere; the human nature was born, yielded obedience, died, and rose again." Yet, there is one person, not two. The divine nature and the human nature, and all that characterizes the two, are united in the same Christ. Stated otherwise, it is the "same Christ, that acts all these things,—the one nature being his no less than the other."[43]

Third,

> the perfect, complete work of Christ, in every act of his mediatory office,— in all that he did as the King, Priest, and Prophet of the church,—in all that he did and suffered,—in all that he continueth to do for us, in or by virtue of whether nature soever it be done or wrought,—is not to be considered as the act of this or that nature in him alone, but it is the act and work of the whole person,—of him that is both God and man in one person.[44]

In order to understand this third point, Owen gives us four other points to provide clarity: First, this does not mean that Scripture never speaks of the person of Christ "wherein the enunciation is verified with respect *unto one nature only.*" For example, consider texts like John 1:1 ("The Word was with God, and the Word was God"), John 8:58 ("Before Abraham was, I am"), or Hebrews 1:3 ("Upholding all things by the word of his power"). These texts, and many others, refer to the person of Christ, and yet the divine nature in particular, not the human nature, is in view when the eternity, power, and divinity of the Son are referenced. Quite the reverse is the case in other texts, like Isaiah 9:6 ("Unto us a child is born, unto us a son is given") and Isaiah 53:3 ("A man of sorrows, and acquainted with grief"). "They are spoken of the person of Christ, but are verified in human nature only, and the person on the account thereof."[45]

Second, and on the other hand, sometimes something is spoken of the person of Christ without belonging "distinctly and originally" to either nature, but rather belonging to Christ "on the account of their *union* in him." For example, Christ is said to be the "Head, the King, Priest, and Prophet of the church; all which offices he bears, and performs the acts of them, not

---

[43] Ibid.
[44] Ibid.
[45] Ibid.

on the singular account of this or that nature, but of the *hypostatical* union of them both."[46]

Third, at other times Scripture speaks of the person of Christ "being denominated from one nature" in which "the properties and acts of the other are assigned unto it." Owen gives the tremendous example of the death of Christ:

> He is the Lord of glory on the account of his divine nature only; thence is his person denominated when he is said to be crucified, which was in the human nature only. So God purchased his church "with his own blood," Acts 20:28. The denomination of the person is from the divine nature only—he is God; but the act ascribed unto it, or what he did by his own blood, was of the human nature only. But the purchase that was made thereby was the work of the person as both God and man.[47]

Fourth, and last, Scripture can also refer to the "person being denominated from one nature, that is ascribed unto it which is common unto both; or else being denominated from both, that which is proper unto one only is ascribed unto him." For example, Paul writes in Romans 9:5 that to the Jews belong the patriarchs and that it is from their race that Christ came in the flesh, who is "over all, God blessed for ever." Here, in just one verse, we see how Christ's humanity and deity are recognized, yet within the context of his one, undivided person.[48]

Christ's Person the Cause of True Religion

How then does this robust, orthodox, Reformed christology affect the Christian life? "The person of Christ," says Owen, "is the most glorious and ineffable effect of divine wisdom, grace, and power."[49] Therefore, Christ is the "next foundation" of acceptable religion and worship. The first foundation is God the Father. To him is due all worship and honor and glory, since we are his creatures and he is our Creator. Through the created order God has manifested himself, that is, his "Divine Being, existence, excellencies, and properties" (cf. Rom. 1:18–22). However, none of this compares to his special revelation of himself through his Son, Christ Jesus. Christ is the

---

[46] Ibid.
[47] Ibid., 1:235.
[48] For other places where Owen unfolds his christology, see ibid., 1:37–44.
[49] Ibid., 1:44.

"foundation of the new creation" and he is "most ineffable and glorious."[50] "God was manifested in the flesh" (1 Tim. 3:16), and he did so for us and our salvation. Christ is the Word who was made flesh in order to dwell among us (John 1:14). But, asks Owen, "what Word was this?"

> That which was in the beginning, which was with God, which was God, by whom all things were made, and without whom was not any thing made that was made; who was light and life. This Word was made flesh, not by any change of his own nature or essence, not by a transubstantiation of the divine nature into the human, not by ceasing to be what he was, but by becoming what he was not, in taking our nature to his own, to be his own, whereby he dwelt among us. This glorious Word, which is God, and described by his eternity and omnipotency in works of creation and providence, "was made flesh,"—which expresseth the lowest state and condition of human nature. Without controversy, great is this mystery of godliness![51]

No wonder Isaiah, predicting the coming of this long-awaited Messiah, titles him "Wonderful, Counsellor, The Mighty God, The everlasting Father, The Prince of Peace" (Isa. 9:6).[52]

For Owen, this is the "glory of the Christian religion—the basis and foundation that bears the whole superstructure" and what sets Christianity apart from every false religion. The Son of God, taking on our human flesh, becoming a man in order to save us from sin and condemnation, uniting us to himself—this doctrine is certainly the foundation of our entire faith, a foundation that cannot be shaken. Whatever beauty and glory there was in that initial relation between man and God in the garden (Genesis 1–2), "it was all but an obscure representation of the exaltation of our nature in Christ—as the apostle declares, Heb. 2:6–9."[53] In our union with Christ we have a far greater bond than before. Nothing compares with the union we have with the Son of God, who has manifested himself in the flesh through the "subsistence of the divine and human natures in the same single individual person."[54]

The beauty of our union becomes even more apparent when we consider the state of humanity after the fall. It is true, says Owen, that there was "true religion in the world after the fall, both before and after the giving of the Law; a religion built upon and resolved into divine revelation." However, with

---

[50] Ibid., 1:45.
[51] Ibid., 1:46–47.
[52] Ibid., 1:48. Owen will also appeal to Heb. 1:1–3.
[53] Ibid.
[54] Ibid.

the coming of Christ we have something "far more glorious, beautiful, and perfect, than that state of religion was capable of, or could attain."[55] Hebrews 1:1–3 and Colossians 2:17 demonstrate Owen's point. Though God, in times past, spoke through his prophets, in these last days he has spoken directly through his own Son, who is the "brightness of his glory" and through whom our sins are "purged." Therefore, while the promise was given through the prophets, it is with the advent of Christ that God fulfills that promise, establishing a new covenant through the blood of his Son. Thus, says Owen, "as all the religion that was in the world after the fall was built on the promise of this work of God, in due time to be accomplished; so it is the actual performance of it which is the foundation of the Christian religion, and which gives it the pre-eminence above all that went before it."[56] Naturally, if we take away Christ—both who he is and what he has accomplished—we "despoil the Christian religion of all its glory, debasing it unto what Mohammedanism pretends unto, and unto what in Judaism was really enjoyed."[57]

Christ the Object of Our Worship

If Christ is our Savior, it follows that he is also the object of our faith, a truth Scripture everywhere supports. What this means is that Christ is to be embraced by faith. It also means that Christ is the object of our worship. Such a claim is possible only if Christ is, as we saw earlier, fully divine. In other words, everything hinges on the person of Christ. Therefore, Owen can draw a direct line from the person of Christ to the Christian religion as a whole.

> The glory, life, and power of Christian religion, as Christian religion, and as seated in the souls of men, with all the acts and duties which properly belong thereunto, and are, therefore, peculiarly Christian, and all the benefits and privileges we receive by it, or by virtue of it, with the whole of the honour and glory that arise unto God thereby, have all of them their formal nature and reason from their respect and relation unto the person of Christ; nor is he a Christian who is otherwise minded.[58]

The first priority in the Christian life is giving honor, glory, and praise to the Son for who he is and what he has done. In other words, Christ is the ob-

---

[55] Ibid.
[56] Ibid., 1:49.
[57] Ibid.
[58] Ibid., 1:104.

ject of our worship owing to his "divine nature" and "infinite excellencies."[59] Owen detests those who would claim that they can deny Christ's divine nature and still claim him as the object of their worship and adoration. No, says Owen, they are instead worshiping a "golden calf of their own setting up; for a Christ who is not over all, God blessed for ever, is not better."[60] Furthermore, a contradiction is at play as well. How is it that any creature could be "the immediate, proper object of divine worship; unless the divine essential excellencies be communicated unto it, or transfused into it, whereby it would cease to be a creature"?[61]

In order for us to understand why Jesus is so worthy of our worship, Owen asks us to consider Christ in his "whole entire person, the Son of God incarnate, 'God manifest in the flesh.'" As we saw, the "infinite condescension" of the Son, by which he assumed our human nature, in no way divested him of his "divine essential excellencies."[62] Yes, his divine attributes were "shadowed and veiled" from those who saw him, especially since he "made himself of no reputation, and took on him the form of a servant." However, though he took the form of a servant, at the same time he "eternally and unchangeably continued 'in the form of God,' and 'thought it not robbery to be equal with God,'" as Philippians 2:6–7 says. Therefore, Owen asserts, "He can no more really and essentially, by any act of condescension or humiliation, cease to be God, than God can cease to be."[63] How does this relate to our worship? Our worship is not lessened by Christ's clothing himself with our human nature, but actually "adds an effectual motive unto it." "He is, therefore, the immediate object of all duties of religion, internal and external; and in the dispensation of God towards us, none of them can be performed in a due manner without a respect unto him."[64] It is not surprising then that we read from John 5:23 that it is the Father's will "that all men should honour the Son, even as they honour the Father. He that honoureth not the Son, honoureth not the Father which hath sent him." How is it, you might ask, that we honor the Son the way we honor the Father? We do so when we commit all "power, authority, and judgment" to him, as John 5:20–22 explains.[65]

---

[59] Ibid.
[60] Ibid.
[61] Ibid.
[62] Ibid., 1:105.
[63] Ibid.
[64] Ibid.
[65] Owen clarifies: "Not that these things are the *formal* reason and cause of the divine honour which is to be given him; but they are reasons of it, and motives unto it, in that they are evidences of his being the Son of God" (ibid.).

More specifically, Owen lists two duties whereby we "ascribe and express divine honour unto Christ": adoration and invocation. First, consider adoration. Adoration is "the prostration of soul before him as God, in the acknowledgment of his divine excellencies and the ascription of them unto him."[66] We express our adoration when we bow down before Christ as Lord and God, paying reverence to him, and giving him all our worship and praise (Ps. 45:11; Heb. 1:6). One of the greatest pictures of adoration of Christ in the Scriptures is found in Revelation 5:6–14, where John sees the Lamb and those before him falling down in reverence, singing to him that he is worthy to take the book for he was slain and has redeemed us to God by his blood. The many angels cry out: "Worthy is the Lamb that was slain to receive power, and riches, and wisdom, and strength, and honor, and glory, and blessing." Then, says John, the four and twenty elders "fell down and worshipped him that liveth for ever and ever." Are we not to do the same? Owen notes that the *object* of this adoration is Christ, the Lamb. The *motive* for this adoration is the "unspeakable benefits which we receive by his mediation" (i.e., redemption). And the *nature* of this adoration is solemn prostration, ascribing to him all divine honor and glory, and praise by means of a new song.[67]

Adoration of Christ, our Redeemer, is a massive aspect of the Christian life:

> The humbling of our souls before the Lord Christ, from an apprehension of his divine excellencies—the ascription of glory, honour, praise, with thanksgiving unto him, on the great motive of the work of redemption with the blessed effects thereof—are things wherein the life of faith is continually exercised.

Additionally, Owen warns, we can claim no interest in that future heavenly worship of the Lamb if we are not now "exercised" in this worship on earth.[68]

Second, there must be not only adoration but also invocation. Invocation consists of two things. To begin with, there is "an ascription of all divine properties and excellencies unto him whom we invocate." Ascription, Owen remarks, is absolutely essential to prayer. Without it we engage

---

[66] Ibid., 1:107.
[67] Owen makes an important distinction, namely, that this adoration of the Son is different in motive from that of the Father. The Father is adored as God for his work of creation (Eph. 1:4–5; Rev. 4:11). But the motive in adoring the Son is the work of redemption (Rev. 5:9–13).
[68] Owen, *The Person of Christ*, in *Works*, 1:110.

in nothing but "vain babbling." As Owen explains, "Whoever cometh unto God hereby, 'must believe that he is, and that he is the rewarder of them that diligently seek [him].'" Then, there is a "representation of our wills, affections, and desires of our souls, unto him on whom we call, with an expectation of being heard and relieved, by virtue of his infinitely divine excellencies."[69]

Christ is the greatest example of invocation (Ps. 31:5; Luke 23:46; Acts 7:59); and his bride, the church, is characterized by invocation as well, which serves to distinguish her members from the world, as they are those who call on the name of the Lord Jesus Christ (1 Cor. 1:2). Indeed, calling on him is our duty as believers. In calling upon him we express our faith in him (e.g., Rev. 22:20). In calling on him, however, the object and motive is of utmost importance. Christ, of course, is the object, and our motive is redemption. Only through Christ can we be redeemed. But now that we have been redeemed and are making strides in godliness, seeking to be conformed into the image of Christ, our calling on the Lord is a means of petition. We call on him both to worship him and to seek his guidance. Owen is astute to observe the proper Trinitarian relations that come into play at this point. Jesus himself taught us to pray to the Father (Matt. 6:9; John 20:17), but this "invocation is to be by and in the name of the Son, Jesus Christ, through the aid of the Holy Ghost."[70] It is by and in the name of Christ because he is our Mediator before God, and it is through the aid of the Spirit because he is the one who supplies grace, helping and enabling us to perform our Christian duties. If we do not approach God in this way, our invocation, our worship, and our prayers do not look Christian—or as Owen says, "evangelical"—at all.[71]

Scripture repeatedly hints at this Trinitarian invocation. Paul states in Ephesians 2:18 that it is through Christ that "we have access by one Spirit unto the Father." Paul assumes the same in 3:14–16. As Owen explains, "It is through him—that is, by Christ in the exercise of his mediatory office— that we have this access unto the Father." Therefore, we ask in the name of Christ and for the sake of Christ (John 14:13–14; 16:23–24). And the Spirit is by no means left out. The reason we can come to the Father in the name of the Son is that the Spirit enables, aids, and assists. For this reason he is called the "Spirit of grace and supplication" (see Rom. 8:26–27). We pray

---

[69] Ibid.
[70] Ibid., 1:112.
[71] Ibid., 1:113.

and cry out "Abba, Father" by the Spirit of the Son (Gal. 4:6; cf. Heb. 4:15–16; 10:19–22). "Herein," says Owen, "is the Lord Christ considered, not absolutely with respect unto his divine person, but with respect unto his office, that through 'him our faith and hope might be in God,' 1 Peter 1:21."[72]

Never disconnecting theology from the pew, Owen explains how and when and in what manner we invoke the name of Christ. And not just the individual Christian, but the church is in view. What is the "ordinary solemn way of the worship of the church"? Owen gives us five insights.

1. "Times of great distresses in conscience through temptations and desertions, are seasons requiring an application unto Christ by especial invocation."[73] When we are absolutely overwhelmed, we turn to Christ for compassion and deliverance. According to Scripture, when God's children are in the midst of great despair, the "Lord Christ in the Gospel is proposed as full of tender compassion—as he alone who is able to relieve them." Christ suffered and was tempted as we are. He is very familiar with our infirmities and is able to give us relief, deliverance, consolation, refreshment, and comfort. During this time of trouble the believer is to trust in Christ, place his faith in Christ, and depend entirely upon Christ.

2. "Times of gracious discoveries either of the glory of Christ in himself, or of his love unto us, are seasons that call for this duty."[74] Owen observes how the glory of Christ in his person and offices is unchanging. Nonetheless, there are times when God gives to us a special, outstanding affection for Christ, opening our eyes to behold his beauty. Whether this happens through prayer, meditation, or contemplation, we become like Stephen, to whom the heavens were opened to see "the glory of God, and Jesus standing at his right hand" (Acts 7:55–56). God opens the veil and "gives a clear, affecting discovery of his glory unto the minds and souls of believers; and in such seasons are they drawn forth and excited unto invocation and praise."[75] In these times we cannot help but speak of our Savior! Our response to who he is and what he has done for us is worship, praise, and adoration (Rev. 5:3–10). Therefore, when we discover the glory of Christ, we apply ourselves "unto him by invocation or praise."[76]

The same point is apparent when we consider the love of Christ. His love for the church is unchanging and steadfast. But we have seasons in

---

[72] Ibid.
[73] Ibid.
[74] Ibid., 1:114.
[75] Ibid., 1:115.
[76] Ibid.

which we feel his love in a way that we did not before. The love of Christ is shed abroad in our hearts by the Spirit and brings with it a "constraining power, to oblige us to live unto him who died for us, and rose again" (cf. 2 Cor. 5:14–15). There is, no doubt, a mystery here. On the one hand, it is a work of sovereign grace whereby God grants this love to us and even puts this love within us as he sees fit. On the other hand, it is our duty "to dispose our hearts unto its reception."[77] Unfortunately, we are all too often impressed with this world rather than the love of our Savior. As Owen says in one of his most moving statements:

> Were we diligent in casting out all that "filthiness and superfluity of naughtiness" which corrupts our affections, and disposes the mind to abound in vain imaginations; were our hearts more taken off from the love of the world, which is exclusive of a sense of divine love; did we more meditate on Christ and his glory;—we should more frequently enjoy these constraining visits of his love than now we do.[78]

3. "Times of persecution for his Name's sake, and for the profession of the gospel, are another season rendering this peculiar invocation of Christ both comely and necessary."[79] Owen recognizes the reality that so many before him experienced, namely, that the believer will be called upon to suffer for the name of Christ. When this time of persecution comes, those in Christ cannot but "continually think and meditate on him for whom they suffer."[80] In other words, when trouble and hardship come, one's true nature reveals itself. For those who have claimed the name of Christ but have not truly known him, persecution exposes their identity with the world. Not so for those who sincerely love and cherish Christ. When the sword begins to pierce their flesh, they count Christ as worth it and as far more precious than what this world has to give. This is why so many prisons have been filled "with thoughts of Christ and his love." In fact, many Christians have testified that during times of suffering, Christ becomes all the more precious and sweet. They understand that in such suffering, Christ is "full of love, pity, and unspeakable compassion towards them" and, most importantly, "his grace is sufficient for them—that his power shall be perfected in their weakness, to carry them through all their sufferings, unto his and

---

[77] Ibid.
[78] Ibid., 1:116.
[79] Ibid.
[80] Ibid.

their own glory."[81] Therefore, writes Owen, it is impossible for the believer "not to make especial applications continually unto him for those aids of grace—for those pledges of love and mercy—for those supplies of consolation and spiritual refreshments, which their condition calls for."[82] Christ is the believer's refuge, his stronghold, his rock, his fortress, as every martyr knows. This is why the believer who clings to Christ can rejoice in the midst of suffering. Though he takes a beating, he overflows with unspeakable joy. Therefore, Scripture can say that we are more than conquerors.

4. "When we have a due apprehension of the eminent actings of any grace in Christ Jesus, and withal a deep and abiding sense of our own want of the same grace, it is a season of especial application unto him by prayer for the increase of it."[83] In short, when we taste the grace of Christ, we pray and ask God for more. Owen explains,

> Wherefore, when they have a view of the glory of any grace as it was exercised in Christ, and withal a sense of their own defect and want therein—conformity unto him being their design—they cannot but apply themselves unto him in solemn invocation, for a farther communication of that grace unto them, from his stores and fullness.[84]

But how do we do this? How do we petition God for his grace in our time of need? It is by prayer. We simply ask, and we do so having faith that he will give what he has promised. We must be like the disciples who said, "Lord, increase our faith" (Luke 17:5). When we face any temptation, we pray so that we might prevail over it.

5. "The time of death, whether natural, or violent for his sake, is a season of the same nature."[85] Owen once again returns to Stephen's martyrdom. Before he was killed, Stephen prayed, committing his soul to Christ, "Lord Jesus, receive my spirit" (Acts 7:59). Oh, how often Stephen's prayer has been the prayer of saints throughout the centuries! In this life, while we still possess breath, we commit ourselves to Christ, placing our faith in him even in those moments of weakness and struggle. Owen wisely observes, "The more we have been in the exercise of faith on him in our lives, the more ready will it be in the approaches of death."[86] So prepare now. Get

---

[81] Ibid., 1:117.
[82] Ibid.
[83] Ibid.
[84] Ibid., 1:118.
[85] Ibid.
[86] Ibid.

ready. Take these small opportunities of suffering to exercise faith in Christ so that when the final test comes, you, like Stephen, remain faithful.

Honoring Christ by Faith

It is clear so far that Christ is to receive our honor. But what does this mean in its most basic sense? For Owen, the answer is faith in Christ. To honor the person of Christ is to place one's faith in him. From the very beginning, a "first promise" (Gen. 3:15) was given by God, promising deliverance "from that apostasy from God, with all the effects of it, under which our first parents and all their posterity were cast by sin."[87] This first promise is fulfilled in the person of Christ, in his incarnation, through his role as Mediator. He is the "seed of the woman" who crushes the head of the serpent through his suffering, death, and resurrection. The entire Old Testament, especially the sacrificial system, pointed to him who would be called the "Lamb of God" (John 1:29).[88] As 1 Peter 1:19 says, we "were redeemed with the precious blood of Christ, as of a lamb without blemish and without spot" (see also Rev. 5:6; 13:8).

Our first parents, Owen asserts, believed in this promise first given to them in Genesis 3:15, as did many Old Testament saints who followed (e.g., Abel, Enoch, Noah).[89] Owen has no patience for the Socinians, who argue that these Old Testament believers were justified before God not because they believed in God's promise, but rather because they walked according to the light of nature and obeyed.[90] On the contrary, Hebrews 12:1–2, with its great "cloud of witnesses," confirms their faith and justification by grace.[91] Owen draws two conclusions. First, there was "no way of justification and salvation of sinners revealed and proposed from the foundation of the world, but only by Jesus Christ, as declared in the first promise."[92] Second, there was no way for the "participation of the benefits of that prom-

---

[87] Ibid., 1:120.

[88] "All expiatory sacrifices were, from the beginning, types and representations of the sacrifice of Christ; whereon all their use, efficacy, and benefit among men—all their acceptance with God—did depend" (ibid., 1:122).

[89] For Owen's understanding of the relationship between the first promise and the covenants that follow, see ibid., 1:124.

[90] For Owen's refutation of those who seek to separate Christ from the gospel revealed by him, as if one could believe in the latter without the former, by appealing to Old Testament saints, see ibid., 1:127.

[91] Ibid., 1:123. For a more thorough understanding of how Owen views redemptive history, see John Owen, *Biblical Theology: The History of Theology from Adam to Christ* (Grand Rapids: Soli Deo Gloria, 1994). Additionally, to see how Owen views Christ as the fulfillment of these Old Testament promises, and especially his role as the Great High Priest, see Owen, *An Exposition of the Epistle to the Hebrews*, 7 vols. (Edinburgh: Banner of Truth, 1991).

[92] Owen, *The Person of Christ*, in *Works*, 1:125.

ise, or of his work of mediation, but by faith in him as so promised." Faith in him, in other words, was required "from the foundation of the world; that is, from the entrance of sin."[93] Yet Owen is not so naive to ignore the progressive nature of divine revelation. He does realize that the "clearness and fullness of the revelation of the mystery of the wisdom and grace of God in him—as unto the constitution of his person in his incarnation" became more and more evident as the promise came to fruition.[94] Far more is revealed concerning the person of Christ in the New Testament than in the Old Testament (Eph. 3:8–11). Nevertheless, the promise of a Redeemer, a Messiah, was there from the beginning.

Therefore, when the Son does become incarnate, his person is revealed in a way unlike ever before. Those who encounter him are confronted with who he is. For this reason, Jesus can ask the blind man whose eyes he has opened, "Believest thou on the Son of God?" only to hear the response, "'Lord, I believe'; and he worshipped him" (John 9:35, 38). Owen observes, "All divine worship or adoration is a consequent effect and fruit of faith." Consequently, "to adore or invocate any in whom we ought not to believe, is idolatry."[95] How important it is, then, to believe in the person of Christ! If we misunderstand or twist who Christ is, our worship will be idolatrous. As John 3:36 makes clear, "He that believeth on the Son hath everlasting life: and he that believeth not the Son shall not see life; but the wrath of God abideth on him." Owen puts everything into perspective when he writes, "Deny his person to be the proper and immediate object of this faith, and all these things are utterly overthrown—that is, the whole spiritual life and eternal salvation of the church."[96]

Love, the Fire That Kindles Obedience to Christ

So far much has been made of "faith" in the person of Christ. But what about obedience and love? Do these have a proper place in the Christian life?[97] Yes, indeed, they do. The two relate to one another in the most critical way. As Owen explains, what enlivens and animates our obedience is love.[98] Christ himself makes this clear when he says, "If ye love me, keep

---

[93] Ibid., 1:126.
[94] Ibid.
[95] Ibid.
[96] Ibid., 1:130.
[97] To be clear, here we are referring to sanctification, not justification.
[98] Under the Old Testament, says Owen, the law had two parts: (1) moral preceptive part, and (2) the institutions of worship. For Owen's view of both, see Owen, *The Person of Christ*, in *Works*, 1:134–39. On

my commandments" (John 14:15). In other words, love is the very foundation of our obedience. "He accepts no obedience," Owen observes, "unto
his commands that doth not proceed from love unto his person. That is
no love which is not fruitful in obedience; and that is no obedience which
proceeds not from love."[99] Owen notes that the love of God was the "life and
substance of all obedience" in the Old Testament.

What does all of this have to do with the person of Christ? Owen answers poetically: the "person of Christ is the especial object of this divine
love, which is the fire that kindles the sacrifice of our obedience unto him."[100]
So central is love to obedience that Paul says in 1 Corinthians 16:22, "If any
man love not the Lord Jesus Christ, let him be Anathema Maranatha." Paul's
words could not be stronger. His point is clear: love for Christ is essential
and indispensable. To be a Christian is to love the Lord Jesus with our whole
heart. Therefore, Owen proposes that there "ought to be, in all believers, a
divine, gracious love unto the person of Christ, immediately fixed on him,
whereby they are excited unto, and acted in, all their obedience unto his
authority."[101]

First, Owen argues that there are many who are under a "false pretence
of love unto Christ."[102] There are hypocrites in our churches, and a false
pretense of love for Christ is at the root of their hypocrisy. Judas, the be-
trayer, is a perfect example. "The first great act of hypocrisy, with respect
unto Christ, was treachery, veiled with a double pretence of love."[103] Judas
cried, "Hail, Master! And kissed him." This was the kiss of betrayal, though
it gave the false appearance of love. As Owen explains the scene, "His words
and actions proclaimed love, but deceit and treachery were in his heart."
This is why the apostle Paul prayed that believers in the church would not
have corrupt affections (Eph. 6:24). So vile, so poisonous is an insincere
love. "This falsely pretended love is worse than avowed hatred."[104] Jesus
talks about such hypocrisy in Matthew 7:21–23. On the day of judgment
some will say, "Lord, Lord, have we not prophesied in thy name? and in thy
name have cast out devils? and in thy name done many wonderful works?"
But Jesus will say in return, "I never knew you: depart from me, ye that

---

Owen's understanding of the law, see Sinclair B. Ferguson, *John Owen on the Christian Life* (Edinburgh:
Banner of Truth, 1987), 48–53.
[99] Owen, *The Person of Christ*, in *Works*, 1:139.
[100] Ibid.
[101] Ibid., 1:140.
[102] Ibid.
[103] Ibid.
[104] Ibid.

work iniquity." Why? Because though they called him "Lord," they did not do the will of the Father in heaven. Therefore, Owen concludes, regardless of what they say, they do not truly love Christ if they do not keep his commandments.

Each of us can easily fall into this trap. Certainly, those who claim on the last day to have done mighty works in the Lord's name are, at least to some degree, sincere. But their sincerity misleads them. They are deceived because, though they possess some measure of sincerity, their love for Christ is neither pure nor true to the "principles and rules of the Gospel." "They may think that they love Christ, but indeed do not." Owen gives five ways one falls into this dangerous trap:

1. "That love is not sincere and incorrupt which proceedeth not from—which is not a fruit of faith." In other words, "Those who do not first really believe on Christ, can never sincerely love him. . . . Where the faith of men is dead, their love will not be living and sincere."[105]
2. "That love is not so which ariseth from false ideas and representations that men make of Christ, or have made of him in their minds."[106] Therefore, getting the person of Christ right is absolutely essential! How prone we are to "draw images" in our minds of what we "most fancy." Owen warns against presenting Christ—as he says some Roman Catholic missionaries (i.e., Jesuits) did to the Indians—as a "glorious person exalted in heaven at the right hand of God," but all the while neglecting his natures, his offices, and especially his cross and sufferings.[107] If we develop a false and even blasphemous notion of Christ's person, the love that follows will not be real, let alone approved by God. To be more specific, it is precisely our false notions of Christ's person that corrupt our love for him. Owen has the Arians of the fourth century and the Socinians in his own day in mind when he writes, "Shall we think that they love Christ by whom his divine nature is denied?" The same can be said of those who deny his human nature, or the union of the divine nature and human nature in the one person. "There cannot be true evangelical love unto a false Christ, such as these imaginations do fancy."[108]
3. Scripture alone gives us the "nature, rules, and bounds of sincere spiritual love." Scripture tells us the proper motives of our love, so that if

---

[105] Ibid., 1:141.
[106] Ibid.
[107] Ibid., 1:141, 431.
[108] Ibid., 1:141.

"either the acts or effects of it will not endure a trial thereby, they are false and counterfeit."[109]

4. False love "fixeth itself on undue objects, which, whatever is pretended, are neither Christ nor means of conveying our love unto him."[110] Here Owen has the Roman Catholic Church in view, whose members express "devotion to images of Christ, as they fancy, of Christ; crucifixes, pretended relics of his cross, and the nails that pierced him, with the like superstitious representations of him, and what they suppose he is concerned in." Though they have "ardent affections"— they kiss these relics, prostrate themselves, even having tears in their eyes—it is not Christ that they are cleaving to, but a "cloud of their own imaginations."[111] Owen compares Rome to the idolater in Isaiah 44:17, who carves out of a tree a god for himself and worships this god, prays to this god, and cries out to this god for deliverance. But all along, even though his devotion to it is steadfast and his affections for it are strong, it is a false god.

5. "I acknowledge there have been great pretences of such a love unto Christ as cannot be justified." Owen again aims at Rome. He notes that there are raptures, ecstasies, self-annihilations, immediate adhesions and enjoyments, yet "without any act of the understanding, and with a multitude of other swelling words of vanity" used to "set off what they fancy to be divine love."[112] But where is truth in all of this? Where is Scripture? Why have we not directed our love to the person of Christ and him alone?[113]

Owen concludes that there ought to be in all believers a "religious, gracious love unto the person of Christ."[114] The church must be characterized by this Christ-centered love. "Love unto the person of Christ, proceeding from faith, is their life, their joy, and glory."[115]

Scripture, furthermore, promises that it is through this type of love that we receive peace, safety, and consolation in this world. Love is that divine quality which not only characterizes the Trinity and the three persons' relations to one another, but also is directed toward us who are covered in the blood of the Lamb.[116] As Jesus says in John 14:21, "He that loveth

---

[109] Ibid., 1:142.
[110] Ibid.
[111] Ibid.
[112] Ibid.
[113] Ibid., 1:142–43.
[114] Ibid., 1:143.
[115] Ibid., 1:148.
[116] On how the members of the Trinity love one another, see ibid., 1:144–49.

me, shall be loved of my Father, and I will love him, and manifest myself unto him." And again, "My Father will love him, and we will come unto him, and make our abode with him" (14:23). With these verses in mind, Owen overflows with joy:

> What heart can conceive, what tongue can express, the glory of these promises, or at the least part of the grace that is contained in them? Who can conceive aright of the divine condescension, love, and grace that are expressed in them? How little a portion is it that we know God in these things! But if we value them not, if we labour not for an experience of them according unto our measure, we have neither lot nor portion in the gospel. The presence and abode of God with us as a Father, manifesting himself to be such unto us, in the infallible pledges and assurances of our adoption—the presence of Christ with us, revealing himself unto us, with all those ineffable mercies wherewith these things are accompanied—are all contained in them. And these promises are peculiarly given unto them that love the person of Christ, and in the exercise of love towards him.[117]

Just how important is the person of Christ to the Christian life? According to Owen, the two are intimately intertwined and inseparable. All our "spiritual comforts" depend upon our love for and obedience to the Lord Jesus.[118]

Tragically, however, the unbeliever applies his love to everything but Christ. The "depravation of our natures by sin" and the "degeneracy of our wills from their original rectitude" are exposed in our proneness to love other things, seeking satisfaction "where it is not to be obtained." Our wretched depravity is apparent in how difficult it is "to raise our hearts unto the love of God." "Were it not for that depravation, he would always appear as the only suitable and satisfactory object unto our affections."[119] This reminds us that God's love is the cause of our love. "Herein is love, not that we loved God, but that he loved us, and sent his Son to be the propitiation for our sins" (1 John 4:10). God is love and he has displayed his love toward us in the atoning sacrifice of his own Son for the forgiveness of our sins. Apart from this divine, redeeming love manifested to us, we cannot love God. "This is the cause, the spring and fountain, of all our love to him."[120]

---

[117] Ibid., 1:149.
[118] Ibid., 1:150.
[119] Ibid., 1:151. For Owen's extensive overview of the nature, operations, and causes of divine love, see ibid., 1:150–61. And for our motives in loving Christ, see ibid., 1:161–69.
[120] Ibid., 1:152. As seen in chap. 3, Owen goes on to observe that nothing in us moves God to love us (see ibid., 1:166).

Beholding the Glory of Christ

As seen so far, the person of Christ is the object of our faith, worship, obedience, and love. In all of this Christ is the focus. This brings us to the essence of the Christian life: beholding the glory of Christ. As Owen points out in *Meditations and Discourses on the Glory of Christ*, Jesus himself prays with this goal in mind. He says, in John 17:24, "Father, I will that they also whom thou hast given me be with me where I am; that they may behold my glory, which thou hast given me" (cf. John 1:14, 29–33). Therefore, says Owen, beholding the glory of Christ is one of the "greatest privileges and advancements of believers, both in this world and unto eternity."[121] Why this is the case is something we must take time to explore.

To begin with, Owen is on solid biblical ground to claim that this is one of our greatest privileges as believers. Along with John 17:24, 2 Corinthians 4:6 lends support. There Paul says, "For God, who commanded the light to shine out of darkness, hath shined in our hearts, to give the light of the knowledge of the glory of God in the face of Jesus Christ." God brings us from darkness to light, and he does so by shining light into our hearts. What is this light? Paul tells us it is the "knowledge of the glory of God in the face of Jesus Christ." So when the sinner is awakened to see this light for the first time, it is Christ whom he sees and, for the first time, cherishes. From this point forward, the believer is not satisfied without Christ. He must have Christ. Christ is everything. Or as Owen states:

> For being once touched by the love of Christ, receiving therein an impression of secret ineffable virtue, they will ever be in motion, and restless, until they come unto him, and behold his glory. That soul which can be satisfied without it,—that cannot be eternally satisfied with it,—is not partaker of the efficacy of his intercession.[122]

How we behold the glory of our Savior is especially important to Owen. To begin with, we behold his glory by faith. "No man shall ever behold the glory of Christ by sight hereafter, who doth not in some measure behold it by faith here in this world."[123] Grace, says Owen, is absolutely necessary in our "preparation for glory, and faith for sight." Unless our soul is "seasoned with grace and faith," we will not be capable of beholding his glory. Those

---

[121] Owen, *Meditations and Discourses on the Glory of Christ*, in *Works*, 1:286.
[122] Ibid. Also see 1:384–85.
[123] Ibid., 1:289.

not "disposed" here and now to behold Christ will not, no matter what they say or "pretend," desire him on that future day.[124]

Owen gives us a rare glimpse into his own personal desires at this point. He is very serious about knowing Christ in this present life and concerned over the many temptations by which the world amuses us, distracting us away from our Savior.[125] Owen's words, sounding much like Paul's in Philippians 3:8, are penetrating:

> If, therefore, we desire to have faith in its vigour or love in its power, giving rest, complacency, and satisfaction unto our own souls, we are to seek for them in the diligent discharge of this duty [of beholding the glory of Christ];—elsewhere they will not be found. Herein would I live;—herein would I die;—hereon would I dwell in my thoughts and affections, to the withering and consumption of all the painted beauties of this world, unto the crucifying all things here below, until they become unto me a dead and deformed thing, no way meet for affectionate embraces.[126]

Therefore, in this life we are being prepared for heaven, where we will behold the glory of Christ like never before—our sight being immediate, direct, intuitive, steady, and constant.[127] Just as music has no pleasure to those who cannot hear, just as color is not beautiful to those who cannot see, so we will not see Christ as magnificent unless the faculties of our soul are exercised and our faith is made strong.[128] "Heaven itself would not be more advantageous unto persons not renewed by the Spirit of grace in this life."[129]

Additionally, it is into the image of Christ that we are being transformed in this life. As Paul tells the Corinthians, "We all, with open face beholding as in a glass the glory of the Lord, are changed into the same image from glory to glory, even as by the Spirit of the Lord" (2 Cor. 3:18). Fundamentally, we are seeking to be spiritually minded in this life. In

---

[124] Owen believes Rome has fallen prey to this danger (see ibid.; cf. 1:393).

[125] See especially ibid., 1:388.

[126] Ibid., 1:291.

[127] Ibid., 1:378. Also see 1:376, 378, 384.

[128] Owen does give several ways we can focus our gaze upon the glory of Christ's person: (1) "Let us get it fixed on our souls and in our minds, that this glory of Christ in the divine constitution of his person is the best, the most noble, useful, beneficial object that we can be conversant about in our thoughts, or cleave unto in our affections." (2) We must *diligently study the Scripture,* and the revelations that are made of this glory of Christ therein." (3) Having "attained the light of the knowledge of the glory of Christ from the Scripture, or by the dispensation of the truth in the preaching of the gospel, we *would esteem it our duty frequently to meditate thereon.*" (4) "Let your *occasional thoughts of Christ be many,* and multiplied every day. He is not far from us; we may make a speedy address unto him at any time." (5) "The next direction is, that all our thoughts concerning Christ and his glory should be accompanied with *admiration, adoration, and thanksgiving*" (ibid., 1:312–22).

[129] Ibid., 1:291.

doing so, by God's grace and by the power of the Spirit, our minds are filled not with the darkness that characterizes this lost and perishing world, but rather with the "great worth, beauty, and glory" of our Lord and what he has in store for us (Phil. 3:7–11).[130] Ineffable joy, as well as the "peace of God, which passeth all understanding" (Phil. 4:7), characterizes those occupied in this life with the glory of Jesus. This is why Scripture can say of believers, "Christ, in you, the hope of glory" (Col. 1:27). Here and now we have but a foretaste of the harvest to come.[131]

Fixated on the Beauty of Christ

In thinking through how Christ became our Mediator via the incarnation, Owen is simply in awe and cannot help but praise God for who Christ is and what he has done. After reflecting on the condescension of the Son (Phil. 2:5–8), Owen writes:

> How glorious, then, is the condescension of the Son of God in his suscep-tion of the office of mediation! For if such be the perfection of the divine nature, and its distance so absolutely infinite from the whole creation,—and if such be his self-sufficiency unto his own eternal blessedness, as that nothing can be taken from him, nothing added unto him, so that every regard in him unto any of the creatures is an act of self-humiliation and condescension from the prerogative of his being and state,—what heart can conceive, what tongue can express, the glory of that condescen-sion in the Son of God, whereby he took our nature upon him, took it to be his own, in order unto a discharge of the office of mediation on our behalf?[132]

In light of the glory and beauty of who Christ is and what he has done, how can the Christian avoid having his mind drawn to his Savior at all times?[133] Owen goes so far as to say that while one Christian may exceed

---

[130] Owen, in describing how we will one day behold Christ, is referring to the "Beatific Vision," which, he says, "is the sole fountain of all the actings of our souls in the state of blessedness." However, we shall not see God "in his immense essence," which is invisible to our "corporeal eyes" and incomprehensible to our minds. Because of this, our vision will always be "in the face of Jesus Christ." "Therein will that manifestation of the glory of God, in his infinite perfections, and all their blessed operations, so shine into our souls, as shall immediately fill us with peace, rest, and glory" (ibid., 1:292–93).

[131] Far more can be said. Owen goes on to answer three questions: "1. *What* is that glory of Christ which we do or may behold by faith? 2. *How* do we behold it? 3. *Wherein* our doing so differs from immediate vision in heaven?" For Owen's answers, see ibid., 1:293–415.

[132] Ibid., 1:325.

[133] "He is no Christian who lives not much in the meditation of the mediation of Christ, and the especial acts of it." Owen, *The Person of Christ*, in *Works*, 1:52.

another in his thoughts of Christ, anyone who never finds himself fixated on the beauty of Christ should question whether or not he is truly a Christian. Owen's words are indeed sobering:

> Some may more abound in that work than others, as it is fixed, formed and regular; some may be more able than others to dispose their thoughts concerning them into method and order; some may be more diligent than others in the observation of time for the solemn performance of this duty; some may be able to rise to higher and clearer apprehensions of them than others. But as for those, the bent of whose minds doth not lie towards thoughts of them—whose hearts are not on all occasions retreating unto the remembrance of them—who embrace not all opportunities to call them over as they are able—on what grounds can they be esteemed Christians? How do they live by the faith of the Son of God? Are the great things of the Gospel, of the mediation of Christ, proposed unto us, as those which we may think of when we have nothing else to do, that we may meditate upon or neglect at our pleasure—as those wherein our concernment is so small as that they must give place unto all other occasions or diversions whatever? Nay, if our minds are not filled with these things—if Christ doth not dwell plentifully in our hearts by faith—if our souls are not possessed with them, and in their whole inward frame and constitution so cast into this mould as to be led by a natural complacency unto a converse with them—we are strangers unto the life of faith. And if we are thus conversant about these things, they will engage our hearts into the love of the person of Christ. To suppose the contrary, is indeed to deny the truth and reality of them all, and to turn the Gospel into a fable.[134]

How can we identify those who are followers of Christ? It is easy; they are those possessed with thoughts of him so that the gospel is always on their minds and lips. They are those who find their greatest delight to be in Jesus Christ.

Without question, this was true of Owen. The day he died, his friend William Payne came to visit him at home in the "quiet village of Ealing." Payne brought news that Owen's *Meditations and Discourses on the Glory of*

---

[134] Ibid., 1:164. In this passage Owen reiterates in very personal language what he says in the quote that prefaces this chapter. He says elsewhere: "I shall only say, that those who are inconversant with these objects of faith—whose minds are not delighted in the admiration of, and acquiescency in, things incomprehensible, such as is this constitution of the person of Christ—who would reduce all things to the measure of their own understandings, or else willfully live in the neglect of what they cannot comprehend—do not much prepare themselves for that vision of these things in glory, wherein our blessedness doth consist" (ibid., 1:52).

Christ was en route to publication. Owen was glad. But his gladness reached a new height that day as he prepared to meet Christ face-to-face. "I am glad to hear it; but, O brother Payne! The long wished for day is come at last in which I shall see that glory in another manner than I have ever done, or was capable of doing in this world."[135]

---

[135] Ibid., 1:ciii.

CHAPTER 5

CRUSHED FOR OUR INIQUITIES

He who by his own blood and death paid the price of our redemption to God, in that he underwent what was due to us, and procured our liberty and deliverance thereby, he made satisfaction properly for our sins; but when we were captives for sin to the justice of God, and committed thereon to the power of sin and Satan, Christ by his death and blood paid the price of our redemption to God, and procured our deliverance thereby: therefore he made satisfaction to God for our sins.[1]

John Owen's writings on the priesthood of Christ, as well as Christ's atoning work on the cross, brought him into controversy with many forms of opposition to Reformed orthodoxy, including Arminianism, Socinianism, and Roman Catholicism. As Carl R. Trueman explains:

> The Arminian ordering of decrees, which placed individual election after faith, clearly precluded any direct causal relationship between the priestly work of Christ and the salvation of any particular individual. The Socinians, by denying that Christ was divine in the traditional sense, radically reduced the objective importance of the atonement. The Catholics were problematic on various fronts, particularly in the relationship they drew

---

[1] Owen, *Vindiciae Evangelicae; The Mystery of the Gospel Vindicated and Socinianism Examined*, in *Works*, 12:524; except for general references to this title, hereafter this work is cited as *The Mystery of the Gospel*.

between Christ's death and the Mass, and also in the development of Pelagianizing tendencies within their ranks, tendencies susceptible to the same strictures from the Orthodox viewpoint as those of the Arminians.[2]

Trueman goes on to observe that the priesthood of Christ had first importance in Owen's theology from the very beginning of his career; and for good reason too, since Christ's mediation and intercession for sinners is at the very center of the gospel itself. Therefore, when the nature of Christ's priesthood came under attack, for Owen such a threat was not minor by any means, but an assault on the very focal point of Christianity, precisely because what Christ accomplished on the cross as High Priest is the most important and central event in the drama of redemption.[3] This chapter, therefore, is a window into Owen's theology of the cross as we explore not only how Owen understood the nature of Christ's sacrificial death, but also what the atonement has to do with the Christian life.[4]

Christ's Threefold Office

If we are to rightly understand what Christ has accomplished for the salvation of God's elect, we need to recognize that threefold office of Christ which is so integral to his person as God incarnate. As Owen puts the matter:

> It is by the exercise and discharge of the office of Christ—as the king, priest, and prophet of the church—that we are redeemed, sanctified, and saved. Thereby doth he immediately communicate all Gospel benefits unto us—give us an access unto God here by grace, and in glory hereafter; for he saves us, as he is the mediator between God and man.[5]

---

[2] Carl R. Trueman, *The Claims of Truth: John Owen's Trinitarian Theology* (Carlisle: Paternoster, 1998), 188. Owen also came into conflict with others who did not neatly fit into these three categories. Consider, for example, Hugo Grotius, *A Defense of the Catholic Faith concerning the Satisfaction of Christ against Faustus Socinus* (1617), which argues for a governmental view of the atonement, a view that differed substantially from Owen's satisfaction view. Also Richard Baxter, dissatisfied with Owen's *The Death of Death in the Death of Christ* (1647), responded to Owen in an appendix in *Aphorismes of Justification* (1649). Though he does not mention him, Owen is certainly responding to Grotius in *Of the Death of Christ* (1650), in *Works*, 10:429–79. Baxter continued the debate in his *Confession of his Faith* (1655), which Owen addressed, along with Socinianism, in *Of the Death of Christ, and of Justification*, attached to the end of *The Mystery of the Gospel* (1655), in *Works*, 12:591–617. On Baxter, see J. I. Packer, *The Redemption and Restoration of Man in the Thought of Richard Baxter* (Vancouver, BC: Regent College Publishing, 2001); and Trueman, *Claims of Truth*, 206–26. For the relationship of Owen and Baxter, see especially Tim Cooper, *John Owen, Richard Baxter and the Formation of Nonconformity* (Burlington, VT: Ashgate, 2011).
[3] Trueman, *Claims of Truth*, 189.
[4] In this chapter we focus mostly on Owen's *The Mystery of the Gospel*. But also see Owen, *A Brief Declaration and Vindication of the Doctrine of the Trinity as Also of the Person and Satisfaction of Christ*, in *Works*, 2:419–39; Owen, *The Death of Death in the Death of Christ*, in *Works*, 10:274–86; Owen, *Of the Death of Christ*, in *Works*, 10:429–79.
[5] Owen, *The Person of Christ*, in *Works*, 1:85.

As our Mediator, therefore, Christ's office is threefold: prophet, priest, and king. Or perhaps the order should be changed to priest, king, prophet, reflecting God's work in redemptive history. Owen gives this justification: "The first promise made of him [Christ] by God to Adam was of him generally as a mediator, particularly as a priest, as he was to break the head of Satan by the bruising of his own heel."[6] Here Owen has in mind Genesis 3:15, the *protoevangelium*, where God promises, "I will put enmity between thee and the woman, and between thy seed and her seed; it shall bruise thy head, and thou shalt bruise his heel." The seed who crushes the serpent's head is Christ. So even from the beginning, immediately after the fall into sin, the gospel of Christ is there and as the narrative unfolds, this promise matures until it fully blooms at the cross and resurrection. The point is that Christ's priestly role is hinted at from the start.

Christ's kingly and prophetic offices are also foreshadowed in the Old Testament with figures like Abraham and Moses. Abraham was a king, "taking all nations to be his inheritance" (see Gen. 12:2–3). Moses, after giving God's law to Israel, was very much "a prophet to teach and instruct his [God's] redeemed people" (see Deut. 18:18).[7] Owen identifies these figures as types of the antitype (Christ) to come. Other examples could be included: "Christ was like to Moses as he was a prophet, and like to Aaron as he was a priest, and like to David as he was a king; that is, he was represented and typified by all these, and had that likeness to them which the antitype (as the thing typified is usually but improperly called) hath to the type."[8] But, says Owen, Christ is not merely like these types—whether prophet, priest, or king—as if he simply shares their general office corresponding to his office. Rather, as we shall see, Christ is far greater, both in his person, as the God-man, and in the work of redemption that he accomplishes.[9]

It is important to understand why these offices are so vital to Owen, especially Christ's role as High Priest.[10] Remember, Owen's christological

---

[6] Owen, *The Mystery of the Gospel*, in *Works*, 12:348.

[7] Ibid.

[8] Ibid., 12:349.

[9] Owen is careful to clarify, however, that not just anyone can fulfill this role as Mediator, as if we just needed another king, or prophet, or priest. To the contrary, it is the very person of Christ who is necessary, as the one who is both fully God and fully man in one person. As Owen says, "It is evident, therefore, that the redemption and salvation of the church do not depend merely on this—that God hath given one to be the king, priest, and prophet of the church, by the actings of which offices it is redeemed and saved; but on the person of him who was so given unto us: as is fully attested, Isa. 9:6, 7." Owen, *The Person of Christ*, in *Works*, 1:86.

[10] The following will focus on Owen's work, *The Person of Christ* (the fuller title being *Christologia; or, A Declaration of the Glorious Mystery of the Person of Christ—God and Man*). However, Owen also treats the priesthood of Christ in his commentary on Hebrews. See Owen, *Hebrews*, in *Works*, 18:3–262. Also see

treatises were molded and formed in the midst of theological controversy, especially with Socinianism. The deity of Christ was under attack by voices of Socinianism like Biddle and the Racovian Catechism. Moreover, as Trueman observes, the nature of the threefold office of Christ was reinterpreted by Socinians so that, for example, "Christ's primary, if not his only, importance lies in his task of revealing the Father's will to humanity through example and teaching, i.e. those tasks covered by the prophetic office." However, as important as Christ's prophetic office is in demonstrating his divinity in revealing the Father, his humanity being the "medium of that revelation" (e.g., Heb. 1:1–2),[11] for Owen "it is Christ's work in expiating sin through his position as mediator between God and humanity that serves as the basic premise for his understanding of the person of Christ, and it is this soteriological concern that finds its most detailed exposition in the threefold office."[12] Christ, for Owen, is more than a teacher, prophetically pointing us to the Father's will.[13] Not only does he come revealing the Father to sinners, but also he himself is the sinless High Priest who mediates on behalf of the elect, obeying the law in our stead as the God-man, and substituting himself as the perfect, once-for-all sacrifice for the forgiveness of our sins.

In that light, therefore, Christ's office as the great High Priest deserves our attention as we give special focus to what he accomplishes for us and our salvation by means of the cross.[14]

Our Great High Priest

Scripture places great emphasis on the mediation of Christ as High Priest, as well as its centrality to the gospel and the Christian faith.[15] Christ dem-

---

his commentary in vols. 20–22. For a more in-depth treatment of Owen on the threefold office of Christ, see Trueman, *Claims of Truth*, 168–98.

[11] Trueman, *Claims of Truth*, 173.

[12] Ibid. The Socinians also attacked Christ's kingly office, arguing that he did not become king until after he ascended to the right hand of the Father. He is king, in other words, not by nature, but by his human achievements. Biddle's *Twofold Catechism*, for example, makes this argument. For Owen's response, see Owen, *The Mystery of the Gospel*, in *Works*, 12:373.

[13] Even concerning Christ's prophetic office, Owen has serious disagreements with Socinianism. For Owen, Christ's prophetic role demonstrates both his humanity and his deity. "While the divinity of Christ secures his knowledge of the Father's will, it is his humanity which is necessary for the communication of that knowledge to other human beings." Trueman, *Claims of Truth*, 171.

[14] For Owen's defense of Christ as prophet and king, see Owen, *The Mystery of the Gospel*, in *Works*, 12:348–96; Owen, *The Person of Christ*, in *Works*, 1:85–100.

[15] Owen's affirmation of Christ's priestly office comes to us in the context of his refutation of Biddle's Socinianism, which Owen addresses in his book *Vindiciae Evangelicae; The Mystery of the Gospel Vindicated and Socinianism Examined*. Owen rejects the Socinian argument that Christ is High Priest only in a metaphorical sense. See Trueman, *Claims of Truth*, 185–98 for a fuller treatment than that given here.

onstrates that he is the great High Priest by offering himself as the sacrifice for our sins. Paul says in Ephesians 5:2, "Christ hath loved us, and hath given himself for us as an offering and a sacrifice to God for a sweet-smelling savour." Paul's description fits the definition of the high priest outlined in Hebrews 5:1, which says that he is one "taken from amongst men" and "ordained to offer both gifts and sacrifices for sins." Certainly this is the case with Christ, who mediates on behalf of God's people and offers up a sacrifice, though the sacrifice is himself, the spotless Lamb who is slain for our transgressions (John 1:29) and crushed for our iniquities (Isa. 53:5).[16]

Christ, by virtue of his priesthood, prays on behalf of God's people, and makes supplication for them. Christ, a "priest for ever after the order of Melchisedec" (Heb. 5:6; cf. Ps. 110:4), is described as he who, "in the days of his flesh . . . offered up prayers and supplications with strong crying and tears unto him that was able to save him from death" (Heb. 5:7). When did Christ do this? Owen answers that it was "before his death and at his death." Notice, observes Owen, that Christ's prayers and tears "were not for himself, but for his church, and the business that for their sakes he had undertaken."[17]

Christ exercises his priesthood by purging our sins through sacrifice. As Hebrews 1:3 testifies, when Christ "had by himself purged our sins," he then "sat down on the right hand of the Majesty of high." Other texts are supportive as well. First John 1:7 says that Christ's blood cleanses us from all sin, and Hebrews 10:10 says that we are "sanctified through the offering of the body of Jesus Christ once for all." "Christ, then, offering this sacrifice whilst he was on the earth, was a priest in so doing."[18] However, what sets Christ apart is that unlike the high priests in the Old Testament, who had to first offer a sacrifice for their own sins before they could make an offering on behalf of the people's sins, Christ is sinless, and therefore need not atone for his own sin, but rather can offer himself once for all for the sins of his people, as Hebrews 7:27 explains. Furthermore, Hebrews 9:12 says of Christ, "Neither by the blood of goats and calves, but by his own blood he entered in once into the holy place, having obtained eternal redemption for us." Owen elaborates, "Redemption is everywhere in Scripture ascribed

---

[16] Other passages Paul mentions include Rom. 4:25; 8:32; Gal. 2:20; Eph. 5:25. Owen, *The Mystery of the Gospel*, in *Works*, 12:408.

[17] Ibid., 12:409.

[18] Ibid.

to the blood of Christ; and himself abundantly manifesteth in what account it is to be had, when he says that 'he gave his life a ransom,' or 'a price of redemption.'" It is clear, argues Owen, that Christ laid down his life and, therefore, our redemption is accomplished by means of the offering he made for us. As Hebrews 9:26 says, "He put away sin by the sacrifice of himself."[19]

Additionally, Christ demonstrates his priestly office because he offers himself "once for all." In other words, unlike the sacrifices of the Old Testament, which had to be offered continually and without end, Christ offers himself up just once, and his one-time sacrificial death is sufficient for redemption (see Heb. 7:27; 9:26; 10:10–14).[20] Owen concludes that Christ's death was an offering that could not be repeated. "We do not deny that Christ offers himself in heaven,—that is, that he presents himself as one that was so offered to his Father; but the offering of himself, that was on earth: and therefore there was he a priest."[21]

Finally, the sacrifices in the Old Testament also prefigured the ultimate, once-for-all sacrifice of Christ. As Owen says, those Old Testament sacrifices were offered daily and were "types of the sacrifice of Christ," which is final and complete in every way.[22] This point especially leads us to the nature of the death and sacrifice of this Great High Priest.[23]

Crushed for Our Iniquities

How are we to understand the death of Christ? Owen is particularly disturbed by Socinianism because it has rejected the death of Christ as a "satisfaction," an atonement, that Christ has made "for us."[24] For Owen, however, this is exactly what took place on the cross. Texts like 2 Corinthians 5:18–21 and 1 Peter 3:18, he argues, most definitely support the substitutionary and sacrificial nature of the cross. Owen defends his view of the death of Christ by looking to three different concepts Scripture uses to describe the cross: price, sacrifice, and penalty.

---

[19] Ibid., 12:409–10.
[20] Ibid., 12:410.
[21] Ibid., 12:411.
[22] Ibid.
[23] For more on Christ's role as Mediator, see Owen, *The Person of Christ*, in *Works*, 1:164–69, 252–72, 323ff., 338ff.
[24] To fully understand the Socinian argument, see Alan W. Gomes, "*De Jesu Christo Servatore*: Faustus Socinus on the Satisfaction of Christ," *The Westminster Theological Journal* 55 (1993): 209–31; Trueman, *Claims of Truth*, 206–10.

Price

First, Scripture speaks of Christ's death as a price. "Ye are bought with a price," says Paul in 1 Corinthians 6:20. What is this price, one might ask? Owen believes that the Holy Spirit informs us in 1 Peter 1:18–19: "Ye were not redeemed with corruptible things, as silver and gold, . . . but with the precious blood of Christ." Likewise, Matthew 20:28 and 1 Timothy 2:6 affirm that Christ came to lay down his life as a ransom for sinners.[25]

The concept of "ransom" or "price" is not an invention of the New Testament, but finds its origins in the Old. Exodus 21:30, for example, says, "If there be laid on him a sum of money, then he shall give for the ransom of his life whatsoever is laid on him." Owen also points to Psalm 49:9, a passage demonstrating that there is, he says, a "valuable price, to be paid for the deliverance of that which, upon guilt, became obnoxious to death."[26] Likewise, in Isaiah 43:3 the Lord, who is the Savior of Israel, says to his people, "I gave Egypt for thy ransom, Ethiopia and Seba for thee."

While Owen looks into the different words used in both Hebrew and Greek, his main point is that this concept of "ransom" and "price" in the Old Testament is applied in the New Testament to the cross of Christ. "It denotes properly a price of redemption, a valuable compensation made by one thing for another."[27] Since the sinner is guilty before God, condemned for his sin, deserving the eternal judgment and wrath of God, there must be a price of redemption. And that price is Christ himself who substitutes himself in the sinner's place in order to absorb the wrath of God and turn away his divine anger toward him for the forgiveness of his sins. Therefore, Jesus can say that the Son of Man "came not to be ministered unto, but to minister, and to give his life a ransom for many" (Matt. 20:28).

While words like "price" and "ransom" tell us the means by which the sinner is liberated, behind these terms sits the far more encompassing concept of redemption. As Owen defines it, redemption

> is the deliverance of any one from bondage or captivity, and the misery attending that condition, by the intervention or interposition of a price or ransom, paid by the redeemer to him by whose authority he is detained,

---

[25] Owen, *The Mystery of the Gospel*, in *Works*, 12:419–21.
[26] Ibid., 12:419. For Owen's in-depth treatment of the Hebrew and Greek origins behind the terms surrounding the concept of price, see ibid., 12:419–21.
[27] In regard to the atonement "the death of Christ was a price of ransom" (ibid., 12:421).

that, being delivered, he may be in a state of liberty, at the disposal of the redeemer.[28]

Christ has obtained an "eternal redemption" by his blood (Heb. 9:12). Moreover, our justification, says Paul, is "through the redemption that is in Christ Jesus" (Rom. 3:24). Again Paul can say, "We have redemption through his blood, the forgiveness of sins" (Eph. 1:7; cf. Col. 1:14). Elsewhere Paul will say in no uncertain terms that Christ is "made unto us . . . redemption" (1 Cor. 1:30).

But what exactly does it mean to be ransomed, redeemed by the blood of Christ? As the definition above states, redemption consists in *deliverance from captivity*.[29] In other words, Christ delivers sinners from their captivity and bondage. Paul tells the Galatians, "[He] gave himself for our sins, that he might deliver us" (Gal. 1:4; cf. Luke 1:74; Rom. 7:6; Col. 1:13; 1 Thess. 1:10; Heb. 2:15). The concept of deliverance is implied in John 3:14–15 as well: "As Moses lifted up the serpent in the wilderness, even so must the Son of man be lifted up: That whosoever believeth in him should not perish, but have eternal life." Of course, Jesus has in mind Numbers 21:9, where the sin of the people brought upon them the just judgment and wrath of God. God provided a way of deliverance, however, by instructing Moses to erect a bronze serpent on a pole, so that if anyone bitten by a serpent looked up at it, they would be healed of their infirmity. Typologically, this incident points forward to the cross of Christ. As Jesus says, he is lifted up so that those who are perishing might look to him by faith and live (cf. Isa. 52:13; John 3:14–15). The death of Jesus delivers and ransoms the sinner from his captivity.

Still, why do we need deliverance, and what do we need to be delivered from? Owen's answer gets to the very heart of the matter. All humanity, he argues, is in a "state of sin and alienation from God" and therefore "in captivity."[30] Scripture calls us "captives," those "bound in prison" (Isa. 61:1). The work of Christ "is to 'bring out the prisoners from the prison, and them that sit in darkness' (that is, in the dungeon) 'out of the prison-house'" (Isa. 42:7).[31] Our only escape is the blood of the covenant (Heb. 10:29; cf. Isa. 49:25–26; Zech. 9:9–12). Hence, Christ arrives on the scene and proclaims

---

[28] Ibid., 12:509–10.
[29] Ibid., 12:510, 513.
[30] Ibid., 12:513.
[31] Ibid.

"liberty to the captives" (Isa. 61:1; Luke 4:18). And upon his death, Scripture says, he "led captivity captive" (Ps. 68:18; Eph. 4:8). Therefore, while we were prisoners and captives, "Christ gave us liberty from that yoke of bondage" (Gal. 5:1; Heb. 2:15).[32]

To be more precise, we can explain human captivity as having several causes. To begin with, we are captive to sin, which is our master.[33] Inescapably, we are in great debt, "whereof God is the creditor."[34] Therefore, we desperately need to have our sins forgiven (Matt. 6:12; 18:23–35). Owen explains, "Debt makes men liable to prison for non-payment; and so doth sin (without satisfaction made) to the prison of hell" (cf. Matt. 5:25–26).[35] Everyone, therefore, is a prisoner, enslaved to sin. "They are bound in the prison-house because they have wasted the goods of their Master, and contracted a debt that they are no way able to pay; and if it be not paid for them, there they must lie to eternity."[36]

Also, and most fundamentally, since it is against God that people have rebelled, transgressing God's law, the "principal cause of this captivity and imprisonment" is God.[37] Owen gives several reasons why:

1. God is the "creditor to whom these debts are due" (see Matt. 6:9–12; Ps. 51:4). Therefore, we owe a debt we can never repay.[38]
2. God is the "great king, judge, and governor of the world, who hath given his law for the rule of our obedience." To "sin is to rebel, and to transgress, and to perverse, to turn aside from the way, to cast off the yoke of the Lord" (see Gen. 18:25; Deut. 27:26; Pss. 1:6; 10:16; Rom. 1:32; James 2:10–12; 4:12). Therefore, "who should commit the rebel that offends, who should be the author of the captivity and imprisonment of the delinquent, but he who is the king, judge, and lawmaker?"[39]
3. God is the one who has "shut up all under disobedience" (Rom. 11:32), and they shall not be released unless satisfaction is made on their

---

[32] Ibid., 12:514. Do not be mistaken, however, into thinking that man is a poor victim. Quite the contrary, his captivity is willful, and he is a rebel against God and his kingdom.
[33] Elsewhere Owen also includes the "world" as something to which we are captive, based on Gal. 4:5 (ibid., 12:521).
[34] Ibid., 12:514.
[35] Ibid.
[36] Ibid., 12:514–15.
[37] Ibid., 12:515. Owen astutely avoids the caricature that would make God a tyrant who conquers, captures, and imprisons man. He explains, "God was not our detainer in captivity as a sovereign conqueror, that came upon us by force and kept us prisoners, but as a just judge and lawgiver, who had seized on us for our transgressions: so that not his power and will were to be treated withal, but his law and justice; and so the ransom was properly paid to him in the undergoing that penalty which his justice required" (ibid., 12:522; cf. 523).
[38] Ibid., 12:515.
[39] Ibid.

behalf (see Matt. 5:25; 18:21–35). Therefore, God is the one who can "cast both body and soul into hell fire" (Matt. 10:28; cf. 2 Thess. 1:9). "In brief, God is the judge, the law is the law of God; the sentence denounced is condemnation from God; the curse inflicted is the curse of God; the wrath wherewith men are punished is the wrath of God; he that finds a ransom is God: and therefore it is properly and strictly he to whom sinners are prisoners and captives" (see 2 Pet. 2:4).[40]

But what about Satan? Certainly Scripture says that we are in bondage to the Devil prior to our salvation. Owen agrees; Scripture often speaks of Christ's delivering the sinner from Satan, as, for example, in Colossians 1:13–14. But how, exactly, does God deliver us from the power of Satan? Owen answers:

> Even as he who delivers a captive from the judge by a price delivers him also from the jailer who kept him in prison. By his death (which, as hath been showed, was a price and a ransom), he deprived Satan of all his power over us; which is called his destroying of him, Heb. 2:14,—that is, not the devil as to his essence and being, but as to his power and authority over those who are made partakers of his death.[41]

Or, to state the matter differently, "legally, juridically, and authoritatively" our captivity is to God (for we are in debt to him), but instrumentally our captivity is to Satan, the law, and the fear of death (Heb. 2:14–15). Satan, in other words, is in "subservience to the authority" of God himself.[42]

Moreover, Owen's cautiousness in clarifying Satan's role also leads him to reject a ransom-to-Satan theory, as if Christ on the cross is paying a ransom price to Satan himself. Instead, Owen intentionally remains within the bounds of a satisfaction view of the atonement, while simultaneously refusing to diminish Scripture's emphasis on Christ's victory over Satan. For example, while acknowledging Satan's role in our captivity—one that is

---

[40] Ibid. For Owen, the biblical evidence that it is God who is paid this ransom is overwhelming: "He is the great householder that calls his servants, that do or should serve him, to an account, συνᾶραι λόγον, Matt. 18:23, 24; and wicked men are κατάρας τέκνα, 2 Pet. 2:14, the children of his curse, obnoxious to it. It is *his judgment* 'that they which commit sin are worthy of death,' Rom. 1:32; and Christ is a propitiation to 'declare *his righteousness*,' chap. 3:25; and it is *his wrath* from which we are delivered by this ransom, chap. 2:5, 1 Thess. 1:10; the *law was his* to which Christ was made obnoxious, Gal. 4:4; the *curse his* which he was made, chap. 3:13; it was his will he came to do and suffer, Heb. 10:7,—it was *his will* that he should drink off the cup of his passion, Matt. 26:42; it pleased him to bruise him, Isa. 53:10; he made all our iniquities to meet upon him, verse 6: so that, doubtless, this ransom was paid to him" (ibid., 12:523).
[41] Ibid., 12:519.
[42] Ibid., 12:517. Owen goes on to say that while our lawful captivity is *directly* to God and then Satan, the law, and the fear of death, it is *consequently*, or by accident, to sin and the world.

subordinate to God himself—Owen is certain to point out that the ransom price Christ pays is not to Satan but to God.[43] It is not Satan we have disobeyed, nor is he the judge who sentences us to prison, spiritually speaking. No, Satan is merely the jailer! Rather, it is God and his law that we have violated, and he is the Judge to whom we are accountable.

Furthermore, that the price is paid to God, not Satan, is manifested in what Christ accomplishes in regard to our sin. Titus 2:14 says that Christ gave himself for us, and thereby he "redeemed us from all iniquity" (cf. 1 Pet. 1:18–19). Owen observes that being redeemed from our sin involves two things: the *guilt* of our sins, "that they should not condemn us," and the *power* of our sins, "that they should not rule in us."[44] Concerning the former, Owen argues that we have been redeemed from the "curse of the law" (Gal. 3:13; cf. Deut. 27:26), and for the "redemption of transgressions" (Heb. 9:15). God is a God of justice, and his will and law are holy, which means he requires a punishment for sin. Therefore, Scripture can speak of the vengeance and wrath of God inflicted for sin (Rom. 1:18). His holy wrath is his "justice and indignation against sin."[45] Owen remarks, "In this sense, to 'redeem us from the curse of the law,' is to make satisfaction to the justice of God, from whence that curse doth arise, that it should not be inflicted on us."[46] Certainly Owen is highlighting the substitutionary and penal nature of the atonement. We are delivered from this penalty by "this ransom-paying of Christ," who takes our penalty and redeems us from the curse of the law by becoming a curse in our place (Gal. 3:13).

Finally, what about the "power" of our sin? This too, says Owen, is met by the cross. "Now, we are redeemed from the power of our sins by the blood of Christ, not immediately, but consequentially, as a captive is delivered from his fetters and filth upon the payment of his ransom." Owen continues:

> Christ's satisfying the justice of God, reconciling him to us by his death, hath also procured the gift of his Spirit for us, to deliver us from the power of our sins. The foundation of this being laid in the blood of Christ, and the price which thereby he paid, our delivery from our sins belongs to his redemption.[47]

---

[43] This ran contrary to Socinus, whom Owen quotes as saying that the ransom price was paid not to Satan or God, but to no one at all, since redemption is to be understood metaphorically (ibid., 12:519).
[44] Ibid.
[45] Ibid., 12:520.
[46] Ibid.
[47] Ibid.

In summary, such a serious and unbreakable captivity, based upon our debt due to sin, means that our only way of deliverance is through God himself providing a Deliverer who can pay our debt as prisoners and set us free to serve a new Master (see Rom. 3:23–25). Therefore, a satisfaction is necessary for redemption and ransom, which leads us to Owen's next two concepts: sacrifice and penalty.

Sacrifice

Already underlined in the death of Christ as a ransom that involves a *price* is the notion of *sacrifice*. Similarly, Owen's affirmation of Christ as the Great High Priest directs our attention to the death of Christ as a sacrificial offering (e.g., Heb. 8:3). "If he be a priest, he must have a sacrifice," explains Owen. "The whole and entire office and employment of a high priest, as a priest, consists in offering sacrifice, with the performance of those things which did necessarily precede and follow that action. It is of necessity, then, that he should also have somewhat to offer as a sacrifice to God."[48]

What is so shocking is that Christ, our Great High Priest, *is* the sacrifice. In other words, not only does Christ mediate on behalf of God's people, but, more precisely, he mediates *by* offering up himself unto death. Whereas the priest on the Day of Atonement (Lev. 16:30) made atonement for the people by offering the sacrifice, Christ comes both as the High Priest and as the sacrifice, undergoing the penalty of death for the forgiveness of our sins. And how necessary this was, for the blood of bulls and goats could not take away sin (Heb. 10:4).

> It cost more to redeem our souls. . . . The sacrifices instituted by the law could not effect or work that which Christ, our high priest, was to accomplish by his sacrifice; and therefore he was not to offer them, but they were to be abolished, and something else to be brought in that might supply their room and defect.[49]

Therefore, the sacrifices in the Old Testament pointed forward and were but a shadow of the final and ultimate sacrifice to come. Once again appealing to the imagery of the Day of Atonement (Leviticus 16), Owen explains, "This sacrifice of Christ was typified by the two goats: his body, whose blood was shed, by the goat that was slain visibly; and his soul by *azazel* [scapegoat],

---

[48] Ibid., 12:421.
[49] Ibid. As to why these Old Testament sacrifices could not take away sin, see ibid., 12:422–25.

on whose head the sins of the people were confessed, and he sent away into the wilderness, to suffer there by a fall or famishment."[50]

Deep within this idea of sacrifice is the concept of reconciliation. Owen defines reconciliation as "the renewal of lost friendship and peace between persons at variance."[51] Within the biblical storyline, reconciliation is front and center. In the beginning Adam and Eve were created in a state of friendship and peace with God. "God had no enmity against his creature; he approved him to be good, and appointed him to walk in peace, communion, confidence, and boldness with him, Gen. 2."[52] Likewise, man did not have any enmity against his "Creator, God, and Rewarder." Written on his heart was the "law and love of his Maker."[53]

Tragically, everything changed in an instant when Adam and Eve sinned. Nothing would be the same again. Suddenly there was division between God and the human race. There was a severe and irreparable separation, a "breach of peace and friendship." And with Adam, our federal representative, fell all of humankind (Rom. 5:12–19). Consequently, every one of us is a rebel against his Maker. As we read in Isaiah 59:2, "Your iniquities have separated between you and your God, and your sins have hid his face from you." And again, "There is no peace, saith my God, to the wicked" (Isa. 57:21).

What is the result of this breach? "By this breach of peace and friendship with God, God was alienated from the sinner, so as to be angry with him, and to renounce all peace and friendship with him."[54] Therefore, Jesus says in John 3:36, "He that believeth not . . . the wrath of God abideth on him." And as Paul says in Ephesians 2:3, by nature we are "children of wrath." All of mankind is "obnoxious to the wrath of God, that abides upon unbelievers."[55] The unbeliever, therefore, is the "unreconciled" person.

In order to understand this enmity, we need to grasp the significance of God's holiness and purity. God is perfect in holiness and therefore he "cannot admit a guilty, defiled creature to have any communion with him."[56] Furthermore, his holiness and justice demand the punishment of sin for breaking his law, and that punishment is death. As Paul explains in Romans 1:32, "It is the judgment of God, that they which commit sin are worthy of

---

[50] Ibid., 12:431.
[51] Ibid., 12:531.
[52] Ibid. On Owen's understanding of the covenant of works, see Sinclair B. Ferguson, *John Owen on the Christian Life* (Edinburgh: Banner of Truth, 1987), 22–24.
[53] Owen, *The Mystery of the Gospel*, in *Works*, 12:531.
[54] Ibid.
[55] Ibid., 12:532.
[56] Ibid.

death" (cf. 2 Thess. 1:6). Such a penalty was promised from the beginning (Gen. 2:17), and consequently everyone is cursed who is a lawbreaker (Deut. 27:26; Gal. 3:13). As a result, God's righteous wrath remains on every sinner (Ps. 1:4–6; Prov. 15:8–9), and he "prepares wrath and vengeance for them, to be inflicted in his appointed time" (Rom. 2:5).

To be clear, God is the offended party. Man, on the other hand, is the offender. Therefore, given what Owen has said about God's holiness and righteousness, if reconciliation is to take place there must be a propitiation that turns "away the anger of the person offended," bringing the "offender into favour with him again."[57] This propitiation takes place in the sacrificial death of God's Son, Christ Jesus. Romans 5:10 states, "When we were enemies, we were reconciled to God by the death of his Son." To be reconciled to God, says Owen, is to be "brought again into his favour." And how did this occur but by the death of Christ, whose sacrifice satisfied and appeased the wrath of God that we deserve. God displays his deep love for us in that while "we were yet sinners, Christ died for us" (Rom. 5:8). While we were still weak, Christ gave his life for us, the ungodly (Rom. 5:6). On that account, we have been "justified by the blood of Christ" (Rom. 5:9).

Therefore, Hebrews 10:26–27 highlights the great importance of Christ's sacrifice by explaining what an awful state we are left in without it. Where there is no sacrifice for sin, there "remaineth nothing to sinners but a certain fearful looking for judgment and fiery indignation, which shall devour the adversaries." How then, one might ask, can "this jealous God, this holy God and just Judge," command some to "beseech sinners to be reconciled to him"? Owen answers, "It is because he reconciles us to himself by Christ, or in Christ; that is, by Christ his anger is pacified, his justice satisfied, and himself appeased or reconciled to us."[58] Owen believes this is Paul's message in 2 Corinthians 5:18–21. Christ's death as a "sacrifice" means that he gave himself up to death, and in doing so he bore our transgressions. In Owen's words, God "hath made Christ to be sin for us,—that is, either a sacrifice for sin, or as sin,—by the imputation of our sin to him." But not only is our sin imputed to Christ; Christ's righteousness is also imputed to us. Therefore, Owen exclaims:

> He was "made sin for us," as we are "made the righteousness of God in
> him." Now, we are made the righteousness of God by the imputation of his

---

[57] Ibid.
[58] Ibid., 12:537.

righteousness to us: so was he made sin for us by the imputation of our sin to him. Now, for God to reconcile us to himself by imputing our sin to Christ, and thereon not imputing it to us, can be nothing but his being appeased and atoned towards us, with his receiving us into his favour, by and upon the account of the death of Christ.[59]

Penalty

Thus far Owen has outlined the nature of Christ's atonement as *price* and *sacrifice*. Yet there is a third category, namely, a *penalty* that characterizes the death of Christ. This third category gets to the heart of Owen's view of the atonement, which, as we have seen, is a penal-substitutionary view. Essential to this view is the concept of "penalty," that is, a penalty that must be paid on our behalf and for our sins.

Owen begins by defining punishment, in the most basic sense, as "an evil of suffering inflicted for doing evil." To elaborate, it is "an effect of justice in him who hath sovereign power and right to order and dispose of offenders, whereby he that doth contrary to the rule of his actions is recompensed with that which is evil to himself, according to the demerit of his fault."[60] Several things stand out in this definition.

First, punishment is an effect of divine justice. Scripture refers to God as inflicting his anger. For example, Paul asks in Romans 3:5, "Is God unrighteous, who inflicteth anger?" Or consider Romans 1:18: "The wrath of God is revealed from heaven." In other words, God's "vindictive justice against sin is manifested by its effects."[61]

Second, God, being God, has "sovereign power" and "judiciary right" to punish those who have offended him, broken his law, transgressed his commandments.[62] He does so directly (e.g., James 4:12) or through secondary causes (e.g., human rulers and governors; see John 19:11).

Third, the nature of this punishment consists in God's inflicting evil, either by "corrupting, vexing, and destroying," or by "the subtraction of that which is cheering, useful, good, and desirable."[63] Since sin is, by definition, a "transgression of the law," an "inconformity to the law," this punishment is just and deserved.[64] In short, there must be a "suffering of evil for doing evil."

---

[59] Ibid., 12:537–38.
[60] Ibid., 12:433.
[61] Therefore, we would be on target to substitute the word *vengeance* in a passage like Rom. 3:5 (ibid., 12:434).
[62] Ibid.
[63] Ibid.
[64] Ibid.

Fourth, punishment always is because of a procuring cause. This is what makes the punishment just, namely, that a wicked act was committed. There is an offender and his offense precedes punishment. Sin and punishment, therefore, go together, the former being the procuring cause of the latter.[65]

Fifth, the measure of the penalty is the "demerit of the offense." In other words, God is rendering to the offender what he deserves for his evil works. Thus, Paul can say in Romans 1:32 that those who commit sin "are worthy of death." Likewise, there is a judgment coming (Rom. 2:5–11), one in which the world will know God's justice and vengeance, whereby he will render to each person according to his deeds (Rom. 2:6).[66] All of this is to say that God, in punishing the wicked, satisfies his justice (Rom. 2:5–11).

But what does all of this have to do with the death of Christ? Owen explains that the death of Christ "was a punishment."[67] However, Christ was sinless. The prophet Isaiah notes that all of this suffering, all of this punishment, was not for Christ's own sin, for he "had done no violence, neither was any deceit in his mouth" (Isa. 53:9). Jesus was "perfectly innocent, so that he had no need of any chastisement for his amendment."[68] Therefore, it was not a punishment for his own sin. Instead, Christ was punished for the sins of God's elect. Christ, says Owen, was "punished and broken for us and our sins." He was wounded, bruised, chastised, cut off, killed, and slaughtered in order that he might be sacrificed, making an "offering for sin." He underwent such miserable affliction for the "justification and salvation of believers," as Isaiah 53:3–6 extensively demonstrates.[69]

Owen rejects the view that the punishment of Christ is merely an example to us (i.e., the moral-example theory of the atonement). Yes, says Owen, Christ set us an example by his obedience, but "he was not punished for an example." Rather, the text says, "He shall justify many, for he shall bear their iniquities" (Isa. 53:11). Therefore, the cross is about Christ's bearing the punishment of our sin, taking upon himself the wrath of God that

---

[65] Ibid., 12:435.
[66] Ibid., 12:437–38.
[67] Ibid., 12:439.
[68] Ibid., 12:441.
[69] Ibid. Owen spends considerable space refuting Grotius's interpretation of Isaiah 53 (see ibid., 12:455–85). Also see Owen, *A Review of the Annotations of Hugo Grotius in Reference unto the Doctrine of the Deity and Satisfaction of Christ; with a Defence of the Charge Formerly Laid against Them*, in Works, 12:617–39.

we deserve, so that we can be forgiven and justified in God's sight (Rom. 5:6–8; 1 Pet. 2:24).[70]

Given the substitutionary and penal nature of the cross, the word *propitiation* is especially important to Owen. Scripture says that God set forth Christ "to be a propitiation" by his blood (Rom. 3:25). Christ became a merciful and faithful High Priest to make reconciliation or propitiation for the sins of the people (Heb. 2:17). This is the very reason the Father, out of love for us, sent his Son to be the propitiation for our sins (1 John 4:10; cf. 2:2).[71] It is hard to think of a doctrine more precious and relevant to the Christian life than this one. As Owen observes:

> He [Christ] then took a view of all our sins and iniquities. He knew what was past and what was to come, knowing all our thoughts afar off. Not the least error of our minds, darkness of our understandings, perverseness of our wills, carnality of our affections, sin of our nature or lives, escaped him. . . . God, I say, made them all to meet on Christ, in the punishment due to them.[72]

The Covenant of Redemption

For Owen, this great doctrine of the atonement, which takes place in time and space on the cross, is also something that reveals the grand scheme of redemptive history. What Christ accomplished was planned in eternity past. A covenant was made between the Father and the Son for the sake of our salvation. In Reformed thought this covenant has been called the *pactum salutis*, or the "covenant of redemption."[73]

Owen sees this covenant of redemption (i.e., compact) as the very

---

[70] Owen, *The Mystery of the Gospel*, in *Works*, 12:442. Owen also makes his case from Lev. 16:5 (see ibid., 12:476–77).

[71] Owen also looks at Heb. 9:5, which tells us that "mercy seat" in the Old Testament is applied to Christ. Owen explains the connection: "The mercy-seat declared God to be appeased; but how? By the blood of the sacrifice that was offered without, and brought into the holy place. The high priest never went into that place about the worship of God but it was with the blood of that sacrifice, which was expressly appointed to make atonement, Lev. xvi. God would not have the mercy-seat once seen, nor any pledge of his being atoned, but by the blood of the propitiatory sacrifice. So it is here. God sets out Jesus Christ as a propitiation, and declares himself to be appeased and reconciled; but how? By the blood of Christ, by the sacrifice of himself, by the price of redemption which he paid. This is the intendment of the apostle: Christ by his blood, and the price he paid thereby, with the sacrifice he made, having atoned God, or made atonement with him for us, God now sets him forth, the veil of the temple being rent, to the eye of all believers, as the Mercy-seat wherein we may see God fully reconciled to us" (ibid., 12:529–30).

[72] Ibid., 12:448.

[73] The following will focus on Owen's *The Mystery of the Gospel*. However, Owen also treats the covenant of redemption in *The Person of Christ*, in *Works*, 1:55; and Owen, *Hebrews*, in *Works*, 18:42–97. On the covenant of redemption in Owen and his seventeenth-century context, see Trueman, *Claims of Truth*, 133–43; and Ferguson, *John Owen on the Christian Life*, 20–36. Also see Owen, *The Death of Death in the Death of Christ*, in *Works*, 10:170–200.

ground of Christ's mediation and punishment on our behalf. What took place in time and space was planned in eternity past, before the foundation of the world. Owen describes the covenant of redemption as that "compact, covenant, convention, or agreement, that was between the Father and the Son, for the accomplishment of the work of our redemption by the mediation of Christ, to the praise of the glorious grace of God."[74] Owen goes on to explain that it was the will of the Father to appoint the Son to be the "head, husband, deliver[er], and redeemer of his elect, his church, his people, whom he did foreknow," to which the Son responded voluntarily, "freely undertaking that work and all that was required thereunto."[75]

Several aspects of this covenant need unfolding. First, there is a "voluntary concurrence" and "distinct consent" between the Father and Son for the purpose of bringing about and accomplishing redemption, which brings sinners peace with God. "There are the Father and the Son as distinct persons agreeing together in counsel for the accomplishment of the common end,—the glory of God and the salvation of the elect."[76]

Second, this compact or covenant between the Father and Son means that the Son, Christ Jesus, submits himself to the Father's plan, which includes his sacrificial, atoning death on the cross. Or as Owen says:

> For the accomplishment of this work, the Father, who is principal in the covenant, the promiser, whose love "sets all on work," as is frequently expressed in Scripture, requires of the Lord Jesus Christ, his Son, that he shall do that which, upon consideration of his justice, glory, and honour, was necessary to be done for the bringing about the end proposed, prescribing to him a law for the performance thereof; which is called his "will" so often in Scripture.[77]

That Christ did fulfill his role in this regard is evident in a passage like Philippians 2:6–7: "Being in the form of God, and equal with God, he

---

[74] Owen clarifies, however, that there is but one will in God, corresponding to the one nature in God who is triune in person. Owen, *The Mystery of the Gospel*, in *Works*, 12:497. Also see Owen, *Hebrews*, in *Works*, 18:87–88.

[75] Owen, *The Mystery of the Gospel*, in *Works*, 12:497. Owen argues that biblical support is found in Heb. 10:7 and Ps. 40:7–8. In *The Death of Death in the Death of Christ*, in *Works*, 10:170, he also appeals to Isa. 49:6–12. On how the covenant of redemption grounds our election and justification, see Trueman, *Claims of Truth*, 133–42.

[76] Owen, *The Mystery of the Gospel*, in *Works*, 12:500–501. Passages Owen appeals to include Ps. 50:14; Prov. 8:22–31; Isa. 9:6; Zech. 6:13; 13:7; Heb. 2:9–10; 12:2.

[77] Ibid., 12:501.

made himself of no reputation, but took upon him the form of a servant, and was made in the likeness of men." "He did it," remarks Owen, "upon his Father's prescription, and in pursuit of what God required at his hands."[78] Therefore, Christ comes to do and accomplish the will of the Father (Heb. 10:9).

Third, the Father makes many promises to the Son for the purpose of accomplishing this work of redemption. For example, given the extreme difficulty Christ will have to undergo, the Father promises his presence, which will carry Christ "through all perplexities and trials."[79] As he prophesies through the prophet Isaiah, "I the LORD have called thee in righteousness, and will hold thy hand, and will keep thee, and give thee for a covenant of the people" (see Isa. 42:6). And again in Psalm 16:10, "I will not leave thy soul in hell, nor suffer mine Holy One to see corruption." Or consider Psalm 89:28: "My mercy will I keep for him for evermore, and my covenant shall stand fast with him." The Father promises, in other words, that he will not forsake his Son in his work, but will carry him through, support him, and uphold him until he successfully accomplishes that for which he was sent.[80]

Owen also observes that these promises guaranteed the Father's preservation both of the Son and of the work itself, namely, that it would "thrive and prosper in his hand" (Ps. 22:30–31; Isa. 53:10–11). On this basis, says Owen, Hebrews 12:2 can say that for the "joy that was set before him [Christ]"—that is, the joy of "bringing many sons unto glory"—"he endured the cross, and despised the shame" (Isa. 42:1–4).[81]

Fourth, the Lord Jesus delightfully and with great pleasure and joy accepts the condition and the promise of his Father in this covenant. Owen applies Psalm 40:7–8 to Christ: "Then said I, Lo, I come: . . . I delight to do thy will, O my God: yea, thy law is within my heart" (cf. Isa. 50:5; Phil. 2:6–8).[82]

Fifth, the Father, as the one who has made such promises, accepts and approves the performance of the Son that he has prescribed (Isa. 49:5–9). Owen especially sees this last truth in the resurrection of Christ from the grave. Owen appeals to Acts 13:33 and explains, "God by the resurrection

---

[78] Ibid., 12:502.
[79] Ibid., 12:504.
[80] Ibid.
[81] Ibid.
[82] Owen also notes that Christ's compact was voluntary, but once he committed to it, he was then obligated (ibid., 12:505).

from the dead gloriously manifested him to be his Son, whom he loved, in whom he was well pleased, and who did all his pleasure."[83]

Why is this covenant of redemption so important? It is important, Owen explains, because it not only demonstrates the eternal and Trinitarian nature of our salvation, but is also the very foundation, the rock upon which our redemption is then accomplished. Owen argues:

> Here lies the ground of the righteousness of the dispensation treated of, that Christ should undergo the punishment due to us: It was done voluntarily, of himself, and he did nothing but what he had power to do, and command from his Father to do. "I have power," saith he, "to lay down my life, and I have power to take it again; this commandment have I received of my Father"; whereby the glory both of the love and justice of God is exceedingly exalted.[84]

The Extent of the Atonement

What has been under the surface and certainly engrafted into everything we have said so far is Owen's understanding of the extent and efficacy of the atonement. In perhaps one of his most famous (and rigorous!) books, *The Death of Death in the Death of Christ*, Owen makes a biblical, theological, and logical case for the particularity of Christ's work on the cross, namely, that Christ died only for God's elect.[85] As Trueman observes, for Owen, "Christ's death is part of his priesthood; his priesthood is part of his mediatorial office; and the mediatorial office is created and defined by the covenant of redemption."[86] Therefore, there is a direct line from the covenant of redemption to the efficacy of the atonement. The Son, before

---

[83] Ibid., 12:506. Owen also observes that though the compact was one of grace, the reward is of debt. "Look, then, whatever God promised Christ upon his undertaking to be a Saviour, that, upon the fulfilling of his will, he merited. That himself should be exalted, that he should be the head of his church, that he should see his seed, that he should justify and save them, sanctify and glorify them, were all promised to him, all merited by him" (ibid., 12:508).

[84] Ibid., 12:507. The covenant of redemption reminds us once again that for Owen our salvation, whether in election, atonement, or justification, has an intentional Trinitarian and christological structure. See Trueman, *Claims of Truth*, 138–39.

[85] Owen, *The Death of Death in the Death of Christ*, in *Works*, 10:139–428. For a more succinct case, see Owen, *A Display of Arminianism*, in *Works*, 10:87–100. The best introduction to Owen on the extent of the atonement is J. I. Packer, *A Quest for Godliness: The Puritan Vision of the Christian Life* (Wheaton, IL: Crossway, 1990), 125–48. See also Andrew David Naselli, "John Owen's Argument for Definite Atonement in *The Death of Death in the Death of Christ*: A Brief Summary and Evaluation," *Southern Baptist Journal of Theology* 14, no. 4 (2010): 60–82; and Carl R. Trueman, "Atonement and the Covenant of Redemption: John Owen on the Nature of Christ's Satisfaction," in *From Heaven He Came and Sought Her: Definite Atonement in Historical, Biblical, and Theological Perspective*, ed. David Gibson and Jonathan Gibson (Wheaton, IL: Crossway, 2013), 201–26.

[86] Trueman, *Claims of Truth*, 205.

the foundation of the world, compacted with the Father that he would, at the proper time, and due to human sinfulness, offer himself up as an atoning sacrifice for those whom the Father predestined. In short, those whom the Father elected, the Son agreed to ransom. Owen explains, "Christ died for them whom God gave unto him to be saved: 'Thine they were, and thou gavest them me,' John 17:6. He layeth down his life for the sheep committed to his charge, chap. 10:11."[87] This covenant of redemption, which results in the atonement, was designed not to make men savable, but to actually save all those whom the Father had chosen before the foundation of the world.[88]

Certainly the particularity and efficacy of the atonement follow from everything Owen has said about Christ thus far. They follow from Christ's inauguration of the new covenant.

> The proper counsel and intention of God in sending his Son into the world to die was, that thereby he might confirm and ratify the new covenant to his elect, and purchase for them all the good things which are contained in the tenure of that covenant. . . . that by his death he might bring many (yet some certain) children to glory, obtaining for them that were given unto him by his Father (that is, his whole church) reconciliation with God, remission of sins, faith, righteousness, sanctification, and life eternal.[89]

As John 17:2 says, Christ died to "give eternal life to as many as God gave him."

The particularity and efficacy of the atonement also follow from Christ's role as High Priest and Mediator. "He is an 'advocate' for every one for whose sins his blood was a 'propitiation,' 1 John 2:1, 2," and "he 'maketh intercession' only for them who 'come unto God by him,' Heb. 7:25."[90] Christ, as Mediator, "doth not intercede and pray for all, as himself often witnesseth, John 17; he 'made intercession' only for them who 'come unto God by him,' Heb. 7:25."[91] Therefore, since Christ, as High Priest, "doth not intercede and pray for every one, he did not die for every one."[92]

Particular redemption follows from the nature of the cross as a penal

---

[87] Owen also appeals to John 10:28–29 and 17:2. Owen, *A Display of Arminianism*, in *Works*, 10:92.

[88] How drastically different this is from the Arminian view, which, as Owen explains, argues that (1) "Christ died for all and every one," and (2) "he died for no one man at all in that sense Christians have hitherto believed that he laid down his life, and submitted himself to bear the burden of his Father's wrath for their sakes" (ibid., 10:88; also see 10:94–97).

[89] Ibid., 10:90.

[90] Ibid., 10:91.

[91] Ibid.

[92] Ibid., 10:92.

and substitutionary satisfaction and atonement as well. The one who truly limits the atonement is not the Calvinist, but the Arminian. The Arminian, argues Owen, limits the efficacy of the atonement in making it for everyone, including those who never believe. "For though the Arminians pretend, very speciously, that Christ died for all men, yet, in effect, they make him die for no one man at all."[93] On the contrary, says Owen, Scripture teaches that Christ actually substituted himself for specific sinners and in doing so bore the wrath that they deserve, taking the penalty for their sin. Given the penal and substitutionary nature of the cross, Owen "cannot conceive an intention in God that Christ should satisfy his justice for the sin of them that were in hell some thousands of years before, and yet be still resolved to continue their punishment on them to all eternity." "No, doubtless: Christ giveth life to every one for whom he gave his life; he loseth not one of them whom he purchased with his blood."[94] As Scripture teaches:

> Christ hath, by his righteousness, merited for us grace and glory; that we are blessed with all spiritual blessings, in, through, and for him; that he is made unto us righteousness, and sanctification, and redemption; that he hath procured for us, and that God for his sake bestoweth on us, every grace in this life that maketh us differ from others, and all that glory we hope for in that which is to come; he procured for us remission of all our sins, an actual reconciliation with God, faith, and obedience.[95]

It is clear, therefore, that Christ "died to procure for us an actual reconciliation with God, and not only a power for us to be reconciled unto him" (see Rom. 3:24–25; 5:10; 2 Cor. 5:21; Heb. 9:15).[96]

What do the extent and efficacy of the atonement have to do with the Christian life? Everything! First, Owen appeals to every Christian's conscience,

> whether they do not suppose the very foundation of all their consolation to be stricken at, when they shall find those places of Scripture [Heb. 9:12–28; Isa. 53:10; 1 John 2:2, etc.] that affirm Christ to have died to take away our sins, to reconcile us unto God, to put away or abolish our transgres-

---

[93] Ibid., 10:93.
[94] Ibid., 10:88.
[95] Ibid., 10:93.
[96] Ibid., 10:97.

sions, to wash and regenerate us, perfectly to save us, and purchase for us an everlasting redemption, whereby he is become unto us righteousness, and redemption, and sanctification, the Lord our righteousness, and we become the righteousness of God in him, to be so wrested as if he should be said only to have done something from which these things might happily follow?[97]

Second, if we deny this doctrine, do we not impair our love for Christ and weaken our faith in Christ? Indeed, this is exactly what happens when God's people are taught that

> Christ hath done no more for them than for those that are damned in hell; that, be their assurance never so great that Christ died for them, yet there is enough to be laid to their charge to condemn them; that though God is said to have reconciled them unto himself in Christ, Col. 1:19, 20, yet indeed he is as angry with them as with any reprobate in the world; that God loveth us not first, but so long as we continue in a state of enmity against him, before our conversion, he continues our enemy also, so that the first act of friendship or love must be performed on our part, notwithstanding that the Scripture saith, "When we were enemies, we were reconciled unto God," Rom. 5:10?[98]

Third, and most personally, the efficacy and particularity of the atonement grounds our assurance that Christ did, indeed, die *for us*. Owen asks

> whether they have not hitherto supposed themselves bound to believe that Christ died for their sins, and rose for their justification? Do they not think it lawful to pray that God would bestow upon them grace and glory for Christ's sake? and to believe that Jesus Christ was such a mediator of the new covenant as procured for the persons covenanted withal all the good things comprehended in the promise of that covenant?[99]

Conclusion

Carl Trueman has boldly claimed that Owen's theology "seeks all means at its disposal to place Christ at the centre of a soteriological scheme

---

[97] Ibid., 10:98.
[98] Ibid.
[99] Ibid.

determined by a Trinitarian God."[100] It is difficult to think of a doctrine where Christ is more central than in his atonement and satisfaction on behalf of sinners. Indeed, the cross of Christ is the focal point and most important event in the drama of redemption. For in it the Christian finds life eternal.

---

[100] Trueman, *Claims of Truth*, 231.

CHAPTER 6

SALVATION BELONGS TO THE LORD

Amidst all our afflictions and temptations, under whose pressure we should else faint and despair, it is no small comfort to be assured that we do nor can suffer nothing but what his hand and counsel guides unto us, what is open and naked before his eyes, and whose end and issue he knoweth long before; which is a strong motive to patience, a sure anchor of hope, a firm ground of consolation. [1]

One of the most difficult obstacles surrounding the word *predestination* is that when people hear it, they often assume the worst. Predestination is thought to be a cold, dark, awful doctrine, and most definitely absent from Scripture. After all, could there be a doctrine more harmful and antithetical to the love at the heart of the Christian life? But when we open the Scriptures we see a very different picture. For example, in Ephesians 1 Paul not only teaches the doctrine of predestination, but also uses some of the most beautiful, warm, Trinitarian, and gospel-saturated language to do so! John Owen knew this truth well. For him, predestination was not some abstract doctrine, unrelated to the Christian life, but the muscle behind it.

---

[1] Owen, *A Display of Arminianism*, in *Works*, 10:29.

Poor Naked Truth

Owen was deeply bothered by the Arminianism of his age. Looking back on the debate over divine sovereignty and human freedom among the British divines, particularly with the rise of Arminianism under William Laud, Owen concluded that Arminianism "beat poor naked truth into a corner"[2] by stripping God of his power and instead giving man "self-sufficiency" and autonomous freedom. Therefore, Owen took up his pen, defending divine sovereignty in salvation in the midst of this heated polemical context. The book he devoted to the issue was A Display of Arminianism, first published in 1643.[3]

In it he says, first, that Arminians "exempt themselves from God's jurisdiction" and "free themselves from the supreme dominion of his all-ruling providence." Human beings, they argue, do not live and move in God, but instead have "an absolute independent power in all their actions, so that the event of all things wherein they have any interest might have a considerable relation to nothing but chance, contingency, and their own wills."[4] It should not surprise us that Owen sees such a view as "most nefarious" and "sacrilegious"! Owen considers his reaction justified given four beliefs of his opponents. To be fair, Owen does acknowledge that some of these are not directly taught by Arminians but rather are consequences of their views that, in Owen's mind, cannot be avoided.[5]

To begin with, argues Owen, "they deny the eternity and unchangeableness of God's decrees." If the purposes of the "Strength of Israel" are eternal and immutable, then "free-will must be limited, their independency prejudiced." So instead Arminians argue that God's decrees must be "temporary and changeable." Furthermore, when he does change his decrees, he does so "according to the several mutations he sees in us."

Additionally, "they question the prescience or foreknowledge of God."

---

[2] Ibid., 10:4, 8.
[3] In Puritan fashion, Owen's full title conveys his discontent: A Display of Arminianism: Being a discovery of the old Pelagian idol free will, with the new goddess contingency, advancing themselves into the throne of the God of heaven, to the prejudice of his grace, providence, and supreme dominion over the children of men; wherein the main errors by which they are fallen off from the received doctrine of all the Reformed Churches, with their opposition in divers particulars to the doctrine established in the Church of England, are discovered and laid open out of their own writings and confessions, and confuted by the Word of God.
[4] Owen, A Display of Arminianism, in Works, 10:12.
[5] Some have criticized Owen for portraying the theology of Arminianism in a way that is Pelagian or semi-Pelagian rather than accurately describing the theology of Arminius (who was not Pelagian). While it is true enough that Arminius was not teaching Pelagianism, this criticism of Owen tends to ignore Owen's context. We must remember that Owen is responding specifically to the Arminianism and Arminians of his own day, which at times did look Pelagian and semi-Pelagian, detracting from Arminius on certain points, though being consistent with him on others.

If God knows all things that come to pass, then there is an "infallibility of event upon all their actions, which encroaches upon the large territory of their new goddess, contingency." Exhaustive foreknowledge, in other words, would "quite dethrone the queen of heaven, and induce a kind of necessity of our doing all, and nothing but what God foreknows."[6]

Moreover, "they depose the all-governing providence of this King of nations." How do they do this? By denying his "energetical, effectual power, in turning the hearts, ruling the thoughts, determining the wills, and disposing the actions of men." They grant nothing to his providence "but a general power and influence, to be limited and used according to the inclination and will of every particular agent; so making Almighty God a desirer that many things were otherwise than they are, and an idle spectator of most things that are done in the world."

Also, "they deny the irresistibility and uncontrollable power of God's will." Instead, they affirm that

> oftentimes he seriously willeth and intendeth what he cannot accomplish, and so is deceived of his aim; nay, whereas he desireth and really intendeth, to save every man, it is wholly in their own power whether he shall save any one or no; otherwise their idol free-will should have but a poor deity, if God could, how and when he would, cross and resist him in his dominion.[7]

Second, the "new doctrine of the Arminians" aims to "clear human nature from the heavy imputation of being sinful, corrupted, wise to do evil but unable to do good." Their aim is to "vindicate unto themselves a power and ability of doing all that good which God can justly require to be done by them." On this basis, Owen criticizes them because they have ascribed the "first and chiefest part in the work of their salvation" to themselves.[8] They do this by rejecting unconditional election, as well as by denying original sin and the efficacy of the death of Christ. They do not claim that free will has a "saving power, but they do want to affirm that it is "very active and operative in the great work of saving our souls." How so? First, says Owen,

---

[6] Later, however, Owen qualifies that the Arminians have not technically denied God's foreknowledge, but rather it is something he believes they cannot affirm, given their view of human freedom, as well as their view of God's decrees. See Owen, *A Display of Arminianism*, in *Works*, 10:22. For Owen's critique, see ibid., 10:22–30.

[7] These four points can be found in ibid., 10:12.

[8] Owen is so angered by how such a move ascribes the credit of salvation to man rather than God that he calls it a "proud Luciferian endeavour!" (ibid., 10:13).

they believe free will prepares us for the grace of God, so much so that grace is due to us! Second, it takes an active role in the "effectual working of our conversion."[9]

While far more could be said, these points introduce us to the type of Arminianism Owen confronts in the seventeenth century and the type of consequences he believes follow from it. Now we must see how Owen responds and why he believes getting all of this right actually has a significant impact upon the Christian life.

The Decrees of God

Christians throughout the ages have believed that God's decrees are unchangeable and irrevocable, Owen argues. But now the Arminians have started questioning such a belief, instead ascribing "mutability to the divine essence."[10] First, God's purpose, they say, is diverse and even dependent upon us. In the ordering of God's decrees, some of his purposes precede our actions, and some of them follow our actions. This distinction in God's decrees is described as God's *antecedent will* and his *consequent will*. Take election, for example. Antecedent to God foreseeing who will and will not believe, he wills that all people be saved. However, consequent to foreseeing that some will reject him and others will place their faith in him, he wills the election of those whom he foresees will believe.

Owen regards such a view as seriously problematic, for it compromises the eternal and immutable nature of God's saving purpose. God does not develop a second decree, which surely could not be eternal, once he sees that his first decree will fail. Far from it. Paul says that we were "chosen before the foundation of the world" (Eph. 1:4; cf. 2 Tim. 1:9; 2 Pet. 1:10), and that God's choice in election is not based on anything Jacob or Esau will do, so that his purpose might stand (Rom. 9:11).[11] God's purpose of salvation and his decision to save are not thwarted or dependent on what we will do. If it were, then it would be subject to change, and it could not be called eternal.

Therefore, when the question is asked, Does anything come into God's mind that changes his will? Owen rejects the answer of Arminius: "Yes. He would have all men to be saved; but, compelled with the stubborn and incorrigible malice of some, he will have them to miss it."[12] Such a response,

---

[9] Ibid., 10:13–14.
[10] Ibid., 10:14.
[11] Ibid., 10:16.
[12] Ibid.

Owen remarks, denies "God a power to do what he will" and it instead belittles God as one who must be "contented to do what he may, and not much repine at his hard condition."[13] In short, God is made our debtor. We can make our own election void. We can frustrate God's original purpose and intention. But Owen is confident that God is sovereign and his saving purpose will not fail or falter. Those whom he has chosen will be redeemed, for he has not elected them based on foreseen faith or foreseen perseverance in that faith, but purely on the basis of his good pleasure and will. Accordingly, God's decrees are eternal and immutable, everlasting and unshakable.[14]

Furthermore, Owen differentiates between God's *secret will* and God's *revealed will*, concepts Owen believes go a long way in helping us understand both the biblical text and God's operation in our daily lives. To appreciate this distinction, we must grasp Owen's dissatisfaction with the Arminian view.

> For having made his decrees mutable, his prescience fallible, and almost quite divested him of his providence, as the sum and issue of all their endeavours, they affirm that his will may be resisted, he may fail of his intentions, be frustrate of his ends,—he may and doth propose such things as he neither doth nor can at any time accomplish, and that because the execution of such acts of his will might haply clash against the freedom of the will of men.[15]

For Owen, this view is unacceptable, especially given what we have seen from Scripture already, namely, that God is in heaven and does whatever he pleases (Ps. 115:3).

So what does Owen suggest instead? He recommends the Reformed distinction between God's secret and revealed wills.[16] Owen defines both:

> The secret will of God is his eternal, unchangeable purpose concerning all things which he hath made, to be brought by certain means to their

---

[13] Ibid.

[14] Owen supports his argument by appealing to 1 Sam. 15:29; Job 23:13; Ps. 115:3; Isa. 14:24–27; 46:10; 48:14; Heb. 6:17.

[15] Owen, *A Display of Arminianism*, in *Works*, 10:44.

[16] Since God has only one will, and this will cannot be divided, Owen is careful to qualify himself. By "distinction" he refers to the "signification of the word" rather than "of the thing." For more on this qualification, see ibid. Later Owen makes it clear that he is not incredibly impressed with the phrases "*secret* will" and "*revealed* will," but nonetheless uses them. Here we see the limitations of our language to describe the complexity of God's will (see ibid., 10:45).

appointed ends: of this himself affirmeth, that "his counsel shall stand, and he will do all his pleasure," (Isa. 46:10). This some call the absolute, efficacious will of God, the will of his good pleasure, always fulfilled; and indeed this is the only proper, eternal, constant, immutable will of God, whose order can neither be broken nor its law transgressed, so long as with him there is neither change nor shadow of turning.

The revealed will of God containeth not his purpose and decree, but our duty,—not what he will do according to his good pleasure, but what *we* should do if we will please him; and this, consisting in his word, his precepts and promises, belongeth to us and our children, that we may do the will of God.[17]

We see this distinction at work in regard to both "acts and their objects." First, consider "acts." On the one hand, the secret will of God can be identified with his "eternal decree and determination concerning any thing to be done in its appointed time." On the other hand, God's revealed will is an "act whereby he declareth himself to love or approve any thing, whether ever it be done or no." Second, consider the "objects" of these acts. "The object of God's purpose and decree is that which is good in any kind, with reference to its actual existence, for it must infallibly be performed." However, the object of his revealed will "is that only which is morally good (I speak of it inasmuch as it approveth or commandeth), agreeing to the law, and the gospel, and that considered only inasmuch as it is good." But do not miss the difference. God's moral will or revealed will does not concern "whether it be ever actually performed or no," for this is "accidental to the object of God's revealed will."[18]

This distinction alone can do justice to the diversity of biblical texts. For example, in Genesis 22 we read that God orders Abraham to sacrifice his son Isaac, and that it is "well-pleasing unto God that he should accomplish what he was enjoined." By preparing to sacrifice his son, Abraham is obeying the will of God. But as the event unfolds, God stops Abraham short, commanding him not to lay a hand on the boy. "The event plainly

---

[17] To clarify, the former is referred to as God's "secret" will, but there are ways in which it is not always secret. (1) There are places in Scripture where God chooses to make manifest his decree. Surely this is the case with the future resurrection of the dead, for example. And many more examples could be multiplied (e.g., return of Christ, final judgment). (2) Though his secret will remains secret, once it is accomplished in time and space, then it has been made known. Therefore, we can know God's secret will after the fact, particularly by its effects. For example, Joseph, looking back and seeing the effects of God's providence, can say that though his brothers intended evil, it was God's will (Gen. 45:5) (see ibid.). For an excellent contemporary defense of these distinctions, see John Piper, *Does God Desire All to Be Saved?* (Wheaton, IL: Crossway, 2013).
[18] Owen, *A Display of Arminianism*, in *Works*, 10:47.

manifesteth that it was the will of God that Isaac should not be sacrificed."[19] If we understand God's will in only one simple sense, then we have a divine contradiction. But if we understand that on the one hand it was God's *revealed* will, his moral command and precept, for Abraham to sacrifice his son, while on the other hand, according to his *secret* will (sometimes referred to as his decretive will), the incident was a test of Abraham's faith and God intended to stop the sacrifice short all along, then the tension or contradiction is resolved.

Likewise, consider God's actions with Pharaoh. On the one hand, God commands Pharaoh to let his people go. This is God's moral, revealed will at play. In fact, when Pharaoh rebels against God's command, he is sinning, for it has clearly been presented to him as God's will. At the same time, we see God's secret will at work, for God tells Moses, even before Moses goes to Pharaoh, that he will harden Pharaoh's heart. Or as Owen states, "Yet God affirms that he would harden his heart, that he should not suffer them to depart until he had showed his signs and wonders in the land of Egypt."[20]

God's secret will and revealed will are again indisputable in the proclamation of the gospel. On the one hand, God commands all to believe, reflecting his revealed will. But whether it is God's purpose that certain sinners believe, and that he create faith in them so that they do believe, is left up to God's secret will. Where the gospel is preached, people are commanded to believe, and where they in fact do believe, then God's revealed and secret will coincide. But this is not always the case, as there are many times when he commands sinners to repent and believe but they do not, nor is it his will—his secret will that is—for them to do so. Indeed, many "are commanded to believe on whom God never bestoweth faith."[21]

Therefore, we must distinguish between our moral duty (made evident in God's revealed will) and his divine intention (which is hidden from us, left to his secret will). For example, consider Judas. According to God's revealed will, it was Judas's duty to believe and follow Christ. When he did not do so he sinned, and we can say in the most genuine sense that he violated God's revealed will. However, was it God's purpose and will all along that Judas betray Christ for the purposes of bringing to fruition his

---

[19] Ibid., 10:44.
[20] Ibid., 10:45.
[21] Ibid., 10:47.

plan of salvation through the cross of Christ?[22] Absolutely! Owen, quoting Gregory, writes, "'Many fulfil the will of God' (that is, his intentions) 'when they think to change it' (by transgressing his precepts); 'and by resisting imprudently, obey God's purpose.'"[23]

Owen, therefore, has no patience for those who claim that "God may fail in his purposes, come short of what he earnestly intendeth, or be frustrated of his aim and end: as if, [when] he should determinately resolve the faith and salvation of any man, it is in the power of that man to make void his determination, and not believe, and not be saved."[24] Scripture gives us a very different picture of God. He is the omnipotent God. Therefore, when he converts sinners by his grace he does so efficaciously. He cannot fail for he is the one whose counsel will stand and who will do all that he pleases (Isa. 46:10; Dan. 4:25).[25]

The Providence of God

Owen's affirmation of God's eternal and immutable decrees, as well as his exhaustive foreknowledge of the future, means that his providence is meticulous, sovereign, and infallible.[26] Not only is God's decree, issued before the foundation of the world, indestructible, unwavering, and irreversible, but his implementation of that plan in time and space is equally unfailing and effectual. He is a God who "worketh all things according to his decree, or the counsel of his will" (Eph. 1:11; cf. Ps. 115:3).[27]

Owen defines the providence of God as his ineffable act or work "whereby he cherisheth, sustaineth, and governeth the world, or all things by him created, moving them, agreeably to those natures which he endowed them withal in the beginning, unto those ends which he hath proposed."[28] Owen believes that God's providential control and reign extend to all people, and over both good and evil. His "eyes are in every place, beholding the evil and the good" (Prov. 15:3) and "none can hide himself in secret places that he shall not see him" (Jer. 23:24; cf. Ex. 4:11; Job 5:10–11; Acts 17:24). Indeed, he is the one who "formeth the light, and createth dark-

---

[22] Ibid., 10:48.
[23] Ibid.
[24] Ibid., 10:49.
[25] Ibid., 10:51.
[26] For an in-depth treatment of Owen on divine providence, see Carl R. Trueman, *The Claims of Truth: John Owen's Trinitarian Theology* (Carlisle: Paternoster, 1998), 102–50.
[27] Owen, *A Display of Arminianism*, in *Works*, 10:31.
[28] Ibid.

ness: he maketh peace, and createth evil: he doeth all these things" (Isa. 45:6–7).[29] Therefore, the wicked do not escape his purview, his dominion, and his "almighty hand."

However, God's universal and common governance does not preclude his acting in a special way toward particular people. He has a unique love and care for his church on earth, whom he governs and among whom he "most eminently showeth his glory, and exerciseth his power." His care for his church is steadfast and a steady stronghold against the gates of hell (Matt. 16:18; 28:20). He forbids any to "touch his anointed ones" (Ps. 105:15), for they are the "apple of his eye" (Zech. 2:8).[30]

On the basis of these biblical truths, Owen points out several different ways God exercises his providential control in the universe. First, he *sustains* all things. God is "sustaining, preserving, and upholding of all things by his power" (Heb. 1:3), and by his power he continues "their being, natural strength, and faculties, bestowed on them at their creation" (Acts 17).[31] In sustaining all things God often works with and through secondary causes.[32]

Additionally, God *determines* all things—even those things that appear to be random (Job 14:5; Prov. 16:33)—and he does so for his own glory.[33] Owen states, "His supreme dominion exerciseth itself in disposing of all things to certain and determinate ends for his own glory, and is chiefly discerned advancing itself over those things which are most contingent, and making them in some sort necessary, inasmuch as they are certainly disposed of to some proposed ends."[34]

Furthermore, God works effectually in men's wills to bring his eternal purposes to pass, but he does so in a way that they are not compelled but remain free and willing agents. According to Owen, God has predestined all things, and he works effectually to bring all things to their appointed end.

---

[29] Ibid., 10:32–33.
[30] Ibid., 10:33.
[31] Ibid., 10:34–35.
[32] Ibid., 10:35. Therefore, says Owen, two extremes must be avoided: "So that he doth neither work all himself in them, without any co-operation of theirs, which would not only turn all things into stocks, yea, and take from stocks their own proper nature, but also is contrary to that general blessing he spread over the face of the whole world in the beginning, 'Be fruitful, and multiply,' Gen. 1:22;—nor yet leave them to a self-subsistence, he in the meantime only not destroying them; which would make him an idle spectator of most things in the world, not to 'work hitherto,' as our Saviour speaks, and grant to divers things here below an absolute being, not derivative from him: the first whereof is blasphemous, the latter impossible" (ibid., 34–35).
[33] Owen also appeals to: Achan in Josh. 7:16–18; Saul in 1 Sam. 10:2–21; Jonathan in 1 Sam. 14:41–42; Jonah in Jonah 1:7; Matthias in Acts 1:26.
[34] Owen, *A Display of Arminianism*, in *Works*, 10:35.

This includes the wills of men. It is not that they are "compelled," but rather they are "inclined and disposed to do this or that, according to their proper manner or working, that is, most freely." Such control cannot be chalked up to a "naked permission," as if it were a government merely of "external actions" or "general influence." To the contrary, not even the innermost chamber of the human heart is hidden from God's providential control.[35]

Owen was opposed to those who sought to elevate the human will to such an extent that it was autonomous and outside divine determination. To be clear, Owen does not deny human freedom. As seen already, individuals do choose most freely, but freedom is never to be defined as liberation from God's providence. Owen appeals to Augustine, who blamed Cicero for teaching a type of freedom that made people sacrilegious "by denying them to be subject to an overruling providence." This, says Owen, is a "gross error."[36] Such a view ascribes to a person's will an "independent liberty," yes, even independent of God. Though God has his purposes and seeks to accomplish his plans, man decides by his own power whether he will do them or not, and there is nothing God can do about it. Such a power of the will exempts individuals from "any effectual working or influence of the providence of God into the will itself, that should sustain, help, or co-operate with it in doing or willing any thing."[37]

From Owen's point of view, a divine providence that is not exhaustive, meticulous, and powerful, but "general and indifferent" in its influence, "always waiting and expecting the will of man to determine itself to this or that effect, good or bad" is unbiblical.[38] Such a God is "always ready at hand to do that small part which he hath in our actions, whensoever we please to use him, or, if we please to let him alone, he no way moveth us to the performance of any thing."[39] Owen believes this view effectively removes God from his throne, and instead institutes the human will as the commander in chief. In contrast, Scripture depicts a God who acts effectually and powerfully, influencing the wills and actions of men, even directing them to a "voluntary performance of what he hath determined."[40]

Owen has a number of arguments that establish his point. In "innumerable places it is punctual that his providence doth not only bear rule

---

[35] Ibid., 10:36.
[36] Ibid.
[37] Ibid., 10:37.
[38] Ibid. For Owen's elaboration on the Arminian view, see ibid., 10:40.
[39] Ibid., 10:37.
[40] Ibid.

in the counsels of men and their most secret resolutions," but also prove "effectual even in the hearts and wills of men to turn them which way he will, and to determine them to this or that in particular, according as he pleaseth." Concerning the former, the counsels of men, Owen appeals to texts like Jeremiah 10:23, where we learn that "the way of man is not in himself" and that "it is not in man that walketh to direct his steps." Or consider Solomon, who says that "a man's heart deviseth his way, but the LORD directeth his steps" (Prov. 16:9). David likewise states that "the LORD bringeth the counsel of the heathen to nought" and "maketh the devices of the people of none effect," but "his own counsel standeth for ever, the thoughts of his heart to all generations" (Ps. 33:10–11; cf. 2 Sam. 15:31). Concerning the latter, the hearts and wills of men, Owen also finds support from Proverbs 16:1, "The preparations of the heart in man, and the answer of the tongue, is from the LORD." Owen is baffled by how the Arminian, were he to apply his views consistently, would have to interpret Jacob's prayer in Genesis 43:14. His prayer would have to sound like this: "Grant, O Lord, such a general influence of thy providence, that the heart of that man may be turned to good towards my sons, or else that it may not, being left to its own freedom."[41] But, says Owen, what a "strange request"! Certainly Jacob prayed and believed that it was in God's power to "incline and unalterably turn and settle the heart of Joseph to favour his brethren."[42] Therefore, Solomon can say that "the king's heart is in the hand of the LORD like the rivers of water: he turneth it whithersoever he will" (Prov. 21:1).

Additionally, throughout Scripture the saints pray and ask that God would be pleased to "determine their hearts, and bend their wills, and wholly incline them to some one certain thing, and that without any prejudice to their true and proper liberty."[43] For example, Owen takes David's prayer in Psalm 119:36 ("Incline my heart unto thy testimonies and not to covetousness") and argues that this is typical of the scriptural posture of prayer, where the believer prays that God would "powerfully bend his heart and soul unto his testimonies, and work in him an actual embracing of all the ways of God, not desiring more liberty, but only enough to do it willingly."[44] Therefore, Solomon and his people ask that the Lord "incline their heart unto him, to keep his statutes and walk in his commandments" (1 Kings 8:57–58), and

---

[41] Ibid., 10:40.
[42] Ibid.
[43] Ibid., 10:41.
[44] Ibid.

David cries out in repentance, asking God to create a clean heart and renew a right spirit within him (Ps. 51:10). At other times God's people pray that he would "put his fear into their hearts" (Jer. 32:40) and "unite their hearts to fear his name" (Ps. 86:11). Their petitions, in every way, intend God to "work in them both the will and the deed, an actual obedience unto his law," which in no way can merely "aim at nothing but a general influence, enabling them alike either to do or not to do what they so earnestly long after."[45]

Moreover, the very promises and warnings of God rely upon his power to determine and turn the wills and hearts of people however he pleases. So those who fear the Lord are promised that they will find favor in the eyes of men (Prov. 3:4). But how, if God cannot operate powerfully and effectually in their hearts, can he genuinely make such a promise or guarantee it? As Owen points out, if the Arminian perspective is true, then the success of God's promise lies entirely in the hands of men. Owen notes how contrary this is to Scripture. For example, when Jacob wrestled with God, demanding God's blessing, he never questioned whether God could perform it or not (Gen. 32:12). Rather, his wrestling with God communicated the exact opposite, namely, his belief that God can do whatever he pleases, especially bringing to fruition his own promises (Genesis 33). After all, Jacob knew firsthand how the Lord turned his brother's heart so that Esau would not kill but pity him. We see throughout Scripture that this is something God often does for the sake of his own people, fulfilling his covenant promises to them (Ps. 106:46; Job 12:17; 20:21). Therefore, Owen concludes,

> there is no prophecy nor prediction in the whole Scripture, no promise to the church or faithful, to whose accomplishment the free actions and concurrence of men are required, but evidently declareth that God disposeth of the hearts of men, ruleth their wills, inclineth their affections, and determines them freely to choose and do what he in his good pleasure hath decreed shall be performed.[46]

Notice how carefully Owen chooses his words. Man is not a block of wood or a stone. He does choose. But such choice is always according to God's will and purpose. So God inclines and determines human affections, but in such a way that a person chooses freely, according to what he or she most

---

[45] Ibid.
[46] This much is evident, says Owen, in the prophecies that God would deliver his people from the Babylonians via Cyrus (Isaiah 45), convert the Gentiles, build and protect his church (Matthew 16), and destroy Jerusalem through the Romans (Matthew 24) (ibid., 10:42).

desires. And all along, the person's voluntary and willful choice is what God has decreed from the beginning.[47]

Finally, Owen lists three reasons why he is convinced Scripture does not teach a mere general providence of God that precludes God from moving effectually on the human will:

1. It would mean that there are many good things that God is not the author of, including those "special actions," which apparently would be performed apart from God's "special concurrence."[48] A general providence is in direct conflict with the apostle Paul when he affirms that "of him are all things."

2. It denies God's authorship of all "moral goodness." Instead, the goodness of an action is attributed first and foremost, if not *entirely*, to the will of man. "The general influence of God moveth him no more to prayer than to evil communications tending to the corruption of good manners."[49]

3. It makes all of God's decrees, whose "execution dependeth on human actions, to be altogether uncertain, and his foreknowledge of such things to be fallible and easily to be deceived."[50]

It should be noted, therefore, that a general providence removes the believer's confidence and assurance. God's actions are "altogether uncertain." On the other hand, how great is the Christian's faith who has trusted in a God who is sovereign Lord over all things.

> Amidst all our afflictions and temptations, under whose pressure we should else faint and despair, it is no small comfort to be assured that we do nor can suffer nothing but what his hand and counsel guides unto us, what is open and naked before his eyes, and whose end and issue he knoweth long before; which is a strong motive to patience, a sure anchor of hope, a firm ground of consolation.[51]

The Glorious Doctrine of Predestination

For Owen, predestination is a part of God's providence, falling under its wider umbrella.[52] While providence addresses God's actions in relation to

---

[47] It seems that Owen was very much what we call today a "compatibilist."
[48] Owen, *A Display of Arminianism*, in *Works*, 10:42.
[49] Ibid.
[50] Ibid.
[51] Ibid., 10:29.
[52] For more on Owen's ordering of predestination under providence, see Trueman, *Claims of Truth*, 121–22.

all things, predestination zeroes in on his "rational creatures" and their ends. Predestination concerns the "counsel, decree, or purpose of Almighty God concerning the last and supernatural end of his rational creatures, to be accomplished for the praise of his glory."[53] More specifically, Owen defines predestination thus:

> This election the word of God proposeth unto us as the gracious, immutable decree of Almighty God, whereby, before the foundation of the world, out of his own good pleasure, he chose certain men, determining to free them from sin and misery, to bestow upon them grace and faith, to give them unto Christ, to bring them to everlasting blessedness, for the praise of his glorious grace.[54]

With this definition in place, Owen presents several arguments for a Reformed understanding of predestination. First, predestination is an *eternal* and *unconditional* decree that God makes before the foundation of the world. As Paul says in Ephesians 1:4, "He hath chosen us in him before the foundation of the world." And when referring to Jacob and Esau in Romans 9:11–12, Paul indicates that God made his choice before they were born and had done anything good or evil. Again, to Timothy he states, "We are called with an holy calling, not according to our works, but according to his own purpose and grace, which was given us in Christ Jesus before the world began" (2 Tim. 1:9). What these passages demonstrate, says Owen, is that "no good thing in us can be the cause of our election."[55]

Second, predestination is *constant*, which means that it is an *immutable* decree. His decision is final; and praise God that it is, for those who are his can have every assurance that the God who predestined them will also preserve them until the end. God does not elect some individuals and have them fail to be saved in the end. To the contrary, his election is meticulous, predestining both the ends and the means to the appointed ends. For example, Acts 13:48 says that as many as were "ordained to eternal life" believed. Likewise, Jesus himself promises that he gives God's elect eternal life and they will never perish, for no one will snatch Christ's sheep out of his hand or the Father's hand (John 10:28–29). Furthermore, says Owen,

---

[53] Owen, *A Display of Arminianism*, in *Works*, 10:54. We must not forget that for Owen there is a strong Trinitarian and christological emphasis when it comes to the doctrine of predestination. On Owen's christological emphasis, especially in regard to predestination and the covenant of redemption, see Trueman, *Claims of Truth*, 128–42.

[54] Owen, *A Display of Arminianism*, in *Works*, 10:54.

[55] Ibid., 10:55.

Paul tells us in 2 Timothy 2:19 that "God's purpose of election is sealed up" and "therefore cannot be revoked" but it must "stand firm," as Paul makes clear in Romans 9:11 also.[56]

Third, the object of predestination is some (not all) men and women chosen out of the human race. In other words, election is *particular*, not universal. Scripture often uses language to indicate the selectivity of electing grace. There is, says Paul in Romans 11:5, a "remnant according to election." There are those whom "the Lord knoweth to be his" (2 Tim. 2:19). These are men "ordained to eternal life" (Acts 13:48; cf. Rom. 8:39), those "written in the Lamb's book of life" (Rev. 21:27). Therefore, the number of the elect is "certain," and specific persons have been chosen and no others, something that "cannot be altered."[57]

Fourth, the only cause of election is God's own counsel. Stated otherwise, election is not based on divine foreknowledge of a person's faith, but is instead unconditional, based on God's good pleasure and will alone. Owen puts it this way:

> It recounteth no motives in us, nothing impelling the will of God to choose some out of mankind, rejecting others, but his own decree,—that is, his absolute will and good pleasure; so that as there is no cause, in any thing without himself, why he would create the world or elect any at all,—for he doth all these things for himself, for the praise of his own glory,—so there is no cause in singular elected persons why God should choose them rather than others. He looked upon all mankind in the same condition, vested with the same qualifications, or rather without any at all; for it is the children not yet born, before they do either good or evil, that are chosen or rejected, his free grace embracing the one and passing over the other.[58]

The passage Owen has in mind here is Romans 9, where Paul says God loved Jacob and hated Esau. God's choice, as Paul makes clear, was before either of them had done anything good or evil. The emphasis, in other words, is on the unconditionality of God's choice, something that is not based on anything within either man, including faith or the lack thereof. If we condition God's choice on something within us, says Owen, we "rob him of

---

[56] Ibid., 10:57.
[57] Ibid.
[58] Ibid., 10:60.

his glory," for he is the God who has "mercy on whom he will have mercy," loving us "without our desert before the world began."[59]

Owen realizes that we, like Paul's audience in Romans 9, naturally protest the idea that God did not base his choice on anything in us. The Arminian must claim his own faith as the cause that moved God to choose him. Faith, the argument goes, is not the fruit of election but its preceding cause. Notice, says Owen, that faith is "required [not only] as a necessary condition in him that is to be chosen, but as a cause moving the will of God to elect him that hath it."[60] As one Remonstrant, Simon Episcopius, states, "The one only absolute cause of election is, not the will of God, but the respect of our obedience."[61]

That God is moved by nothing but his sheer mercy and grace is proved throughout Scripture. In Matthew 11:26 Jesus declares that God reveals the gospel to some while hiding it from others. In Luke 12:32 we discover that God's will and good pleasure are the only cause of granting some sinners entrance into the kingdom of God, rather than others.[62] Ephesians 1:11 is very direct, stating that we are "predestined according to the purpose of him who worketh all things after the counsel of his own will." Owen plays Devil's advocate, asking, "But did not this counsel of God direct him to choose us rather than others because we had something to commend us more than they?" Quoting Deuteronomy 7:7–8, Owen answers, "No; 'The LORD did not set his love upon you, nor choose you, because ye were more in number than any people; but because the LORD loved you.'"[63] And as we saw, Paul is clear that God's choice was before either Jacob or Esau was born (Rom. 9:11–13). Works are explicitly ruled out by Paul. Nor will it do to slip faith in there instead. Owen explains:

> Wherever there is any mention of election or predestination, it is still accompanied with the purpose, love, or will of God; his foreknowledge, whereby he knoweth them that are his; his free power and supreme dominion over all things. Of our faith, obedience, or any thing importing so much, not one syllable, no mention, unless it be as the fruit and effect thereof. It is the sole act of his free grace and good pleasure, that "he might make known the riches of his glory on the vessels of mercy," Rom. 9:23.[64]

---

[59] Ibid.
[60] Ibid., 10:61.
[61] Ibid.
[62] Ibid., 10:62.
[63] Ibid., 10:63.
[64] Ibid.

If Paul was not clear enough in Romans 9, he surely is in 2 Timothy 1:9, where he says that God has "saved us, and called us with an holy calling, not according to our works, but according to his own purpose and grace, which was given us in Christ Jesus before the world began." So even our "calling" is "free and undeserved" since it flows out of that "most free grace of election."[65]

With the doctrine of predestination firmly established, it naturally follows to see how this great, sovereign God actually saves sinners in time and space by his Holy Spirit.

The Holy Spirit and the Application of Redemption

We cannot forget that for Owen our salvation is Trinitarian through and through. Those whom the Father has chosen in Christ Jesus are then redeemed by Christ himself, who has covenanted with the Father in eternity past to redeem God's elect. Furthermore, the Holy Spirit, who is sent by the Father and the Son, effectually calls and regenerates those whom the Son has purchased, bringing God's elect from spiritual death to spiritual life. In our transition from election to regeneration, it is the third person of the Trinity, the Holy Spirit, who takes center stage.

Foundational to Owen's understanding of the doctrine of salvation is a biblical portrayal of the person of the Holy Spirit. For Owen, the *person* of the Holy Spirit is the very basis for understanding the *work* of the Spirit. Therefore, in his *Discourse on the Holy Spirit* Owen begins by devoting considerable space first to defending the deity of the Spirit.[66] Then, having established the deity of the Spirit, Owen is able to move to the work of the Spirit in applying redemption to God's elect. The Spirit, says Owen, is sent from the Father and the Son with a mission to call, regenerate, convert, justify, sanctify, preserve, and glorify all those whom the Father has elected before the foundation of the world.[67] In all of this, the Spirit's aim is to unite the sinner to Christ.

Given the Spirit's focal role in our salvation, it is important to emphasize how Owen understands the Spirit's role in the context of the Trinity. As mentioned in chapter 3, Owen is a firm believer in the Patristic and Re-

---

[65] Ibid. Owen also concludes his work by giving six reasons why election is unconditional (see ibid., 10:63–67).

[66] Owen, *A Discourse concerning the Holy Spirit*, in Works, 3:14–124.

[67] Before addressing these specific doctrines in the order of salvation, however, Owen takes one step back and first addresses the general manner of the Spirit's work. "God's disposal of the Spirit unto his work is five ways expressed in the Scripture: for he is said,—1. To *give* or bestow him; 2. To *send* him; 3. To *minister* him; 4. To *pour* him out; 5. To *put* him on us. And his own application of himself unto his work is likewise five ways expressed: for he is said,—1. To *proceed*; 2. To *come*, or come upon; 3. To *fall* on men; 4. To *rest*; and, 5. To *depart*" (ibid., 3:105).

formed slogan *opera ad extra trinitatis indivisa sunt*—the external works of the Trinity are indivisible—and this is noticeable once again as he begins his *Discourse on the Holy Spirit*. As Owen explains, "There is no such division in the external operations of God that any one of them should be the act of one person, without the concurrence of the others; and the reason of it is, because the nature of God, which is the principle of all divine operations, is one and the same, undivided in them all."[68] In other words, the unity that exists among the persons of the Trinity in the one divine essence or nature is displayed and consistent with the unity that exists among the three persons in their work of redemption. And yet, writes Owen, although all three persons of the Trinity are united and participatory at every stage in our salvation, nonetheless one person may become the focal agent.[69]

Surely this is the case with the Son in his incarnation. While the Father and the Spirit have a role to play at this stage in redemptive history, it is the Son in particular who takes on human flesh, is crucified, and rises again, not the Father or the Spirit. Likewise, with the application of salvation: while the Father *plans* our redemption, and while the Son *accomplishes* our redemption, it is the Holy Spirit in particular who *applies* redemption. Or as Owen states, the Holy Spirit of God is the "immediate *operator* and efficient cause."[70] The Father's will, counsel, love, grace, authority, purpose, and design are the foundation of the whole work of salvation, and the Son "condescendeth, consenteth, and engageth to do and accomplish in his own person the whole work which, in the authority, counsel, and wisdom of the Father was appointed for him" (Phil. 2:5–8).[71] But it is the Holy Spirit who immediately works and effects "whatever was to be done in reference unto the person of the Son or the sons of men, for the perfecting and accomplishment of the Father's counsel and the Son's work, in an especial application of both unto their especial effects and ends."[72]

---

[68] Ibid., 3:162. This unity, which removes any division between the persons, also means that any one work of redemption can be credited to the entire Trinity in some sense. Owen uses an analogy to drive the point home: "Whereas, therefore, they are the effects of divine power, and that power is essentially the same in each person, the works themselves belong equally unto them: as, if it were possible that three men might see by the same eye, the act of seeing would be but one, and it would be equally the act of all three" (ibid.).

[69] "Yea, and there is such a distinction in their operations, that one divine act may produce a peculiar respect and relation unto one person, and not unto another; as the assumption of the human nature did to the Son, for he only was incarnate" (ibid., 3:162; also see 3:190, 198–201, 291–92).

[70] Ibid., 3:126. It would be a mistake to conclude from this that the Spirit, for Owen, is not present until Pentecost. Quite the contrary, Owen argues that the Spirit was active in the Old Testament, preparing the way for Christ, whether through prophecy, the inspiration of the Scriptures, or miracles (see ibid., 3:126–51).

[71] Ibid., 3:158.

[72] Ibid., 3:159; cf. 3:190. It follows, naturally, that this should be the case for he is the Spirit *of the Father and the Son*. He is the third person of the Trinity, following a certain "order of his subsistence in the holy Trinity" (ibid., 3:162).

Consequently, Owen can conclude that the Spirit is the "sole cause and author of all the good that in this world we are or can be made partakers of."[73] In fact, no good is communicated to us from God unless it is "bestowed on us or wrought in us by the Holy Ghost." No "gift, no grace, no mercy, no privilege, no consolation, do we receive, possess, or use, but it is wrought in us, *collated on us*, or manifested unto us, by him alone."[74] Furthermore, if there is any good in us toward God—including faith, love, duty, or obedience—it is there because it was "effectually wrought in us" by the Holy Spirit, and him alone. In our flesh, no good thing dwells within us, nor can we do any good thing toward God. But when the Spirit comes, he works within us, changes us, makes us new creatures in Christ. Therefore, whether the topic is faith, love, or our obedience toward God, all these "things are from him and by him."[75]

It would be difficult to place too much emphasis on the importance of the Spirit. For Owen, while we cannot come to the Father but by the Son (John 14:6; 1 Pet. 1:21), it is also the case that we cannot come to the Father or the Son "unless we are enabled thereunto by the Spirit, the author in us of faith, prayer, praise, obedience, and whatever our souls tend unto God by."[76] It is not merely that God the Father descends toward us in love and grace through the person and work of the Spirit; but likewise we ascend toward him only by the Spirit.[77] Therefore, Owen will identify the Spirit as the immediate author and cause of regeneration.[78]

Regeneration

Regeneration and Total Depravity

Why is regeneration by the Spirit so necessary? Owen's answer is simple and drawn from the biblical text itself. It is necessary because every aspect of our being is depraved.[79] No part of us—mind, will, affections, etc.—

---

[73] Ibid., 3:157.
[74] Ibid.
[75] Ibid.
[76] Ibid., 3:200.
[77] Hence, he is titled the "Spirit of adoption" for good reason, for it is only through the Spirit that we can cry out, "Abba, Father" (Rom. 8:15; Gal. 4:6).
[78] Owen, *A Discourse concerning the Holy Spirit*, in *Works*, 3:299. Owen also clearly affirmed what the Reformed labeled "effectual calling." In the Westminster Confession regeneration seems to be assumed under (and synonymous with) effectual calling. It is unclear whether Owen thought of the two as synonymous or entirely distinct. Either way, they are closely related and are the cause of conversion. For Owen's description of effectual calling, which closely parallels what we are describing here as "regeneration," see Owen, *The Greater Catechism*, in *Works*, 1:486; Owen, *A Display of Arminianism*, 10:134–35.
[79] Owen's treatment of human depravity and bondage is extensive. See Owen, *A Discourse concerning the Holy Spirit*, in *Works*, 3:203, 242–97.

escapes the clutches of sin. There is not even the slightest ability within us to do what is spiritually pleasing toward God. Owen explains, "There was a spiritual darkness and death came by sin on all mankind; neither was there in any man living the least principle of spiritual life, or any disposition thereunto."[80] And again, "Men are not able of themselves to attain unto regeneration, or complete conversion to God, without an especial, effectual, internal work of the Holy Spirit of grace on their whole souls."[81] Where there was darkness, the Spirit creates light. Where there was only death, the Spirit creates new life. And he does so in an effectual and ineffable way, liberating us from our bondage to sin.[82]

We must not miss Owen's emphasis on both spiritual "darkness" and spiritual "death," two words Scripture uses to speak of human corruption and bondage to sin. Concerning the former Owen writes, "Spiritual darkness is in and upon all men, until God, by an almighty and effectual work of the Spirit, shine into them, or create light in them."[83] In regard to spiritual things, everyone is blind (John 9:40–41). He is a natural man, not accepting the things of the Spirit of God, which are foolishness to him. He is not able to understand these things because they are spiritually discerned (1 Cor. 2:14).[84] As Scripture attests, "The light shined in the darkness, and the darkness comprehended it not" (John 1:5). This much is overt in Paul's gospel mission to "open the eyes of men, and to turn them from darkness to light" (Acts 26:18; cf. Eph. 5:8). Indeed, when Scripture speaks of how God has saved us, it says he has "delivered us from the power of darkness" (Col. 1:13), and "called us out of darkness into his marvelous light" (1 Pet. 2:9). Paul can, therefore, speak of regeneration as the creation of new light in the dark soul, much like the creation of the universe. "God, who commanded the light to shine out of darkness, shines in the hearts of men, to give them the light of the knowledge of his glory in the face of Jesus Christ" (2 Cor. 4:6; cf. Gen. 1:2). The work of the Spirit in this new creation work is pivotal. "It is the work of the Holy Spirit to remove and take away this darkness; which until it is done no man can see the kingdom of God, or enter

---

[80] Ibid., 3:207.
[81] Ibid., 3:231.
[82] Ibid., 3:212. Also see 3:201 on the efficacious nature of grace.
[83] Ibid., 3:246.
[84] Owen elaborates elsewhere, "There is in the minds of unregenerate persons a moral impotence, which is reflected on them greatly from the will and affections, whence the mind never will receive spiritual things,—that is, it will always and unchangeably reject and refuse them,—and that because of various lusts, corruptions, and prejudices invincibly fixed in them, causing them to look on them as foolishness" (ibid., 3:267; also see 3:245–52, 277, 281).

into it."[85] This darkness is powerful indeed, and until the Spirit penetrates this darkness, a person remains "in a constant and unconquerable aversion from God and the gospel."[86]

Scripture also speaks of sinners as being spiritually dead. Owen explains that because of this condition there needs to be an "internal, powerful, effectual work of the Holy Ghost on the souls of men, to deliver them out of this state and condition by regeneration."[87] It must be internal, powerful, and effectual because the unsaved are not merely injured or sick, but rotting away in their tombs, spiritually lifeless. They have no "disposition active and inclining unto life spiritual." Each person is like dead Lazarus before Jesus raised him from the grave.[88] Or as Paul explains, "Ye were dead in trespasses and sins" (Eph. 2:1; cf. 2:5), "dead in your sins, and the uncircumcision of your flesh" (Col. 2:13; cf. Rom. 5:12, 15). Due to the depraved nature mankind inherits from Adam, the unregenerate are "utterly disabled from doing any thing that is spiritually good, until they are quickened by the almighty power and irresistible efficacy of the Holy Ghost."[89]

Spiritual darkness and death also mean that there is a bondage of the will to sin, a spiritual inability. However, the common objection, which Owen anticipates, is that everywhere in Scripture sinners are commanded to repent and believe; does this not assume a spiritual ability? Owen recognizes this faulty argument, namely, that *ought* implies *can*, and that commands imply ability and power. He responds that these exhortations, promises, and threatenings address our *duty*, not our ability. "Their end is, to declare unto us, not what we can do, but what we ought to do."[90] Whenever we think we have the power to fulfill these commands, we "evacuate

---

[85] Ibid., 3:247.

[86] Ibid., 3:269.

[87] Ibid., 3:282.

[88] Ibid., 3:295. Elsewhere in his *Discourse concerning the Holy Spirit* Owen says of the vivification or quickening, basing his argument on passages like John 5:25, Rom. 6:11, and Eph. 2:5: "Now, no such work can be wrought in us but by an effectual communication of a principle of spiritual life; and nothing else will deliver us. Some think to evade the power of this argument by saying that 'all these expressions are metaphorical, and arguings from them are but fulsome metaphors': and it is well if the whole gospel be not a metaphor. But if there be not an impotency in us by nature unto all acts of spiritual life, like that which is in a dead man unto the acts of life natural; if there be not an alike power of God required unto our deliverance from that condition, and the working in us a principle of spiritual obedience, as is required unto the raising of him that is dead,—they may as well say that the Scripture speaks not truly as that it speaks metaphorically. And that is the almighty power, the 'exceeding greatness of God's power,' that is put forth and exercised herein; we have proved from Eph. 1:19, 20; Col. 2:12, 13; 2 Thess. 1:11; 2 Pet. 1:3. And what do these men intend by this quickening, this raising us from the dead by the power of God? A persuasion of our minds by rational motives taken from the word, and the things contained in it! But was there ever heard such a monstrous expression, if there be nothing else in it?" (ibid., 3:329).

[89] Ibid., 3:283. Owen notes that this death is not only spiritual but legal, as evidenced in Gen. 2:17; Rom. 5:12; 2 Cor. 5:14. We can be delivered from this legal death only by justification (Rom. 8:1).

[90] Ibid., 3:289.

the grace of God, or at least make it only useful for the more easy discharge of our duty, not necessary unto the very being of duty itself; which is the Pelagianism anathematized by so many councils of old." Sounding much like Augustine before him, Owen asserts that "the command directs our duty, but the promise gives strength for the performance of it."[91] Furthermore, says Owen, we cannot compromise or bend God's commands, his holy standard, or the conditions of gospel conversion simply because we cannot attain to them by no fault but our own. "Preachers of the gospel and others have sufficient warrant to press upon all men the duties of faith, repentance, and obedience, although they know that in themselves they have not a sufficiency of ability for their due performance."[92] Besides, to "make a judgment of men's ability, and to accommodate the commands of God unto them accordingly, is not committed unto any of the sons of men."[93] How low would this accommodation have to be? Very low indeed, for "in the flesh there dwelleth no good thing," and "that which is born of the flesh is flesh."[94]

In short, to deny this bondage is to deny the corruption of our nature.[95] Owen qualifies himself, recognizing that we all possess the faculties of personhood, including mind, will, and affections. Otherwise, we would be reduced to brute beasts or stones.[96] But if one infers from the mere faculties of personhood the spiritual power to initiate conversion or obey God's commands, Owen denies it, for such a view ignores the reality of "the corruption of our nature by the entrance of sin," rendering "the grace of Christ useless."[97]

Lest one think such a bondage is not willful on our part, Owen responds

---

[91] Ibid., 3:290. Owen also answers another objection: "That if men are thus utterly devoid of a principle of spiritual life, of all power to live unto God,—that is, to repent, believe, and yield obedience,—is it righteous that they should perish eternally merely for their disability, or their not doing that which they are not able to do?" Owen responds, "Men's disability to live to God is their sin. Whatever, therefore, ensues thereon may be justly charged on them. It is that which came on us by the *sin of our nature* in our first parents, all whose consequents are our sin and our misery, Rom. 5:12. Had it befallen us without a guilt truly our own, according to the law of our creation and covenant of our obedience, the case would have been otherwise; but on this supposition (sufficiently confirmed elsewhere), those who perish do but feed on the fruit of their own ways." Owen goes on to explain that the bondage of man is a *willful* bondage and therefore their condemnation is well-deserved (ibid., 3:290–91).

[92] Ibid., 3:295.

[93] Ibid.

[94] Ibid.

[95] Owen goes further, believing it strikes at the gospel itself. "To say that we have a sufficiency in ourselves so much as to think a good thought, or to do any thing as we ought, any power, any ability that is our own, or in us by nature, however externally excited and guided by motives, directions, reasons, encouragements, of what sort soever, to believe or obey the gospel savingly in any one instance, is to overthrow the gospel and the faith of the catholic church in all ages" (ibid., 3:292).

[96] Ibid., 3:261.

[97] Ibid., 3:262.

that our enslavement to sin is just that, a real, genuine enslavement, and at the same time we are absolutely complicit and willing. In other words, our bondage is voluntary. Therefore, as Scripture affirms, it is not just that we *cannot* please God, but we *will not*. "As 'they cannot come to Christ except the Father draw them,' so 'they will not come that they may have life'"; and consequently "destruction is just and of themselves."[98]

In summary, each person is in desperate need of God's supernatural grace in the new birth. Without "an infused habit of internal inherent grace, received from Christ by an efficacious work of the Spirit, no man can believe or obey God, or perform any duty in a saving manner, so as it should be accepted with him."[99]

The Scriptural Affirmation of Regeneration

Seeking to prove his view of regeneration from Scripture, Owen first turns to John 3:3–6, where Nicodemus approaches Jesus only to discover that one must be born again to see the kingdom of God. This new birth is not of the flesh, but of the Spirit. There is clearly a cause and effect. The Spirit is the principal and "efficient cause" (John 3:8), and our spiritual birth is the effect.[100] Moreover, the Spirit's work in the new birth is rightly called efficient because there is no synergism or cooperation between God and us. Rather, and as we will explore in more depth shortly, the new birth is monergistic, meaning that God alone acts on our dead souls. The "whole efficiency of the new birth is ascribed unto God alone."[101] Appealing to texts like John 1:13, Owen argues that there is no role for the will of man; rather, the individual is passive while God is the one at work, bringing about life where there was only spiritual death.

This new birth or regeneration—at times Owen will also use words like "vivification" or "quickening"—is also affirmed in a variety of other texts.[102] For example, Paul states in Titus 3:4–6, "But after the kindness and love of God our Saviour toward man appeared, not by works of righteousness

---

[98] Ibid., 3:291.

[99] Ibid., 3:292.

[100] Owen also notes that water is mentioned as "the pledge, sign, and token of it, the initial seal of the covenant." But there is a "redoubled expression" at work when Jesus refers to "water and Spirit" for the Spirit is being "signified by the water also" (ibid., 3:208).

[101] Ibid.

[102] It is hard to pin down an exact definition of regeneration from Owen, but he comes close in this statement: "I have proved before that this [regeneration] consists in a new, spiritual, supernatural, vital principle or habit of grace, infused into the soul, the mind, will, and affections, by the power of the Holy Spirit, disposing and enabling them in whom it is unto spiritual, supernatural, vital acts of faith and obedience" (ibid., 3:329).

which we have done, but according to his mercy he saved us, by the washing of regeneration, and renewing of the Holy Spirit; which he shed on us richly through Jesus Christ our Saviour."[103] Likewise, a number of texts say we are "born of God" and "begotten again of his own will" (John 1:13; James 1:18; 1 John 3:9).[104] These texts only serve to complement John 3:3–6 and Titus 3:5, where the new birth is clearly affirmed.[105]

Regeneration, a Spiritual Renovation of Our Nature

In Owen's day the Socinians posed a serious threat to many Christian doctrines. Regeneration was no exception. Owen considered the Socinians to be modern-day Pelagians, and he thought their understanding of regeneration to be unbiblical and dangerous to the church, leading people astray, even contradicting the gospel itself. More specifically, what disturbed Owen was how the Socinians in his day believed regeneration consists in a moral reformation of life (*morali reformatione vitae*). In contrast, Owen argued that the new birth consists in a spiritual renovation of our nature (*spirituali renovatione naturae*). What is the difference between the two? In promoting the former, the Socinians treated regeneration more like sanctification, an ongoing process of moral transformation. But when applied to the new birth, such a view removes God from the picture almost entirely and places the power within the human will. Regeneration no longer is supernatural, a miracle that the Spirit accomplishes in the heart of the sinner. Instead, regeneration is the process by which one helps himself become a better person.

To be clear, Owen was not denying the importance of moral reformation in the life of the believer. But moral reformation is always the result of the Spirit's antecedent and initial work of spiritual renovation within our nature.[106] In other words, prior to conversion we sinners need a new heart before we can act and behave in a new way as new creatures in Christ. This was the essence of the problem with the Socinians, for they denied the doctrine of original sin or "an inherent, habitual corruption of nature."[107] However, Owen believed he was on firm biblical ground (e.g., Rom. 5:12–19;

---

[103] Ibid., 3:209. Owen goes on to emphasize the Trinitarian nature of this regenerating work.
[104] Ibid., 3:300.
[105] Other texts speak of this new birth as hearing the voice of the Son of God and living (John 5:25), or being made "alive unto God through Jesus Christ" (Rom. 6:11).
[106] "Now, as we grant that this spiritual renovation of nature will infallibly produce a moral reformation of life; so if they will grant that this moral reformation of life doth proceed from a spiritual renovation of our nature, this difference will be at the end." Owen, *A Discourse concerning the Holy Spirit*, in *Works*, 3:219.
[107] Ibid., 3:223.

Eph. 2:1–3) in affirming humanity's inherited pollution from Adam. In *A Discourse concerning the Holy Spirit*, Owen explains how the Socinians' denial of original sin alters their view of regeneration:

> For if man be not originally corrupted and polluted, if his nature be not depraved, if it be not possessed by, and under the power of, evil disposi-tions and inclinations, it is certain that he stands in no need of an inward spiritual renovation of it. It is enough for such an one that, by change of life, he renounce a custom of sinning, and reform his conversation according to the gospel; which in himself he hath power to do. But as it hath been in part already manifested, and will fully, God assisting, be evinced afterward, that in our regeneration the native ignorance, dark-ness, and blindness of our minds are dispelled, saving and spiritual light being introduced by the power of God's grace into them; that the pravity and stubbornness of our wills are removed and taken away, a new prin-ciple of spiritual life and righteousness being bestowed on them; and that the disorder and rebellion of our affections are cured by the infusion of the love of God into our souls: so the corrupt imagination of the con-trary opinion, directly opposite to the doctrine of the Scriptures, the faith of the ancient church, and the experience of all sincere believers, hath amongst us of late nothing but ignorance and ready confidence produced to give countenance unto it.[108]

The Socinians, much like the Pelagians before them, have overthrown "original sin and the grace of our Lord Jesus Christ!"[109] In contrast, Owen appeals to Scripture to make the argument for regeneration as a supernatu-ral, instantaneous, effectual, and necessary work in the heart of the sinner. What we need is to be made new creatures in Christ Jesus (2 Cor. 5:17). As those who belonged to the "old creature," we lacked any spiritual power, disposition, ability, or inclination for God. Therefore, a "new spiritual prin-ciple or nature" must be "wrought in us by the Spirit of God" (e.g., Eph. 2:10). An internal change must occur. "This new creature, therefore, doth not consist in a new course of actions, but in renewed faculties, with new dispositions, power, or ability to them and for them."[110] Such a change is not a process, but is instantaneous since it is a creative act of the Spirit. It occurs in an instant and therefore "cannot consist in a mere formation of

---

[108] Ibid., 3:224.
[109] Ibid., 3:221.
[110] Ibid.

life."[111] Therefore, if there is any obedience, holiness, righteousness, virtue, or any other good in us, it is always "the consequent, product, and effect" of being made a new creature, never its cause.

In order to make his case for the grace of regeneration, Owen appeals to passages like Ezekiel 36:25–27 and Jeremiah 31:33 and 32:39–40. There we discover that God must take out our heart of stone and replace it with a heart of flesh, one that is alive, not dead. He must put his Spirit within and write his law on our heart. In doing so, God causes us to walk in his statues, "keep his judgments and do them,—that is, reform our lives, and yield all holy obedience unto God."[112] If we reverse the cause (God's grace) with the effect (obedience), we will only distort and remove grace from the picture altogether.[113]

Regeneration, the Work of God Alone

Is regeneration a cooperation or synergism between God and us? Or is regeneration the work of God alone? Is the new birth something God works within us efficaciously, without fail? Or is it something that we can resist and thwart, something that is conditioned upon our willingness to believe? Against the Arminians of his day who assert the latter, Owen answers by affirming the former, namely, that the new birth is "infallible, victorious, irresistible, or always efficacious."[114] It is "always prevalent or effectual, and cannot be resisted, or it will effectually work what God designs it to work: for wherein he 'will work, none shall let him'; and 'who hath resisted his will.'"[115]

Owen proves the efficacious nature of regeneration in several ways. To begin with, he appeals to Scripture, which says in texts like Ezekiel 36:26–27 not merely that God replaces the heart of stone with a heart of flesh, but also that he will do so without question or dependence upon human consent. Owen could not be more straightforward than when he writes:

> He doth not say that he will endeavour to take it away, nor that he will use such or such means for taking of it away, but absolutely that he will take it away. He doth not say that he will persuade men to remove it or do it

---

[111] Ibid., 3:222. Owen appeals to Rom. 6:6; 12:2; Eph. 1:19; 4:22–24; Col. 2:12–13; 2 Thess. 1:11; 2 Pet. 1:4.
[112] Ibid., 3:223.
[113] Owen also appeals to Rom. 6:3–6; Eph. 2:10; 5:23–25; Col. 3:1–5.
[114] Owen, *A Discourse concerning the Holy Spirit*, in *Works*, 3:317. On irresistible grace, see ibid., 3:200–201.
[115] Ibid., 3:318. Owen also has an excellent defense of monergism in *A Display of Arminianism*, in *Works*, 10:100–137.

away, that he will aid and help them in their so doing, and that so far as
that it shall wholly be their own fault if it be not done,—which no doubt it
is where it is not removed; but positively that he himself will take it away.
Wherefore, the act of taking it away is the act of God by his grace, and not
the act of our wills but as they are acted thereby; and that such an act as
whose effect is necessary. It is impossible that God should take away the
stony heart, and yet the stony heart not be taken away. What, therefore,
God promiseth herein, in the removal of our natural corruption, is as
unto the event infallible, and as to the manner of operation irresistible.[116]

Owen goes on to argue that God's implanting of a new spirit within the
human frame cannot be limited by or conditioned on a person's will of re-
fusal. Furthermore, by implanting a new spirit within, God does not merely
give someone the power to obey, as if the individual can accept or refuse,
but rather God works actual obedience within so that one certainly will
obey. And God does so, says Owen, with a "real efficiency of internal grace,
taking away all repugnancy of nature unto conversion, curing its depravation actually and effectually, and communicating infallibly a principle of
scriptural obedience."[117]

To be more precise, regeneration is a renewal of (1) the mind, (2) the
will, and (3) the affections. Prior to regeneration, the mind or understanding is in a state of corruption, vitiated by the fall, and therefore is possessed by spiritual blindness and darkness, "filled with enmity against
God and his law, esteeming the things of the gospel to be foolishness;
because it is alienated from the life of God through the ignorance that is
in it."[118] But when the Spirit regenerates, he is said to give us a new understanding (1 John 5:20). There is an "effectual, powerful, creating act of
the Holy Spirit" in our minds that enables us to "discern spiritual things."[119]
This renovation of our minds is a work of transforming power "peculiarly
ascribed unto the Holy Spirit" (Titus 3:5). Whereas before we lived in darkness, God has now shined in our hearts to give us the "light of the knowledge of the glory of God in the face of Jesus Christ" (2 Cor. 4:6).

Not just our mind, but also our will is impacted. By nature we are dead in
sin. Our will, therefore, is necessarily and irreversibly inclined toward sin.
But when grace appears, the will is renewed by an "effectual implantation" of

---

[116] Owen, *A Discourse concerning the Holy Spirit*, in *Works*, 3:327.
[117] Ibid., 3:328.
[118] Ibid., 3:331.
[119] Ibid., 3:332.

"spiritual life."[120] And not just our will, but our affections are also renewed. Like the Spirit's work on our mind and will, a "prevailing love is implanted upon the affections by the Spirit of grace, causing the soul with delight and complacency to cleave to God and his ways." The heart is circumcised (Deut. 30:6), which "consists in the 'putting off the body of the sins of the flesh'" (Col. 2:11). The flesh, the affections, and our lusts are crucified. When this occurs, says Owen, the Spirit removes from the affections the "enmity, carnal prejudices, and depraved inclination."[121] In their place the Spirit "fills us with *holy spiritual love, joy, fear, and delight,* not changing the being of our affections, but sanctifying and guiding them by the principle of saving light and knowledge."[122] And he does so "effectually, powerfully, and irresistibly."[123]

But what about those who resist the gospel when they hear it? What are we to make of them? According to Owen, since God's saving grace is effectual and "his will shall not be frustrated in any instance," where "any work of grace is not effectual, God never intended it should be so, nor did put forth that power of grace which was necessary to make it so." Owen goes on, "Wherefore, in or towards whomsoever the Holy Spirit puts forth his power, or acts his grace for their regeneration, he removes all obstacles, overcomes all oppositions, and infallibly produceth the effect intended."[124]

One might protest, however, that this is coercive and does violence to our faculties. Not so, says Owen. God does not work in a coercive manner, doing violence to our will. Quite the contrary. Since we are absolutely opposed to God—our will being "in the depraved condition of fallen nature," "habitually filled and possessed with an aversion from that which is good spiritually" (alienated from the life of God), and also continually acting with a "carnal mind" as belonging to those who are at enmity with God, as is observable in how men everywhere "resist the Holy Spirit" (e.g., Acts

---

[120] Owen does not hesitate to call the will "determined," though he qualifies that this determination of the will by the Spirit does not impeach freedom (ibid., 3:334).

[121] Owen adds, however, that these are not removed "absolutely and perfectly" this side of heaven (ibid., 3:335).

[122] Ibid.

[123] Ibid., 3:335–36. He adds, "From the whole it appears that our *regeneration* is a work of the Spirit of God, and that not any *act of our own,* which is only so, is intended thereby. I say it is not *so our own* as by outward helps and assistance to be educed out of the principles of our natures." Owen appeals to Matt. 16:17; John 1:13; 3:5–6, 8; Eph. 2:9–10; Titus 3:5; James 1:18; 1 Pet. 1:3, 23; 1 John 3:9. Owen then puts the burden of proof on those who would contradict these Scriptures. "It is, therefore, incumbent on them who plead for the active interest of the will of man in regeneration to produce some testimonies of Scripture where it is assigned unto it, as the effect unto its proper cause. Where is it said that a man is born again or begotten anew by himself? And if it be granted,—as it must be so, unless violence be offered not only to the Scripture but to reason and common sense,—that whatever be our duty and power herein, yet these expressions must denote an act of God, and not ours, the substance of what we contend for is granted, as we shall be ready at any time to demonstrate" (ibid., 3:336).

[124] Ibid., 3:318. Also see ibid., 3:327–37.

7:51)—he must work powerfully in putting forth his grace. Yet, while there is efficacy, there is no coercion. How so? According to Owen, God's grace can be efficacious and not simultaneously coercive because God works to renew our will, not do violence to it. In other words, God works within, in and by our natural faculties.[125] He does not destroy our will, but reorients, renews, reforms, and re-inclines our will toward him, so that whereas before we hated Christ, now we find Christ our sweetest delight and salvation.

Additionally, Owen observes, since the new birth is not a cooperation between God and us, it is instead the work of God *alone*. This means that we are passive in the new birth. We become active only as a result of the Spirit's invincible work. In the logical order of salvation, God's regenerating grace is always antecedent to our "acting," even though in real time everything appears to happen simultaneously and instantly.[126] There is an "inward almighty secret act of the power of the Holy Ghost," an act that is effectual in nature, and it is this act that brings about our acting, an acting that is most free and natural, owing to the work of the Spirit that preceded it. So powerful, so effectual, so great is this work of the Spirit that Owen can compare it to nothing else than raising the dead.

> The power here mentioned hath an "exceeding greatness" ascribed unto it, with respect unto the effect produced by it. The power of God in itself is, as unto all acts, equally infinite,—he is omnipotent; but some effects are greater than others, and carry in them more than ordinary impressions of it. Such is that here intended, whereby God makes men to be believers, and preserves them when they are so. And unto this power of God there is an actual operation or efficiency ascribed,—the "working of his mighty power." And the nature of this operation or efficiency is declared to be of the same kind with that which was exerted in the raising of Christ from the dead; and this was by a real physical efficiency of divine power.

Whenever Scripture speaks in reference to our new birth, it ascribes to God the efficacy, for "he creates us anew, he quickens us, he begets us of his

---

[125] "He doth not act in them any otherwise than they themselves are meet to be moved and move, to be acted and act, according to their own nature, power, and ability. . . . for as it [God's persuading and alluring] is certainly effectual, so it carries no more repugnancy unto our faculties than a prevalent persuasion doth" (ibid., 3:318; cf. 3:319).

[126] Ibid., 3:320. It should be observed that at times Owen uses the terms *regeneration* and *conversion* synonymously, while at other times he seems to distinguish between them. With the former use, *regeneration* is understood more broadly, while in the latter use, *regeneration* is understood in a more narrow sense. Therefore, context is key in determining how Owen is using these terms. On their usage as synonymous, see, for example, ibid., 3:336–37.

will." Therefore, "it is plain in the Scripture that the Spirit of God works internally, immediately, efficiently, in and upon the minds of men in their regeneration." So powerful is his work in the new birth that it is "the effect of an act of his power and grace; or, no man is born again but it is by the inward efficiency of the Spirit."[127]

Owen turns not only to various biblical texts to prove his point, but also to the practice of prayer, a spiritual discipline that is integral to the Christian life. For Owen, the efficacy of God in the new birth is apparent in our everyday life, particularly in evangelism and missions. For example, when one prays for an unbelieving neighbor or a lost people on the mission field, one always assumes effectual grace must be true. In other words, while one may publicly deny that God works effectually in the souls of his elect, when one prays for the lost, one always believes in God's effectual work. We "beg effectual grace" for the lost. We never pray that God would respect the will of man to resist his gospel. We never pray that God would just give someone enough grace to decide for himself whether he wants God or not—or worse, to do whatever is within his capacity. Rather, we pray that God would work powerfully and without fail. We pray continually "that God would effectually work" in the hearts of the lost. Convert them! Create a clean heart and renew a right spirit in them! Give them faith for Christ's sake![128] In short, we beg God to save them, not merely to make them savable.

Soli Deo Gloria

Why is this issue so important for Owen? Much like Calvin before him, Owen believes the glory of God is at stake.[129] Whether one is a Pelagian and believes that the initiative and power lie within the unregenerate, or a semi-Pelagian, who believes that the unsaved can initiate salvation but nonetheless need God's grace to come alongside and assist them due to humanity's injury from the fall, both views agree on one thing:

> It is absolutely in the power of the will of man to make use of it [grace] or not,—that is, of the whole effect on them, or product in them, of this grace communicated in the way described; for notwithstanding anything

---

[127] Ibid., 3:317.
[128] Ibid., 3:312.
[129] For Calvin, see John I. Hesselink, *Calvin's First Catechism: A Commentary* (Louisville, KY: Westminster John Knox, 1997), 72.

wrought in us or upon us thereby, the will is still left various, flexible, and undetermined.

In other words, whichever view one takes, at the moment of choice, man has the final say, the determinative power, to cooperate with or resist God. What is the problem with this conclusion?

> This ascribes the whole glory of our regeneration and conversion unto ourselves, and not to the grace of God; for that act of our wills, on this sup-position, whereby we convert unto God is merely an act of our own, and not of the grace of God. This is evident; for if the act itself were of grace, then would it not be in the power of the will to hinder it.

But there is an even worse consequence, says Owen:

> This would leave it absolutely uncertain, notwithstanding the purpose of God and the purchase of Christ, whether ever any one in the world should be converted unto God or no; for when the whole work of grace is over, it is absolutely in the power of the will of man whether it shall be effectual or no, and so absolutely uncertain: which is contrary to the covenant, promise, and oath of God unto and with Jesus Christ.[130]

Grace is reduced to a mere illumination, all for the sake of the human will, which "is at perfect liberty to make use of or to refuse at pleasure." What could be a greater threat to God's glory? Owen explains:

> Now this, in effect, is no less than to overthrow the whole grace of Jesus Christ, and to render it useless; for it ascribes unto man the honour of his conversion, his will being the principal cause of it. It makes a man to beget himself anew, or to be born again of himself,—to make him-self differ from others by that which he hath not in an especial manner received.[131]

Owen concludes:

> It makes the act of living unto God by faith and obedience to be a mere natural act, no fruit of the mediation or purchase of Christ; and allows the Spirit of God no more power or efficacy in or towards our regeneration

---

[130] Owen, *A Discourse concerning the Holy Spirit*, in *Works*, 3:308.
[131] Ibid., 3:311.

than is in a minister who preacheth the word, or in an orator who eloquently and pathetically persuades to virtue and dehorts from vice. And all these consequences, it may be, will be granted by some amongst us, and allowed to be true; to that pass are things come in the world, through the confident pride and ignorance of men. But not only it may be, but plainly and directly, the whole gospel and grace of Christ are renounced where they are admitted.[132]

On the contrary, says Owen, God's glory and power must not be diminished to somehow make room for man to have the determinative power in the matter. That would rob God of his glory in salvation and give man the credit instead. Exposing the consequences of such a view, Owen's conclusion is sobering:

For if the Holy Ghost do not work immediately and effectually upon the will, producing and creating in it a principle of faith and obedience, infallibly determining it in its free acts, then is all the glory of our conversion to be ascribed unto ourselves, and we make ourselves therein, by the obediential actings of our own free will, to differ from others who do not so comply with the grace of God; which is denied by the apostle, 1 Cor. 4:7. Neither can any purpose of God concerning the conversion of any one soul be certain and determinate, seeing after he hath done all that is to be done, or can be done towards it, the will remaining undetermined, may not be converted, contrary to those testimonies of our Saviour, Matt. 11:25, 26; John 6:37; Rom. 8:29. Neither can there be an original infallibility in the promises of God made to Jesus Christ concerning the multitudes that should believe in him, seeing it is possible no one may so do, if it depend on the undetermined liberty of their wills whether they will or no. And then, also, must salvation of necessity be "of him that willeth, and of him that runneth," and not "of God, that showeth mercy on whom he will have mercy," contrary to the apostle, Rom. 9:15, 16. And the whole efficacy of the grace of God is made thereby to depend on the wills of men; which is not consistent with our being the "workmanship of God, created in Christ Jesus unto good works," Eph. 2:10. Nor, on this supposition, do men know what they pray for, when they pray for their own or other men's conversion to God; as hath been before declared. There is, therefore, necessary such a work of the Holy Spirit upon our wills as may cure and take away the depravation of them before described, freeing us from the state

---
[132] Ibid.

of spiritual death, causing us to live unto God, and determining them in and unto the acts of faith and obedience. And this he doth whilst and as he makes us new creatures, quickens us who are dead in trespasses and sins, gives us a new heart and puts a new spirit within us, writes his law in our hearts, that we may do the mind of God and walk in his ways, worketh in us to will and to do, making them who were unwilling and obstinate to become willing and obedient, and that freely of choice.[133]

Faith and Repentance

If regeneration is the work of God alone, then what are we to make of faith and repentance, or someone's conversion? While the human will is passive in the new birth, as a result of the new birth a person becomes active, repenting of his or her sin and trusting in Christ for the very first time. Yet, even here in conversion Owen is very careful to define our act of believing. It is not as if God places his offer of grace in front of us and then leaves it up to us to will belief. Rather, "the act of believing, or faith itself, is expressly said to be of God, to be wrought in us by him, to be given unto us from him."[134] In other words, God does not merely offer faith, but he actually works faith within us, so that we will believe. "Scripture says not that God gives us ability or power to believe only,—namely, such a power as we may make use of if we will, or do otherwise; but faith, repentance, and conversion themselves are said to be the work and effect of God."[135] Those who object that a person must have within him the power to believe before he actually does so are mistaken, argues Owen. The reason is that "the act of God working faith in us is a creating act" (Eph. 2:10; 2 Cor. 5:17).[136]

The fact that faith is not merely a gift offered or a gift that makes us savable, but one that God actually works within us so that we will believe is conspicuous in passages like Philippians 1:29, "Unto you it is given in the behalf of Christ, not only to believe on him, but also to suffer for his sake." Owen comments, "To 'believe on Christ' expresseth saving faith itself. This is 'given' unto us. And how is it given us? Even by the power of

---

[133] Ibid., 3:334–35.

[134] Ibid., 3:320. Owen also has an excellent defense of the Reformed view of faith and repentance in *A Display of Arminianism*, in *Works*, 10:100–108, 114–37.

[135] Owen, *A Discourse concerning the Holy Spirit*, in *Works*, 3:320.

[136] At this point it seems that Owen objects to what would today be labeled "prevenient grace" by Wesleyan Arminians and classical Arminians: "Notwithstanding, therefore, all these preparatory works of the Spirit of God which we allow in this matter, there is not by them wrought in the minds and wills of men such a *next power*, as they call it, as should enable them to believe without farther actual grace working faith itself. . . . That there is a power or faculty of believing given unto all men unto whom the gospel is preached, or who are called by the outward dispensation of it, some do pretend" (ibid., 3:321–22).

God 'working in us both to will and to do of his good pleasure,' chap. 2:13."[137] Or as Jesus explains in John 6:65, "And no man can come unto me, except it be given unto him of my Father." No one, says Owen, "can believe, can come to Christ, unless faith itself be 'given unto him,'—that is, be wrought in him by the grace of the Father, Phil. 1:29."[138] Owen appeals to Ephesians 2:8 as well and explains Paul's logic: "Our own ability, be it what it will, however assisted and excited, and God's gift, are contradistinguished. If it be 'of ourselves,' it is not 'the gift of God'; if it be 'the gift of God,' it is not 'of ourselves.'"[139] How exactly is faith wrought in us, one might ask? By the creating act of God. As Paul states in Ephesians 2:10, "We are his workmanship, created in Christ Jesus."

Not only is faith an effectual gift from God, but the same can be said of repentance. Passages like 2 Timothy 2:25 and Acts 9:18 demonstrate that "God in our conversion, by the exceeding greatness of his power, as he wrought in Christ when he raised him from the dead, actually worketh faith and repentance in us, gives them unto us, bestows them on us; so that they are mere effects of his grace in us." If we question whether God does this unfailingly, Owen clarifies: "And his working in us infallibly produceth the effect intended, because it is actual faith that he works, and not only a power to believe, which we may either put forth and make use of or suffer to be fruitless, according to the pleasure of our own wills."[140] So God does not merely make us capable of believing and repenting, but actually creates faith and repentance within.

Furthermore, argues Owen, God works faith and repentance within by "a *power infallibly efficacious*, and which the will of man doth never resist; for this way is such as that he thereby takes away all repugnancy, all resistance, all opposition, every thing that lieth in the way of the effect intended."[141] Passages like Deuteronomy 29:4 and 30:6, Isaiah 44:3–5, Jeremiah 24:7 and 31:33, Ezekiel 36:26–27, and Colossians 2:11 all demonstrate that when the Lord creates faith and repentance, he does so without failure, for he removes any and all obstacles and hindrances. The Spirit gives us a new circumcised heart, something we could not do for ourselves. "No man ever circumcised his own heart. No man can say he began to do it by the power of his own will, and then God only helped

---

[137] Ibid., 3:323.
[138] Ibid.
[139] Ibid.
[140] Ibid., 3:323–24.
[141] Ibid., 3:324.

him by his grace." Just as physical circumcision is an act performed *on* the child, not *by* the child, so also in spiritual circumcision one is passive, which conveys that this is "the act of God, whereof our hearts are the subject."[142] And how can we resist? After all, the Spirit comes and takes away our "blindness, obstinacy, and stubbornness in sin that is in us by nature, with the prejudices which possess our minds and affections, which hinder us from conversion unto God."[143] How can our hearts resist God's work of grace "when that whereby it should resist is effectually taken away"?[144]

Though Owen places great emphasis on divine sovereignty in conversion, he does not neglect to emphasize that faith and repentance, unlike regeneration, do involve the human will. Though God is the one who works faith and repentance within, it truly is the sinner who feels sorrow for his sin and turns to Christ in belief. Therefore, while a person is totally passive in regeneration, in conversion he or she is active, though enabled by God to repent and trust in Christ.

Perseverance of the Saints and the Covenant of Grace

God's sovereign grace is made visible not only in election, regeneration, and conversion, but also in sanctification. God, who has chosen his elect, purchased them by the blood of his own Son, and brought them from spiritual death to new life by the power of the Holy Spirit, will indeed preserve his elect unto glory. To use contemporary theological language, God's elect will not lose their salvation or fall away from the faith, but God will keep and sustain them to the end, working within them his sanctifying grace by the power of the Spirit. This is the Reformed doctrine of the perseverance of the saints; or to highlight God's sovereignty in sanctification, it is sometimes called the *preservation* of the saints.[145]

While Owen's affirmation of perseverance can be seen in a number of his writings, his entire argument is most palpable in his massive 1654

---

[142] Ibid.
[143] Ibid.
[144] Ibid.
[145] Here we briefly treat perseverance. However, for Owen's view of assurance and apostasy, see Sinclair B. Ferguson, *John Owen on the Christian Life* (Edinburgh: Banner of Truth, 1987), 99–124, 232–61 (and for more on Owen's understanding of perseverance, see 262–79); Joel R. Beeke, "John Owen," in *The Quest for Full Assurance: The Legacy of Calvin and His Successors* (Edinburgh: Banner of Truth, 1999), 165–213. For Owen on assurance, see Owen, *A Practical Exposition upon Psalm 130*, in *Works*, 6:379–606; Owen, *A Discourse concerning the Holy Spirit*, in *Works*, 4:352–419); Owen, *A Treatise of the Dominion of Sin and Grace*, in *Works*, 7:500–560. For Owen on apostasy, see *Nature and Causes of Apostasy from the Gospel*, in *Works*, 7:2–261.

tome *The Doctrine of the Saints' Perseverance Explained and Confirmed*. He wrote this polemical treatise in response to Arminian John Goodwin and his book *Redemption Redeemed* (1651). Dedicating this work to Oliver Cromwell, Owen reveals his objective:

> That you and all the saints of God may yet enjoy that peace and consolation which is in believing that the eternal love of God is immutable, that he is faithful in his promises, that his covenant, ratified in the death of his Son, is unchangeable, that the fruits of the purchase of Christ shall be certainly bestowed on all them for whom he died, and that every one who is really interested in these things shall be kept unto salvation, is the aim of my present plea and contest.[146]

Here we see the framework and structure of Owen's argument. The doctrine of perseverance is not only manifested in legions of biblical texts, but also necessarily follows from certain theological pillars. Among them are the immutability of the divine nature, the immutability of the purposes of God, the saving nature of the covenant of grace, the efficacy of the promises of God, and the substitutionary nature and particular design of the mediation and intercession of Christ, as well as the indwelling of the Holy Spirit, the Trinitarian agent who will not lose those whom the Father has chosen and the Son has purchased. Each of these doctrines solidifies and supports the biblical affirmation of perseverance. As a result, to abandon the doctrine of perseverance is to rupture the nature of redemptive history, particularly what the Father has planned and the Son has accomplished. It is to divide the members of the Trinity, as if the Spirit can fail at applying the redemptive work the Father has decreed and the Son has accomplished.

Consider, for example, how the covenant of grace reinforces the doctrine of perseverance. For Owen, this covenant is immutable, for as Scripture everywhere says, it is an everlasting covenant. In contrast to God's covenant with Adam, the covenant of grace is one in which "God himself hath undertaken the whole, both for his continuing with us and our continuing with him."[147] This covenant and all of its requirements have been fulfilled by Christ, our Mediator, on our behalf. Therefore, as Ferguson explains, according to Owen, "The result is that, to the believer, this covenant

---

[146] Owen, *The Doctrine of the Saints' Perseverance Explained and Confirmed*, in *Works*, 11:5–6.
[147] Ibid., 11:264.

is an unconditional promise of grace and perseverance. In this way, God reveals his special faithfulness as the God who keeps covenant."[148]

The natural question at this point is whether God's promise to preserve his elect leads to laxness in piety and the pursuit of holiness. Certainly this was the argument Goodwin sought to advance against Owen, namely, that the doctrine of perseverance would lead men to be careless and licentious since they have already been justified and have been promised eternal life. Like many Reformed theologians before him, Owen demonstrates that such an argument is unbiblical in countless ways. Indeed, Goodwin's protest is the same as those who opposed the apostle Paul and said, "Let us continue in sin, because we are not under the law, or the condemning power of it for sin, but under grace" (Rom. 6:14–15). But Paul answered, "God forbid!" Sin shall not have dominion over us, "because we are not under the law, but under grace."[149] Christ has redeemed his elect from the curse of the law by becoming a curse for us (Gal. 3:13). As a result, we have been redeemed from sin's reign over us. Furthermore, the Spirit of Christ, who indwells every believer, leads us to mortify the flesh (Rom. 8:13). "It is the Spirit of Christ alone that is able to do this great work."[150] Owen explains:

> It is the Spirit of Christ alone that hath sovereign power in our souls of killing and making alive. As no man quickeneth his own soul, so no man upon any consideration whatsoever, or by the power of any threatenings of the law, can kill his own sin. There was never any one sin truly mortified by the law or the threatening of it. All that the law can do of itself is but to entangle sin, and thereby to irritate and provoke it, like a bull in a net, or a beast led to the slaughter. It is the Spirit of Christ in the gospel that cuts its throat and destroys it.[151]

As those who are in Christ (i.e., united with Christ), we are now new creatures. The old has passed away, and the new has come (2 Cor. 5:17). Paul says in Galatians 6:14, "By the cross of Christ is the world crucified unto us, and we unto the world." Therefore, not only does Christ atone for our sins so that there is no longer any condemnation for God's elect (Rom. 8:1, 31), but from him also comes the promised Holy Spirit, who works

---

[148] Ferguson, *John Owen on the Christian Life*, 265. See Owen, *The Doctrine of the Saints' Perseverance Explained and Confirmed*, in *Works*, 11:211–18. For more on Owen's view of the covenant of grace, as well as other covenants, see Ferguson, *John Owen on the Christian Life*, 20–36.
[149] Owen, *The Doctrine of the Saints' Perseverance Explained and Confirmed*, in *Works*, 11:392.
[150] Ibid.
[151] Ibid., 11:392–93.

within to mortify the flesh in the process of sanctification. And since we are dead to sin and alive to God (Rom. 6:11), we have been overtaken with the love of Christ, which "constraineth us" (2 Cor. 5:14–15). In short, Christ not only has purchased redemption for us and is now interceding on our behalf, but also has procured the Spirit and given him to us as a free gift. The Spirit indwells the believer, seals the believer, and works within the believer a sanctifying grace, renewing him or her into the image of Christ.[152] In doing so, the Spirit brings every believer to the finish line to behold the glory of God in the face of Christ. Therefore, divine sovereignty in sanctification does not undermine gospel holiness, but actually is the impetus for it.

It must be noted, since this is a book on Owen's understanding of the *Christian life*, that in his "Epistle Dedicatory" Owen says that the "doctrine asserted and the error opposed are the concernment of the common people of Christianity."[153] In other words, perseverance is a doctrine that concerns every Christian in the local church. Owen is especially concerned with how Arminianism has "crept into the bodies of sundry congregations."[154] To abandon the doctrine of perseverance is to unleash havoc on the Christian life. Without the doctrine of perseverance, there can be no assurance that the God who began this work of salvation will bring it to completion. And if there is no guarantee or assurance, what hope and confidence does the believer have in the midst of intense battles against sin and temptation? Without the doctrine of perseverance, any hope we do have lies not in a sovereign God who has promised to bring us through the fire of life's trials to see the glory of his Savior. Rather, our security rests in ourselves. As John Goodwin would have it, "God hath promised believers shall persevere in case they persevere."[155] To the contrary, says Owen, believers persevere in God's grace and favor and continue in faith and obedience precisely because God has promised that he will do it!

Conclusion

Owen led the way both in defending the doctrines of grace and in teaching others why doctrines like predestination, regeneration, and perseverance matter so much to the Christian life. Without them, the sovereignty of God

---

[152] Ibid., 11:336–50.
[153] Ibid., 11:16.
[154] Ibid.
[155] Ibid., 11:248.

is lost, our salvation is placed in our own hands, and we become the masters of our fate. Christianity, in this scheme, is turned inward, toward the self. But what is so refreshing about Owen is that he not only recognized this danger in his own day, but was courageous enough to take on all criticism in order to lift our eyes to God, giving us a glimpse of just how big our God is. He is not a God who is weak, dependent upon us for his success in salvation, but rather a God who is absolutely omnipotent, strong to save. For Owen, salvation belongs to the Lord (Ps. 3:8; Jonah 2:9). Apart from this truth, the Christian life has much to do with us and little to do with the God whom Scripture portrays as one in sovereign control of all things for his own glory and the good of those who love him (Rom. 8:28).

CHAPTER 7

JUSTIFICATION BY FAITH ALONE AND CHRISTIAN ASSURANCE

For the doctrine of justification is directive of Christian practice, and in no other evangelical truth is the whole of our obedience more concerned; for the foundation, reasons, and motives of all our duty towards God are contained therein. Wherefore, in order unto the due improvement of them ought it to be taught, and not otherwise. That which alone we aim (or ought so to do) to learn in it and by it, is how we may get and maintain peace with God, and so to live unto him as to be accepted with him in what we do. To satisfy the minds and consciences of men in these things, is this doctrine to be taught.[1]

The doctrine of justification proved to be a controversial issue in John Owen's day, just as it had been during the era of the Reformation. Defending the traditional Protestant doctrine of justification by faith alone, as well as the imputation of Christ's righteousness, placed Owen in the middle of a firestorm, surrounded on all sides by a host of conflicting voices.[2]

First, Socinianism compromised justification in major ways, as it did

---

[1] Owen, *The Doctrine of Justification by Faith*, in *Works*, 5:10.
[2] For in-depth coverage of Owen's theological context with regard to justification, see Carl R. Trueman, *John Owen: Reformed Catholic, Renaissance Man* (Hampshire: Ashgate, 2007), 108–21.

almost every other doctrine. Socinianism viewed the imputation of Christ's righteousness, which Reformed theologians like Owen believed to consist of Christ's active obedience (i.e., his fulfilling the law on our behalf) and passive obedience (i.e., his taking the penalty for our sin), as an "impossible" doctrine. Socinius argued that Christ needed to obey for the sake of his own salvation. Therefore, he died for himself, and God approved of his death and made him his son.[3] Underlying all of this is a denial of Christ's full deity, as well as his vicarious, substitutionary sacrifice. Christ's death is merely an example, as the Racovian Catechism argues (see chap. 5). The Socinians viewed a vicarious atonement not only as impossible, says Owen, but also as "fallacious, erroneous, and very pernicious"! Hence, justification cannot involve the imputation of Christ's righteousness.[4]

Second, there was the ongoing challenge from Rome. As we will see, Owen went to great lengths to refute the Roman Catholic view of justification. From Rome's point of view, justification, regeneration, and sanctification were intertwined so that justification was understood not as an instantaneous legal, forensic declaration, but as a process of inner renewal and transformation. In this view, God did not impute the alien righteousness of Christ to the sinner's account, but infused grace, particularly by means of the sacraments. Cooperating with this infused grace, the sinner is made righteous, and on this basis he is pardoned before God. Therefore, justification is not by faith alone, but faith is accompanied by works of merit.

Third, Arminianism also posed a threat. For a number of Puritans like Owen, Arminianism was the close cousin of Roman Catholicism. As J. I. Packer explains, many Arminians argued that faith itself is counted for righteousness because "it is in itself actual personal righteousness, being obedience to the gospel viewed as God's new law." Therefore, the "argument against both Romans and Arminians was that by finding the ground of justification in the believer himself they ministered to human pride on the one hand, and on the other hand robbed the Son of God of the glory which was his due."[5] In contrast, the Reformed argued that Christ alone

---

[3] The covenant of redemption proves an important doctrine in Owen's arsenal for refuting this Socinian argument. Owen writes, "The compact between the Father and the Son as unto his undertaking for us . . . undeniably proves all that he did in the pursuit of them to be done for us, and not for himself." Owen, *The Doctrine of Justification by Faith*, in *Works*, 5:258–59. Also see Trueman, *John Owen*, 110–11.

[4] Carl Trueman reminds us that a denial of the active obedience of Christ for our justification would characterize some Arminians and other moderate Puritans (e.g., Richard Baxter). Trueman, *John Owen*, 108–9.

[5] J. I. Packer, *A Quest for Godliness: The Puritan Vision of the Christian Life* (Wheaton, IL: Crossway, 1990), 153.

(*solus Christus*), specifically his salvific-redemptive work on our behalf, is the basis of our justification, meaning not only that our sins have been forgiven, but also that his perfect righteousness is credited to us; faith is merely the instrumental cause of our justification.

Additionally, while Arminianism viewed faith as a gift, it is a mere offer left up to the individual to decide whether or not he will accept as his own. While God takes the initiative via prevenient grace, faith remains man's part, his work in the matter. The Reformed argued, however, that faith is not merely offered, but is a gift in the sense that God actually works faith within. In other words, those whom God effectually calls and monergisti- cally regenerates will believe (see chap. 6). While in Arminianism there was no guarantee that prevenient grace would result in faith (i.e., God's saving grace was conditioned upon a person's choice), for the Reformed there was every guarantee, for those whom the Father had elected and the Son had purchased the Spirit would regenerate, resulting in repentance and trust in Christ.[6] As Packer explains, while justification and regeneration are distinct, the "former cannot take place without the latter."[7] Therefore, the Reformed understood regeneration and justification in vastly different ways than did their Arminian counterparts.[8]

Moreover, some (though certainly not all) Arminians redefined the atonement as well. The atonement was viewed as universal in its extent and this made men savable, but did not actually guarantee the salvation of any- one. It made salvation possible, not actual. Therefore, a penal substitution- ary atonement had to be rejected, for it drew a direct correlation between the atonement and the salvation of the elect. As Packer explains, "Substi- tution is, by its very nature, an effective relationship, securing actual im- munity from obligation for the person in whose place the substitute acts."[9] As an alternative then, some Arminians adopted a governmental view of the atonement, most famously advocated by Hugo Grotius (1583–1645). It is no surprise that in their rejection of the penal and substitutionary nature of the atonement, justification likewise would need modification as well.

Fourth, certain Puritans deviated from the Reformed view of justifica-

---

[6] The Puritans, says Packer, "emphasized that justifying faith is given by God through effectual calling, which includes regeneration—that is, vitalizing union with the risen Christ through the sovereign work of the Spirit, from which, as a work of new creation, flows the sinner's response to the gospel" (ibid., 154).
[7] Ibid.
[8] Packer elaborates: "Thus the Arminians appeared to Reformed thinkers to be playing into Rome's hands at this point: Rome complained that justification according to Protestants was divorced from subjective renewal, and Arminianism admitted that faith might fail to produce good works every time" (ibid.).
[9] Ibid., 156.

tion by affirming eternal justification. Justification from eternity is just what it sounds like: the sinner is counted righteous in eternity past. In this view, justification is absorbed and swallowed up by election. Packer explains,

> William Twisse, first prolocutor of the Assembly, had maintained this as part of his case against Arminianism, but in addition to being unscriptural the idea is pastorally disastrous, for it reduced justifying faith to discovering that one is justified already, and so sets seekers waiting on God for assurance instead of exerting active trust in Christ.[10]

The Westminster Confession would correct such a view: "God did, from all eternity, decree to justify all the elect . . . nevertheless they are not justified until the Holy Spirit doth in due time actually apply Christ unto them" (11.4). Owen's Savoy Declaration would follow suit.

In an interesting turn of events, Richard Baxter would accuse Owen of falling prey to such a view, a charge of which Owen cleared himself. Ironically, while Baxter pointed the finger at Owen, it was Baxter himself who diverted from Reformed orthodoxy in considerable ways. He imbibed Amyraldianism (retaining particular election, effectual calling, and perseverance, while rejecting definite atonement), and combined it with Grotius's governmental view of the atonement, which fit well with Baxter's political theology. One of the consequences was that justification was reconfigured. Packer captures Baxter's neonomianism:

> God should be thought of as governor, and the gospel as part of his legal code. Our salvation requires a double righteousness: Christ's which led to the enacting of God's new law, and our own, in obeying that new law by genuine faith and repentance. Faith is imputed for righteousness because it is real obedience to the gospel, which is God's new law. Faith, however, involves a commitment to keep the moral law, which was God's original code, and every believer, though righteous in terms of the new law, needs pardon every moment for his shortcomings in relation to the

---

[10] Ibid., 155. Packer also lists antinomianism as a second trap some Puritans fell into (though he argues that no Puritans of notable mention adopted such a view). In this view "God takes no notice of the sins of the justified." In their liberty they failed to see that "the moral law still binds believers, as expressing God's will for his adopted children, and that the Father-son relationship between him and them will be spoiled if his will is ignored or defiled" (ibid.). The Westminster Confession counters: "God doth continue to forgive the sins of those that are justified: and although they can never fall from the state of justification, yet they may by their sins fall under God's fatherly displeasure, and not have the light of His countenance restored unto them, until they humble themselves, confess their sins, beg pardon, and renew their faith and repentance" (11.5).

old law. Jesus Christ, who procured the new law for mankind by satisfying the prescriptive and penal requirements of the old one, should be thought of as Head of God's government, enthroned to pardon true believers. . . . Baxter was convinced that those who held the ground and formal cause of our justification to be the imputing to us of Christ's own righteousness (i.e., his fulfillment of the precept and penalty of the moral law) were logically committed to Antinomianism, on the "payment-God-cannot-twice-demand" principle. At this point in his thinking (though not else-where) Baxter assumed, with his Roman and Socinian contemporaries, that law-keeping has no relevance for God or man save as work done to earn acceptance and salvation, so that if the law has been kept once in our name no basis remains for requiring us to keep it a second time in our own persons.[11]

It is no wonder that Baxter found Owen disagreeable, accusing him not only of eternal justification, but of antinomianism as well![12] With good reason Packer describes Baxter as a "great and saintly man," truly brilliant in pastoral matters, but theologically "something of a disaster."[13]

Owen, of course, rejected each of these views, and in his book *The Doctrine of Justification by Faith, through the Imputation of the Righteousness of Christ; Explained, Confirmed, and Vindicated* (1677) he takes them on, while simultaneously defending, both biblically and theologically, the Reformed orthodox view. But long before Owen's 1677 work on justification, one can see his view in the Savoy Declaration of 1658. This confession of faith was an adaption of the Westminster Confession for those committed, as Owen

---

[11] Packer, *A Quest for Godliness*, 158. For others who address Baxter's theology, see Hans Boersma, *A Hot Pepper Corn: Richard Baxter's Doctrine of Justification in Its Seventeenth-Century Context of Controversy* (Zoetermeer: Boekencentrum, 1993), 257–330; Tim Cooper, *John Owen, Richard Baxter and the Formation of Nonconformity* (Burlington, VT: Ashgate, 2011), 75–80; J. V. Fesko, *Beyond Calvin: Union with Christ and Justification in Early Modern Reformed Theology (1517–1700)*, Reformed Historical Theology 20 (Göttingen: Vandenhoeck & Ruprecht, 2012), 300–317.

[12] The debate between Baxter and Owen was an undying one. Baxter, dissatisfied with Owen's *The Death of Death in the Death of Christ* (1647), responded to Owen in an appendix in *Aphorismes of Justification* (1649). Owen responded in *Of the Death of Christ* (1650) (see *Works*, 10:429–79). Baxter continued the debate in *Richard Baxter's Confession of His Faith* (1655), which Owen addressed, along with Socinianism, in *Of the Death of Christ, and of Justification*, attached to the end of *Vindiciae Evangelicae* (1655) (see *Works*, 12:591–617). For the relationship of Owen and Baxter, see especially Tim Cooper, *John Owen, Richard Baxter and the Formation of Nonconformity*.

[13] Packer, *A Quest for Godliness*, 159. Packer goes so far as to say: "Thus Baxter, by the initial rationalism of his 'political method,' which forced Scripture into an *a priori* mould, actually sowed the seeds of *moralism* with regard to sin, *Arianism* with regard to Christ, *legalism* with regard to faith and salvation, and *liberalism* with regard to God. . . . What we see in Baxter is an early stage in the decline, not simply of the doctrine of justification among the Puritans, but of the Puritan insight into the nature of Christianity as a whole" (ibid., 160). For an extensive treatment of the Baxter-Owen debate, see Trueman, *John Owen*, 113–21; Trueman, *The Claims of Truth: John Owen's Trinitarian Theology* (Carlisle: Paternoster, 1998), 140–43, 203–10, 214–26; Cooper, *John Owen, Richard Baxter and the Formation of Nonconformity*. Cooper points out that personality issues also figured in the disagreement between Baxter and Owen.

was, to Congregationalism. Owen was certainly one of the main authors of this Declaration, along with Thomas Goodwin. In it we witness not only Owen's ecclesiology, but also his soteriology. Indeed, where the Westminster Confession is ambiguous when it comes to justification, the Savoy Declaration is far more specific, affirming and specifically naming the active and passive righteousness of Christ.[14] It reads:

> Those whom God effectually calleth, he also freely justifieth, not by infusing righteousness into them, but by pardoning their sins, and by accounting and accepting their persons as righteous, nor for any thing wrought in them, or done by them, but for Christ's sake alone; nor by imputing Faith itself, the act of believing, or any other Evangelical obedience to them, as their righteousness, but by imputing Christ's active obedience unto the whole Law, and passive obedience in his death for their whole and sole righteousness, they receiving and resting on him and his righteousness by Faith; which Faith they have not of themselves, it is the gift of God.[15]

As we will discover in this chapter, such a biblically minded and orthodox definition of justification would distinguish Owen's theology from the various positions mentioned above.

In the sixteenth century Martin Luther called justification by faith alone the doctrine on which the church stands or falls.[16] Owen said the same, but what made his fight all the more complicated was that he, unlike Luther, was facing not merely one major opponent (i.e., Rome), but a theological hydra, the monster with many heads. Cut one head off and two more would take its place! Furthermore, the stakes were very high indeed. Not only was the debate over justification a serious exegetical and theological matter, but the consequences of this biblical idea for the Christian life were enormous (and still are today). As we will now see, and as the quote at

---

[14] There was debate at Westminster over the active and passive righteousness of Christ. William Twisse and Thomas Gataker, for example, affirmed only passive righteousness. However, Daniel Featley defended active righteousness, and the majority sided with him, affirming the phrase the "whole obedience and satisfaction." Strangely, the word "whole" is left out in the final version of the Westminster Confession (see 11.3), though questions 70–73 of the Larger Catechisms leave no doubt as to where the divines stood on the matter. Trueman notes that the omission is insignificant and may be due to an attempt to accommodate Twisse and Gataker. Trueman, *John Owen*, 105–6. See also Chad van Dixhoorn, ed., *The Minutes and Papers of the Westminster Assembly, 1643–1652*, 5 vols. (Oxford: Oxford University Press, 2012), 2:48–58. For help with this reference, we are indebted to Trey Moss of the archives of the James P. Boyce Library, The Southern Baptist Theological Seminary, Louisville, Kentucky.

[15] *A Declaration of the Faith and Order Owned and Practiced in the Congregational Churches in England* (London, 1658), 11.1.

[16] Owen, *The Doctrine of Justification by Faith*, in *Works*, 5:67.

the beginning of this chapter reveals, the Christian life hung in the balance of these debates over justification. What one believes about justification in large part determines whether one will also have a biblical understanding of Christian obedience, assurance, and the gospel itself.

Justification and the Christian Life

The doctrine of justification for Owen is not one reserved for conversations in the ivory tower of academia. Quite the contrary, justification has massive implications for the common Christian. At the very opening of *The Doctrine of Justification by Faith*, Owen addresses the sinner who is "pressed and perplexed with a sense of the guilt of sin."[17] Owen's first concern, in other words, is the "proper relief of the conscience."[18] How is it that a sinner, condemned before a holy God, ridden with guilt for his sin, can be justified in God's sight? Owen believes the answer lies in the doctrine of justification itself. "For justification is the way and means whereby such a person doth obtain acceptance before God, with a right and title unto a heavenly inheritance."[19]

This is not merely Owen's concern, but the New Testament's as well. Owen explains that we sinners are described as "ungodly" (Rom. 4:5) and "guilty before God" (Rom. 3:19). Those who commit sin are guilty and therefore worthy of death (Rom. 1:32). Everyone is under the "curse" and "wrath of God" (John 3:18, 36; Gal. 3:10), "without plea, without excuse, by any thing in and from himself, for his own relief."[20] The sinner's mouth is stopped (Rom. 3:19) and in every way "'shut up under sin' and all the consequents of it" (Gal. 3:22).[21] Therefore, the most fundamental question must be "Sirs, what must I do to be saved?" (Acts 16:30), along with "How shall man be just with God?" (Job 9:2). Again, the answer is in the doctrine of justification, whereby "God pardoneth all their sins, receiveth them into his favour, declareth or pronounceth them righteous and acquitted from all guilt, removes the curse, and turneth away all his wrath from them, giving them right and title unto a blessed immortality or life eternal."[22]

The controversial question, however, is this:

---

[17] Ibid., 5:7.
[18] Ibid.
[19] Ibid.
[20] Ibid.
[21] Ibid., 5:8.
[22] Ibid.

Whether it be any thing in ourselves, as our faith and repentance, the renovation of our natures, inherent habits of grace, and actual works of righteousness which we have done, or may do? Or whether it be the obedience, righteousness, satisfaction, and merit of the Son of God our mediator, and surety of the covenant, imputed unto us?

Owen undoubtedly affirms the latter against his Roman Catholic opponents, who argue for the former. But before we can investigate such a matter, we must begin with Adam's fall. If we do not first understand our identity in Adam, we will not be able to make sense of our identity in Christ. Or, to state the issue more acutely, unless one first feels the weight of one's peril in Adam, one will never see his need for a Savior in Christ, the second Adam.

The Imputation of Adam's Sin

"A clear apprehension and due sense of the greatness of our apostasy from God, of the depravation of our natures thereby, of the power and guilt of sin, of the holiness and severity of the law, are necessary unto a right apprehension of the doctrine of justification."[23] This is exactly what Owen believes the Pelagians of old and the Socinians of his own day lack. They do not have a clear apprehension of their own depravity and wretchedness before a holy God and his perfect law, unlike the apostle Paul (e.g., Rom. 1:17). The consequences, argues Owen, are enormous, for when they do not apprehend "the dread of our original apostasy from God, nor the consequence of it in the universal depravation of our nature, they disown any necessity either of the satisfaction of Christ or the efficacy of divine grace for our recovery and restoration."[24] The Socinians of Owen's day deny the imputation of the "actual apostasy and transgression of Adam, the head of our nature, whereby his sin became the sin of the world."[25] In doing so they remove the very ground and necessity of justification, whereby one is "made righteous by the obedience of another," as demonstrated in Romans 5:12–19, a passage we will return to.[26] Owen laments, "And small hope is there to bring such men to value the righteousness of Christ, as imputed to

---

[23] Ibid., 5:20.
[24] Ibid.
[25] Ibid., 5:21.
[26] Ibid. Owen goes on to explain that some Socinians deny not only the imputation of the guilt of Adam's sin to his posterity, but also his corruption. And if they do not deny it, says Owen, they "so extenuate it as to render it a matter of no great concern unto us."

them, who are so unacquainted with their own unrighteousness inherent in them." And here is Owen's key point: "Until men know themselves better, they will care very little to know Christ at all."[27]

But what exactly is our connection to Adam, and how does our identity in Adam impact our status before God? Adam acted as our federal head and representative. Therefore, Owen makes the case, especially on the basis of passages like Romans 5:12–19 and 1 Corinthians 15:22, that the guilt and corruption (pollution) from Adam's first sin are imputed to all of his children (i.e., all humanity). Here we see Owen's doctrine of original sin, one very much in line with his Reformed predecessors. First, the guilt of Adam's first sin is imputed to us. We "were all in covenant with him; he was not only a natural head, but also a federal head unto us."[28] Adam is our representative, so that when he sinned he plunged all of humanity into condemnation along with him (Rom. 5:12, 18–19). Owen concludes from Romans 5 that the transgression of Adam is reckoned (imputed) to all humanity. Conversely, the obedience of Christ is reckoned (imputed) to those who believe.

Second, not only is Adam's guilt imputed to his posterity, but so also is the *"derivation* of a polluted, corrupted nature" (e.g., Job 14:4; John 3:6; Rom. 8:7).[29] A "polluted fountain will have polluted streams," Owen remarks. "The first person corrupted nature, and that nature corrupts all persons following."[30] So not only does every person born into this world inherit the guilt of his father Adam, but it is on the basis of this imputed guilt that all

---

[27] Ibid. Owen explains: "The consciences of men are kept off from being affected with a due sense of sin, and a serious consideration how they may obtain acceptance before God. Neither the consideration of the holiness or terror of the Lord, nor the severity of the law, as it indispensably requireth a righteousness in compliance with its commands; nor the promise of the gospel, declaring and tendering a righteousness, the righteousness of God, in answer thereunto; nor the uncertainty of their own minds upon trials and surprisals, as having no stable ground of peace to anchor on; nor the constant secret disquietment of their consciences, if not seared or hardened through the deceitfulness of sin, can prevail with them whose thoughts are pre-possessed with such slight conceptions of the state and guilt of sin to fly for refuge unto the only hope that is set before them, or really and distinctly to comport with the only way of deliverance and salvation." Owen continues, "So insensibly are the minds of men diverted from Christ, and seduced to place their confidence in themselves. Some confused respect they have unto him, as a relief they know not how nor wherein; but they live in that pretended height of human wisdom, *to trust in themselves*" (ibid., 5:23).

[28] Owen, *Of Communion with God*, in *Works*, 2:64.

[29] Ibid., 2:64–65.

[30] Ibid. Preserving the sinlessness of Christ, however, Owen explains that Christ is free from the imputation of Adam's guilt and corruption. The guilt of sin is imputed to Christ not as a child of Adam, but rather as our Mediator so that he could take away the sin of the world (John 1:29). "Though he was in Adam in a natural sense from his first creation, in respect of the purpose of God, Luke 3:23, 38, yet he was not in him in a law sense until after the fall: so that, as to his own person, he had no more to do with the first sin of Adam, than with any personal sin of [any] one whose punishment he voluntarily took upon him; as we are not liable to the guilt of those progenitors who followed Adam, though naturally we were no less in them than in him." Owen also explains how Christ is not susceptible to the imputation of Adam's corrupt nature. He appeals to the Holy Spirit's work in the virgin birth (see Luke 1:35). See chap. 5 for further details of the sinlessness of Christ.

have consequently inherited Adam's corrupt nature as well. Owen explains, "As he [Adam] was after the fall, so are we by nature, in the very same state and condition."[31]

The Basis of Justification

So far we have seen that for Owen every person stands before God guilty and condemned, possessing a corrupt nature, and is therefore inclined in every aspect of his being toward sin rather than God. Not only is everyone a child of Adam (inheriting his guilt and corruption), but to make matters even worse, each person has committed actual sin as well, rebelling against the law of God, violating God's commandments. As a lawbreaker, idolater, and covenant transgressor, one finds his remedy only in Christ, clothed in his righteousness, not his own. Christ alone can deal with our sin and our need for a righteous standing before a holy God. Therefore, it is the work of Christ on the sinner's behalf that becomes the very basis of justification. Thus, as we will soon discover, it is Christ, and Christ alone, who is the object of our faith.[32]

Owen begins his study on the relationship between the believer and Christ by turning to what we might call the doctrine of double imputation, that is, the imputation of the believer's sin to Christ and Christ's righteousness to the believer. Scripture teaches everywhere that there is a "communication between Christ and believers, as unto sin and righteousness; that is, in the imputation of their sins unto him, and of his righteousness unto them."[33] Owen starts with Leviticus 16:21–22 and the Day of Atonement, when Aaron, as high priest, laid both of his hands on the head of the goat, confessing all the sins of Israel, "putting them upon the head of the goat" which then bore the people's iniquities. Aaron did not "transfuse" sin from the people into the goat, Owen observes, but "transferred the guilt of it" from the people to the goat. Therefore, the sacrifice itself was called "sin" and "guilt" (Lev. 4:29; 7:2; 10:17).

Owen's main point in addressing Leviticus 16 is, however, to demonstrate the parallel to Christ, who acts as an atoning sacrifice on whom the sins of his people are transferred. Owen explains the connection to Christ:

---

[31] Also see Owen, *The Doctrine of Justification by Faith*, in Works, 5:77.

[32] "In this lost, forlorn, hopeless condition, God proposeth the promise of redemption by Christ unto him [the sinner]. And this was the object of that faith whereby he was to be justified" (ibid., 5:76).

[33] Ibid., 5:34.

Whether this goat sent away with this burden upon him did live, and so was a type of the life of Christ in his resurrection after his death; or whether he perished in the wilderness, being cast down the precipice of a rock by him that conveyed him away, as the Jews suppose; it is generally acknowledged, that what was done to him and with him was only a representation of what was done really in the person of Jesus Christ.[34]

That Christ is an atoning sacrifice in line with Leviticus 16 is also perceptible in a number of other passages. For example, according to Isaiah 53 God lays on the suffering servant (i.e., Christ) the iniquities of "us all," so that "by his stripes we might be healed." Owen comments: "Our iniquity was laid on him, and he bare it, verse 11; and through his bearing of it we are freed from it. His stripes are our healing. Our sin was his, imputed unto him; his merit is ours, imputed unto us."[35] Or consider Romans 3:24–25, "being justified freely by his grace, through the redemption that is in Christ Jesus: whom God hath set forth to be a propitiation through faith in his blood." Not only does Paul affirm that justification is by grace, not by works, but he also explicitly affirms that our justification is through the blood of Christ. In other words, God the Father, out of love for his elect, gave his Son to bear the penalty and wrath that we deserve, so that in turn we would have our sins forgiven and receive the righteousness of Christ.[36]

Owen also appeals to 2 Corinthians 5:21, "He [Christ] was made sin for us, who knew no sin; that we might become the righteousness of God in him." God does not impute our sin to us but instead imputes the righteousness of Christ! This was possible only because our sin was imputed to Christ in the first place. As Owen remarks, "All the guilt of our sins was laid on him, and he bare all our iniquities."[37] Therefore, it is by the blood of Christ, by his atoning death, that our sins are forgiven. In summary, we are justified by faith in the blood of Christ alone. And it is because our justification is based on Christ alone that we not only are accepted with God but have peace with him, for his wrath has been turned away by Christ's propitiationary atonement. "It is by the blood of Christ that we are 'made nigh,' who were 'far off,' Eph. 2:13. By the blood of Christ are we reconciled,

---

[34] Ibid.
[35] Ibid., 5:35.
[36] Ibid., 5:119–20.
[37] Ibid., 5:120.

who were enemies, verse 16. By the blood of Christ we have redemption, Rom. 3:24, 25; Eph. 1:7, etc. This, therefore, is the object of faith."[38]

Consider also Romans 8:3–4, "God sending his own Son in the likeness of sinful flesh, and for sin, condemned sin in the flesh; that the righteousness of the law might be fulfilled in us." Owen interprets Paul as saying:

> The sin was made his, he answered for it; and the righteousness which God requireth by the law is made ours: the righteousness of the law is fulfilled in us, not by our doing it, but by his. This is that blessed change and commutation wherein alone the soul of a convinced sinner can find rest and peace.[39]

Once again, for Owen the issue is extremely pastoral. The sinner's rest and peace depend on what Christ has done on his behalf. Owen also finds support for this great exchange in Galatians 3:13–14, where Paul says that Christ "hath redeemed us from the curse of the law, being made a curse for us, that the blessing of Abraham might come on us." Certainly the curse of the law "contained all that was due to sin."[40] "This belonged unto us; but it was transferred on him. He was made a curse; whereof his hanging on a tree was the sign and token." Therefore, Christ is said to "bear our sins in his own body on the tree" (1 Pet. 2:24), since Christ "hanging on the tree was the token of his bearing the curse" (see Deut. 21:23).[41]

Now, if the basis or grounding of our justification is the work of Christ, what role does faith play in the believer's justification? And where does repentance fit in?

Faith and Repentance

Owen identifies three things that must be present for there to be true, genuine repentance and conviction of sin. First, there must be a "displicency [i.e., dissatisfaction, discontentment] and sorrow that we have sinned." One must have a "dislike of sin, and of himself that he hath sinned, shame of it, and sorrow for it."[42] As Scripture makes clear (e.g., Jer. 36:24), anyone who is not convinced of sin has not truly been affected, regardless of what he

---

[38] Ibid., 5:121.
[39] Owen, *Of Communion with God*, in *Works*, 2:35.
[40] Ibid.
[41] Ibid.
[42] Owen, *The Doctrine of Justification by Faith*, in *Works*, 5:77.

might say or confess in public. Second, there must be a "fear of punishment due to sin." Here Owen connects our sin to the law of God:

> For conviction respects not only the instructive and preceptive part of the law, whereby the being and nature of sin are discovered, but the sentence and curse of it also, whereby it is judged and condemned, Gen. 4:13, 14. Wherefore, where fear of the punishment threatened doth not ensue, no person is really convinced of sin; nor hath the law had its proper work towards him, as it is previous unto the administration of the gospel.

Owen concludes, "And whereas by faith we 'fly from the wrath to come,' where there is not a sense and apprehension of that wrath as due unto us, there is no ground or reason for our believing."[43] Third, "a desire of deliverance from that state wherein a convinced sinner finds himself upon his conviction is unavoidable unto him." There should be various degrees of fear, solicitude, and restlessness, says Owen, that move the individual to desire liberation and redemption from his condemned state.[44]

These three aspects characterize repentance. To drive the point home, Owen uses the example of Adam when he sinned. First, Adam's eyes were opened and suddenly he saw the "filth and guilt of sin in the sentence and curse of the law applied unto his conscience, Rom. 7:9, 10." Of course, our first reaction to the guilt of sin is to think merely of our state as "evil and dangerous," as if we simply need to do our "duty to better it" by applying ourselves and trying harder. "But all these things, as to a protection or deliverance from the sentence of the law, are no better than fig-leaves and hiding."[45] Second, God shuts our mouths. Utilizing the law, revealing our incapability to keep it, God exposes our helpless state. We are cornered since our guilt is unmistakable and we can find no relief from our efforts to improve ourselves. We cannot redeem ourselves. Third, in this condition "it is a mere act of sovereign grace, without any respect unto these things foregoing, to call the sinner unto believing, or faith in the promise unto the

---

[43] Ibid., 5:77–78.

[44] Owen observes that if these three internal characteristics are present, certain external effects will follow, including "abstinence from known sin unto the utmost of men's power," and the "duties of religious worship, in prayer and hearing of the word, with diligence in the use of the ordinances of the church." Owen is quick to clarify, however, that these things are never to be considered meritorious or conditions of our justification. "But yet it must be said, that they are neither severally nor jointly, though in the highest degree, either necessary dispositions, preparations, previous congruities in a way of merit, nor conditions of our justification" (ibid., 5:78; cf. 5:79).

[45] Ibid., 5:79.

justification of life."[46] The order is important: nothing prior to God's calling us to himself possesses "causality." In other words, nothing we do can bring about faith. It is purely and only a sovereign gift from God.

As for faith, Owen begins by defining it in regard to what it is not. Faith is no mere assent.[47] It is not as if one must merely assent cognitively to the teachings of the church or divine revelation. No, there must be far more to faith than merely understanding. There must be belief, which is an act of the heart. As Paul affirms, "With the heart man believeth unto righteousness" (Rom. 10:10).[48] Belief from the heart is rooted specifically in Christ. Owen explains,

> I say, therefore, that the Lord Jesus Christ himself, as the ordinance of God, in his work of mediation for the recovery and salvation of lost sinners, and as unto that end proposed in the promise of the gospel, is the adequate, proper object of justifying faith, or of saving faith in its work and duty with respect unto our justification.[49]

So the faith that is from the heart is directed toward Christ entirely. When we believe, our faith is specifically and wholly in him, in his name, receiving him, and looking to him for the promise of justification and eternal life. "Faith is that act of the soul whereby convinced sinners, ready otherwise to perish, do look unto Christ as he was made a propitiation for their sins; and who so do 'shall not perish, but have everlasting life.'"[50] Or as Paul expresses it, "being justified freely by his grace through the redemption that is in Christ Jesus; whom God hath set forth to be a propitiation through faith in his blood; to declare his righteousness for the remission of sins" (Rom. 3:24–25). And again, "He hath made us accepted in the Beloved; in whom we have redemption through his blood, according to the riches of his grace" (Eph. 1:6–7). Owen concludes, "Christ as a propitiation

---

[46] Ibid., 5:80.

[47] Owen is responding to the Roman Catholic view, particularly that of Robert Bellarmine. See ibid., 5:80–81.

[48] Belief from the heart involves an act of the will, though Owen is careful to qualify that it is not *merely* an act of the will (i.e., God's grace is primary). "But without an act of the will, no man can believe as he ought" (John 1:12; 5:40; 6:35). "We come to Christ in an act of the will; and 'let whosoever will, come.'" This much is obvious when we examine the opposite: unbelief. Unbelief is considered disobedience (Heb. 3:18–19), and therefore it is implied that man is held responsible for his unbelief (ibid., 5:84).

[49] Ibid., 5:85–86.

[50] Ibid., 5:91. Owen does nuance himself, explaining that Christ is the object of our faith unto justification not *absolutely*, but as the *ordinance of God*, in his work of mediation. In other words, Scripture speaks of the Father as the immediate object of faith (John 5:24; 6:29; Rom. 3:23–24; 1 Pet. 1:21). On other objects of our faith, such as love, mercy, the benefits of Christ, divine promises, pardon of sin, and eternal life, see ibid., 5:86–93.

is the cause of our justification, and the object of our faith, or we attain it by faith in his blood."[51]

And yet, Owen does not simply describe faith as belief from the heart focused on Christ and his redemptive work. Faith also includes a "sincere renunciation of all other ways and means for the attaining of righteousness, life, and salvation."[52] Thus the psalmist cries out, "I will make mention of thy righteousness, even of thine only" (Ps. 71:16; cf. Jer. 3:23; Hos. 14:2–3; Acts 4:12). Many things present themselves to the unbeliever, particularly his own righteousness (Rom. 10:3). True faith is a renunciation of them all, especially one's own righteousness (Isa. 50:10–11).

Additionally, faith involves the will's consent, meaning that "the soul betakes itself cordially and sincerely, as unto all its expectation of pardon of sin and righteousness before God, unto the way of salvation proposed in the gospel."[53] Owen believes that this is what Scripture has in mind when it speaks of the sinner "coming unto Christ," "receiving of him," "believing in him," or "believing on his name." As Jesus says in John 14:6, "I am the way, the truth, and the life: no man cometh unto the Father, but by me."

Moreover, faith is an "acquiescency of the heart in God, as the author and principal cause of the way of salvation prepared, as acting in a way of sovereign grace and mercy towards sinners."[54] Peter addresses readers "who by him [Christ] do believe in God, that raised him up from the dead, and gave him glory; that your faith and hope might be in God" (1 Pet. 1:21; cf. Isa. 42:1; 49:3). It is this "acquiescency of the heart in God," says Owen, that is the "immediate root" of the Christian's patience, long-suffering, and hope, all of which are the effects of justifying faith (Heb. 6:12–19). Faith is an act that results in rest for the soul. "For all our rest in this world is from trust in God; and the especial object of this trust, so far as it belongs unto the nature of that faith whereby we are justified, is 'God in Christ reconciling the world unto himself' [2 Cor. 5:19]."[55]

Finally, faith is trust in God. Or to be more specific, faith is trust in the "grace and mercy of God in and through the Lord Christ, as set forth to be a propitiation through faith in his blood."[56] Faith as trust means that it is an act that results in *rest* for the soul. "For all our rest in this world is from

---

[51] Ibid., 5:89. Owen lays out a long list of biblical texts in support of his argument; see 5:90–93.
[52] Ibid., 5:100.
[53] Ibid., 5:101.
[54] Ibid.
[55] Ibid.
[56] Ibid.

trust in God; and the especial object of this trust, so far as it belongs unto the nature of that faith whereby we are justified, is 'God in Christ reconciling the world unto himself.'"[57]

With these necessary characteristics of faith in mind, Owen makes his case for why faith is the instrumental cause of our justification.[58] To be clear, God alone is the principal or efficient cause of our justification. God is the one who "justifieth us by faith" (see Acts 15:9; Rom. 3:30; Gal. 3:8; Eph. 2:8). Therefore, "faith, in some sense, may be said to be the instrument of God in our justification, both as it is the means and way ordained and appointed by him on our part whereby we shall be justified"; and also because "he bestoweth it on us, and works it in us unto this end, that we may be justified."[59] Hence, faith is simultaneously our duty and God's free gift. Or as Owen states the mystery, appealing to Romans 3:24, "It is, therefore, the ordinance of God prescribing our duty, that we may be justified freely by his grace, having its use and operation towards that end, after the manner of an instrument."[60] In this sense, then, it is appropriate to call faith the instrumental means of our justification, though God himself is always the efficient cause. Owen believes Scripture is very much on his side as well. By faith we "receive Christ" (John 1:12; Col. 2:6), the "word of promise" (Acts 2:41), the "word of God" (Acts 8:14; 1 Thess. 1:6; 2:13), the "atonement made by the blood of Christ" (Rom. 5:11), the "forgiveness of sins" (Acts 10:43; 26:18), the "promise of the Spirit" (Gal. 3:14), and all the "promises" of God (Heb. 9:15). Owen concludes, "There is, therefore, nothing that concurreth unto our justification, but we *receive* it by faith."[61]

One reason it is important to acknowledge the instrumentality of faith is that if we are justified by an inherent righteousness of our own, then faith ceases to be instrumental in the biblical sense. But if, as Owen believes, we are "justified through the imputation of the righteousness of Christ, which faith alone apprehends and receives, it will not be denied but that it is rightly enough placed as the instrumental cause of our justification." Conversely, if we are "justified by an inherent, evangelical righteousness of our own, faith may be the condition of its imputation, or

---

[57] Ibid.
[58] Owen breaks down the causality of justification as follows: (1) the moving cause is God, (2) the meritorious cause is the work of Christ, and (3) the instrumental cause is faith (ibid., 5:360).
[59] Ibid., 5:110; cf. 5:112.
[60] Ibid., 5:111.
[61] Ibid. Owen's point is proved when we look in the opposite direction as well, for unbelief is spoken of as not receiving (John 1:11; 3:11; 12:48; 14:17).

a disposition for its introduction, or a congruous merit of it, but an instrument it cannot be."[62]

Justification: A Legal Declaration

In all that Owen has said so far it is implied that justification by faith is a forensic or legal matter. In other words, justification refers not to a moral transformation over time, but to an instantaneous, legal declaration that the sinner is not guilty, but now has a righteous status before God. Moreover, contrary to Roman Catholicism, justification does not involve an infusion of grace, but rather an imputation or reckoning of Christ's righteousness to the sinner's account (which we will explore later). Owen protests those medieval schoolmen and Roman Catholic theologians of his own day who viewed justification as an "internal change from inherent unrighteousness unto righteousness likewise inherent."[63] Justification is mixed with sanctification and considered the "making of a man to be inherently righteous, by the infusion of a principle or habit of grace, who was before inherently and habitually unjust and unrighteous."[64]

The fact that justification is forensic and judicial rather than transformative is proved throughout Scripture. Owen appeals to the original languages, examining both Hebrew and Greek, to demonstrate that a host of passages support a forensic, legal definition.[65] For example, he draws attention to Proverbs 17:15 ("He that justifieth the wicked, and he that condemneth the just, even they both are abomination to the LORD") and concludes that the passage means to "show or declare one righteous; to appear righteous; to judge any one righteous."[66] Likewise, citing Job 13:18

---

[62] Ibid., 5:112. There is, nevertheless, a sticky question that Owen anticipates, namely, should faith be considered a "condition"? Owen does not want to quibble about words and terms, as long as an agreement can be reached. If by "condition" one means it is man's duty, required by God, then Owen believes we can comfortably affirm faith as a condition of justification. Without faith, in other words, justification will not occur, and this is something all of Scripture supports. For uses of the word "condition" that Owen does not accept, see ibid., 5:113.

[63] Ibid., 5:124.

[64] Ibid.; also see 5:207, 218.

[65] Ibid., 5:125–30.

[66] Ibid., 5:125. Owen clarifies on 126: "Not he that maketh the *wicked inherently righteous*, not he that changeth him *inherently* from unrighteous unto righteousness; but he that, without any ground, reason, or foundation, acquits him in judgment, or *declares* him to be righteous 'is an abomination unto the Lord.' And although this be spoken of the judgment of men, yet the judgment of God also is according unto this truth: for although he *justifieth the ungodly*,—those who are so in themselves,—yet he doth it on the ground and consideration of a *perfect righteousness* made theirs by imputation; and by another act of his grace, that they may be meet subjects of this righteous favour, really and *inherently changeth* them from unrighteousness unto holiness, by the renovation of their natures. And these things are singular in the actings of God, which nothing amongst men hath any resemblance unto or can represent; for the *imputation of the righteousness of Christ* unto a person in himself ungodly, unto his justification, or that

("Behold, now I have ordered my cause; I know that I shall be justified") he says, "The ordering of his cause (his judgment), his cause to be judged on, is his preparation for a sentence, either of absolution or condemnation: and hereon his confidence was, that he should be justified; that is, absolved acquitted, pronounced righteous."[67]

In his extensive study of the Old Testament, Owen concludes that the meaning of *justify* is to "absolve, acquit, esteem, declare, pronounce righteous, or to impute righteousness."[68] In other words, the forensic sense is in view. On such a basis, Owen believes that the most fundamental and primary issue with those in the church of Rome is not that they oppose justification by faith through the imputation of Christ's righteousness, but that they

> deny that there is any such thing as justification: for that which they call the first justification, consisting in the infusion of a principle of inherent grace, is no such thing as justification: and their second justification, which they place in the merit of works, wherein absolution or pardon of sin hath neither place nor consideration, is inconsistent with evangelical justification.[69]

In other words, Rome affirms an understanding of justification that cannot be substantiated biblically, and therefore, before we can even discuss issues like legal imputation, we must acknowledge, argues Owen, that Rome does not affirm justification at all, at least in the biblical sense of the word.[70]

That the forensic sense, rather than a physical operation, transfusion, or transmutation, is in view is also evident in the New Testament. For example, in Luke 18:14 Jesus declares that the publican went down to his house justified, that is, "acquitted, absolved, pardoned, upon the confession of his sin, and supplication for remission."[71] Appealing to an overwhelming list of passages that likewise communicate a judicial, forensic, and legal meaning to the concept of justification, Owen concludes, in con-

---

he may be acquitted, absolved, and declared righteous, is built on such foundations, and proceedeth on such principles of righteousness, wisdom, and sovereignty, as have no place among the actions of men, nor can have so; as shall afterward be declared." Other Old Testament passages Owen appeals to include: Gen. 44:16; Ex. 23:7; Deut. 25:1; 2 Sam. 15:4; 1 Kings 8:31–32; 2 Chron. 6:22–23; Job 27:5; Ps. 82:3; Isa. 5:23; 53:11; Dan. 12:3.

[67] Ibid., 5:125.
[68] Here Owen makes his case from the *hiphil* and *hithpael* in Hebrew (ibid.).
[69] Ibid., 5:126. For Owen's critique of the double justification of Rome, see ibid., 5:137–52.
[70] Ibid., 5:141.
[71] Ibid., 5:129.

trast to Roman Catholic theologians like Robert Bellarmine (1542–1621), that in "no one of these instances can it admit of any other signification, or denote the making of any man righteous by the infusion of a habit or principle or righteousness, or any internal mutation whatever."[72]

Before moving on, we must observe that justification is not only legal or forensic, but instantaneous as well. "Justification," Owen says, "is such a work as is at once completed in all the causes and the whole effect of it, though not as unto the full possession of all that it gives right and title unto."[73] How different this is from Rome, which sees justification not only as transformative, but also as progressive over time. Owen gives several arguments in response. To begin with, "all our sins, past, present, and to come, were at once imputed unto and laid upon Jesus Christ" (see Isa. 53:5–6; 1 Pet. 2:24). Christ did "at once 'finish transgression, make an end of sin, make reconciliation for iniquity and bring in everlasting righteousness,' Dan. 9:24. At once he expiated all our sins" (cf. Heb. 1:3; 10:10, 14). Christ never has to do anything more than what he has already done in expiating all our sins from the "first to last; 'for there remaineth no more sacrifice for sin.'"[74] However, this does not mean that

> our justification is complete [at the cross], but only, that the meritorious procuring cause of it was at once completed, and is never to be renewed or repeated any more; all the inquiry is concerning the application of it unto our souls and consciences, whether that be by faith alone, or by works of righteousness which we do.[75]

Moreover, when we actually believe, with a "justifying faith," in Christ, "we do receive him" and become sons of God (John 1:12), heirs of God and joint heirs with Christ (Rom. 8:17). "Hereby we have a right unto, and an

---

[72] The array of biblical passages Owen appeals to throughout his *Doctrine of Justification by Faith* in order to verify the judicial meaning is extensive (see ibid.). Owen's case is also buttressed by the fact that *condemnation* is likewise used by Scripture in a legal, declarative sense (Prov. 17:15; Isa. 50:8–9; Rom. 5:16, 18; 8:33–34) (ibid., 5:135). Additionally, argues Owen, many other phrases only add their support: the "imputation of righteousness without works" (Rom. 4:6, 11), "reconciliation with God" (Rom. 5:9, 10; 2 Cor. 5:20, 21), "save" and "salvation" (Matt. 1:21; Acts 13:39; 15:11; Gal. 2:16; Eph. 2:8–9), "remission of sins" (Rom. 4:5–6), "receiving the atonement" (Rom. 5:11), not "coming into judgment" or "condemnation" (John 5:24), "blotting out sins and iniquities" (Ps. 51:9; Isa. 43:25; 44:22; Jer. 18:23; Acts 3:19), "casting them into the bottom of the sea" (Mic. 7:19), and finally "many shall be made righteous" (Rom. 5:19), which insinuates a "juridical trial in open court" where one "is absolved and declared righteous." For ten other themes concerning justification that are proposed in Scripture under a "juridical scheme" or "forensic trial and sentence," see ibid., 5:135–36.

[73] Ibid., 5:143.

[74] Ibid., 5:144.

[75] Ibid.

interest in, all the benefits of his mediation; which is to be at once completely justified" (Acts 13:39; 26:18; Eph. 1:3; Col. 2:10). At the moment we believe in Christ, all our sins are forgiven! As we learn from the apostle Paul, "He hath quickened you together with him, having forgiven you all trespasses" (Col. 2:13–15), and "in him we have redemption through his blood, even the forgiveness of sins, according unto the riches of his grace" (Eph. 1:7). Those who have been justified have nothing to be laid at their charge. Why? Because "he that believeth hath everlasting life, and shall not come into condemnation, but is passed from death unto life" (John 5:24). As Paul says in Romans 8:33–34, "Who shall lay any thing to the charge of God's elect? It is God that justifieth; it is Christ that died." Or as he states in Romans 8:1, "There is no condemnation unto them that are in Christ Jesus." Therefore, "being justified by faith, we have peace with God" (Rom. 5:1; cf. 4:5–6).

Sola Fide

Whether or not justification is by faith alone becomes clear when the condition of humanity is considered. As discussed already, each human being is in the same "state that Adam was in after the fall," and the only solution to such a state is one God himself proposed in Genesis 3:15 and manifested at the proper time (Heb. 1:1), namely, at the "incarnation and suffering of Christ."[76] Furthermore, as mentioned, not only is everyone born into a state of guilt and wrath, but he is also born with a depraved nature, controlled by the power of sin, so much so that his whole soul is defiled. In other words, so depressing is each person's state that justification by works or by an inherent righteousness is absolutely removed from the picture and in no way a possibility.

Therefore, justification by works of the law is precluded.[77] Works, no matter what type, are excluded from our justification before God.[78] Paul states in Romans 3:20, "Therefore by the deeds of the law there shall no

---

[76] Ibid., 5:118.

[77] For Owen's definition and articulation of the "law," see ibid., 5:286ff.

[78] Owen rejected the Roman Catholic argument that Paul excludes only works that come before believing, works done in the "strength of our own wills and natural abilities, without the aid of grace." But, says Rome, Paul does not exclude works that are aided by grace or enabled by grace, works necessary for meriting justification. No, says Owen, Paul does exclude all works. It will not do to appeal to works mixed in with some grace, because justification, in the Roman Catholic view, is still conditioned upon one's good works and merit, even if they be enabled by grace. On the contrary, the "apostle [Paul] excludeth all works, without distinction or exception." In doing so, Paul leaves no ground for boasting (Rom. 3:27; 4:2; Eph. 3:9; 1 Cor. 1:29–31) (ibid., 5:282–83).

flesh be justified in his sight; for by the law is the knowledge of sin" (cf. Rom. 3:22; 4:5; 11:6; Eph. 2:8–9; Phil. 3:8–9; Titus 3:5). Suitably, it is not by our personal righteousness that we are justified in God's sight.[79] The law does not save us, but instead exposes our sinfulness, our failure to uphold God's moral standard, and thereby condemns us before a holy God (Rom. 3:19; Gal. 2:19–21).[80]

How then, if not by works of the law, can a sinner be justified in God's sight? Owen finds the answer in Romans 3:21–23:

> But now the righteousness of God without the law is manifested, being witnessed by the law and the prophets; even the righteousness of God, which is by faith of Jesus Christ unto all and upon all them that believe; for there is no difference: for all have sinned, and come short of the glory of God; being justified freely by his grace, through the redemption that is in Christ Jesus; whom God hath set forth to be a propitiation through faith in his blood, to declare his righteousness for the remission of sins that are past, through the forbearance of God.

Therefore, says Owen:

> That which a guilty, condemned sinner, finding no hope nor relief from the law of God, the sole rule of all his obedience, doth betake himself unto by faith, that he may be delivered or justified,—that is the especial object of faith as justifying. But this is the grace of God alone, through the redemption that is in Christ; or Christ proposed as a propitiation through faith in his blood. Either this is so, or the apostle doth not aright guide the souls and consciences of men in that condition wherein he himself doth place them. It is the blood of Christ alone that he directs the faith unto all them that would be justified before God. Grace, redemption, propitiation, all through the blood of Christ, faith doth peculiarly respect and fix upon.[81]

How is a sinner justified before a holy God? To echo the Reformers, it is by grace alone, through faith alone, in the work of Christ alone.[82] As already

---

[79] Ibid., 5:156. Stated otherwise, "If we are saved by grace, through faith in Christ, exclusively unto all works of obedience whatever, then cannot such works be the whole or any part of our righteousness unto the justification of life: wherefore, another righteousness we must have, or perish for ever" (ibid., 5:361).
[80] Ibid., 5:278–79. Or as Owen says elsewhere, "The reason why no man can be justified by the law, is because no man can yield perfect obedience thereunto; for by perfect obedience the law will justify, Rom. 2:13, 10:5" (ibid., 5:284). For other places where Owen gives a thorough refutation of justification as that which is conditioned upon works, see ibid., 5:288–89, 309–13.
[81] Ibid., 5:119.
[82] Concerning *sola gratia*, Owen states, "The grace of God, the promise of mercy, the free pardon of sin, the blood of Christ, his obedience, and the righteousness of God in him, rested in and received by faith

discussed, Christ's work is the basis for justification. But now Owen gets to the heart of the matter: Justification occurs through faith alone.[83]

Owen's defense of *sola fide* is saturated with biblical support. The faith through which we are justified is spoken of in a number of ways in the New Testament. First, faith is *receiving* Christ (John 1:12; 3:11; 12:48; 14:17; Acts 26:18; Rom. 5:17; Col. 2:6). Such a "receiving" and "reception" is not from our own nature or our own willpower. Rather, God is the one who works faith within, for it is his gift. Furthermore, our justification is something that we receive, for it is "freely granted, given, communicated, and imputed unto us,—that is, of Christ, of the atonement, of the gift of righteousness, of the forgiveness of sins." Therefore, all our "works" have no "influence into our justification, nor are they causes and conditions" of our justification.[84]

Second, faith is *looking* to Christ (Num. 21:8–9; Ps. 123:2; Isa. 17:7; 45:22; Zech. 12:10; John 3:14–15; 8:28; 12:32; 1 Cor. 10:11). Owen explains the relationship between "looking" and *sola fide*:

> Now, if faith, whereby we are justified, and in that exercise of it wherein we are so, be a looking unto Christ, under a sense of the guilt of sin and our lost condition thereby, for all, for our only help and relief, for deliverance, righteousness, and life, then is it therein exclusive of all other graces and duties whatever; for by them we neither look, nor are they the things which we look after. . . . Faith is that act of the soul whereby they who are hopeless, helpless, and lost *in themselves*, do, in a way of expectancy and trust, *seek for all help and relief in Christ alone*, or there is not truth in it.[85]

Third, faith is *coming* to Christ (Matt. 11:28; John 6:35–65; 7:37). "To come unto Christ for life and salvation, is to believe on him unto the justification of life." Owen explains the connection between "coming" and *sola fide*:

---

are everywhere asserted as the causes and means of our justification, in opposition unto any thing in ourselves, so expressed as it useth to express the best of our obedience, and the utmost of our personal righteousness. Wherever mention is made of the duties, obedience, and personal righteousness of the best of men, with respect unto their justification, they are all renounced by them, and they betake themselves unto sovereign grace and mercy alone." The passages Owen brings to his defense are numerous: Gen. 3:15; 15:6; Lev. 16:21–22; Job 4:18–19; Pss. 71:16; 130:3–4; 143:2; Isa. 27:4–5; 45:24–25; 53:6, 11; 64:6; Jer. 23:6; Dan. 9:24; John 1:12; 3:14–15; Acts 13:38–39; 26:18; Rom. 3:24–28; 4:2–8; 5:15–19; 8:1–4; 10:4; 11:6; 1 Cor. 1:30; 2 Cor. 5:21; Gal. 2:16; 3:11–13; Eph. 2:8–10; Phil. 3:8–9; 2 Tim. 1:9; Titus 3:7; Heb. 9:26–28; 10:14; 1 John 1:7; Rev. 1:5–6. Therefore, Owen can refer to this doctrine as the "gratuitous imputation" of Christ's righteousness to the believer, something that occurs "freely by his grace," removing all of our boasting (ibid., 5:339). Consequently, the only boasting the believer has is a boasting in the righteousness of Christ, which is imputed to us by the grace of God (ibid., 5:345; also see 5:314–15).
[83] Ibid., 5:317.
[84] Ibid., 5:292.
[85] Ibid., 5:293.

He who hath been convinced of sin, who hath been wearied with the burden of it, who hath really designed to fly from the wrath to come, and hath heard the voice of Christ in the gospel inviting him to come unto him for help and relief, will tell you that this coming unto Christ consisteth in a man's going out of himself, in a complete renunciation of all his own duties and righteousness, and betaking himself with all his trust and confidence unto Christ alone, and his righteousness, for pardon of sin, acceptance with God, and a right unto the heavenly inheritance.[86]

Fourth, faith is *fleeing for refuge* in Christ (Prov. 18:10; Heb. 6:18). Therefore, says Owen, some have defined faith as "the flight of the soul unto Christ for deliverance from sin and misery."[87] Once again, Owen demonstrates what fleeing for refuge in Jesus has to do with *sola fide*:

For herein it is supposed that he who believeth is antecedently thereunto convinced of his lost condition, and that if he abide therein he must perish eternally; that he hath nothing of himself whereby he may be delivered from it; that he must betake himself unto somewhat else for relief; that unto this end he considereth Christ as set before him, and proposed unto him in the promise of the gospel; that he judgeth this to be a holy, a safe way, for his deliverance and acceptance with God, as that which hath the characters of all divine excellencies upon it: hereon he fleeth unto it for refuge, that is, with diligence and speed, that he perish not in his present condition; he betakes himself unto it by placing his whole trust and affiance thereon.[88]

Fifth, faith is *leaning* on God or Christ (Song 8:5; Mic. 3:11), *rolling* or *casting ourselves and our burden* on Christ (Ps. 22:8; 37:5), *resting* on God or Christ (2 Chron. 14:11; Ps. 37:7), *cleaving* to Christ (Deut. 4:4; Acts 11:23), and *trusting, hoping, and waiting* in and on Christ. In other words, sinners declare themselves "to be lost, hopeless, helpless, desolate, poor, orphans" and, instead of relying on their own works, which are useless and nothing but filthy rags, place all their "hope and expectation on God alone."[89]

These five biblical descriptions of faith, Owen concludes, show us that the

---

[86] Ibid.
[87] Ibid., 5:294.
[88] Ibid.
[89] Ibid.

faith whereby we believe unto the justification of life . . . is such an act of the whole soul whereby convinced sinners do wholly go out of themselves to rest upon God in Christ for mercy, pardon, life, righteousness, and salvation, with an acquiescency of heart therein; which is the whole of the truth pleaded for.[90]

In the end, while Owen believes good works are essential, they are not the cause of justification but rather the effect. In other words, good works are the fruit of justification, not the cause, means, or condition.[91] Justification is, therefore, distinct from sanctification, the latter being the consequence of the former, not vice versa. To confuse the two, as Owen believes Rome does, is to be left with no justification at all![92]

The Forgiveness of Sins and the Imputation of Christ's Righteousness

As seen already, humanity stands condemned before God. Everyone has failed to uphold the law perfectly, and therefore the law exposes our sin and condemns us in God's sight. Furthermore, Scripture tells us that the penalty for sin, for breaking the law of God, is death. If anyone is to be delivered from this charge, Christ must take upon himself the penalty of the sinner, thereby satisfying the wrath of God. As discussed in chapter 5, this is exactly what Christ did, his death being a propitiation for God's elect. Owen writes:

When the Lord Christ died for us, and offered himself as a propitiatory sacrifice, "God laid all our sins on him," Isa. 53:6; and he then "bare them all in his own body on the tree," 1 Pet. 2:24. Then he suffered in our stead, and made full satisfaction for all our sins; for he "appeared to put away sin by the sacrifice of himself," Heb. 9:26; and "by one offering he hath perfected for ever them that are sanctified," chap. 10:14. He whose sins were

---

[90] Ibid. One of Owen's main proof texts is Luke 18:9–14. For his exegesis, see ibid., 5:303.

[91] Ibid., 5:151, 156.

[92] In this light, Owen can say Rome has done away with justification entirely. "This *inherent righteousness*, taking it for that which is habitual and actual, is the same with our *sanctification*; neither is there any difference between them, only they are diverse names of the same thing. For our sanctification is the inherent renovation of our natures exerting and acting itself in newness of life, or obedience unto God in Christ and works of righteousness. But sanctification and justification are in the Scripture perpetually distinguished, whatever respect of *causality* the one of them may have unto the other. And those who do confound them, as the Papists do, do not so much dispute about the *nature of justification*, as endeavour to prove that indeed there is no such thing as justification at all; for that which would serve most to enforce it,—namely, the pardon of sin,—they place in the exclusion and extinction of it, by the infusion of inherent grace, which doth not belong unto justification" (ibid., 5:155). Elsewhere in his *Doctrine of Justification by Faith*, Owen also argues that Rome goes wrong in making our work or obedience something that is even included in faith itself. See ibid., 5:103ff.

not actually and absolutely satisfied for in that one offering of Christ, shall never have them expiated unto eternity; for "henceforth he dieth no more," there is "no more sacrifice for sin."[93]

Just who are those who have their sins pardoned by the offering of Christ? They are those who trust in Christ alone for the forgiveness of their sins and the promise of life everlasting. Those who have received Christ are justified, having their iniquities forgiven by God. The implication, therefore, is that the forgiveness of sins is part and parcel with justification.

As important as it is to affirm that justification is the forgiveness of sins, we cannot limit justification merely to forgiveness. It is not enough to have our debt forgiven and removed.[94] We need a positive righteousness to speak for us before a holy God. Owen says it best: "Now, to be justified is to be freed from the guilt of sin, or to have all our sins pardoned, and to have a righteousness wherewith to appear before God, so as to be accepted with him, and a right to the heavenly inheritance."[95] Indeed, so important is the doctrine of justification by the imputation of the righteousness of Christ that Owen can say, much like Luther before him, that "the life and continuance of any church on the one hand, and its apostasy or ruin on the other, do depend in an eminent manner on the preservation or rejection of the truth in this article of religion."[96]

Owen begins with the meaning of the word itself. To *impute* righteousness is to count or reckon the righteousness of one, in this case Christ, to the account of another, namely, the believer.[97] Scripture does not have in mind, Owen argues, a transfusion or infusion of righteousness, as Rome assumes.[98] Rather, imputation is legal, forensic, and judicial. It is not the infusion of a habit of grace into one's nature that is in view, but the reckoning of a righteous status—namely, Christ's righteous status—to the sinner

---

[93] Ibid., 5:216.
[94] Ibid., 5:159.
[95] Ibid., 5:117.
[96] Ibid., 5:165. That said, however, Owen is not without nuance. For example, he writes, "Men may be really saved by that grace which doctrinally they do deny; and they may be justified by the imputation of that righteousness which, in opinion, they deny to be imputed: for the faith of it is included in that general assent which they give unto the truth of the gospel, and such an adherence unto Christ may ensue thereon, as that their mistake of the way whereby they are saved by him shall not defraud them of a real interest therein. And for my part, I must say, that notwithstanding all the disputes that I see and read about justification (some whereof are full of offence and scandal), I do not believe but that the authors of them (if they be not Socinians throughout, denying the whole merit and satisfaction of Christ) do really trust unto the mediation of Christ for the pardon of their sins and acceptance with God, and not unto their own works or obedience; nor will I believe the contrary, until they expressly declare it" (ibid., 5:164).
[97] Ibid., 5:165–66.
[98] Ibid., 5:173.

as he stands before God who is his Judge. Only then can "the most holy and righteous God justify, or absolve them from sin, pronounce them righteous, and thereon grant unto them right and title unto eternal life."[99]

So not only do we need to have the debt of our iniquities forgiven—which can only happen by our sin being imputed to Christ—but we are in grave need of a perfect righteousness that will grant us favor before God.[100] This is exactly what Christ has earned on our behalf. Because of what Christ, the second Adam, has done on our behalf, earning a perfect righteousness through his obedience in the flesh to the law, we have a plea before the throne of God (Rom. 5:12–19; 2 Cor. 5:21).[101] That plea, however, is not our own righteousness, but rather an alien righteousness, which upon faith is reckoned to us. Owen puts the matter this way:

> The righteousness of Christ (in his obedience and suffering for us) imputed unto believers, as they are united unto him by his Spirit, is that righteousness whereon they are justified before God, on the account whereof their sins are pardoned, and a right is granted them unto the heavenly inheritance.[102]

Or as Paul says in Romans 5:19, "For as by one man's disobedience many were made sinners, so by the obedience of one shall many be made righteous." And again in 2 Corinthians 5:21, "For he hath made him to be sin for us, who knew no sin; that we might be made the righteousness of God in him."[103]

---

[99] Ibid., 5:167.

[100] Owen rejects the opinion of some who argue that if our sins are imputed to Christ, including the guilt of sin, then Christ must inevitably be polluted by them and be "denominated a sinner in every kind." Owen corrects this assumption by pointing out that this would only be the case if "our sins could be communicated unto Christ by *transfusion*, so as to be his inherently and subjectively." However, that is not the case. Instead, they are credited to Christ or imputed to him. So if there is a notion of uncleanness, it is not one where Christ is inherently unclean or defiled. Rather, Christ was "rendered obnoxious unto the curse of the law" (ibid., 5:202; cf. 5:197, 201–2). Additionally, there is a discontinuity between the way our sin is imputed to Christ and the way his righteousness is imputed to us, demonstrating that Christ is not made a sinner in the same sense as we are made righteous. "For our sin was imputed unto Christ only as he was our surety for a time,—to this end, that he might take it away, destroy it, and abolish it. It was never imputed unto him, so as to make any alteration absolutely in his personal state and condition. But his righteousness is imputed unto us to abide with us, to be ours always, and to make a total change in our state and condition, as unto our *relation* unto God. Our sin was imputed unto him only for a *season*, not absolutely, but as he was a surety, and unto the special end of destroying it; and taken on him on this condition, that his righteousness should be made ours for ever" (ibid., 5:203).

[101] Owen goes to great length to demonstrate that Christ is the sinner's "surety" (ibid., 5:182–205).

[102] Ibid., 5:208. Owen states elsewhere, "And as we are made guilty by Adam's actual sin, which is not inherent in us, but only imputed unto us; so are we made righteous by the righteousness of Christ which is not inherent in us, but only imputed unto us. And imputed unto it is, because [he] himself was righteous with it, not for himself, but for us" (ibid., 5:219; cf. 5:221).

[103] Owen also appeals to 1 Cor. 1:30. Here Christ is said to be our righteousness. Owen responds to the objection that this is nonsense since Christ would have to also be our sanctification. He argues that Christ is not our sanctification in the same way that he is our righteousness, and that the text never demands this sort of strict parallel (ibid., 5:346).

Owen concludes that "as the sin of Adam was imputed unto all men unto condemnation, so the righteousness or obedience of Christ is imputed unto all that believe unto the justification of life."[104] This is the great exchange: our guilt was transferred to Christ and his obedience, his righteousness, was transferred to us, that upon faith in him we might be justified.[105] We have no such righteousness in ourselves, Owen explains, but "it is the righteousness of Christ alone, imputed unto us, whereon we are so justified."[106]

Active and Passive Obedience

So far we have learned from Owen that justification means not only the forgiveness of our sins but also the imputation of Christ's righteousness. This, however, raises the penetrating question of what exactly this righteousness consists of. Does the imputed righteousness of Christ include merely his passive obedience (i.e., his suffering the penalty for sin in our stead), or does it also include his active obedience (i.e., his obedience to the law of God on our behalf)?

To begin with, Owen states that this doctrine of imputation has "fallen out in our own days" and to such an extent that "nothing in religion is more maligned, more reproached, more despised, than the imputation of righteousness unto us, or an imputed righteousness."[107] As seen already, Owen most definitely has in mind the "Papists and Socinians," whom he believes "exalt their own merits" and "destroy the merit of Christ."[108] And certainly Owen's debates with seventeenth-century Arminians, as well as Richard Baxter, do not escape his purview on this matter either.

In contrast to these groups, however, Owen affirms both the active and passive obedience of Christ. Indeed, the latter flows logically from the former.

> If it were necessary that the Lord Christ, as our surety, should undergo
> the penalty of the law for us, or in our stead, because we have all sinned,

---

[104] Ibid., 5:322. That Scripture has "guilt" in view, see ibid., 5:197–201.

[105] Ibid., 5:201. Other passages Owen appeals to include Rom. 3:21–22; 4:6; 10:3–4; 1 Cor. 1:30; 2 Cor. 5:21; Gal. 2:16; Eph. 2:8–10; Phil. 3:9. On the transferring of our guilt to Christ, see ibid., 5:349–50.

[106] Ibid., 5:228. He says elsewhere in *The Doctrine of Justification by Faith* that it is "the righteousness of Christ alone, imputed unto us, on the account whereof we are justified before God" (ibid., 5:289). Owen is very careful to clarify that it is not *our faith* that is imputed, but rather the righteousness of Jesus. Nor is it *our obedience*—even if, as some assume, it is Spirit-inspired obedience. If faith itself were imputed, says Owen, then one would be in danger of making faith a work, or something that is meritorious (ibid., 5:168, 172, 317–20).

[107] Ibid., 5:163.

[108] Ibid., 5:165.

then it was necessary also that, as our surety, he should yield obedience unto the preceptive part of the law for us also; and if the imputation of the former be needful for us unto our justification before God, then is the imputation of the latter also necessary unto the same end and purpose.[109]

We have seen so far that Christ suffered the penalty of our sin. So it is not the passive obedience of Christ but his active obedience that is in question. But Owen believes that the active obedience is just as essential as the passive obedience. "That which we plead is, that the Lord Christ fulfilled the whole law for us; he did not only undergo the penalty of it due unto our sins, but also yielded that perfect obedience which it did require."[110]

Owen's case for the active obedience of Christ is multifaceted. First, Owen responds to the attacks of the Socinians against not only the substitutionary nature of Christ's redemptive work, but also his divine person. Since we have seen Owen's defense of the person of Christ in chapter 4, we will not return to it here. Suffice it to say that for Owen, the deity of Christ is foundational to a correct understanding of the work of Christ.

Second, Owen responds to the charge that the active obedience of Christ is "useless unto the persons that are to be justified; for whereas they have in their justification the pardon of all their sins, they are thereby righteous, and have a right or title unto life and blessedness." In this view, to be not unrighteous is the same as to be righteous. If one is not dead, then he is alive. Owen summarizes this notion: "Wherefore, those who have all their sins forgiven have the blessedness of justification; and there is neither need nor use of any farther imputation of righteousness unto them."[111] For several reasons, Owen could not disagree more. First of all, such an argument assumes that if one is pardoned of his sins, then he has

---

[109] Ibid., 5:251.

[110] Ibid., 5:253. Hence, Owen can say elsewhere, "'God imputeth righteousness' unto us, Rom. 4:6; and that righteousness which God imputeth unto us is the righteousness whereby we are justified, for it is imputed unto us that we may be justified;—but we are justified by the obedience and blood of Christ" (ibid., 5:319). This does not mean, however, that Owen is perfectly content with the labels themselves. Typically, active obedience is used to refer to the life of Christ in submission to the law's demands during the incarnation up and until the cross. Then, in the cross we see the passive obedience of Christ take effect, whereby he suffers the penalty for our sin. However, these labels are not perfect, for even in the life of Christ there is suffering, and surely the atonement itself is an obedient act whereby Christ fulfills all righteousness. As Owen explains, Christ "exercised the highest active obedience in his suffering, when he offered himself to God through the eternal Spirit. And all his obedience, considering his person, was mixed with suffering, as a part of his exinanition [i.e., emptying] and humiliation; whence it is said, that 'though he were a Son, yet learned he obedience by the things which he suffered.'" So for Owen the terms—*active* and *passive*—need qualification. But once they are qualified, Owen wholeheartedly argues for Christ's active obedience as that which is essential to imputation. Ibid., 5:254.

[111] Ibid., 5:262.

done all that is required of him. But this is not the case. The "bare pardon of sin will neither make, constitute, nor denominate any man righteous."[112] It is true, says Owen, that the pardoned individual, in the eyes of the law, has been discharged and "looked upon as an innocent man, as unto the punishment that was due unto him." However, "no man thinks that he is made righteous thereby, or is esteemed not to have done that which really he hath done, and whereof he was convicted."[113] Owen drives the point home:

> Wherefore, the pardon of sin dischargeth the guilty person from being liable or obnoxious unto anger, wrath, or punishment due unto his sin; but it doth not suppose, nor infer in the least, that he is thereby, or ought thereon, to be esteemed or adjudged to have done no evil, and to have fulfilled all righteousness.[114]

So while one has been pardoned and guilt has been removed, one has yet to possess righteousness.

Additionally, while the pardoning of sin frees the sinner from the penalty of the law (Eph. 1:7), it does not give the sinner an obedience to the law. This is something he still has yet to perform. Remember, says Owen, the law has two parts or powers. There is a preceptive part, "commanding and requiring obedience, with a promise of life annexed: 'Do this, and live.'" But there is also a "sanction on supposition of disobedience, binding the sinner unto punishment, or a meet recompense of reward: 'In the day thou sinnest thou shalt die.'"[115] Pardon of sin frees us from the "obligation unto punishment," but it does not satisfy the necessary obedience to the law's demands. As sinners, says Owen, we were obnoxious to both the "command and curse of the law." In reference to Christ, by his sufferings "our sins are remitted or pardoned," and we are "delivered from the curse of the law," but this says nothing yet concerning our obligation to fulfill the law's commands and consequently possess an obedience whereby we are considered righteous. That is dependent upon Christ's obeying the law

---

[112] Ibid., 5:263.

[113] Ibid. Owen appeals to the biblical case of Joab and Abiathar the priest, who were both guilty of the same crime. Solomon commands that Joab be executed, but he pardons Abiathar. "Did he [Solomon] thereby make, declare, or constitute him righteous?" asks Owen. Of course not! Solomon says just the opposite, "affirming him to be unrighteous and guilty, only he remitted the punishment of his fault" (see 1 Kings 2:26).

[114] Ibid.

[115] Ibid., 5:264.

perfectly in our place, thereby meriting a righteousness that is credited to us. In other words, it is Christ's suffering that satisfies the curse of the law and his obedience that fulfills the command of the law, and all of this on our behalf.[116]

Owen concludes that the active and passive obedience of Christ are inseparable (Rom. 4:6–8), and they should not be divorced from one another. Yet, they must be distinguished, lest we confuse the two. After all, they are not the same thing. Owen explains:

> It is the imputation of righteousness that gives right unto blessedness; but pardon of sin is inseparable from it, and an effect of it, both being opposed unto justification by works, or an internal righteousness of our own. But it is one thing to be freed from being liable unto eternal death, and another to have right and title unto a blessed and eternal life. It is one thing to be redeemed from under the law,—that is, the curse of it; another, to receive the adoption of sons;—one thing to be freed from the curse; another, to have the blessing of Abraham come upon us.[117]

Having in mind passages like Galatians 3:13–14 and 4:4–5, as well as Acts 26:18, Owen eloquently concludes, "It is one thing to be acquitted before the throne of a king of crimes laid unto the charge of any man, . . . another to be made his son by adoption, and heir unto his kingdom."[118] Or to use another analogy, it is like a man who has his dirty, filthy garments taken away. Now he is no longer defiled by them. But, Owen laughs, neither is he "thereby clothed." What is still needed? The answer is obvious: a new, clean set of garments (cf. Zech. 3:1–5)!

The same reality applies to our justification. Isaiah 61:10, a passage to which the apostle Paul alludes in Philippians 3:9, says, "He hath clothed me with the garments of salvation, he hath covered me with the robe of righteousness." Yes, by the removal of our dirty clothes we are "freed from condemnation." But it is by the gracious gift of new, clean clothes that we have the "right unto salvation" (Ezek. 16:6–12).[119] Therefore, Christ is said to have come to fulfill the law and all righteousness, yielding his "perfect obedience unto it" (Matt. 3:15), and this he did "for us" so that his righteousness is imputed to us (Rom. 5:1–19; Phil. 2:8).

---

[116] Ibid., 5:266.
[117] Ibid., 5:267.
[118] Ibid.
[119] Ibid., 5:268.

Justification and Union with Christ

Finally, it is imperative to set justification within the framework of union with Christ. This union was planned and determined in eternity past (i.e., the covenant of redemption and election), and the basis of this union is to be found in the saving work of Christ in his life, death, and resurrection. But the actualization of this union does not occur until the elect are united to Christ in time and space by the Spirit's sovereign work of effectual calling and regeneration.[120]

From this initial union flow all the benefits of salvation. Or as Owen explains, union with Christ "is the cause of all other graces that we are made partakers of; they are all communicated to us by virtue of our union with Christ. Hence is our adoption, our justification, our sanctification, our fruitfulness, our perseverance, our resurrection, our glory."[121] For Owen, therefore, union with Christ is the "all-encompassing doctrinal rubric that embraces all of the elements of redemption."[122]

Certainly justification is one of those essential elements of redemption, and therefore it must be seen as flowing out of union with Christ.[123] However, justification is not to be randomly placed in the order of salvation (*ordo salutis*)—i.e., the order in which the Holy Spirit works within God's elect to bring them to salvation. For Owen, there is a definite ordering: effectual calling, regeneration, faith, repentance, justification, adoption, and sanctification.[124] Not only do effectual calling and regeneration precede faith and repentance (see chap. 6), but justification precedes sanctification as well. This means that the believer is sanctified because he is justified, not vice versa. This priority of justification to sanctification, both of which flow out of our union with Christ, keeps the forensic or legal nature of justification and transformative nature of sanctification distinct and yet inseparable, thereby guarding us from confusing the two or making our good works the basis of our righteous status.[125]

---

[120] Owen, *The Greater Catechism*, in *Works*, 1:486; Owen, *A Discourse concerning the Holy Spirit*, in *Works*, 3:188–206.

[121] Owen, *Hebrews*, in *Works*, 21:149–50.

[122] J. V. Fesko, "John Owen on Union with Christ and Justification," *Themelios* 37, no. 1 (2012): 12.

[123] One could list "imputation" as well: "The foundation of the *imputation* asserted is union." Owen, *The Doctrine of Justification by Faith*, 5:209; cf. 5:218, 354.

[124] Sinclair B. Ferguson, *John Owen on the Christian Life* (Edinburgh: Banner of Truth, 1987), 35.

[125] "In other words, Owen maintains the classic hallmark of Reformed theology: justification and sanctification are distinct but inseparable benefits of union with Christ, but a person's sanctification (the fruit of which is good works) is not in any way mixed or confused with their justification. Justification logically comes before sanctification because good works are the fruits and evidences of justification, not its antecedent cause." Fesko, "John Owen on Union with Christ and Justification," 9.

In closing, we must not forget what Owen taught us in chapter 3 ("Communing with the Trinity"), namely, that union with Christ is the foundation and cause of our communion with God. As Ferguson observes, union is the "necessary prerequisite for fellowship with God."[126]

Gospel Forgiveness and Christian Assurance

It is fitting to conclude this chapter by reflecting briefly on the relationship between justification and Christian assurance. As mentioned in chapter 1, Owen was no stranger to the internal struggle for assurance. His personal experience (and gain of assurance) was no small factor in his writing a book-length treatment on the subject—*A Practical Exposition upon Psalm 130* (1668)—to help Christians understand the doctrine of assurance better. As the title indicates, Owen's treatment of assurance focuses on Psalm 130, specifically verses 1–8, though verses 3–4 receive the most attention: "If thou, LORD, shouldest mark iniquities, O Lord, who shall stand? But there is forgiveness with thee, that thou mayest be feared."

Drawing from verse 3, Owen demonstrates that the psalmist is indeed right: were the Lord to mark our iniquities, no one could stand. The reason is twofold: (1) God is holy, and (2) we are sinners, guilty of breaking his law, and therefore deserving his just judgment and condemnation.[127] What hope, then, is there for the sinner? Hope, mercy, and grace come only through the propitiation of Jesus Christ, whom God sent out of the infinite goodness of his nature.[128] God's purpose in sending his Son was that Christ's death would be the "means of procuring, of purchasing forgiveness."[129] Because forgiveness is based on what Christ has accomplished, grace comes to us freely. Or as Owen says, "Pardon flows immediately from a sovereign act of free grace."[130] It is appropriate, therefore, to label our pardon "gospel forgiveness." "Indeed, here lies the knot and centre of gospel forgiveness. It flows from the cross, and springs out of the grave of Christ."[131]

If Christ, by his death and resurrection, has secured this gospel forgiveness, how then do we receive it and its benefits? Through faith. As seen already, faith in Jesus results in justification, and justification includes the

---

[126] Ferguson, *John Owen on the Christian Life*, 34.
[127] See Owen's treatment of the law and how it reveals our sin and guilt before God. Owen, *An Exposition upon Psalm 130*, in *Works*, 6:363–68, 386–98.
[128] Ibid., 6:399–401.
[129] Ibid., 6:402–3.
[130] Ibid., 6:402.
[131] Ibid., 6:405. On how the resurrection secures our forgiveness see ibid., 6:491–92.

forgiveness of our sins. And with the realization that one's sins have been forgiven comes gospel assurance. Owen explains, "This discovery of forgiveness in God is a great supportment for a sin-entangled soul."[132] What could be more personally reassuring than Paul's words in Galatians 2:20, "Christ loved me, and gave himself for me"?

Nevertheless, Owen realizes how difficult assurance can be to obtain, and he ascribes this difficulty, at least in part, to a "sinful indulgence to self, or the world, or sloth." So Owen reminds the struggling believer that it is his duty to "labour after an assurance of a personal interest in forgiveness, and to be diligent in the cherishing and preservation of it when it is attained" (Heb. 3:14; 10:22).[133] Certainly such a duty gets at the essence of faith, which is to cleave to the Lord (Deut. 4:4; Josh. 23:8; Acts 11:23).[134] The soul that cleaves to the Lord finds that the greatness of his sin, which troubled him so much, cannot compare to the "infiniteness of forgiveness that he sees in God," providing him with incredible relief.[135] Was this not true for the apostle Paul, who considered himself the worst of sinners (1 Tim. 1:12–16) and yet obtained mercy by cleaving to Christ?[136]

Therefore, Owen encourages the Christian to go to God in prayer that his sins may be pardoned. If we doubt that God would be so merciful, we should consider that God himself has commanded us to do so and that Christ himself has taught us (in the Lord's Prayer—Matt. 6:12) to "pray for the pardon of sin." As a result, we can have "unquestionable security" that forgiveness "may be attained" and "that it is to be found in God."[137] Owen rejoices: "You are not utterly cast off because you are sinners. Let this support and warm your hearts when you go to hear, to pray, or any duty of worship."[138]

How important is this "gospel forgiveness" to assurance of salvation and ongoing fellowship with God? It is the very bedrock. The discovery of gospel forgiveness, says Owen, "is a thing precious and excellent, as being the foundation of all our communion with God here, and of all undeceiving expectation of our enjoyment of him hereafter."[139] Therefore, it is safe to conclude that the doctrine of justification by faith alone—whereby we

---

132 Ibid., 6:413.
133 Ibid.
134 Ibid., 6:415.
135 Ibid., 6:420.
136 Ibid., 6:447.
137 Ibid., 6:468.
138 Ibid., 6:470.
139 Ibid., 6:431.

have forgiveness—is essential to the Christian's confidence that he is a child of God, no longer his enemy. While the Christian may experience nights of great darkness, the light of the gospel shines in, breaking apart the darkness, in order to show the believer that he has been accepted with God because of Christ. It is hard to say the matter more profoundly than Owen does:

> It [evangelical assurance] may be higher or lower, greater or less, obscure or attended with more evidence. It is not quite lost when it is not quite at its highest. God sometimes marvelously raiseth the souls of his saints with some close and near approaches unto them,—gives them a sense of his eternal love, a taste of the embraces of his Son and the inhabitation of the Spirit, without the least intervening disturbance; then this is their assurance. But this life is not a season to be always taking wages in; our work is not yet done; we are not always to abide in this mount; we must down again into the battle,—fight again, cry again, complain again. Shall the soul be thought now to have lost its assurance? Not at all. It had before assurance with joy, triumph, and exultation; it hath it now, or may have, with wrestling, cries, tears, and supplications. And a man's assurance may be as good, as true, when he lies on the earth with a sense of sin, as when he is carried up to the third heaven with a sense of love and foretaste of glory. In brief, this assurance of salvation is such a gracious, evangelical persuasion of acceptance with God in Christ, and of an interest in the promises of preservation unto the end, wrought in believers by the Holy Ghost, in and through the exercise of faith. [140]

---

[140] Ibid., 6:551.

CHAPTER 8

THE INDWELLING SPIRIT, THE MORTIFICATION OF SIN, AND THE POWER OF PRAYER

The spiritual intense fixation of the mind, by contemplation on God in Christ, until the soul be as it were swallowed up in admiration and delight, and being brought unto an utter loss, through the infiniteness of those excellencies which it doth admire and adore, it returns again into its own abasements, out of a sense of its infinite distance from what it would absolutely and eternally embrace. . . . The soul is hereby raised and ravished . . . in all the faculties and affections of it, through the effectual workings of the Spirit of grace and the lively impressions of divine love, . . . [and] is filled with rest, in "joy unspeakable and full of glory."[1]

A concern for biblical piety lies at the very core of English Puritanism, of which Owen's entire theological corpus is a marvelous exemplar.[2] Owen and the Puritans had, in fact, inherited from the continental Reformers of the sixteenth century—John Calvin (1506–1564) in particular—"a constant

---

[1] Owen, *A Discourse concerning the Holy Spirit*, in *Works*, 4:329–30. This treatise also takes in vol. 3 of Owen's *Works*.
[2] Irvonwy Morgan, *Puritan Spirituality* (London: Epworth, 1973), 53–65, esp. 60; Dewey D. Wallace Jr., *The Spirituality of the Later English Puritans: An Anthology* (Macon, GA: Mercer University Press, 1987), xi–xiv; J. I. Packer, *A Quest for Godliness: The Puritan Vision of the Christian Life* (Wheaton, IL: Crossway, 1990), 37–38.

and even distinctive concern" with the person and work of the Holy Spirit.[3]
American historian Richard Lovelace rightly maintains:

> Among the Reformers, John Calvin has been called the theologian of the
> Holy Spirit because his doctrinal work so carefully honors the sovereign
> agency of the Spirit in regeneration and sanctification. This emphasis
> continued in the Reformed tradition, for the English Puritans (particu-
> larly John Owen and Richard Sibbes) have given us the most profound and
> extensive biblical-theological studies of the ministry of the Holy Spirit
> which exist in any language.[4]

Owen's pneumatology (doctrine of the Holy Spirit) takes its start from
the main pneumatological achievement of the ancient church, that which
is found in the creedal statement of the Council of Constantinople in 381:
"[We believe] in the Holy Spirit, the Lord and Giver of Life, who proceeds
from the Father, who with the Father and Son is together worshipped and
glorified, who spoke through the prophets." Owen, like other Puritan theologians, completely embraced as his own this landmark statement of Patristic pneumatology. For example, in *A Brief Declaration and Vindication of
the Doctrine of the Trinity* he declared that the

> first intention of the Scripture, in the revelation of God towards us, is . . .
> that we might fear him, believe, worship, obey him, and live unto him,
> as God. That we may do this in a due manner, and worship the only true
> God, and not adore the false imaginations of our own minds, it [that is,
> the Scripture] declares . . . that this God is one, the Father, Son, and Holy
> Ghost.[5]

And the Holy Spirit he affirmed to be "an eternally existing divine substance, the author of divine operations, and the object of divine and religious worship; that is, 'Over all, God blessed for ever' [Rom. 9:5]."[6]
     Where Owen can claim to be doing pioneering work in biblical pneu-
matology is in his drawing out the implications of classical pneumatology

---

[3] Richard B. Gaffin, "The Holy Spirit," *Westminster Theological Journal* 43 (1980): 61. See also the detailed discussion by Garth B. Wilson, "Doctrine of the Holy Spirit in the Reformed Tradition: A Critical
Overview," in *The Holy Spirit: Renewing and Empowering Presence*, ed. George Vandervelde (Winfield, BC:
Wood Lake Books, 1989), 57–62.
[4] Richard F. Lovelace, *Dynamics of Spiritual Life: An Evangelical Theology of Renewal* (Downers Grove, IL:
InterVarsity Press, 1979), 120.
[5] In *Works*, 2:377–78.
[6] Ibid., 2:399–400.

for faith and practice. Thus, Owen can rightly state, "I know not any who ever went before me in this design of representing the whole economy of the Holy Spirit."[7] Owen is not claiming to be ignorant of or even antagonistic toward the classical pneumatology of the Fathers. As Geoffrey Nuttall, the doyen of Puritan studies in the latter half of the twentieth century, put it, "What is new, and what justifies Owen in his claim to be among the pioneers" in his pneumatological reflections "is the place given . . . to experience."[8]

In chapter 3 we looked at Owen's discussion of the way the believer enters into and maintains communion with the Holy Spirit. In this chapter, we look at some of the key aspects of this communion with the Spirit that are of especial interest to Owen: spiritual experience in general, being spiritually minded, the mortification of sin, and prayer.

Spiritual Experience and Christian Assurance[9]

For Owen, spiritual experience is vital to true Christianity. As he maintained near the end of his life:

> By religion we understand the power of it in the hearts and lives of men, and not any outward profession of it only. . . . The sole use of all outward religious order and profession is lost, where they are not applied unto the ingenerating and promoting of holiness, or evangelical obedience in particular persons.[10]

And Owen asserts that ultimately it is the Holy Spirit who gives the believer, whom he indwells, such experience of "the ingenerating and promoting of holiness, or evangelical obedience." In his words, "He gives unto believers a spiritual sense of the power and reality of the things believed, whereby their faith is greatly established."[11] It is these inner experiences that motivate external observance of the various ordinances of

---

[7] Owen, *A Discourse concerning the Holy Spirit*, in *Works*, 3:7.
[8] Geoffrey F. Nuttall, *The Holy Spirit in Puritan Faith and Experience*, 2nd ed. (Oxford: Basil Blackwell, 1947), 7.
[9] Extremely helpful in summarizing Owen's teaching on biblical piety and pointing out key texts in this regard in Owen's massive corpus has been David M. King, "The Affective Spirituality of John Owen," *Evangelical Quarterly* 68 (1996): 223–33.
[10] Owen, "To the Reader," in James Durham, *The Law Unsealed; or, A Practical Exposition of the Ten Commandments*, 4th ed. (Edinburgh, 1676), xxx–xxxi.
[11] Owen, *A Discourse concerning the Holy Spirit*, in *Works*, 4:64. See also Owen's advice in a sermon that he preached on May 26, 1670: "Sermon XVIII," in *Works*, 9:237: "Get an experience of the power of the gospel, and all the ordinances of it, in and upon your own hearts, or all your profession is an expiring thing."

the Christian life. "Without the internal actings of the life of faith," Owen writes, "external administrations of ordinances of worship are but dead things, nor can any believer obtain real satisfaction in them or refreshment by them without an inward experience of faith and love in them and by them."[12] Inward experience of the power of God is especially important in the context of spiritual warfare, particularly the temptation to doubt God's existence.

> Therefore the way in this case, for him who is really a believer, is, to retreat immediately unto his own experience; which will pour shame and contempt on the suggestions of Satan. There is no believer, who hath knowledge and time to exercise the wisdom of faith in the consideration of himself and of God's dealings with him, but hath a witness in himself of his eternal power and Godhead, as also of all those other perfections of his nature which he is pleased to manifest and glorify by Jesus Christ. Wherefore, on this suggestion of Satan that there is no God, he will be able to say, "He might better tell me that I do not live nor breathe, that I am not fed by my meat nor warmed by my clothes, that I know not myself nor any thing else; for I have spiritual sense and experience of the contrary": . . . "How often," will he say, "have I had experience of the power and presence of God in prayer, as though I had not only heard of him by the hearing of the ear, but also seen him by the seeing of the eye! How often hath he put forth his power and grace in me by his Spirit and his word, with an uncontrollable evidence of his being, goodness, love, and grace! How often hath he refreshed my conscience with the sense of the pardon of sin, speaking that peace unto my soul which all the world could not communicate unto me! In how many afflictions, dangers, troubles, hath he been a present help and relief! What sensible emanations of life and power from him have I obtained in meditation on his grace and glory!"[13]

Similarly Owen can write elsewhere:

> Let a gracious soul, in simplicity and sincerity of spirit, give up himself to walk with Christ according to his appointment, and he shall quickly find such a taste and relish in the fellowship of the gospel, in the communion of saints, and of Christ amongst them, as that he shall come up to such riches of assurance in the understanding and acknowledgment

---

[12] Owen, *The Grace and Duty of Being Spiritually Minded*, in *Works*, 7:435.
[13] Ibid., 7:371.

of the ways of the Lord, as others by their disputing can never attain unto. What is so high, glorious, and mysterious as the doctrine of the ever-blessed Trinity? Some wise men have thought meet to keep it vailed from ordinary Christians, and some have delivered it in such terms as that they can understand nothing by them. But take a believer who hath tasted how gracious the Lord is, in the eternal love of the Father, the great undertaking of the Son in the work of mediation and redemption, with the almighty work of the Spirit creating grace and comfort in the soul; and hath had an experience of the love, holiness, and power of God in them all; and he will with more firm confidence adhere to this mysterious truth, being led into it and confirmed in it by some few plain testimonies of the word, than a thousand disputers shall do who only have the notion of it in their minds. Let a real trial come, and this will appear. Few will be found to sacrifice their lives on bare speculations. Experience will give assurance and stability.[14]

Here then is a strong emphasis upon an experiential Christianity, one that is rooted in the Spirit's application of biblical truth to the heart of the believer. It is this sort of spirituality, Owen argues, that provides assurance against doubt, and ballast against apostasy.[15]

Being Spiritually Minded

One of the ways in which the believer grows in biblical piety is through spiritual-mindedness. Indeed, Owen almost regards the striving to grow in spiritual-mindedness as a mark of conversion.[16] At the core of genuine spiritual-mindedness is meditation, reflection, both cognitive and affective. As Owen writes, "Spiritual affections, whereby the soul adheres unto spiritual things, taking in such a savour and relish of them as wherein it finds rest and satisfaction, is the peculiar spring and substance of our being spiritually minded."[17] True biblical meditation aims at "the affecting of our own hearts and minds with love, delight, and humiliation."[18]

As to the subject of meditation, Owen stresses that especially the person and work of Christ must occupy first place. "If we are spiritually minded, we should fix our thoughts on Christ above, as the center of all

---

[14] Owen, *A Practical Exposition upon Psalm 130*, in *Works*, 6:458–59.
[15] See also Owen, *Nature and Causes of Apostasy from the Gospel*, in *Works*, 7:112–13.
[16] Owen, *The Grace and Duty of Being Spiritually Minded*, in *Works*, 7:274.
[17] Ibid., 7:395.
[18] Ibid., 7:384.

heavenly glory," for it is in Christ that "the beatifical manifestation of God and his glory" is made for all eternity.[19] Owen cautions believers, though, that such meditation on Christ must be according to the Word. "In your thoughts of Christ," he declares, "be very careful that they are conceived and directed according to the rule of the word, lest you deceive your own souls" and do not allow your "affections to be entangled with the paint or artificial beauty of any way or means of giving [your] love unto Christ which are not warranted by the word of truth."[20]

Owen is never slow to enumerate the blessed effects of such Christ-centered meditation. It will, he emphasizes, enable the believer "to endure all [his or her] trials, troubles, and afflictions, with patience unto the end." And it will transform the believer "every day more and more into the likeness of Christ." Thus, Owen can exhort his readers, "Let us live in the constant contemplation of the glory of Christ, and virtue will proceed from him to repair all our decays, to renew a right spirit within us, and to cause us to abound in all duties of obedience."[21] Thus, Owen concludes that such meditation

> will fix the soul unto that object which is suited to give it delight, complacency, and satisfaction. This in perfection is blessedness, for it is caused by the eternal vision of the glory of God in Christ; and the nearer approaches we make unto this state, the better, the more spiritual, the more heavenly, is the state of our souls. And this is to be obtained only by a constant contemplation of the glory of Christ.[22]

Some might feel that Owen's recommendations are unduly subjective. To this criticism, he rightly responds:

> I had rather be among them who, in the actings of their love and affection unto Christ, do fall into some irregularities and excesses in the manner of expressing it (provided their worship of him be neither superstitious nor idolatrous), than among those who, professing themselves to be Christians, do almost disavow their having any thoughts of or affection unto the person of Christ.[23]

---

[19] Ibid., 7:344.
[20] Ibid., 7:345, 346.
[21] Owen, *Meditations and Discourses on the Glory of Christ, Applied unto Unconverted Sinners and Saints under Spiritual Decays*, in *Works*, 1:460–61.
[22] Ibid., 1:461.
[23] Owen, *The Grace and Duty of Being Spiritually Minded*, in *Works*, 7:346.

One final text in this regard—quoted above, but more fully here—provides both a powerful indicator of Owen's own spirituality and a confirmation of the emphasis on piety among those to whom he preached and for whom he wrote:

> The spiritual intense fixation of the mind, by contemplation on God in Christ, until the soul be as it were swallowed up in admiration and delight, and being brought unto an utter loss, through the infiniteness of those excellencies which it doth admire and adore, it returns again into its own abasements, out of a sense of its infinite distance from what it would absolutely and eternally embrace, and, withal, the inexpressible rest and satisfaction which the will and affections receive in their approaches unto the eternal Fountain of goodness, are things to be aimed at in prayer, and which, through the riches of divine condescension, are frequently enjoyed. The soul is hereby raised and ravished, not into ecstasies or unaccountable raptures, not acted into motions above the power of its own understanding and will; but in all the faculties and affections of it, through the effectual workings of the Spirit of grace and the lively impressions of divine love, with intimations of the relations and kindness of God, is filled with rest, in "joy unspeakable and full of glory."[24]

Mortification of Sin "through the Spirit"

Owen wrote three major books on the believer's struggle against sin.[25] *Of Temptation*, first published in 1658 and consisting of sermon material preached during the 1650s, is essentially an exposition of Matthew 26:41, "Watch and pray, that ye enter not into temptation." Owen enumerates four seasons in which believers must exercise special care that temptation not lead them away into sin: times of outward prosperity, times of spiritual coldness and formality, times when one has enjoyed rich fellowship with God, and times of self-confidence, as in Peter's affirmation to Christ "I will not deny thee." Central among the remedies to temptation that Owen recommends is prayer. His pithy remark in this regard is typically Puritan: "If we do not abide in prayer, we shall abide in cursed temptations."[26]

In *The Nature, Power, Deceit, and Prevalency of the Remainders of Indwelling Sin in Believers*, which appeared in 1667, Owen bases his discussion on

---

[24] Owen, *A Discourse concerning the Holy Spirit*, in *Works*, 4:329–30.
[25] All three of these books can be found in vol. 6 of Owen's *Works*.
[26] Owen, *Of Temptation*, in *Works*, 6:126.

Romans 7:21, "I find then a law, that, when I would do good, evil is present with me." Owen shows how sin lies at the heart of even believers' lives and, if not resisted by prayer and meditation, will slowly but surely eat away zeal for and delight in the things of God.

The final work, *Of the Mortification of Sin in Believers*, is in some ways the richest of the three. This treatise was based on a series of sermons on Romans 8:13 that Owen delivered at Oxford and subsequently published in 1656.[27] It details how to fight indwelling sin and ward off temptation. Owen emphasizes that in the fight against sin, the Holy Spirit employs all of our human powers. In sanctifying us, Owen insists, the Spirit works "in us and with us, not against us or without us." Owen would rightly regard as unbiblical those today who talk about "letting go and letting God" take care of the believer's sins. Yet, he is very much aware that the duty of sanctification is also a gift. This duty, he rightly emphasizes, is only accomplished through the Holy Spirit. Not without reason does Owen lovingly describe the Spirit as "the great beautifier of souls." In what follows we look more closely at this important work.[28]

"Vital and crucial to a true understanding of the New Testament doctrine of sanctification" is the way D. Martyn Lloyd-Jones, the twentieth-century preacher and lover of Owen's works, described Romans 8:12–13.[29] Owen would have heartily concurred, as is evident from his *Of the Mortification of Sin in Believers*, particularly his close analysis of Romans 8:13. For Owen this text makes it abundantly clear that the believer has a constant duty to engage in putting to death the sin that still indwells his mortal frame.[30] But equally important for Owen is the fact that, according to this verse, such a duty is possible only in the strength that the Holy Spirit supplies, for he alone is "sufficient for this work."[31] If either of these aspects of the work of mortification is neglected, the doctrine of sanctification cannot escape harm. In our day, the first aspect, the obligation that Romans 8:13 places upon the believer, has often been overlooked, and in its stead there has been substituted an exhortation to give up all of one's known sins, to stop struggling against sin, and, as mentioned above, to "let go and

---

[27] For the date, see Peter Toon, *God's Statesman: The Life and Work of John Owen: Pastor, Educator, Theologian* (Exeter: Paternoster, 1971), 55.

[28] One should also consult Owen, *A Treatise of the Dominion of Sin and Grace*, in *Works*, 7:500–560.

[29] D. Martyn Lloyd-Jones, *Romans, An Exposition of Chapters 8:5–17: The Sons of God* (Grand Rapids: Zondervan, 1975), 118.

[30] Owen, *Of the Mortification of Sin in Believers*, in *Works*, 6:5, 8, 9–16.

[31] Ibid., 6:16.

let God."[32] But in Owen's day, it was the second aspect that seems to have suffered the greater neglect. For among the reasons that Owen gives for his composition of the treatise on mortification is this observation:

> Some men's dangerous mistakes, who of late days have taken upon them to give directions for the mortification of sin, who, being unacquainted with the mystery of the gospel and the efficacy of the death of Christ, have anew imposed the yoke of a self-wrought-out mortification on the necks of their disciples, which neither they nor their forefathers were ever able to bear. A mortification they cry up and press, suitable to that of the gospel neither in respect of nature, subject, causes, means, nor effects; which constantly produces the deplorable issues of superstition, self-righteousness, and anxiety of conscience in them who take up the burden which is so bound for them.[33]

Although many in the church today have erred in the direction opposite to those whom Owen has in mind in this passage, it cannot fail to be profitable to recall some of the more prominent features of Owen's discussion of mortification as a work of the Spirit. For in the attempt to correct the current error with regard to mortification, there is always the danger of overreaction.

Now, Owen's treatment of mortification as a work of the Holy Spirit can be viewed from a number of vantage points. His treatment is especially clear in comments on Romans 8:13, particularly the phrase "through the Spirit." At the beginning of his treatise on mortification Owen notes that the "Spirit" of Romans 8:13 is none other than the Spirit of Christ and of God (see Rom. 8:9, 11), who indwells believers, gives life to them, and makes intercession for them (see Rom. 8:9, 11, 26).[34] And just as regeneration and true intercession are impossible without the Spirit, so mortification of sin can only be performed by the Spirit.

> All other ways of mortification are vain, all helps leave us helpless; it must be done by the Spirit. Men, as the apostle intimates, Romans 9:30–32, may attempt this work on other principles, by means and advantages administered on other accounts, as they always have done, and do: but,

---

[32] For an excellent rebuttal of this view of sanctification, see D. Martyn Lloyd-Jones, *Christ Our Sanctification* (London: Inter-Varsity Fellowship, 1948), 12–21.

[33] Owen, *Of the Mortification of Sin in Believers*, in *Works*, 6:3; see also 6:17.

[34] Ibid., 6:7. Later, in his *Discourse concerning the Holy Spirit* (1674), Owen notes that a different interpretation of the term "Spirit" is possible. It could be taken to mean the "gracious principle of spiritual life in the renovation of our nature." But Owen prefers to be guided by the context of Rom. 8:13 and interpret the term as a reference to the person of the Holy Spirit (in *Works*, 3:547–48).

saith he, "This is the work of the Spirit; by him alone is it to be wrought, and by no other power is it to be brought about."[35]

Owen adduces two reasons for this assertion that the Spirit alone can mortify sin.[36] First, according to a number of Old Testament texts (such as Ezek. 11:19 and 36:26), God the Father promised the gift of the Holy Spirit for the removal of "stubborn, proud, rebellious, unbelieving" hearts, which Owen sees as a description of the work of mortification. Second, the mortification of sin within the believer comes as a gift from Christ. And it is only through the Spirit of Christ that any of Christ's gifts can be actually communicated to believers. Owen writes, "All communications of supplies and relief, in the beginnings, increasings, actings of any grace whatever, from him [i.e., Christ], are by the Spirit, by whom he alone works in and upon believers."[37]

In support of this statement Owen cites Acts 5:31 and then 2:33, which, when taken together, bring to light the fact that repentance (which Owen takes to include mortification) issues from Christ and is made a reality by his Holy Spirit. Owen, of course, is aware of numerous other scriptural texts that speak of the Spirit's accomplishing the work of Christ in the life of the believer. But he is content to indicate this awareness in very general terms by a quotation from the North African theologian Tertullian (fl. 190–215) to the effect that the Spirit has been sent as Christ's deputy, to put into effect in the church all that Christ desires.[38]

Owen's emphasis that only the Spirit is sufficient for the work of mortification should not be taken to mean, however, that the believer should be entirely passive with regard to mortification, "expecting the operation of the Spirit only."[39] Owen takes very seriously the requirement "if ye . . . do mortify the deeds of the body." In his exposition of this Pauline text he is careful to maintain that every believer must make it his daily business to put to death indwelling sin.[40]

Owen, however, is also concerned that Christians might fall into errors

---

[35] Owen, *Of the Mortification of Sin in Believers*, in *Works*, 6:7.
[36] Ibid., 6:18.
[37] Ibid., 6:19.
[38] Ibid. Owen's quotation from Tertullian is not a specific citation from one of Tertullian's works, but, rather, captures the general sense of Tertullian's view of the Holy Spirit as the deputy (*vicarius*) of Christ. For Tertullian's references to the Spirit as the deputy of Christ, see *The Prescription of Heretics* 13.5; 28.1. Owen reiterates this idea of the Spirit as the deputy of Christ in his *Discourse concerning the Holy Spirit*, in *Works*, 3:193.
[39] Owen's point is expressed here by Anthony Burgess, *The True Doctrine of Justification*, quoted in Ernest F. Kevan, *The Grace of Law: A Study in Puritan Theology* (repr., Morgan, PA: Soli Deo Gloria, 1993), 221.
[40] Owen, *Of the Mortification of Sin in Believers*, in *Works*, 6:7–8, 9–16.

similar to those of the early monks, who supposed that mortification of the human body was equivalent to mortification of sin.[41] Some early monks, as well as the Roman Catholic Church of Owen's day and some self-professed Protestants, not only adopted ways and means of mortification that God had not prescribed (for instance, hair shirts, penances, vows), but also regarded means appointed by God (such as prayer, fasting, meditation) as ends in themselves. Consequently, they looked solely to these means to put sin to death, and in doing so, ignored the Spirit, the fountain of mortification.[42] Against such an approach Owen contends that without the Spirit "all ways and means . . . are as a thing of nought."[43] However, as noted, Owen does not swing to the opposite extreme and conclude that the believer must stand passively by and allow the Spirit to mortify the old nature without so much as lifting a finger himself. Rather, the truth of the matter is that the Holy Spirit

> doth not so work our mortification in us as not to keep it still an act of our obedience. The Holy Ghost works in us and upon us, as we are fit to be wrought in and upon; that is, so as to preserve our own liberty and free obedience. He works upon our understandings, wills, consciences, and affections, agreeably to their own natures; he works in us and with us, not against us or without us; so that his assistance is an encouragement as to the facilitating of the work, and no occasion of neglect as to the work itself.[44]

From the same perspective, Owen could later assert in his work on the Spirit that the "Holy Spirit is the author of this work [of mortification] in us, so that although it is our duty, it is his grace and strength whereby it is performed."[45] And as proof of this assertion, Owen can point to Romans 8:13.[46]

Nine Directions in the Fight against Sin

Moreover, Owen provides his readers with a concrete series of nine directions on how exactly he believes Christians can best fight sin. First

---

[41] Ibid., 6:17–18.
[42] Ibid. See also *A Discourse concerning the Holy Spirit*, in *Works*, 3:549: "The foundation of all mortification of sin is from the inhabitation of the Spirit in us."
[43] Owen, *Of the Mortification of Sin in Believers*, in *Works*, 6:16; see also 6:34.
[44] Ibid., 6:20. See also the comments of J. I. Packer, "'Keswick' and the Reformed Doctrine of Sanctification," *Evangelical Quarterly* 27 (1955): 156.
[45] Owen, *A Discourse concerning the Holy Spirit*, in *Works*, 3:547.
[46] Ibid., 3:547–48.

of all, he states that the believer should consider whether or not the sin he or she is seeking to kill displays especially dangerous symptoms. For instance, the "frequency of success in sin's seduction, in obtaining the prevailing consent of the will" is indicative of spiritual ill-health. Is the believer frequently and readily giving into the sin? Another dangerous symptom is when the sin is only avoided out of a fear of punishment. The believer should fight sin out of an abhorrence of sin as sin and a conviction that communion with God is too precious a treasure to be lost.[47] In other words, we are "to cultivate the same hatred of sin that God possesses."[48] Second, Owen recommends that the believer get "a clear and abiding sense upon [the] mind of the guilt, danger, and evil" of the particular sin being fought. For example, Owen urges Christians to think seriously about some of the evils entailed by their allowing unmortified sin to remain in their lives:

1. Christ is wounded afresh when believers harbor sin that he came to destroy.
2. His "tender and loving Spirit, who hath chosen our hearts for a habitation to dwell in" is also grieved and deeply wounded "by our harbouring his enemies, and those whom he is to destroy, in our hearts with him."
3. And such harboring of "spirit-devouring lusts" will cause God to "take away a man's usefulness in his generation."[49]

Third, Owen emphasizes that the believer should reflect on the punishment that sins deserve and how displeased God is with regard to them. Say to your soul, he urges his readers, "What have I done? What love, what mercy, what blood, what grace have I despised and trampled on! Is this the return I make to the Father for his love, to the Son for his blood, to the Holy Ghost for his grace?"[50] Fourth, being thus affected with the gravity of one's sin, Owen then encourages the believer to get "a constant longing, breathing after deliverance from the power of it."[51]

Fifth, the believer should consider whether or not there is a natural or temperamental proneness to the sin with which he or she is troubled. If

---

[47] Owen, *Of the Mortification of Sin in Believers*, in *Works*, 6:43–50.
[48] Joel R. Beeke, *Holiness* (Pensacola, FL: Chapel Library, n.d.), 15.
[49] Owen, *Of the Mortification of Sin in Believers*, in *Works*, 6:55–56.
[50] Ibid., 6:58.
[51] Ibid., 6:59.

so, Owen recommends that the fight against it be accompanied by fasting, whereby "the Spirit may, and sometimes doth, put forth strength for the accomplishing of his own work" of mortification.[52] Owen's sixth direction is to be on guard for occasions and situations that are conducive to giving in to temptation.[53] Seventh, and if one does fall into temptation, Owen emphasized that one should "rise mightily against the first actings" of the sin: "suffer it not to get the least ground." If one allows it one step, it will certainly take another, for, Owen points out, it is "impossible to fix bounds to sin. It is like water in a channel,—if it once break out, it will have its course."[54]

Eighth, Christians should meditate regularly on the "inconceivable greatness of God" and his omnipresence as a way of fighting sin. "Will not a due apprehension of . . . that infinite distance wherein we stand from him," he asks, "fill the soul with a holy and awful fear of him, so as to keep it in a frame unsuited to the thriving or flourishing of any lust whatever?"[55] Finally, Owen urges fellow believers to be careful not to speak peace to their souls before God does, and to note that when "peace is spoken, if it be not attended with the detestation and abhorrency of that sin which was the wound and caused the disquietment, this is no peace of God's creating, but of our own purchasing."[56]

"The Great Beautifier of Souls"[57]

But exactly how does the Spirit effect the mortification of sin? Near the beginning of his treatise on mortification, Owen enumerates three general ways. First, there is what Kenneth Prior has described as strangling: the sinful nature, like a weed in a well-tended garden, is strangled by all that is good and beautiful.[58] The Spirit causes the believer to thrive in grace and the fruit of the Spirit, which are "destructive to all the fruits of the flesh."[59] Second, Owen observes that it is not without reason that the Spirit is described in Isaiah 4:4 as a "Spirit of judgment and burning." For

---

[52] Ibid., 6:60–61.
[53] Ibid., 6:61–62.
[54] Ibid., 6:62.
[55] Ibid., 6:70. The discussion of this "weapon" in the fight against sin takes up nearly seven and a half pages: ibid., 6: 63–70.
[56] Ibid., 6:70, 73.
[57] Owen, *The Nature, Power, Deceit, and Prevalency of the Remainders of Indwelling Sin in Believers*, in *Works*, 6:188.
[58] Kenneth Prior, *The Way of Holiness: A Study in Christian Growth*, rev. ed. (Downers Grove, IL: InterVarsity Press, 1982), 160.
[59] Owen, *Of the Mortification of Sin in Believers*, in *Works*, 6:19. See also Owen, *A Discourse concerning the Holy Spirit*, in *Works*, 3:551–53.

"he is the fire which burns up the very root" and habit of sin.[60] Then, the Spirit brings the believer into communion with the crucified Christ. "He brings the cross of Christ into the heart of a sinner by faith, and gives us communion with Christ in his death, and fellowship in his sufferings."[61] As Sinclair Ferguson notes, "It is in the death of Christ that we find the death of sin."[62]

But at the end of his work on the mortification of sin, Owen expands this list to include the following points about the Spirit's work in mortification.[63] The Spirit reveals Christ's power over sin (see 1 Cor. 2:8–14): though believers may fall and lose various skirmishes against sin, because of their union with Christ, ultimate victory is assured, which gives them hope and sustenance in the fight against sin. Thus, the Spirit encourages the believer to expect aid from Christ (see 2 Cor. 1:21).[64] Then, the Spirit constantly provides believers with the grace to undertake positive acts and duties of holiness (Eph. 3:16–18).[65] Finally, the Spirit, as the "Spirit of supplications" (Zech. 12:10; see also Rom. 8:26), inspires the believer to pray and thereby find strength to overcome temptations. For Owen the enumeration of these various ways in which the Spirit mortifies indwelling sin is a clear demonstration that the work of mortification is "effected, carried on, and accomplished by the power of the Spirit, in all the parts and degrees of it."[66]

In an article on the spirituality of John Owen, Daniel E. Wray has observed that Owen was very concerned "to maintain a balanced and biblical view of the Spirit's place in the Church."[67] Although this section has focused mainly on Owen's description of mortification as a work of the Holy Spirit, an examination of his exposition of the entire text of Romans 8:13 would bear out the truth of Wray's observation. On the basis of this Pauline text Owen expounds the biblical truth that mortification is both a duty and a gift. As the believer undertakes this duty, the Spirit enables him, from start to finish, to carry it out to the glory of God. Thus, it is not

---

[60] Owen, *Of the Mortification of Sin in Believers*, in *Works*, 6:19. This aspect of the Spirit's work in the mortification of sin also probably includes the convicting work of the Spirit, which Owen mentions at the end of his treatise (ibid., 6:85–86).

[61] Ibid., 6:19. See also ibid., 6:86: "The Spirit alone brings the cross of Christ into our hearts with its sin-killing power; for by the Spirit are we baptized into the death of Christ"; and ibid., 6:83: "Mortification of sin is peculiarly from the death of Christ. . . . He died to destroy the works of the devil."

[62] Sinclair B. Ferguson, "John Owen on Christian Piety," *Banner of Truth* 191–92 (1979): 58.

[63] Owen, *Of the Mortification of Sin in Believers*, in *Works*, 6:85–86.

[64] See also Owen, *A Discourse concerning the Holy Spirit*, in *Works*, 3:553–54.

[65] See also ibid., 3:553.

[66] Owen, *Of the Mortification of Sin in Believers*, in *Works*, 6:85.

[67] Daniel E. Wray, "The Spiritual Man in the Teachings of John Owen," *Banner of Truth* 182 (1978): 11.

without reason that Owen can lovingly describe the Holy Spirit as "the great beautifier of souls."[68]

The Holy Spirit and Prayer

In 1657 Owen spoke of the "eminent place of Zech. 12:10," which "is always in our thoughts."[69] This is not surprising, as a number of things in the text appealed especially to Owen's Puritan mind: the idea of the outpouring of the Spirit, the denotation of the Spirit as the "Spirit of grace"—a subject of perennial interest to Calvinists—the prophetic reference to the crucified Christ, and not least, the picture of the Spirit as the inspirer of prayer. Near the end of his life, Owen was able to put into print some of the fruit of what had probably been a lifelong meditation on this Old Testament verse. His major treatise on prayer, *A Discourse of the Work of the Holy Spirit in Prayer* (1682), which became part of his monumental work on the Holy Spirit, took as its theme verse this very text.[70] The Spirit is called a "Spirit of supplication" in this verse, Owen reasons, since the Spirit creates within believers the desire to pray and enables them to engage in prayer: "he both disposeth the hearts of men to pray and enableth them so to do."[71] Left to ourselves, Owen notes, "we are averse from any converse and intercourse with God." For "there is a secret alienation working in us from all duties and immediate communion with him."[72] In other words, if the Spirit did not stir up believers to pray, the remnants of their sinful nature would keep them from communing with God.

Zechariah 12:10, then, was of great significance in helping Owen answer one of the burning questions of his day, namely, the place of written prayers—specifically those of the state church in its Book of Common Prayer—in the Christian life.[73] While many of the Puritans saw no problem

---

[68] Owen, *The Nature, Power, Deceit, and Prevalency of the Remainders of Indwelling Sin in Believers*, in *Works*, 6:188.

[69] Owen, *Of Communion with God*, in *Works*, 2:230.

[70] For helpful studies of Owen's understanding of prayer, see Sinclair B. Ferguson, *John Owen on the Christian Life* (Edinburgh: Banner of Truth, 1987), 224–31; and Daniel R. Hyde, "'The Fire That Kindleth All Our Sacrifices to God': Owen and the Work of the Holy Spirit in Prayer," in *The Ashgate Research Companion to John Owen's Theology*, ed. Kelly M. Kapic and Mark Jones (Burlington, VT: Ashgate, 2012), 249–70. It needs noting that Hyde makes a number of points in his article that we too saw in Owen's work independently.

[71] Owen, *A Discourse concerning the Holy Spirit*, in *Works*, 4:260.

[72] Ibid., 4:257–59.

[73] For the discussion of prayer in this paragraph and the text from Walter Cradock we are indebted to the following sources: Nuttall, *The Holy Spirit in Puritan Faith and Experience*, 62–74; A. G. Matthews, "The Puritans at Prayer," in his *Mr. Pepys and Nonconformity* (London: Independent Press, 1954), 100–122; Horton Davies, *The Worship of the English Puritans* (1948; repr., Morgan, PA: Soli Deo Gloria, 1997), 98–161; Garth B. Wilson, "The Puritan Doctrine of the Holy Spirit: A Critical Investigation of a Crucial Chapter in the History of Protestant Theology" (ThD diss., Knox College, Toronto, 1978), 208–23; Alan L. Hayes, "Spirit and Structure in Elizabethan Public Prayer," in *Spirit within Structure: Essays in Honor of George*

with using written prayers, a goodly number saw little need for them. Walter Cradock (c. 1610–1659), a Welsh Congregationalist preacher who was a friend of Owen, stated forthrightly, "When it may be the (poor Minister) . . . would have rejoiced to have poured out his soul to the Lord, he was tied to an old Service Book, and must read that till he grieved the Spirit of God, and dried up his own spirit as a chip, that he could not pray." Owen similarly maintained that "constant and unvaried use of set forms of prayer may become a great occasion of quenching the Spirit."[74] Owen conceded that the use of written prayers is not intrinsically evil. But since the Spirit whom God had given to the believer is "the Spirit of grace and supplication" (Zech. 12:10), the believer has all the resources he needs for prayer.[75] Moreover, Owen affirmed that the "Holy Ghost, as a Spirit of grace and supplication, is nowhere, that I know of, promised unto any to help or assist them in composing prayers for others; and therefore we have no ground to pray for him or his assistance unto that end in particular."[76]

If there is one Scripture text to which the Puritans gave first place in elucidating a doctrine of prayer, it is Romans 8:26–27.[77] Its highlighting of the inability of believers to pray and the Spirit's intercessory groaning is unique in Scripture. The Puritans, including Owen, had serious difficulties with the idea of the Spirit actually "groaning" and praying for believers. To suppose that the Spirit actually prays for believers, Owen argues, would obviate the need for Christ's intercessory work. It would also indicate, Owen believes, that the Spirit is not fully God, for "all prayer . . . is the act of a nature inferior unto that which is prayed unto."[78] What the passage must then indicate is a parallel to the thought behind Zechariah 12:10: the Spirit is the creator of all genuine prayer. David Clarkson (1622–1686), who assisted John Owen in his ministry to the Leadenhall Street congregation from 1682 to 1683 and then succeeded Owen after his death as the pastor of the church, has a detailed analysis of this passage along these lines in a sermon entitled "Faith in Prayer." He speaks for the Puritan tradition when he states:

> It is his [that is, the Spirit's] function to intercede for us, to pray in us, i.e., to make our prayers. He, as it were, writes our petitions in the heart, we

---

Johnston on the Occasion of His Seventieth Birthday, ed. E. J. Furcha (Allison Park, PA: Pickwick, 1983), 117–32.

[74] Owen, *A Discourse concerning the Holy Spirit*, in *Works*, 4:301.

[75] Ibid., 4:239–41, 338–39.

[76] Ibid., 4:339.

[77] Wilson, "Puritan Doctrine of the Holy Spirit," 222.

[78] Owen, *A Discourse concerning the Holy Spirit*, in *Works*, 4:258.

offer them; he indites a good matter, we express it. That prayer which we are to believe will be accepted, is the work of the Holy Ghost; it is his voice, motion, operation, and so his prayer. Therefore when we pray he is said to pray, and our groans are called his, and our design and intent in prayer his meaning . . . Rom. 8:26, 27.[79]

The first couple of clauses of Romans 8:26–27 indicate why we need the Spirit's help when it comes to praying: we have infirmities and we simply do not know what to pray for as we ought. Numerous Puritan authors commented at length on the meaning of these two clauses. Taking Owen's *Discourse of the Work of the Holy Spirit in Prayer* as representative, we are brought to the very heart of the Puritan case for the vital necessity of the Spirit's aid in prayer.

The believer's consciousness of sin and sense of the awesomeness of God would cause the believer to flee from the divine presence were it not for the Spirit's encouragement and enabling to run in the opposite direction, that is, to God for mercy through the Son. As Owen observes, "It is the work of the Holy Spirit in prayer to keep the souls of believers intent upon Jesus Christ, as the only way and means of acceptance with God."[80] Owen then outlines in Trinitarian terms the subjective element of coming to God as Father. After quoting Ephesians 2:18 ("Through Christ we have access by one Spirit unto the Father"), Owen writes:

No tongue can express, no mind can reach, the heavenly placidness and soul-satisfying delight which are intimated in these words. To come to God as a Father, through Christ, by the help and assistance of the Holy Spirit, revealing him as a Father unto us, and enabling us to go to him as a Father, how full of sweetness and satisfaction is it![81]

No wonder Owen, and his fellow Puritans, prized the work of the Holy Spirit in prayer: it was his help alone that enabled them to find a gracious Father in their union and communion with Christ—an experience "full of sweetness" in this world and a foretaste, by the Spirit (see Eph. 1:13–14), of what they trusted would be their experience in glory of the world to come.

---

[79] *The Practical Works of David Clarkson, B.D.* (Edinburgh: James Nichol, 1864), 1:207. See also Owen, *A Discourse concerning the Holy Spirit*, in *Works*, 4:288–90; Thomas Manton, *Several Sermons upon the Eighth Chapter of Romans* (Worthington, PA: Maranatha, n.d.), 12:226.
[80] Owen, *A Discourse concerning the Holy Spirit*, in *Works*, 4:295.
[81] Ibid., 4:292–93.

CHAPTER 9

LIVING THE CHRISTIAN LIFE AS THE CHURCH UNDER THE STATE

It is the duty of every one who professeth faith in Christ Jesus, and takes due care of his own eternal salvation, voluntarily and by his own choice to join himself unto some particular congregation of Christ's institution, for his own spiritual edification, and the right discharge of his commands.[1]

The Christian life is lived in communion with other believers. As such, it is vital for Christians to think about what the Bible, and especially the New Testament, says about life together in the local church. Inevitably this will mean that we need to think about the question of authority: to whom, under Christ, has God delegated authority in the local church? In the history of Christianity, three broad answers have been given: to the bishop, or to the elders (the presbytery), or to the gathered congregation. Owen, as we shall see in this chapter, was a Congregationalist, and although many evangelicals today are unhappy with the Congregationalist answer, we think Owen's words on this matter have much wisdom to teach us.

The Christian life is also lived in a specific historical context where

---

[1] Owen, "The Duty of Believers to Join Themselves in Church-Order," in *Works*, 15:320.

Christians must relate to the God-given authority of the state. How should they think about political government? Owen lived in times that were as tumultuous as ours: civil war and revolution filled the early years of his career, and brutal state-sponsored persecution filled his latter days. While Owen's thought about the state met resistance from even some Puritans in his day—Richard Baxter and Philip Henry are two who strongly disagreed with him—Owen's passion for religious liberty should be of deep concern to us today, and his thinking about the state not lightly dismissed.

The State of the Church prior to Owen

Although the Puritans were convinced that the Scriptures contain a blueprint with regard to the proper governance of the church, they were unable to agree on all that the blueprint contains.[2] The earliest Puritans, those who emerged during the reign of Elizabeth I, were by and large committed to a Presbyterian model of church government. For example, Thomas Cartwright (c. 1535–1603), deeply impressed by Calvin's Geneva, hoped to "presbyterianize" the Church of England. In 1570, Cartwright began a series of lectures on the book of Acts and became convinced that the church ought to be modeled after the apostolic church, which he deemed to be Presbyterian. Cartwright thus argued that the Church of England needed to totally abolish diocesan episcopacy and concentrate its rule into the hands of its elders.[3]

By the 1580s, however, other Puritan leaders had reached a significantly different perspective on this issue. Robert Browne (c. 1550–1633) proposed setting up completely independent congregations.[4] In his mind, "Christians are a compan[y] or number of bel[i]evers, which by a willing covenant made with their God, are under the government of God and Christ, and [keep] his [Law] in one hol[y] communion."[5] Hence, for Browne, the true church is founded on a covenant, which is "requisite for member-

[2] In this chapter, we are deeply indebted to Baiyu Song for his extensive help in research.
[3] Scott Pearson, *Thomas Cartwright and Elizabethan Puritanism, 1535–1603* (Gloucester, MA: P. Smith, 1966); Steven Paas, *Ministers and Elders: The Birth of Presbyterianism* (Zomba, Malawi: African Books Collective, 2007).
[4] B. R. White, "A Puritan Work by Robert Browne," *The Baptist Quarterly* 18 (1958–1959): 109–17; White, *The English Separatist Tradition from the Marian Martyrs to the Pilgrim Fathers* (London: Oxford University Press, 1971); E. Brooks Holifield, *Covenant Sealed: The Development of Puritan Sacramental Theology in Old and New England, 1570–1720* (Eugene, OR: Wipf & Stock, 1974), 61–73; Michael P. Winship, *Godly Republicanism: Puritans, Pilgrims, and a City on a Hill* (Cambridge, MA: Harvard University Press, 2012), 46–66.
[5] Robert Browne, *A Booke Which Sheweth the Life and Manners of All True Christians, and Howe Unlike They Are unto Turkes and Papistes, and Heathen Folke* (Middleburgh: Richarde Painter, 1582), 2.

ship in the church."[6] True believers ought to separate themselves, therefore, from the Church of England and form congregations bearing the marks of a true church. Separation, then, cannot be an end in itself, but is a means to an end, namely, the creation of a truly Christian congregation.[7] Moreover, while Browne conceded the right of civil authorities to govern, he drew a distinct line between their powers in society at large and their power with regard to local churches. As citizens of the state the individual members of these churches were to be subject to civil authorities. However, he emphasized, these authorities had no right "to compel religion, to plant Churches by power, and to force a submission to ecclesiastical government by laws and penalties."[8] Browne and his followers came to be called Separatists or Brownists, though essentially their model of church government was Congregational.

Under Elizabeth's Act of Uniformity, however, Separatist Congregationalism was not to be tolerated. To curb the growth of the Separatists, state and ecclesiastical authorities passed a law in April 1593 requiring everyone over the age of sixteen to attend their local parish church. Failure to do so for an entire month meant imprisonment. If a person still refused to conform three months following his or her release, the person would be given a choice of exile or death. The Elizabethan church and state hoped to rid itself of the Separatist problem by sending the recalcitrant into exile. Understandably, when faced with a choice of death or exile, most Separatists chose the latter and initially emigrated to Holland. From there, a number of them sailed across the Atlantic in 1620, heading for Virginia. Blown off course, they landed at Plymouth in Cape Cod Bay, Massachusetts, after sixty-six days at sea.

John Cotton's Defense of Congregationalism

A "Middle-way," as Thomas Goodwin (1600–1680) and Philip Nye (1595–1672) later called it, emerged under the leadership of Henry Jacob (1563–1624).[9] In 1616, Jacob sought to implement Cartwright's vision of a church, modeled after the apostolic church, that, while separate from the estab-

---

[6] Jason K. Lee, *Theology of John Smyth: Puritan, Separatist, Baptist, Mennonite* (Macon, GA: Mercer University, 2003), 128.
[7] Kenneth L. Campbell, *Windows into Men's Souls: Religious Nonconformity in Tudor and Early Stuart England* (Lanham, MD: Lexington, 2012), 49.
[8] White, *English Separatist Tradition*, 59.
[9] Thomas Goodwin and Philip Nye, "To the Reader," in John Cotton, *The Keys of the Kingdom of Heaven and the Way of Congregational Churches Cleared* (repr., Weston Rhyn: Quinta, 2008), 10.

lished church, maintained friendly relations with fellow Puritans in the Church of England. In many ways, this can be regarded as the beginning of Congregationalism in England.[10] Before John Owen's treatises on Congregationalism, the ablest defense of this ecclesial position was *The Keys of the Kingdom of Heaven* (1640) by John Cotton (1584–1652).

Born in Derbyshire, Cotton was trained at Cambridge, graduating from Trinity College with a BA (1603) and from Emmanuel College with an MA (1606) and a BD (1613). Under the influence of Puritan divines like William Perkins (1558–1602) and Richard Sibbes (1577–1635), Cotton not only experienced conversion, but also became an influential Puritan preacher and author.[11] Between 1613 and 1615, he struggled with the issue of conformity to the state church. He initially resolved to have "a church within a church," which meant that he would perform both normal services for all parishioners and a separate service for professed believers.[12] Cotton was able to carry on this ecclesial arrangement until William Laud (1573–1645), then bishop of London, summoned him to the Court of High Commission in 1632. Cotton took this as a sign of the coming trouble. After hiding for a few months, he finally decided to leave England. In 1633, Cotton boarded the *Griffin* with his family and other Puritans, including Thomas Hooker (1586–1647). Upon their arrival in New England, Cotton and his family settled in Boston, where Cotton was chosen as the teacher of the First Church of Boston, with John Wilson (c. 1591–1667) as the pastor. It was here, in the safety of Boston, that Cotton wrote and published *The Keys of the Kingdom of Heaven* and *The Way of the Churches of Christ in New England* (1644), two treatises that defended his Congregational convictions.

As divided as the Puritans were regarding the biblical nature of church government, so scholars are not in agreement as to the origins of Congregationalism. On the one hand, Geoffrey L. Barnes has argued from the material noted above that "the origins of congregationalism were essentially English."[13] On the other hand, by using the Bolognese confraternities as an example, Nicholas Terpstra has maintained that Congregationalism should

[10] See Slayden A. Yarbrough, "Ecclesiastical Development in Theory and Practice of John Robinson and Henry Jacob," *Perspectives in Religious Studies* 5 (1978): 183–97; Robert S. Paul, "Henry Jacob and Seventeenth-Century Puritanism," *Hartford Quarterly* 7 (1967): 92–113.

[11] Digby L. James, "Introduction: A Life of John Cotton," in Cotton, *Keys of the Kingdom of Heaven*, vii–viii.

[12] James, "Introduction," x.

[13] Geoffrey L. Barnes, "The English Origins of Congregationalism and Its Beginnings in Australia," *Reformed Theological Review* 37 (1978): 49.

be traced back to Renaissance Italy.[14] And some would see Jean Morély's (c. 1524–c. 1594) *Traicté de la discipline et police Chrestienne* (*A Treatise on Christian discipline and polity*), published in France in 1562, as the fountainhead document. None of these suggestions would satisfy John Cotton. In his *Keys of the Kingdom of Heaven*, Cotton traced Congregationalism back to Matthew 16:19. Cotton pointed out that the power Peter received was "the power of an Apostle," and "so the rest of the Apostles received the same power"; thus "in like sort each Church or Congregation of professed Believers, received that portion also of Church-power which belonged to them."[15] Since it was to the congregation that Christ gave ecclesiastical and spiritual power, the congregation has the right to perform church discipline and elect elders under the sole headship of Jesus Christ. To establish this exegesis, Cotton examined the Patristic era and argued that it was not until the rise of the episcopacy in the third century that the congregational authority was replaced by that of the bishops. However, by retaining church discipline, the pre-Constantinian church was able to hold fast to a state of purity.[16] It was only after Constantine that the church, by abandoning church discipline, truly ceased to be Congregational in its government.

The Magnetism of Congregationalism and Corporate Spirituality

In the same year (1633) that John Cotton arrived in Massachusetts, William Laud was appointed as the archbishop of Canterbury. As a high-church Arminian, Laud sought to purge both the Church of England and the universities, especially Oxford, of Calvinism and reemphasized liturgical ceremony and clerical hierarchy. For Puritans like Owen, the Laudians were attempting to "make the Articles of Religion 'speak good Roman Catholic' and thus lead England back into the arms of the Pope."[17]

Up until 1643, Owen, like most of his fellow Puritans, clearly identified himself with Presbyterianism. In a small volume that he published in 1643, *The Duty of Pastors and People Distinguished*, Owen clearly expressed his adherence to the "presbyterial or synodical" church government, "in opposition to prelatical or diocesan on the one side, and that which is commonly called

---

[14] Nicholas Terpstra, "Renaissance Congregationalism: Organizing Lay Piety in Renaissance Italy," *Fides et Historia* 20 (1988): 31–40.
[15] Cotton, *Keys of the Kingdom of Heaven*, 21.
[16] Ibid., 182.
[17] Peter Toon, *God's Statesman: The Life and Work of John Owen; Pastor, Educator, Theologian* (Exeter: Paternoster, 1971), 9.

independent or congregational on the other."[18] In his later work *A Review of the True Nature of Schism* (1657), Owen stated that when he wrote *The Duty of Pastors and People Distinguished*, he was "a young man" and "the controversy between Independency and Presbytery was young also, nor, indeed, by [him] clearly understood, especially as stated on the congregational side."[19] Furthermore, Owen stated that his arguments on the matter were "purely personal opinions, and [his] sentiment toward Presbyterianism was made without being acquainted with any Congregationalists."[20] As Owen later reviewed his arguments in his *Duty of Pastors and People Distinguished*, he found that his "principles were far more suited to what is the judgment and practices of the congregational men than those of the presbyterian."[21]

After *The Duty of Pastors and People Distinguished* was printed, Owen did not stop searching the Scriptures or researching the matter. And so, in due course, John Cotton's *Keys of the Kingdom of Heaven* came across his path. After a careful examination of Cotton's arguments, Owen found that he was not able to confute them and that he was led to embrace Congregational convictions. With a spot of dry humor, Owen later declared that this "is a course that I would admonish all to be aware of who would avoid the danger of being made Independents"![22]

R. Glynne Lloyd has suggested that besides reading Cotton's *Keys of the Kingdom of Heaven*, there were other factors that led Owen to Congregationalism. Owen's growing commitment to toleration and his observation of intolerance within Presbyterianism also played a role in Owen's ecclesiological change.[23] During the Long Parliament (1640–1648), the Presbyterians gained power politically, since they were in the majority. A number of events during the Long Parliament revealed what Owen came to regard as the intolerant nature of Presbyterianism, such as the publication of the Directory for Public Worship (1645), the abolition of the Book of Common Prayer, and the execution of Laud in 1645.[24] By 1645, Owen clearly favored toleration and liberty of conscience, and when first approached to preach before Parliament the following year, he was a convinced Congregationalist.

---

[18] Owen, *The Duty of Pastors and People Distinguished*, in *Works*, 13:39.
[19] Owen, *A Review of the True Nature of Schism*, in *Works*, 13:222.
[20] Ibid., 13:223.
[21] Ibid.
[22] Ibid., 13:224.
[23] R. Glynne Lloyd, *John Owen: Commonwealth Puritan* (Liverpool: Modern Welsh Publications Ltd., 1972), 50–53.
[24] Ibid., 52.

Defining and Defending Congregationalism

The Nature of the Church

It was essential for the Puritans to determine the origin of the church: does it come from God or from man? Some of their opponents, like John Whitgift (c. 1530–1604), the Elizabethan archbishop of Canterbury, had argued that since the external government of the visible church is helpful but not necessary to salvation, and the Scripture does not clearly lay out details regarding church government, the "outward matters of religion should be determined by human discretion." Owen, however, argued in *An Inquiry into the Original, Nature, Institution, Power, Order, and Communion of Evangelical Churches* (1681) that the churches are "of a divine original, and have the warrant of divine authority."[25] Owen further defined a church as "men associating themselves together, or uniting in such societies for the worship of God, which he requires of them, as may enable them unto an orderly performance of it."[26] More briefly, Owen defined a church as "a society of men united for the celebration of divine worship."[27]

With this understanding, Owen was convinced that "Christ alone is the author, institutor, and appointer, in a way of authority and legislation, of the gospel church-state [or state of the church], its order, rule, and worship, with all things constantly and perpetually belonging thereunto, or necessary to be observed therein."[28] For Owen, the church functions under the direction of both general (the light of nature) and particular (Scripture) revelation. With regard to worship, Owen held to the regulative principle that "only what is commanded in Scripture, or agreeable to the light of nature is acceptable in worship."[29] At the same time, Owen believed that the church also has the freedom, given by Christ in the new covenant, to decide matters like the "time of worship, size of congregation, methods in preaching, etc."[30]

Owen also argued for a threefold understanding of the church:

1. The mystical body of Christ, that is Christ's elect, redeemed, justified, and sanctified ones throughout the world; this is commonly called

---

[25] Sungho Lee, "All Subjects of the Kingdom of Christ: John Owen's Conceptions of Christian Unity and Schism," (PhD diss., Calvin Theological Seminary, 2007), 67–68; John F. H. New, "Whitgift-Cartwright Controversy," *Archiv für Reformationsgeschichte* 59 (1968): 203–12; Owen, *An Inquiry into the Original, Nature, Institution, Power, Order, and Communion of Evangelical Churches*, in *Works*, 15:228.
[26] Ibid.
[27] Ibid., 15:227.
[28] Ibid., 15:244.
[29] Sinclair B. Ferguson, *John Owen on the Christian Life* (Edinburgh: Banner of Truth, 1987), 156. Cf. Owen, *The Duty of Pastors and People Distinguished*, in *Works*, 13:12–19.
[30] Lee, "All Subjects of the Kingdom of Christ," 72.

the church catholic militant and is equivalent to what others called the invisible church.

2. The universality of men throughout the world called by the preaching of the word, visibly professing and yielding obedience to the gospel; this is called the church catholic visible by some.

3. A particular church in a given geographical locale, in which the instituted worship of God in Christ is celebrated according to the Scriptures.[31]

The first two meanings of the term *church* can also be found in the church fathers, many of the Reformers, and most Puritans.[32] Yet, Owen's understanding of the church as a particular congregation that is not merely a local manifestation of the visible church "is unique and forms the crux of his argument."[33] One of Owen's critics, Daniel Cawdrey (1588–1664), noted that Owen's doctrine of the particular church was different from "them of New England . . . who make particular Churches to be Species of the universal Church, as (say they) several drops of water, are Species of water; and also make a man first a member of a particular Church, before he can be a member of the Catholick."[34] For Owen, a visible particular church is "a society of men called by the word to the obedience of the faith in Christ, and joint performance of the worship of God in the same individual ordinances, according to the order by Christ prescribed."[35] In other words, a particular church is a gathered congregation, among whom God is rightfully worshiped, the sacraments of baptism and the Lord's Supper are administered, and church discipline is practiced in love.[36]

Another good place to see Owen's ecclesiology is in "The Branch of the

[31] Owen, *A Review of the True Nature of Schism*, in *Works*, 13:124–25; Owen, *An Inquiry into the Original, Nature, Institution, Power, Order, and Communion of Evangelical Churches*, in *Works*, 15:233.

[32] For example, see Augustine, *On Christian Doctrine* 3.32 and his *On Baptism, against the Donatists* 4.5. On Luther's teaching, see Mark Noll, "Martin Luther and the Concept of a 'True' Church," *Evangelical Quarterly* 50 (1978): 79–85. For John Calvin, see John Calvin, *Institutes of the Christian Religion*, ed. John T. McNeil, trans. Ford Lewis Battles (Philadelphia: Westminster John Knox, 1960), 4.1.3, 7. For the Puritans, see William Ames, *Marrow of Theology*, trans. John D. Eusden (Grand Rapids: Baker 1968), 1.31.24–39; Westminster Confession of Faith 27; and Stuart R. Jones, "The Invisible Church of the Westminster Confession of Faith," *Westminster Theological Journal* 59 (1997): 71–85.

[33] Henry M. Knapp, "John Owen, on Schism and the Nature of the Church," *Westminster Theological Journal* 72 (2010): 346.

[34] Daniel Cawdrey, *Independencie, a Great Schism Proved against Dr. Owen's Apology* (London: John Wright, 1657), 88. Here Cawdrey referenced Thomas Hooker, *A Survey of the Summe of Church-Discipline, wherein the Way of the Congregationall Churches of Christ in New-England, Is Warranted and Cleared, by Scripture and Argument, and All Exceptions of Weight Made Against It by Sundry Learned Divines* (London: John Bellamy, 1648), 260. Also see Geoffrey F. Nuttall, *Visible Saints: The Congregational Way 1640–1660* (Oxford: Basil Blackwell, 1957), 69.

[35] Owen, *A Review of the True Nature of Schism*, in *Works*, 13:174.

[36] Owen, *An Inquiry into the Original, Nature, Institution, Power, Order, and Communion of Evangelical Churches*, in *Works*, 15:233–34; Owen, *A Review of the True Nature of Schism*, in *Works*, 13:179.

Lord the Beauty of Zion; or, The Glory of the Church in Its Relation unto Christ," which he preached as two sermons on Isaiah 56:7 in 1650. Owen explained that the church is like a house, which contains three elements: the foundation, "the materials for a superstruction," and "an orderly framing of both into a useful building."[37] Owen pointed out that Jesus Christ is the foundation of his church, and the visible saints are the living stones that form the superstructure.[38] In another context, Owen stressed that in order for the church to be built, the visible saints had to be "be firmly united in covenant" on the foundation of Jesus Christ.[39] This covenant is "the form of the church while the saints are its matter."[40] And just as the covenant on which the visible catholic church is established is the covenant of grace, so the visible particular church is built on a church covenant. The church covenant consists essentially of two parts, which are obedience to the sovereign commands of Jesus Christ as found in the Scriptures and mutual commitment to the rule of the congregation. Owen was confident that the sole "rule and measure of the government of the church [is] the law of Christ," which is "the intimation and declaration of his mind and will" found only in the Scriptures.[41]

Polity of the Particular Church

According to Owen's *True Nature of a Gospel Church and Its Government* (1689), there are four basic responsibilities of church membership:

(1) Mutual love to one's fellow members to be exercised zealously and continuously.

(2) Personal holiness and moral obedience to the commands of Scripture.

(3) Usefulness toward one's fellow members, toward other churches, and toward all men absolutely, as occasion and opportunity provide.

(4) The performance of all those duties that the members of the church owe to one another according to their calling in the body of Christ.[42]

---

[37] Owen, "The Branch of the Lord the Beauty of Zion; or, The Glory of the Church in Its Relation unto Christ," in *Works*, 8:286–87. These two sermons were preached at Berwick and Edinburgh during 1650 amid the campaign of Cromwell's New Model Army against the Scots, most of whom would have been Presbyterians.
[38] Owen, "The Branch of the Lord the Beauty of Zion; or, The Glory of the Church in Its Relation unto Christ," in *Works*, 8:287–92.
[39] Lee, "All Subjects of the Kingdom of Christ," 87.
[40] Ibid.
[41] Owen, *The True Nature of a Gospel Church*, in *Works*, 16:133, 135.
[42] Ibid., 16:137.

For Owen, members are also subject to church discipline, which is the third mark of the church, along with the proclamation of God's Word and the proper administration of the sacraments.[43]

Here in *True Nature* Owen also gives practical instructions on the officers of the church. He argues that according to the Scripture and "the reason of things from present circumstances," there are only two rightful offices in the church, elders and deacons.[44] Elders are responsible for "the disposal of times, seasons, places, the way and manner of managing all things in church assemblies, the regulation of speeches and actions, the appointment of seasons for extraordinary duties."[45] Owen argues for plural eldership in local churches and specifies that the main duties of elders are shepherding the congregation in teaching sound doctrine according to the Bible and taking care of the souls under their charge.[46]

As for the deacons, Owen states that "the office of deacons is an office of service."[47] According to the Scripture, the main goal of deacons' work is to free the elders from being caught up in mundane, though vital, responsibilities, things such as taking care of the poor, managing church matters—such as "providing for the place of church-assemblies, of the elements for the sacraments"—and the management of church finances.[48]

On Schism

Presbyterian Puritans believed in and hoped for a national church "built upon a system of elected elders, presbyteries, and synods." They "stressed the gift of salvation as apart from, but not unconnected to, a structured church government."[49] As it was contrary to Presbyterian ecclesiology, Congregationalists were labeled as schismatics, especially during Cromwell's Commonwealth and the Protectorate. Such a charge was echoed by the Anglicans after the Restoration of the monarchy (1660). Thus, Congregationalist divines, in response to their accusers, had to demonstrate that a commitment to Congregationalism was not a sinful act of schism, but the "justifiable separation of a gathered church."[50] The charge that Owen was a

---

[43] Stephen Yuille, "John Owen and the Third Mark of the Church," *Puritan Reformed Journal* 2 (2010): 215–27.
[44] Owen, *The True Nature of a Gospel Church*, in *Works*, 16:137.
[45] Ibid.
[46] Ibid., 16:138–43.
[47] Ibid., 16:147.
[48] Ibid.
[49] Knapp, "John Owen, on Schism and the Nature of the Church," 335.
[50] Ibid., 336. See also John Spurr, "Schism and the Restoration Church," *Journal of Ecclesiastical History* 41 (1990): 408–24.

schismatic came mainly through two theologians during the periods of the Commonwealth and Restoration: Daniel Cawdrey, a Presbyterian theologian who made this accusation in the late 1650s, and Bishop Edward Stillingfleet (1635–1699).[51] Owen's response to both was essentially the same: "The guilt of schism lies with those Christian bodies that have departed from the apostolic model, not with the Independents who have preserved the biblical pattern."[52]

In his work *A Review of the True Nature of Schism* (1657), after a careful exegesis of the texts related to schism in 1 Corinthians, Owen gives a biblical definition of schism. It "consists in causeless differences and contentions amongst the members of a particular church, contrary to that [exercise] of love, prudence, and forbearance, which are required of them to be exercised amongst themselves, and towards one another."[53] Thus, schism per se is not about separation from a church, but a division that happens within a church about differences over nonessentials and that leads to a failure of love. While Owen is not prepared to downplay the sinfulness of schism, he is ardent in his defense of Congregationalism from the accusation of being schismatic.

Moreover, Owen argues that the only form of the church appointed by Christ is the particular congregation.[54] Thus, in his refutation of Stillingfleet, *An Inquiry into the Original, Nature, Institution, Power, Order, and Communion of Evangelical Churches*, Owen replies to the bishop's concept that the national church is of divine institution.[55] Unlike Robert Browne, Owen insists on having partial communion with the Church of England, but Owen argues that such communion is in no way of a complete communion.

First, Owen believes that even though the Church of England is in

---

[51] For works by Cawdrey that charged congregationalism with being schismatic, see *Independencie, a Great Schism Proved against Dr. Owen's Apology; Independency Further Proved to Be a Schism; or, A Survey of Dr. Owen's Review of His Tract on Schism* (London: John Wright, 1658). For Owen's responses to Cawdrey, see *A Review of the True Nature of Schism, with a Vindication of the Congregationall Churches in England* (1657), in *Works*, 13:207–75; *An Answer to a Late Treatise of Mr. Cawdrey about the Nature of Schism* (1658), in *Works*, 13:277–302. For works by Stillingfleet on schism, see *The Mischief of Separation* (London: Mortlock, 1680); *The Unreasonableness of Separation; or, An Impartial Account of the History, Nature, and Pleas of the Present Separation from the Communion of the Church of England* (London: Mortlock, 1682). For Owen's responses to Stillingfleet, see *A Brief Vindication of the Nonconformists from the Charge of Schism* (1680), in *Works*, 13:303–42; and *An Inquiry into the Original, Nature, Institute, Power, Order, and Communion of Evangelical Churches* (1681), in *Works*, 15:187–444.

[52] Knapp, "John Owen, on Schism and the Nature of the Church," 337.

[53] Owen, *A Review of the True Nature of Schism*, in *Works*, 13:108–9.

[54] Owen, *An Inquiry into the Original, Nature, Institution, Power, Order, and Communion of Evangelical Churches*, in *Works*, 15:314–19.

[55] Owen, *A Review of the True Nature of Schism*, in *Works*, 13:182–91, 245–50; *An Inquiry into the Original, Nature, Institution, Power, Order, and Communion of Evangelical Churches*, in *Works*, 15:261–76, 313–18.

dire need of reformation, she would not reform herself.[56] And while such need of reformation "is not in itself a cause of withdrawal of communion, . . . it nevertheless shows the disastrous deterioration of the established church."[57]

Second, contrary to Scripture and to Owen's understanding of the particular church, the constitution of the "parochial assemblies" in the Church of England has not followed the pattern of the Bible for divine institutions, but is based on the thinking of men and is thus without authority and lacking divine approval.[58]

Third, the Church of England does not require "a fixed standard of truth, or rule of faith to be professed" by every member.[59] Owen does not believe that the Thirty-Nine Articles are "the *primitive constitution* of the church nor its *legal establishment*."[60] Then, too, church discipline was abandoned in the Church of England, since in the parochial churches, the congregations are "wholly governed and disposed of by others at their pleasure," namely, bishops and state officials, and the churches have therefore lost their "free choice of all their officers."[61] Finally, drawing from his views about conscience and religious toleration, Owen points out that the practice of uniformity by the Church of England would inevitably result in schism.[62]

Congregationalism Extended: Owen on Civil Government

Though Owen was not part of the Westminster Assembly, he was twice invited to preach before the House of Commons during the Long Parliament, in 1646 and 1649. During the Rump Parliament, Owen preached to the Commons on at least eight special occasions. Having become acquainted with Oliver Cromwell, Owen was appointed as Cromwell's chaplain and accompanied him on his campaigns in Ireland and then Scotland. In 1651, Owen was appointed by Parliament as the dean of Christ Church, Oxford. A year later, Cromwell made him the vice-chancellor of Oxford University. As Cromwell desired, Owen and his Puritan colleagues (men such as

---

[56] Owen, *An Inquiry into the Original, Nature, Institution, Power, Order, and Communion of Evangelical Churches*, in *Works*, 15:348–49, 351.
[57] Knapp, "John Owen, on Schism and the Nature of the Church," 352.
[58] Owen, *An Inquiry into the Original, Nature, Institution, Power, Order, and Communion of Evangelical Churches*, in *Works*, 15:354–55.
[59] Ibid., 15:355.
[60] Ibid., 15:356, 357–58.
[61] Ibid., 15:358, 361.
[62] Ibid., 15:362–64.

Thomas Goodwin) tried to reform the university by maintaining its schol-arly esteem.[63] At Oxford, Owen "emphasized the importance of spiritual culture and true scholarship" instead of various "physical observances and customs which smaller minds regarded as having supreme academic significance."[64] Despite such prominent roles in public affairs in the late 1640s and the 1650s, it is unfair to regard Owen as a "political player," or a "political animal." As this final part of this chapter will briefly demon-strate, Owen's political thought was millennium-driven theocratic repub-licanism, which in many ways was tied into his Congregationalism.[65]

S. K. Baskerville has pointed out that Puritans like Owen understood human activities through the lens of providential history, "a conviction that human actions (including political actions) were by nature or design almost certain to create their own opposition, which in turn was destined to be resolved or defeated by the larger purpose of heaven."[66] For most Pu-ritans, this "larger purpose of heaven" was informed by the hope of estab-lishing God's earthly kingdom.[67] Christopher R. Smith's close analysis of three Owen sermons—"The Shaking and Translating of Heaven and Earth" (1649), "The Advantage of the Kingdom of Christ" (1651), and "Christ's Kingdom and the Magistrate's Power" (1652)—reveals at least four impor-tant characteristics in Owen's eschatology:

1. An irenic spirit: Even while formulating his own system to answer vital social and religious questions, Owen acknowledged and re-spected the views of others.[68]
2. Freedom from a nationalistic temper: Even though Owen believed that England had a special, specific role to play in church and salvation history, his eschatology was national without being nationalistic. For Owen, God's Zion was larger than English believers, and Owen thus worked for Zion by dedicating his life to expanding the preaching of the gospel and to training godly ministers.[69]

---

[63] See Blair Worden, *God's Instruments: Political Conduct in the England of Oliver Cromwell* (Oxford: Oxford University Press, 2012), 91–193.
[64] Lloyd, *John Owen*, 92–93.
[65] By observing Owen's actions during the later 1640s and 1650s, Tim Cooper has, for instance, argued that Owen was a man who played politics in order to achieve what he wished. See his *John Owen, Richard Baxter and the Formation of Nonconformity* (Burlington, VT: Ashgate, 2011), 118–24.
[66] S. K. Baskerville, "Puritans, Revisionists, and the English Revolution," *Huntington Library Quarterly* 61 (1998): 156.
[67] Jeffrey K. Jue, "Puritan Millenarianism in Old and New England," in *The Cambridge Companion to Pu-ritanism*, ed. John Coffey and Paul C. H. Lim (Cambridge: Cambridge University Press, 2008), 260–68.
[68] Christopher R. Smith, "'Up and Be Doing': The Pragmatic Puritan Eschatology of John Owen," *Evangeli-cal Quarterly* 61 (1989): 341.
[69] Smith, "Up and Be Doing," 343, 344–45.

3. A positive view of the church: Owen believed Christ's millennial rule would probably be through the church, rather than in person.[70]

4. There was meaning to history: Owen believed that Christ's coming had to be set within history, and that he would not return until it had.[71]

5. The validity of secular vocations: Owen denied the distinction between "sacred" and "secular" worlds or vocations. Thus, the faithful performance of life's duties by any Christian, whether a preacher or a simple laborer, would also help in some way to bring in the kingdom.[72]

Therefore, for Owen, the civil government ought to pursue godliness, while at the same time guaranteeing protection for the preaching of the gospel.[73] This conception of the duty of the civil government is ultimately motivated by Owen's millenarianism. Baskerville was thus right in viewing the Civil War not as "a clash of opposing ideologies but as a fissure between two sides that were moving at different rates in the same ideological direction."[74]

When John Davenport maintained in a 1669 sermon that "the orderly ruling of men over men, in general, is from God, in its root," Owen would have essentially agreed.[75] More than twenty years earlier, on January 31, 1648, Owen preached a sermon to the House of Commons based on Jeremiah 15:19–20, which was later entitled "Righteous Zeal Encouraged by Divine Protection." The day before, Charles I had been executed by Parliament on the charge of high treason. While there was nothing explicit in Owen's sermon—or at least what has come down to us in its printed form—about the execution of the king, Owen did implicitly compare the king to the evil king of Judah, Manasseh. Owen urged the Commons to "discover the vanity and folly of all opposition to men called forth of God to his work, and walking in his ways."[76] Just as Manasseh's "long career of violence and duplicity" ended in disaster for his reign, so, Owen implied, the execution of Charles was a rightful penalty.[77] Magistrates should be "acquainted with the mind of God, to take care that the truth of the gospel be preached to all

---

[70] Ibid., 345.
[71] Ibid., 346.
[72] Ibid., 348–49.
[73] Cf. Owen, "Christ's Kingdom and the Magistrate's Power," in *Works*, 8:390–94.
[74] Baskerville, "Puritans, Revisionists, and the English Revolution," 160.
[75] John Davenport, *A Sermon Preach'd at the Election of the Governour, at Boston in New-England May 19th 1669* (Boston, 1670), 4.
[76] Owen, "Righteous Zeal Encouraged by Divine Protection," in *Works*, 8:153–54.
[77] William H. Goold, "Prefatory Note," in Owen, in *Works*, 8:128.

the people," and if the magistrates neglect their "Master's will," God "will quickly reject them from their power."[78]

Around 1657, the Commons were proposing to restore the House of Lords and offer Cromwell the crown. Knowing Cromwell's struggle regarding the offer, as well as hearing London gossip about how Cromwell would indeed accept the crown (with the suggestion that Philip Nye would be the archbishop of Canterbury and Owen the archbishop of York), Owen became vexed with Cromwell.[79] As it turned out, Cromwell rejected the crown, but Owen's friendship with Cromwell was damaged. Peter Toon explains the reason for Owen's anger:

> He believed that the Republic had been created under the guidance of God in order to fulfill a particular role; he had taken the Engagement to be faithful to the Commonwealth without a King or House of Lords, and he well knew that, in England at least, if past experience was a useful guide, a monarchy and prelacy went hand in hand. Even if Oliver [Cromwell] himself opposed prelacy his successors could so easily reintroduce it and thereby destroy all that which the revolution had achieved.[80]

Politically, Owen was willing to sacrifice his friendship with Cromwell as well as his vice-chancellorship at Oxford for his republican convictions, which went hand in hand with his Congregationalism. As a Congregationalist, Owen had to defend the republic, and this, for him, was ultimately an application of the principles of Congregationalism to civil government.

Conclusion

Whether or not Owen's Congregationalism best captured the polity of the New Testament church—and we believe that it did—it cannot be gainsaid that his thought on this subject played a significant role in developing a key body of believers in the history of Western Christianity. Congregationalism, today found in Baptist and Baptistic congregations around the world, has played a key role in the advance of the church globally and has revealed the key New Testament truth that the Holy Spirit is given to every believer. And it is no accident that the development of Western democracy has vital

---

[78] Owen, "Righteous Zeal Encouraged by Divine Protection," in *Works*, 8:189.
[79] Toon, *God's Statesman*, 99.
[80] Ibid.

roots in this era, for Owen himself wrote in the preface to the Congregationalist Savoy Declaration:

> The Spirit of Christ is in himself too free, great and generous a Spirit, to
> suffer himself to be used by any human arm, to whip men into belief; he
> drives not, but gently leads into all truth, and persuades men to dwell in
> the tents of like precious Faith; which would lose of its preciousness and
> value, if that sparkle of freeness shone not in it.

CHAPTER 10

THE LEGACY OF JOHN OWEN

The fact is . . . Owen is to be bracketed with such as Augustine, Luther, Calvin, Edwards, Spurgeon, and Lloyd-Jones: he is one of the all-time masters. [1]

For twenty-four years I (Michael Haykin) had the inestimable privilege of teaching the adult Sunday school class at Trinity Baptist Church in Burlington, Ontario. Given my love for the history of the church, I frequently interspersed talks on various biblical books with studies in the various epochs and figures of church history. I will never forget one of the first times I spoke on the Puritans. It would probably have been in the early months of 1993, when I taught on the history of English Puritanism from its origins in the mid-sixteenth century to the life of John Bunyan. I did not give a lecture on John Owen on that occasion, though I had been reading and studying Owen for at least ten years at that point. But in the twentieth-century renaissance of interest in Puritanism, especially among Calvinistic-minded Baptists, the figure of Owen loomed large.

On one occasion when I invited questions about a subject I had been teaching, a question came from a bricklayer who was a faithful member of the church. He cited a passage from Owen and inquired about Owen's views. I was taken aback: here was a bricklayer who knew Owen! I was astonished, though I shouldn't have been, for Trinity's pastor at the time,

---

[1] J. I. Packer, introduction to John Owen, *Sin and Temptation: The Challenge to Personal Godliness*, abridged and ed. James M. Houston (Portland, OR: Multnomah, 1983), xxiv.

William Payne (1938–1997), was an ardent Owen aficionado and was not slow to recommend the reading of Owen to his congregation.

Twentieth-Century Influence

Payne was part of that generation in the English-speaking world that rediscovered biblical Calvinism in the 1960s, particularly through various Reformed conferences and through literature published by the Banner of Truth Trust.[2] Around 1969, Payne attended one of the early Reformed Baptist Family conferences at the Pinebrook Bible Conference Center in northeast Pennsylvania, where he saw for the first time the sixteen-volume set of the works of Owen that Banner of Truth had reprinted between 1965 and 1968. As he was looking at the set, a man asked him, "Would you make use of it if you had it?" Payne was quick to reply that he certainly would. "Then it's yours," replied the man, who turned out to be Ernest Reisinger (1919–2004), a key leader in the recovery of biblical Calvinism in the United States. Reisinger loved both good books and giving such away to young men who he thought would benefit from them. And Payne certainly did benefit from the set of Owen. He set himself the goal of reading through the entirety of Owen's corpus, which he accomplished over a number of years. It made him regard Owen as "the prince of the Puritans." Like a number of his generation, Payne was convinced that "most modern works don't come close for the profundity of thought, glowing spirituality and searching practical application" found in Owen. Yes, the Puritan theologian could be "cumbersome in his style," but, using words from Andrew Thomson, Owen's nineteenth-century Scottish biographer, Payne noted, "Owen does not merely touch his subject, but travels through it with the elephant's grave and solid step."[3]

What Payne, like other Calvinists in his day, appreciated about Owen was not only the Puritan's solid Calvinism and his congregational independency, but also his piety found in such works as *Of Communion with God the Father, Son, and Holy Ghost, Of the Mortification of Sin in Believers*, and *The Grace and Duty of Being Spiritually Minded*, which we have explored in previous chapters. It needs noting that certain aspects of Owen's legacy—his political entanglements, his providential reading of history, and his work

---

[2] For the account that follows, see William E. Payne, "My Encounter with John Owen," in *"Declaring the Whole Counsel of God": Celebrating the History of Trinity Baptist Church, Burlington, Ontario, 1972–2012*, ed. Michael A. G. Haykin (Burlington, ON: Trinity Baptist Church, 2012), 75–77.

[3] See Andrew Thomson, *Life of Dr Owen*, in *Works*, 1:xxxviii.

as an educator, for example—have not been prominent in this renaissance of interest in Owen. In other words, it is especially Owen the theologian and spiritual mentor that has been to the fore in recent interest.

The decision of Banner of Truth to reprint the mid-nineteenth-century set of Owen turned out to be a momentous one as it exposed an entire generation of men like Payne to the riches of Owen's works. It is possible that more people were reading Owen in the final half of the twentieth century than at any time before. There is no doubt that J. I. Packer, who played a formative role in the early days of Banner of Truth, had a hand in the decision to reprint the set of Owen.

Packer was first exposed to Owen between 1945 and 1947, when, as the junior librarian of the Inter-Collegiate Christian Union at Oxford University, where he was studying, he came across an uncut set of Owen's works from the nineteenth century, the edition that Banner of Truth would later reprint. Browsing through the titles of Owen's works, he was struck by Owen's treatises on the mortification of sin in volume 6. Up to this point, Packer had held to a view of sanctification propagated by the famous Keswick Conference held annually in England's Lake District since 1875. According to the classic Keswick model, full surrender to Christ would result in ongoing victory over sin in one's life. Packer had embraced this view, but it did not seem to square with reality: his attempts at full consecration did not do the trick—sin was all too present still in his life. Then, reading Owen on the Christian's fight with sin and the duty to kill sin, Packer saw the biblical picture clearly.[4] As Alister McGrath has put it, "The discovery of Owen must be regarded as marking a turning point in Packer's Christian life."[5] It saved his "spiritual sanity," as he put it, and made him a biblical realist when it came to the struggle against indwelling sin.[6]

The reading of these treatises on mortification led Packer to further exploration in Owen's corpus. As he noted in 1983, Owen's impact on him entailed more than "Owen's devotional theology":

> It was Owen's *Death of Death in the Death of Christ* which in 1953 showed me that the habitual form of biblical testimony to the atonement is

---

[4] For Packer's initial discovery of Owen, see his introduction to Owen, *Sin and Temptation*, xxv–xxix. See also J. I. Packer, introduction to John Owen, *The Mortification of Sin* (Fearn, Ross-shire: Christian Focus, 2006), 7–12, 13–15. For more on Packer, see Sam Storms, *Packer on the Christian Life* (Wheaton, IL: Crossway, 2015).

[5] Alister McGrath, *To Know and Serve God: A Life of James I. Packer* (London: Hodder & Stoughton, 1997), 25–26.

[6] Packer, introduction to Owen, *Sin and Temptation*, xvii.

particularistic, thus turning me from a four-point into a five-point Calvinist. It was Owen's *Pneumatologia* that gave me my present understanding of the way to relate regeneration and conversion. And Owen's *True Nature of a Gospel Church*, along with his *Discourse on Spiritual Gifts* and *The Nature of Apostasy*, have done more over the years than any other book to shape my thoughts on what local church life should be. A learned friend who became a seminary professor used to refer to me during the fifties as an Owenian, and I could not deny the justice of the ascription.[7]

Packer's introductory essay to an edition of *The Death of Death in the Death of Christ* that Banner of Truth published in 1959 has itself become something of a minor classic and led numerous people to embrace particular redemption.[8]

Nineteenth- and Eighteenth-Century Influence

The editor of the set of Owen that Bill Payne saw in 1969 and that J. I. Packer discovered in the mid-1940s was a nineteenth-century Scottish Presbyterian named William Henry Goold (1815–1897). Goold was deeply concerned about the fragmentation of Scottish Presbyterianism, and this led him to become an architect of the union of the Reformed Presbyterian Church, his spiritual home, and the Free Church in 1876. This catholicity of outlook was also yoked to a deep conviction of the importance of confessional orthodoxy—a passion that he would have found in Owen's writings.[9] Goold's edition was part of a larger Victorian project to reprint the writings of various Puritan worthies, and here the editions supervised by James Nichol of Edinburgh (1806–1866), who was described after his death as "a man of large conceptions and much originality of idea," especially stand out.[10] Motivating this project was both a respect for the Puritan divines and a larger cultural ambience that reflected a hunger to reproduce the past.[11]

    It is noteworthy that despite this massive reprinting of the works of

---

[7] Ibid., xxv.

[8] McGrath, *To Know and Serve God*, 89–90; see also, 55. Packer has never written a complete volume on Owen. His *A Quest for Godliness: The Puritan Vision of the Christian Life* (Wheaton, IL: Crossway, 1990), which contains a number of chapters on Owen, is the closest he has come to writing a book on the Puritan theologian.

[9] For Goold, see G. J. Keddie, "Goold, William Henry," in *Dictionary of Scottish Church History and Theology*, ed. Nigel M. de S. Cameron, David F. Wright, David C. Lachman, and Donald E. Meek (Downers Grove, IL: InterVarsity Press, 1993), 369.

[10] See the obituary notice in "The Late Mr. James Nichol, Publisher," *The Bookseller*, May 31, 1866.

[11] As one reviewer put it, theirs was an "age of reproduction" when it came to the past. "Nichol's Series of Standard Divines: Puritan Period," *The British Quarterly Review* 45 (January and April 1867): 429.

Owen and other Puritan divines, the impact of this Puritan literature on the larger world of late nineteenth-century evangelicalism was largely muted. There were exceptions, though, a good example of which was Charles Haddon Spurgeon (1834–1892). After his conversion in January 1850, Spurgeon collected original Puritan editions with zest and fervor. Not content with reading the works of these seventeenth-century authors himself, he never ceased to recommend them to his fellow believers. For instance, in a sermon entitled "Paul—His Cloak and His Books," which Spurgeon preached in November 1863, he urged his hearers to follow the apostle Paul's example and to read good books: "Renounce as much as you will all light literature, but study as much as possible sound theological works, especially the Puritanic writers."[12] Spurgeon was especially convinced that wide exposure to the Puritans was a vital part of ministerial training. Thus, at his Pastor's College, founded in 1856, the theology taught was rooted in the Puritans. In defense of this methodology, Spurgeon said:

> We are old-fashioned enough to prefer [Thomas] Manton to [F. D.] Maurice, [Stephen] Charnock to [F. W.] Robertson, and Owen to [Charles] Voysey. Both our experience and our reading of the Scriptures confirm us in the belief of the unfashionable doctrines of grace; and among us, upon those grand fundamentals, there is no uncertain sound.[13]

Spurgeon's use of the terms "old-fashioned" and "unfashionable" with regard to Owen and his fellow Puritans speaks volumes about their modest literary and theological reception in the late Victorian era.

Earlier evangelical eras had been quite different. Within a couple of generations of Owen's death, his works were playing a key role in the conversion and spiritual nurture of the first wave of Anglican leaders in the mid-eighteenth-century evangelical revival. Owen's volume on justification, for instance, was instrumental in the conversion of William Grimshaw (1708–1763), who saw remarkable revival in his parish in Haworth, Yorkshire.[14] And when John Wesley (1703–1791) published a library of recommended reading for his Methodist lay preachers, the fifty-volume *A Christian Library*, he included a number of Owen's works. Obviously Wesley did not include works that highlighted Owen's Calvinism, such as his

---

[12] Charles H. Spurgeon, *The Metropolitan Tabernacle Pulpit*, vol. 9 (London: Passmore and Alabaster, 1864), 668.

[13] *C. H. Spurgeon: The Early Years 1834–1859* (repr., London: Banner of Truth, 1962), 387.

[14] See Faith Cook, *William Grimshaw of Haworth* (Edinburgh: Banner of Truth, 1997), 26–28.

defense of particular redemption *The Death of Death in the Death of Christ*. Rather it was works like *Of Communion with God the Father, Son, and Holy Ghost*, Owen's treatises on the mortification of sin, and *The Person of Christ* (*Christologia*) that Wesley valued and wanted his fellow Methodist preachers to read. But it is noteworthy that Wesley, in some ways theologically poles apart from Owen, nonetheless valued the Puritan as a spiritual mentor.[15]

Later in the eighteenth century, it was a Baptist who was helped by Owen's writings. After his conversion in a hyper-Calvinist environment in 1769, Andrew Fuller (1754–1815) wrestled with the free offer of the gospel. The dominant theological figure in Fuller's world was John Gill (1697–1771), a remarkable theological autodidact—like Fuller himself—but a theologian whose thought so emphasized the sovereignty of God in salvation that human responsibility was diminished. In Owen, Fuller found a guide who helped him reject the hyper-Calvinism of his day and affirm a truly evangelical Calvinism. Fuller's main theological mentor in this endeavor was Jonathan Edwards (1703–1758), but Owen was a close second. As Fuller wrote in his diary on one occasion in 1784 after reading Owen, "[I] feel almost a sacred reverence for his character."[16] It is well known that Fuller went on to play a critical role in the emergence of the modern missionary movement associated with the name of his close friend William Carey (1761–1834). So it was in the eighteenth century that Owen's works had a role to play in revival—what he himself had prayed for in 1674, as we noted in the chapter on Owen's life—and in global mission.

A Guide to Reading Owen Today

Although Owen's works and his massive commentary on Hebrews are readily available today through the Banner of Truth reprint of William Goold's edition, for many it is a daunting prospect to sit down with volume 1 and begin to plow through Owen's corpus volume by volume as Bill Payne did. Where then should one begin? Any selection is bound to reflect a personal bias, and what follows is no exception.[17]

---

[15] On Wesley, see Fred Sanders, *Wesley on the Christian Life* (Wheaton, IL: Crossway, 2013).

[16] Quoted in Andrew Gunton Fuller, "Memoir," in *The Complete Works of the Rev. Andrew Fuller*, ed. Joseph Belcher, 3rd London ed., 3 vols. (1845; repr., Harrisonburg, VA: Sprinkle, 1988), 1:42. For a critical analysis of Fuller's reading of Owen, see Carl R. Trueman, "John Owen and Andrew Fuller," *Eusebeia* 9 (Spring 2008): 53–69. See also Chris Chun, *The Legacy of Jonathan Edwards in the Theology of Andrew Fuller*, Studies in the History of Christian Traditions 162 (Boston: Brill, 2012), 126–31.

[17] For a somewhat different reading guide to Owen, see Sinclair B. Ferguson, "Some Thoughts on Reading the Works of John Owen," *Banner of Truth* 152 (1976): 3–10.

We believe one should begin with Owen's *Of the Mortification of Sin in Believers*, which had such a revolutionary impact on J. I. Packer's life. This small work encapsulates Owen's vision of the Christian life as lifelong warfare with indwelling sin and of how the indwelling Holy Spirit is the believer's great strength in this war. It is available in volume 6 of the *Works* and as a small paperback published by Christian Focus, *The Mortification of Sin* (2006), with an introduction by Packer. A Crossway volume containing all three of Owen's works on mortification is *Overcoming Sin and Temptation* (2006), edited by Kelly M. Kapic and Justin Taylor, with a foreword by John Piper.

Then, Owen's great work on communion with God is an excellent entry into the riches of Owen's Trinitarian spirituality. It can be found in volume 2 of his *Works* and also as a publication by Crossway, *Communion with the Triune God* (2007), edited by Kelly M. Kapic and Justin Taylor, with a foreword by Kevin Vanhoozer. In our opinion, the next Owen work to read is his great treatment on the Holy Spirit. It can be found in volumes 3 and 4 of the *Works* or, again, as a separate volume put out by Christian Focus as *The Holy Spirit: His Gifts and Power* (2004). Additionally, one should read Owen's tremendous *Meditations and Discourses on the Glory of Christ*, which was published posthumously and is contained in volume 1 of the *Works*; it too is a separate Christian Focus volume, *The Glory of Christ: His Office and Grace* (2004). From there, one might also be helped by Owen's articulation of orthodox christology in *A Declaration of the Glorious Mystery of the Person of Christ*, found in volume 1 of the Banner of Truth edition.

Next, one should embark upon reading some of Owen's most famous and rigorous theological and doctrinal treatises. For an introduction to Owen's defense of Calvinism, we commend volume 10 of the Banner of Truth edition, which includes Owen's classic defense of limited (particular) atonement, *The Death of Death in the Death of Christ*, and his first published book, *A Display of Arminianism*. Additionally, we recommend *The Doctrine of Justification by Faith*, in volume 5 in the Banner of Truth edition.[18] Here one will find a very robust defense of the Reformation doctrine of *sola fide*. In our estimation, this is one of Owen's neglected works, and yet it is one of his most impressive accomplishments, one that is relevant for today's debates over the doctrine of justification. For Owen's defense of the

---

[18] Also see the following edition, with an introduction by Carl Trueman: John Owen, *The Doctrine of Justification by Faith* (Grand Rapids: Reformation Heritage, 2006).

perseverance of the saints, as well as his treatment of apostasy and the nature of Christian assurance, see *The Doctrine of the Saints' Perseverance Explained and Confirmed* (in vol. 11) and *Nature and Causes of Apostasy from the Gospel* (in vol. 7). Last, in order to understand the polemical context in which Owen wrote, particularly his refutation of Socinianism, one should read *A Dissertation on Divine Justice* (in vol. 10) and *The Mystery of the Gospel Vindicated* (in vol. 12).

The final major work that we recommend is the Christian Focus publication *The Priesthood of Christ* (2010), which was a major excursus of nearly 260 pages in the second volume of his Hebrews commentary.

And what of his sermons? A good introduction is the first sermon in volume 8, "A Vision of Unchangeable Free Mercy, in Sending the Means of Grace to Undeserving Sinners" (1646), or the *Sacramental Discourses* found in volume 9 of the *Works*—now in a separate Banner of Truth publication: Jon D. Payne, *John Owen on the Lord's Supper* (2004).

Soon after Owen's death, it was said of him that he was "a traveler on earth who grasped God even as one in heaven."[19] So, *tolle lege Johannem Owen*—pick up and read John Owen—and may your mind and heart be blessed!

---

[19] A line from the Latin inscription on his tomb in Bunhill Fields. The Latin runs thus: *in terris viator comprehensori in coelis proximus.* Andrew Thomson, *Life of Dr Owen*, in *Works*, 1:cxiii.

OWEN AS PASTOR TO PILGRIMS

The last word on Owen on the Christian life belongs to Owen himself. Here he speaks to us in two texts: the Lesser Catechism and a delightful and warm pastoral letter to the church meeting in Leadenhall Street, London. But first, a brief word about each is needed if we are to understand the historical significance.

First, let's consider the Lesser Catechism (1645).[1] Owen's christological focus is apparent from the start of his ministry.[2] In 1642, when the twenty-six-year-old Owen began his first pastorate in Fordham, Essex, he found that his people were "grossly ignorant" of Christ and the gospel.[3] To help them, he wrote *Two Short Catechisms, wherein the Principles of the Doctrine of Christ Are Unfolded and Explained. Proper for All Persons to Learn Before They Be Admitted to the Sacrament of the Lord's Supper and Composed for the Use of All Congregations in General*, published in 1645. In these two catechisms, a Lesser Catechism for children and a Greater Catechism for adults, Owen's chief focus is on the person and work of Christ. Here we offer the reader the Lesser Catechism. In doing so, we desire the reader to see just how central the person and work of Christ is to the Christian life in Owen's estimation.

---

[1] Owen, *The Lesser Catechism*, in *Works*, 1:467–69.
[2] For a recent study of this theme, see Suzanne McDonald, "Beholding the Glory of God in the Face of Jesus Christ: John Owen and the 'Reforming' of the Beatific Vision," in *The Ashgate Research Companion to John Owen's Theology*, ed. Kelly M. Kapic and Mark Jones (Burlington, VT: Ashgate, 2012), 141–58.
[3] Owen, *The Lesser Catechism*, in *Works*, 1:465.

Of course, Owen does not limit himself to the person and work of Christ, but expands the catechism to questions and answers concerning the entire scope of the Christian faith.

Second, we would like to also include Owen's "Letter to the Church Meeting in Leadenhall Street, London" (1680). For men and women like John Owen, who were determined to obey their Lord before any earthly monarch, the twenty-eight years following the return of the monarchy in 1660 were extremely difficult—a time of persecution, imprisonment, and trial. Truly, in this era the Puritans found themselves a church under the cross. That they bore such sufferings with remarkable fortitude is due in part to the leadership of men like Owen, a leadership powerfully manifested in the letter reproduced below. Owen encourages his fellow believers to join with him in suffering for the glory of Christ. This letter also well displays Owen's deep conviction that the Christian life is not a solitary life: we need the help of other believers to walk through the wilderness of this world.

The Lesser Catechism (1645)

To my loving neighbours and Christian friends.

Brethren,
My heart's desire and request unto God for you is, that you may be saved. I say the truth in Christ also, I lie not, my conscience bearing me witness in the Holy Ghost, that I have great heaviness, and continual sorrow in my heart, for them amongst you who, as yet, walk disorderly, and not as beseemeth the Gospel, little laboring to acquaint themselves with the mystery of godliness; for many walk, of whom I have told you often weeping, and now tell you again with sorrow, that they are the enemies of the cross of Christ, whose end is destruction, whose god is their belly, who mind earthly things.

You know, brethren, how I have been amongst you, and in what manner, for these few years past, and how I have kept back nothing (to the utmost of the dispensation to me committed) that was profitable unto you; but have showed you, and taught you publicly and from house to house, testifying to all repentance towards God, and faith towards our Lord Jesus

Christ. Now, with what sincerity this hath been by me performed, with what issue and success by you received, God the righteous Judge will one day declare; for before him must both you and I appear to give an account of the dispensation of the glorious Gospel amongst us;—in the meanwhile, the desire of my heart is, to be servant to the least of you in the work of the Lord; and that in any way which I can conceive profitable unto you—either in your persons or your families.

Now, amongst my endeavours in this kind, after the ordinance of public preaching the Word, there is not, I conceive, any more needful (as all will grant that know the estate of this place, how taught of late days, how full of grossly ignorant persons) than catechising; which hath caused me to set aside some hours for the compiling of these following, which also I have procured to be printed, merely because the least part of the parish are able to read it in writing;—my intention in them being, principally, to hold out those necessary truths wherein you have been in my preaching more fully instructed. As they are, the use of them I shall briefly present unto you:—

1. The Lesser Catechism may be so learned of the younger sort, that they may be ready to answer to every question thereof.
2. The Greater will call to mind much of what hath been taught you in public, especially concerning the Person and Offices of Jesus Christ.
3. Out of that you may have help to instruct your families in the Lesser, being so framed, for the most part, that a chapter of the one is spent in unfolding a question of the other.
4. The texts of Scripture quoted are diligently to be sought out and pondered, that you may know indeed whether these things are so.
5. In reading the Word, you may have light into the meaning of many places, by considering what they are produced to confirm.
6. I have been sparing in the doctrine of the Sacraments, because I have already been so frequent in examinations about them.
7. The handling of moral duties I have wholly omitted, because, by God's assistance, I intend for you a brief explication of the Lord's Prayer, and the Ten Commandments, with some articles of the Creed, not unfolded in these, by themselves, by the way of question and answer.

Now, in all this, as the pains hath been mine, so I pray that the benefit may be yours, and the praise His, to whom alone any good that is in this or any thing else is to be ascribed. Now, the God of heaven continue that peace, love, and amity, amongst ourselves, which hitherto hath been unshaken, in these divided times, and grant that the scepter and kingdom of his Son may be gloriously advanced in your hearts that the things which concern your peace may not be hidden from your eyes in this your day; which is the daily prayer of

Your servant in the work of the Lord,

J. O.

From my Study,
September the last, [1645.]

The Lesser Catechism

Ques. Whence is all truth concerning God and ourselves to be learned?
Ans. From the holy Scripture, the Word of God.

Q. What do the Scriptures teach that God is?
A. An eternal, infinite, most holy Spirit, giving being to all things, and doing with them whatsoever he pleaseth.

Q. Is there but one God?
A. One only, in respect of his essence and being, but one in three distinct persons, of Father, Son, and Holy Ghost.

Q. What else is held forth in the Word concerning God, that we ought to know?
A. His decrees, and his works.

Q. What are the decrees of God concerning us?
A. His eternal purposes, of saving some by Jesus Christ, for the praise of his glory, and of condemning others for their sins.

Q. What are the works of God?
A. Acts or doings of his power, whereby he createth, sustaineth, and governeth all things.

Q. What is required from us towards Almighty God?
A. Holy and spiritual obedience, according to his law given unto us.

Q. Are we able to do this of ourselves?
A. No, in no wise, being by nature unto every good work reprobate.

Q. How came we into this estate, being at the first created in the image of God, in righteousness and innocency?
A. By the fall of our first parents, breaking the covenant of God, losing his grace, and deserving his curse.

Q. By what way may we be delivered from this miserable estate?
A. Only by Jesus Christ.

Q. What is Jesus Christ?
A. God and man united in one person, to be a Mediator between God and man.

Q. What is he unto us?
A. A King, a Priest, and a Prophet.

Q. Wherein doth he exercise his kingly power towards us?
A. In converting us unto God by his Spirit, subduing us unto his obedience, and ruling in us by his grace.

Q. In what doth the exercise of his priestly office for us chiefly consist?
A. In offering up himself an acceptable sacrifice on the cross, so satisfying the justice of God for our sins, removing his curse from our persons, and bringing us unto him.

Q. Wherein doth Christ exercise his prophetical office towards us?
A. In revealing to our hearts, from the bosom of his Father, the way and truth whereby we must come unto him.

Q. In what condition doth Jesus Christ exercise these offices?
A. He did in a low estate of humiliation on earth, but now in a glorious estate of exaltation in heaven.

Q. For whose sake doth Christ perform all these?
A. Only for his elect.

Q. What is the church of Christ?
A. The universal company of God's elect, called to the adoption of children.

Q. How come we to be members of this church?
A. By a lively faith.

Q. What is a lively faith?
A. An assured resting of the soul upon God's promises of mercy in Jesus Christ, for pardon of sins here and glory hereafter.

Q. How come we to have this faith?
A. By the effectual working of the Spirit of God in our hearts, freely calling us from the state of nature to the state of grace.

Q. *Are we accounted righteous for our faith?*
A. No, but only for the righteousness of Christ, freely imputed unto us, and laid hold of by faith.

Q. *Is there no more required of us but faith only?*
A. Yes; repentance also, and holiness.

Q. *What is repentance?*
A. A forsaking of all sin, with godly sorrow for what we have committed.

Q. *What is that holiness which is required of us?*
A. Universal obedience to the will of God revealed unto us.

Q. *What are the privileges of believers?*
A. First, union with Christ; secondly, adoption of children; thirdly, communion of saints; fourthly, right to the seals of the new covenant; fifthly, Christ liberty; sixthly, resurrection of the body to life eternal.

Q. *What are the sacraments, or seals, of the new covenant?*
A. Visible seals of God's spiritual promises, made unto us in the blood of Jesus Christ.

Q. *Which be they?*
A. Baptism and the Lord's supper.

Q. *What is baptism?*
A. A holy ordinance, whereby, being sprinkled with water according to Christ's institution, we are by his grace made children of God, and have the promises of the covenant sealed unto us.

Q. *What is the Lord's supper?*
A. A holy ordinance of Christ, appointed to communicate unto believers his body and blood spiritually, being represented by bread and wine, blessed, broken, poured out, and received of them.

Q. *Who have a right unto this sacrament?*
A. They only who have an interest in Jesus Christ by faith.

Q. *What is the communion of saints?*
A. A holy conjunction between all God's people, partakers of the same Spirit, and members of the same mystical body.

Q. *What is the end of all this dispensation?*
A. The glory of God in our salvation.

Glory be to God on high!

Letter to the Church Meeting in
Leadenhall Street, London [1680][4]

Beloved in the Lord,

Mercy, grace and peace be multiplied to you from God our Father and from our Lord Jesus Christ, by the communication of the Holy Ghost. I thought and hoped that by this time I might have been present with you, according unto my desire and resolution; but it hath pleased our holy and gracious Father otherwise to dispose of me, at least for a season. The continuance of my painful infirmities and the increase of my weaknesses will not allow me at present to hope that I should be able to bear the journey. How great an exercise this is to me, considering the season, he knows, to whose will I would in all things cheerfully submit myself.

But although I am absent from you in body, I am in mind, affection and spirit present with you, and in your assemblies; for I hope you will be found my crown and rejoicing in the day of the Lord: and my prayer for you night and day is, that you may stand fast in the whole will of God, and maintain the beginning of your confidence without wavering, firm unto the end. I know it is needless for me at this distance to write to you about what concerns you in point of duty at this season, that work being well supplied by my brother in the ministry;[5] yet give me leave, out of my abundant affections towards you, to bring some few things to your remembrance as my weakness will permit.

And in the first place, I pray God it may be fixed and rooted in our minds, that the shame and loss we may undergo for the sake of Christ and the profession of the Gospel, is the greatest honour which, in this life, we can be made partakers of. Hence it is reckoned to the Philippians in a peculiar manner, that it was given unto them, not only to believe in Christ, but also to suffer for him;[6] That it is far more honourable to suffer with Christ than to reign with the greatest of his enemies. If this be fixed by faith in our

---

[4] From *The Correspondence of John Owen (1616–1683)*, ed. Peter Toon (Cambridge: James Clarke, 1970), 170–72. Spelling has been modernized. For the date of this letter, see Mark Burden, "John Owen, Learned Puritan," Centre for Early Modern Studies, accessed June 17, 2013, http://www.cems-oxford.org/projects/lucy-hutchinson/john-owen-learned-puritan.

[5] In the latter days of his ministry, Owen had a number of ministerial assistants. In 1680, when he wrote this letter, Isaac Loeffs was his assistant.

[6] See Phil. 1:29.

minds, it will tend greatly to our encouragement. I mention these things only, as knowing that they are more at large pressed on you.

And secondly, the next thing I would recommend unto you at this season is the increase of mutual love among yourselves. For every trial of our faith towards our Lord Jesus Christ is also a trial of our love towards the brethren. This is that which the Lord Christ expects from us, namely, that when the hatred of the world doth openly manifest and act itself against us all, we should evidence an active love among ourselves. If there have been any decays, any coldness herein, if they are not recovered and healed in such a season, it can never be expected. I pray God therefore that your mutual love may abound more and more in all the effects and fruits of it towards the whole society and every member thereof. You may justly measure the fruit of your present trial by the increase of this grace amongst you: in particular have a due regard to the weak and tempted that "that which is lame may not be turned out of the way, but rather let it be healed."[7]

Furthermore, brethren, I beseech you to hear a word of advice in case the persecution increases, which it is like to do for a season. I could wish that because you have no ruling elders, and your teachers cannot walk about publicly with safety, that you would appoint some among yourselves, who may continually as their occasions will admit, go up and down from house to house and apply themselves peculiarly unto the weak, the tempted, the fearful, those who are ready to despond, or to halt, and to encourage them in the Lord. Choose out those unto this end who are endued with a spirit of courage and fortitude; and let them know that they are happy whom Christ will honour with his blessed work. And I desire the persons may be of this number who are faithful men, and know the state of the church; by this means you will know what is the frame of the members of the church, which will be a great direction to you, even in your prayers.

Watch now, brethren, that if it be the will of God, not one soul may be lost from under your care. Let not one be overlooked or neglected. Consider all their conditions, and apply yourselves to all their circumstances.

Finally brethren that I be not at present further troublesome to you, examine yourselves, as to your spiritual benefit which you have received or do receive, by your present fears and dangers, which will alone give you the true measure of your condition. For if this tends to the exercise of your faith and love and holiness, if this increases your valuation of the privileges

---

[7] Heb. 12:13.

of the gospel, it will be an undoubted token of the blessed issue which the Lord Christ will give unto your troubles.

Pray for me as you do, and do it the rather, that if it be the will of God, I may be restored to you. And if not, that a blessed entrance may be given to me into the kingdom of God and glory. Salute all the church in my name. I take the boldness in the Lord to subscribe myself,

Your unworthy pastor and your servant for Jesus sake,
J. Owen

Postscript

I humbly desire you would remember in your prayers the family where I am;[8] from whom I have received and do receive great Christian kindness. I may say as the Apostle of Onesiphorus: the Lord give unto them that they may find mercy of the Lord in that day; for they have often refreshed me in my great distress.[9]

---

[8] Owen was staying at the home of Lord Philip Wharton (1613–1696), who was regarded by many in his day as a supporter of the Congregationalists like Owen, but who actually seems to have held an ecclesiological position midway between Presbyterianism and Congregationalism. He supported numerous Nonconformist ministers after the restoration of the monarchy in 1662. The Latin epitaph on his tomb noted that Wharton was an "advocate and patron of the Reformed Religion, a model alike of good works, and of a true and living faith. His doors stood open to outcast ministers of God's Word, affording them shelter and hospitality." Quoted in K. W. Wadsworth, "Philip, Lord Wharton—Revolutionary Aristocrat?" (annual lecture of the United Reformed Church Society, 1990), http://www.ravenstonedale.org/history_archive/docs/folder9_wharton.pdf, pp. 8–9. For a brief biography of Wharton, see Sean Kelsey, "Wharton, Philip, Fourth Baron Wharton (1613–1696)," in *Oxford Dictionary of National Biography* (Oxford: Oxford University Press, 2004); online ed., January 2008; accessed June 16, 2013, http://www.oxforddnb.com.libaccess.lib.mcmaster.ca/view/article/29170.

[9] See 2 Tim. 1:18.

I am going to him whom my soul hath loved, or rather who hath loved me with an everlasting love; which is the whole ground of all my consolation. . . . I am leaving the ship of the church in a storm, but whilst the great Pilot is in it the loss of a poor under-rower will be inconsiderable. Live and pray and hope and wait patiently and do not despair; the promise stands invincible that he will never leave thee nor forsake thee.

JOHN OWEN, LETTER TO CHARLES FLEETWOOD,
AUGUST 22, 1683

SELECT BIBLIOGRAPHY

This bibliography is intentionally limited. For an extensive bibliography, see Kelly M. Kapic and Mark Jones, eds., *The Ashgate Research Companion to John Owen's Theology* (Burlington, VT: Ashgate, 2012), 297–328.

Abbott, John. "John Owen and the Basis of Christian Unity." In *Out of Bondage*. London: Westminster Conference, 1983.

Barcellos, Richard C. "John Owen and New Covenant Theology." *Reformed Baptist Theological Review* 1, no. 2 (2004): 12–46.

Barraclough, Peter. *John Owen, 1616–1683*. London: Independent Press, 1961.

Beeke, Joel R., and Mark Jones. *A Puritan Theology: Doctrine for Life*. Grand Rapids: Reformation Heritage, 2012.

Brown, Michael. "The Covenant of Works Revived: John Owen on Republication in the Mosaic Covenant." *The Confessional Presbyterian* 4 (2008): 151–61, 310.

Cleveland, Christopher. *Thomism in John Owen*. Hampshire: Ashgate, 2013.

Coffey, John. "John Owen and the Puritan Toleration Controversy, 1646–59." In *The Ashgate Research Companion to John Owen's Theology*, edited by Kelly M. Kapic and Mark Jones, 227–48. Burlington, VT: Ashgate, 2012.

Cooper, Tim. *John Owen, Richard Baxter and the Formation of Nonconformity*. Burlington, VT: Ashgate, 2011.

———. "Owen's Personality: The Man behind the Theology." In *The Ashgate Research Companion to John Owen's Theology*, edited by Kelly M. Kapic and Mark Jones, 215–26. Burlington, VT: Ashgate, 2012.

———. "State of the Field: John Owen Unleashed: Almost." *Conversations in Religion and Theology* 6, no. 2 (2008): 226–57.

———. "Why Did Richard Baxter and John Owen Diverge? The Impact of the First Civil War." *Journal of Ecclesiastical History* 61, no. 3 (2010): 496–516.

Crisp, Oliver D. *Revisioning Christology: Theology in the Reformed Tradition*. Burlington, VT: Ashgate, 2011.

Daniels, Richard. *The Christology of John Owen*. Grand Rapids: Reformation Heritage, 2004.

Entwistle, F. R. "Some Aspects of John Owen's Doctrine of the Person and Work of Christ." In *Faith and a Good Conscience*. London: Westminster Conference, 1962.

Eveson, Philip. "The Case for Forensic Justification in John Owen." In *Seeing the Lord*. London: Westminster Conference, 2000.

Ferguson, Sinclair. "John Owen and the Doctrine of the Holy Spirit." In *John Owen: The Man and His Theology*, edited by Robert W. Oliver, 101–29. Phillipsburg, NJ: P&R, 2002.

———. "John Owen and the Doctrine of the Person of Christ." In *John Owen: The Man and His Theology*, edited by Robert W. Oliver, 69–100. Phillipsburg, NJ: P&R, 2002.

———. "John Owen on Conversion." *Banner of Truth* 134 (1974): 20–25.

———. "John Owen on Piety." *Banner of Truth* 191 (1979): 47–60; and 194 (1979): 6–19.

———. *John Owen on the Christian Life*. Edinburgh: Banner of Truth, 1987.

———. "John Owen on the Spirit in the Life of Christ." *Banner of Truth* 293 (1988): 10–15; and 294 (1988): 10–14.

———. "Some Thoughts on Reading the Works of John Owen." *Banner of Truth* 152 (1972): 3–10.

Gatiss, Lee. "From Life's First Cry: John Owen on Infant Baptism and Infant Salvation." In *The Ashgate Research Companion to John Owen's Theology*, edited by Kelly M. Kapic and Mark Jones, 271–81. Burlington, VT: Ashgate, 2012.

Gleason, Randall C. *John Calvin and John Owen on Mortification: A Comparative Study in Reformed Spirituality*. New York: Peter Lang, 1995.

Golding, Peter. "Owen on the Mortification of Sin." *Banner of Truth* 321 (1990): 13–16; and 322 (1990): 20–24.

Griffiths, Steve. *Redeem the Time: The Problem of Sin in the Writings of John Owen*. Fearn, Ross-shire: Mentor, 2001.

Guelzo, Allen C. "John Owen, Puritan Pacesetter." *Christianity Today* 20 (May 21, 1976): 14–16.

Gundry, Stanley N. "John Owen on Authority and Scripture." In *Inerrancy and the Church*, edited by John D. Hannah, 189–221. Chicago: Moody, 1984.

Hannah, John D. "The Cure of Souls; or, Pastoral Counseling: The Insight of John Owen." *Reformation and Revival Journal* 5, no. 2 (1996): 71–92.

———. "Insights into Pastoral Counseling from John Owen." In *Integrity of Heart, Skillfulness of Hands*, edited by Charles Dyer and Roy Zuck, 348–60. Grand Rapids: Baker, 1994.

Harrison, Graham S. "John Owen's Doctrine of the Church." In *John Owen: The Man and His Theology*, edited by Robert W. Oliver, 159–90. Phillipsburg, NJ: P&R, 2002.

Howson, Barry H. "The Puritan Hermeneutics of John Owen: A Recommendation." *Westminster Theological Journal* 63 (2001): 351–76.

Hunsinger, George. "Justification and Mystical Union with Christ: Where Does Owen Stand?," In *The Ashgate Research Companion to John Owen's Theology*, edited by Kelly M. Kapic and Mark Jones, 199–211. Burlington, VT: Ashgate, 2012.

Hyde, Daniel R. "'The Fire That Kindleth All Our Sacrifices to God': Owen and the Work of the Holy Spirit in Prayer." In *The Ashgate Research Companion to John Owen's Theology*, edited by Kelly M. Kapic and Mark Jones, 249–70. Burlington, VT: Ashgate, 2012.

Jones, D. Martyn Lloyd. "John Owen on Schism." In *Diversity in Unity*. London: Westminster Conference, 1963.

Kapic, Kelly. "Communion with God by John Owen (1616–1683)." In *The Devoted Life: An Invitation to the Puritan Classics*, edited by Kelly M. Kapic and Randall Gleason, 167–82. Downers Grove, IL: InterVarsity Press, 2004.

———. *Communion with God: The Divine and Human in the Theology of John Owen*. Grand Rapids: Baker Academic, 2007.

———. "Evangelical Holiness: Assumptions in John Owen's Theology of Christian Spirituality." In *Life in the Spirit: Spiritual Formation in Theological Perspective*, edited by Jeffrey P. Greenman and George Kalantzis, 97–114. Downers Grove, IL: InterVarsity Press, 2010.

———. "Introduction: Life in the Midst of Battle: John Owen's Approach to Sin, Temptation, and the Christian Life." In *John Owen, Overcoming Sin and Temptation: Three Classic Works by John Owen*, edited by Kelly M. Kapic and Justin Taylor, 23–36. Wheaton, IL: Crossway, 2006.

———. "The Spirit as Gift: Explorations in John Owen's Pneumatology." In *The Ashgate Research Companion to John Owen's Theology*, edited by Kelly M. Kapic and Mark Jones, 113–40. Burlington, VT: Ashgate, 2012.

Kapic, Kelly, and Mark Jones, eds. *The Ashgate Research Companion to John Owen's Theology*. Burlington, VT: Ashgate, 2012.

Kay, Brian. *Trinitarian Spirituality: John Owen and the Doctrine of God in Western Devotion*. Milton Keynes: Paternoster, 2007.

Kelly, Ryan. "Reformed or Reforming? John Owen and the Complexity of Theological Codification for Mid-Seventeenth-Century England." In *The Ashgate Research Companion to John Owen's Theology*, edited by Kelly M. Kapic and Mark Jones, 3–30. Burlington, VT: Ashgate, 2012.

King, David M. "The Affective Spirituality of John Owen." *Evangelical Quarterly* 68 (1996): 223–33.

Knapp, Henry M. "Augustine and Owen on Perseverance." *Westminster Theological Journal* 62 (2000): 65–88.

———. "John Owen, On Schism and the Nature of the Church." *Westminster Theological Journal* 72 (2010): 333–58.

——. "John Owen's Interpretation of Hebrews 6:4–6: Eternal Perseverance of the Saints in Puritan Exegesis." *Calvin Theological Journal* 34 (2003): 29–52.

Letham, Robert. "John Owen's Doctrine of the Trinity and Its Significance for Today." In *Where Reason Fails*. London: Westminster Conference, 2006.

——. "John Owen's Doctrine of the Trinity in Its Catholic Context." In *The Ashgate Research Companion to John Owen's Theology*, edited by Kelly M. Kapic and Mark Jones, 185–98. Burlington, VT: Ashgate, 2012.

Lim, Paul. "The Trinity, Adiaphora, Ecclesiology, and Reformation: John Owen's Theory of Religious Toleration in Context." *Westminster Theological Journal* 67 (2005): 281–300.

Lloyd, R. Glynne. *John Owen—Commonwealth Puritan*. Pontypridd: Modern Welsh Publications, 1972.

Macleod, Jack N. "John Owen and the Death of Death." In *Out of Bondage*. London: Westminster Conference, 1983.

Mayor, Stephen. "The Teaching of John Owen concerning the Lord's Supper." *Scottish Journal of Theology* 18 (1965): 170–81.

McDonald, Suzanne. "Beholding the Glory of God in the Face of Jesus Christ: John Owen and the 'Reforming' of the Beatific Vision." In *The Ashgate Research Companion to John Owen's Theology*, edited by Kelly M. Kapic and Mark Jones, 141–58. Burlington, VT: Ashgate, 2012.

——. "The Pneumatology of the 'Lost' Image in John Owen." *Westminster Theological Journal* 71 (2009): 323–35.

McGrath, Gavin J. *"But We Preach Christ Crucified": The Cross of Christ in the Pastoral Theology of John Owen, 1616–1683*. London: Needham, 1994.

McGraw, Ryan M. "John Owen on the Study of Theology." *The Confessional Presbyterian* 5 (2010): 180–96.

——. "Thoughts on Using Owen on Hebrews." *Banner of Truth* (2010): 13–16.

McKim, Donald K. "John Owen's Doctrine of Scripture in Historical Perspective." *Evangelical Quarterly* 45 (1973): 195–207.

Moore, Jonathan. "John Owen and Knowing the Mind of God." In *Knowing the Mind of God*. London: Westminster Conference, 2003.

Najapfour, Brian G. "An Analysis of John Owen's View of the Mosaic Covenant." *Scottish Bulletin of Evangelical Theology* 29 (2011): 196–204.

Naselli, Andrew David. "John Owen's Argument for Definite Atonement in *The Death of Death in the Death of Christ*: A Summary and Evaluation." *Southern Baptist Journal of Theology* 14, no 4 (2010): 60–82.

Oliver, Robert W. "John Owen—His Life and Times." In *John Owen: The Man and His Theology*, edited by Robert W. Oliver, 9–39. Phillipsburg, NJ: P&R, 2002.

——, ed. *John Owen: The Man and His Theology*. Phillipsburg, NJ: P&R, 2002.

Packer, J. I. "Introduction." In John Owen, *The Mortification of Sin: A Puritan's View of How to Deal with Sin in Your Life*. Fearn, Ross-shire: Christian Heritage, 1996.

———. "Introductory Essay." In John Owen, *The Death of Death in the Death of Christ*. Edinburgh: Banner of Truth, 1959.

———. "A Puritan Perspective: Trinitarian Godliness according to John Owen." In *God the Holy Trinity: Reflections on Christian Faith and Practice*, edited by Timothy George, 91–108. Grand Rapids: Baker Academic, 2006.

———. *A Quest for Godliness: The Puritan Vision of the Christian Life*. Wheaton, IL: Crossway, 1990.

Parsons, Burk, ed. "John Owen 1616–1683." *Tabletalk* 28, no. 10 (2004).

Payne, Jon D. *John Owen on the Lord's Supper*. Edinburgh: Banner of Truth, 2004.

Piper, John, *Contending for Our All: Defending Truth and Treasuring Christ in the Lives of Athanasius, John Owen and J. Gresham Machen*. Wheaton, IL: Crossway, 2011.

Rehnman, Sebastian. *Divine Discourse: The Theological Methodology of John Owen*. Grand Rapids: Baker Academic, 2002.

———. "John Owen: A Reformed Scholastic at Oxford." In *Reformation and Scholasticism: An Ecumenical Enterprise*, edited by Willem J. van Asselt and Eef Dekker, 181–203. Texts and Studies in Reformation and Post-Reformation Thought. Grand Rapids: Baker Academic, 2002.

———. "John Owen on Faith and Reason." In *The Ashgate Research Companion to John Owen's Theology*, edited by Kelly M. Kapic and Mark Jones, 31–48. Burlington, VT: Ashgate, 2012.

Smith, Christopher R. "'Up and Be Doing': The Pragmatic Puritan Eschatology of John Owen." *Evangelical Quarterly* 61 (1989): 335–49.

Spence, J. Alan. "Christ's Humanity and Ours: John Owen." In *Persons, Divine and Human*, edited by C. Schwöbel and Colin Gunton, 74–97. Edinburgh: T&T Clark, 1991.

———. *Incarnation and Inspiration: John Owen and the Coherence of Christology*. London: T&T Clark, 2007.

———. "John Owen and Trinitarian Agency." *Scottish Journal of Theology* 43 (1990): 157–73.

———. "The Significance of John Owen for Modern Christology." In *The Ashgate Research Companion to John Owen's Theology*, edited by Kelly M. Kapic and Mark Jones, 171–84. Burlington, VT: Ashgate, 2012.

Tay, Edwin. "Christ's Priestly Oblation and Intercession: Their Development and Significance in John Owen." In *The Ashgate Research Companion to John Owen's Theology*, edited by Kelly M. Kapic and Mark Jones, 159–69. Burlington, VT: Ashgate, 2012.

Thomson, Andrew. *John Owen: Prince of Puritans*. Fearn, Ross-shire: Christian Focus, 1996.

Timmins, William. "John Owen and the Problem of Indwelling Sin." In *Puritans and Spiritual Life*. London: Westminster Conference, 2001.

Toon, Peter. *God's Statesman: The Life and Work of John Owen: Pastor, Educator, Theologian*. Exeter: Paternoster, 1971.

———. "New Light on Dr. John Owen." *Baptist Quarterly* 22 (1968): 443–46.

Troxel, Craig A. "'Cleansed Once for All': John Owen on the Glory of Gospel Worship in Hebrews." *Calvin Theological Journal* 32 (1997): 468–79.

Trueman, Carl R. *The Claims of Truth: John Owen's Trinitarian Theology.* Carlisle: Paternoster, 1998.

———. "Faith Seeking Understanding: Some Neglected Aspects of John Owen's Understanding of Scriptural Interpretation." In *Interpreting the Bible: Historical and Theological Studies in Honour of David F. Wright*, edited by A. N. S. Lane, 147–62. Leicester: Apollos, 1997.

———. "John Owen as a Theologian." In *John Owen: The Man and His Theology*, edited by Robert W. Oliver, 41–68. Phillipsburg, NJ: P&R, 2002.

———. "John Owen on Justification." In *Justified in Christ: God's Plan for Us in Justification.* Fearn, Ross-shire: Mentor, 2007.

———. *John Owen: Reformed Catholic, Renaissance Man.* Hampshire: Ashgate, 2007.

———. "John Owen's Dissertation on Divine Justice: An Exercise in Christocentric Scholasticism." *Calvin Theological Journal* 33 (1988): 87–103.

Tweeddale, John W. "John Owen's Commentary on Hebrews in Context." In *The Ashgate Research Companion to John Owen's Theology*, edited by Kelly M. Kapic and Mark Jones, 49–64. Burlington, VT: Ashgate, 2012.

van den Brink, Gert. "Impetration and Application in John Owen's Theology." In *The Ashgate Research Companion to John Owen's Theology*, edited by Kelly M. Kapic and Mark Jones, 85–96. Burlington, VT: Ashgate, 2012.

Vries, Pieter de. "The Significance of Union and Communion with Christ in the Theology of John Owen (1616–1683)." *Reformed Theological Journal* 17 (2001): 75–89.

———. "Union and Communion with Christ in the Theology of John Owen." *Reformed Theological Journal* 15 (1999): 77–96.

Wallace, Dewey D. "The Life and Thought of John Owen to 1660: A Study of the Significance of Calvinist Theology in English Puritanism." PhD diss., Princeton University, 1965.

———. *Puritans and Predestination: Grace in English Protestant Theology, 1525–1695.* Chapel Hill: North Carolina University Press, 1982.

———. *Shapers of English Calvinism, 1660–1714: Variety, Persistence, and Transformation.* Oxford Studies in Historical Theology. Oxford: Oxford University Press, 2011.

Westcott, Stephen P. *By the Bible Alone: John Owen's Puritan Theology for Today's Church.* Fellsmere, FL: Reformation Media & Press, 2010.

Wray, Daniel E. "The Spiritual Man in the Teachings of John Owen." *Banner of Truth* 182 (1978): 10–20.

Yarhouse, Mark A. "John Owen on Spiritual Mindedness." *Psychology and Christianity* 20 (2001): 342–50.

GENERAL INDEX

Abraham, 123
active and passive righteousness of
Christ, 186n3, 190n14, 211–14
Act of Uniformity (1662), 31, 239
actual sin, 194
Adam
as federal head, 133, 193
in Paradise, 49
promise to, 110, 123
sin of, 192–94, 197, 210–11
adoption, 73n86, 82–83
adoration, of Christ, 105
affections, renewal of, 172
alienation from God, 133
alien righteousness, 210
Amyraldianism, 188
anointing, by the Spirit, 85
antinomianism, 188n10
anti-Trinitarianism, 54
apostasy, 16–17, 179n145, 260
argument, 13
Arianism, 54, 93–94, 97, 189n13
Arminianism, 121–22, 146–48, 211
on efficacy of the atonement, 142
on faith, 160
on justification, 186–87
on perseverance, 182
on prevenient grace, 177n136
on providence, 155
on regeneration, 170

on universal atonement, 187
Arminius, 146n5, 148
assurance, 16, 26, 179n145, 216–18,
260
Athanasius, 94
atonement, 16, 122, 132
efficacy of, 141–43
extent of, 140–43
Augustine, 13, 15, 58, 154, 166
authority, 35
autonomy, 154

backsliding, 81
Banner of Truth Trust, 254–55
baptism, 244
Baptist congregations, 251
Barnes, Geoffrey L., 240
Baskerville, S. K., 249, 250
Bauman, Richard, 41
Baxter, Richard, 46–47, 122n2, 186n3,
188–89, 211, 238
Beatific Vision, 118n130
beauty of Christ, 118
belief, 198–99
Bellarmine, Robert, 198n47, 203
Best, Paul, 54
Biddle, John, 54, 90, 124
blessedness, 118n130
blood of Christ, 57, 195–96, 198–99,
212n110

SCRIPTURE INDEX

WISDOM FROM THE PAST FOR LIFE IN THE PRESENT

Other volumes in the Theologians on the Christian Life series

AUGUSTINE

BAVINCK

BONHOEFFER

CALVIN

EDWARDS

LUTHER

NEWTON

OWEN

PACKER

SCHAEFFER

WARFIELD

WESLEY

Visit crossway.org/TOCL for more information.